READINGS IN SCHOOL LEARNING

David P. Ausubel
THE CITY UNIVERSITY OF NEW YORK

READINGS IN SCHOOL LEARNING

HOLT, RINEHART AND WINSTON, INC.
NEW YORK CHICAGO SAN FRANCISCO ATLANTA
DALLAS MONTREAL TORONTO LONDON SYDNEY

Library of Congress Catalog Card Number 69–17646
03–080890–1
Printed in the United States of America

90123 68 987654321

To
Theresa and Herman Ausubel

Preface

This reader in educational psychology is primarily designed to supplement Ausubel and Robinson's *School Learning: An Introduction to Educational Psychology*. Thus, for purposes of convenience, it is organized along lines parallel to those adopted in the latter textbook.

Even if a textbook does not attempt more than an integrated presentation of just a single point of view in the field, it is necessarily limited in what it can hope to accomplish. Inevitably, for understandable reasons of economy, it is obliged to telescope ideas, arguments, and evidence. Hence a collection of representative selections from original sources in the discipline can serve at least four useful purposes for beginning students in educational psychology. First, it can furnish more definitive and detailed empirical support for the particular theoretical position adopted by the textbook. Second, it can provide some examples and flavor of the research strategy and methodology of educational psychology as an experimental empirical discipline. To fulfill this objective, original articles must obviously remain unabridged and unsimplified even if they are somewhat difficult for the beginning student. Third, it can discuss in greater depth some of the salient theoretical and pedagogic issues which, for considerations of space, receive less extended coverage in the textbook. Finally, it can make available to all of the students in the course original articles which are either unobtainable at all or obtainable in insufficient copies in college libraries.

The reason only a single author and his co-workers are represented in this book of readings is fairly self-evident. Like the textbook itself, it does not purport to sample different points of view in educational psychology, but rather to make the best possible case for the particular point of view advanced by Ausubel and Robinson. In line with this objective it can be plausibly argued that a given author is the best spokesman for his own point of view.

As in any book of readings, the particular topics and articles chosen for this reader are intended to be representative rather than exhaustive in nature. Since a certain amount of arbitrariness, as well as the particular research and theoretical interests of the author, inevitably enter into such choice, a good case could be made for including many other topics or articles. Also, some quite long articles—longer than those typically found in books of readings—have been selected. Their inclusion was thought justified on the grounds that each either embraces several issues or provides the kind of supplementary argumentation in depth that is one of the prime objectives of this reader.

I am grateful to my colleague Dr. Floyd G. Robinson, co-author of *School Learning: An Introduction to Educational Psychology*, for contributing an article to this collection.

NEW YORK *D. P. A.*
JANUARY 1969

Contents

READINGS
IN
SCHOOL LEARNING

PART I THE SCOPE AND FIELD OF EDUCATIONAL PSYCHOLOGY

Much controversy has arisen in recent years over whether there really is such a discipline as educational psychology and, if there is, what it consists of. Is it a discipline in its own right with its own body of theory and distinctive research methodology? Or does it merely consist of general psychology applied to problems of education? Three basic positions are adopted in the following article.

First, it is argued that educational psychology must be *restricted* to the nature, conditions, determinants, and evaluation of the kinds of meaningful learning that occur in school and similar learning environments, that it should not be permitted to constitute a watered-down version of general psychology inclusive of diverse types of learning, developmental psychology, social psychology, evaluation and measurement, and the psychology of adjustment.

Second, it is maintained that educational psychology is an applied science and hence must employ an applied research strategy studying problems of learning in the complex and practical contexts in which they exist in the school, rather than employ a basic science research strategy studying highly simplified kinds of learning which are not representative of what pupils learn in school.

Last, it is proposed that, as an applied discipline, educational psychology does not consist of general psychological theory applied to education, but, like medicine, possesses an independent body of applied theory explaining the distinctive phenomena in its own field, in addition to being related in a more general way to its parent discipline.

1 Is There a Discipline of Educational Psychology?

David P. Ausubel

Is there such a discipline as educational psychology? I have a very strong personal stake in hoping to be able to convince you that there is, because if I fail in this attempt I shall be concomitantly demonstrating that as a scholar, a researcher, and a theorist, I myself do not exist. For however else I may perceive my academic and professional role, I regard myself primarily as an educational psychologist. It is certainly not the case that I perceive this question as irrelevant or irreverent. Quite the contrary, it follows very pertinently if one examines many textbooks of educational psychology that were written during the past thirty years. In fact, from the conception of educational psychology inferable from analysis of the contents of these textbooks—that is, as a superficial, ill-digested, and typically disjointed and watered-down miscellany of general psychology, learning theory, developmental psychology, social psychology, psychological measurement, psychology of adjustment, mental hygiene, client-centered counseling and child-centered education—one would be hard put not to give a negative answer to the question raised by the title of my paper.

Definition of the Field

My thesis, in brief, is that educational psychology is that special branch of psychology concerned with the nature, conditions, outcomes, and evaluation of school learning and retention. As such, the subject matter of educational psychology consists primarily of the theory of meaningful learning and retention and the influence of all significant variables—cognitive, developmental, affective, motivational, personality, and social—on school learning outcomes, particularly the influence of those variables that are manipulable by the teacher, by the curriculum developer, by the programmed instruction specialist, by the educational technologist, by the school psychologist or guidance counselor, by the educational administrator, or by society at large.

Psychology versus Educational Psychology

Since both psychology and educational psychology deal with the problem of learning, how can we distinguish between the special theoretical and research interests of each discipline in this area? As an applied science, educational psychology is not concerned with general laws of learning *per se,* but only with those properties of learning that can be related to efficacious ways of *deliberately* effecting stable cognitive changes which have social value (Ausubel, 1953). Education, therefore, refers to guided or manipulated learning directed toward specific practical ends. These ends may be defined as the long-term acquisition of stable bodies of knowledge and of the capacities needed for acquiring such knowledge.

The psychologist's interest in learning, on the other hand, is much more *general.* Many aspects of learning, other than the efficient achievement of the above-designated competences and capacities for growth in a directed context, concern him. More typically, he investigates the nature of simple, fragmentary, or short-term learning experiences, which are presumably more representative of learning in general, rather than the kinds of long-term learning involved in assimilating extensive and organized bodies of knowledge.

The following kinds of learning problems, therefore, are particularly indigenous to psychoeducational research: (a) discovery of the *nature* of those aspects of the learning process affecting the acquisition and long-term retention of organized bodies of knowledge in the learner; (b) long-range improvement of learning and problem-solving capacities; (c) discovery of which cognitive and personality characteristics of the learner, and of which interpersonal and social aspects of the learning environment, affect subject-matter learning outcomes, motivation for learning, and typical ways of assimilating school material; and (d) discovery of appropriate and maximally efficient ways of organizing and presenting learning materials and of deliberately motivating and directing learning toward specific goals.

Another way of epitomizing the difference between the two disciplines is to say that *general* aspects of learning interest the psychologist, whereas *classroom* learning, that is, deliberately guided learning of subject matter in a social context, is the special province of the educational psychologist. The subject matter of educational psychology, therefore, can be inferred directly from the problems facing the classroom teacher. The latter must generate interest in subject matter, inspire commitment to learning, motivate pupils, and help induce realistic aspirations for educational achievement. He must decide what is important for pupils to learn, ascertain what learnings they are ready for, pace instruction properly, and decide on the appropriate size and difficulty level of learning tasks. He is expected to organize subject matter expeditiously, present materials clearly, simplify learning tasks at initial stages of mastery, and integrate current and past learnings. It is his responsibility to arrange practice schedules and reviews, to offer confirmation, clarification, and correction, to ask critical questions, to provide suitable rewards, to evaluate learning and development, and where feasible, to promote discovery learning and problem-solving ability. Finally, since he is concerned with teaching groups of students in a social environment, he must grapple with problems of group instruction, individualization, communication, and discipline.

Thus the scope of educational psychology as an applied science is exceedingly broad, and the potential rewards it offers in terms of the social value of facilitating the subject-matter learning of pupils are proportionately great.

In What Sense is Educational Psychology an "Applied" Discipline?

Few persons would take issue with the proposition that education is an applied or engineering science. It is an *applied science* because it is concerned with the realization of certain practical ends which have social value. The precise nature of these ends is highly controversial, in terms of both substance and relative emphasis. To some individuals the function of education is to transmit the ideology of the culture and a core body of knowledge and intellectual skills. To others, education is primarily concerned with the optimal development of potentiality for growth and achievement—not only with respect to cognitive abilities, but also with respect to personality goals and adjustment. Disagreement with respect to ends, however, neither removes education from the category of science nor makes it any less of an applied branch of knowledge. It might be mentioned in passing that automobile engineers are also not entirely agreed as to the characteristics of the "ideal" car; and physicians disagree violently in formulating a definition of health.

Regardless of the ends it chooses to adopt, an applied discipline becomes a science only when it seeks to ground proposed means to ends on empirically validatable propositions. The operations involved in such an undertaking are commonly subsumed under the term "research." The question under discussion here relates to the nature of research in applied science, or, more specifically, in education. Is educational research a field in its own right with theoretical problems and a methodology of its own, or does it merely involve the operation of applying knowledge from "pure" scientific disciplines to practical problems of pedagogy?

Despite the fact that education is an applied science, educational psychologists have manifested a marked tendency uncritically to extrapolate research findings from laboratory studies of simplified learning situations to the classroom learning environment. This tendency reflects the fascination which many research workers feel for the "basic-science" approach to research in the applied sciences, as well as their concomitant failure to appreciate its inherent limitations. They argue that progress in educational psychology is made more rapidly by focusing indirectly on basic-science problems in general psychology than by trying to come to grips directly with the applied problems that are more indigenous to the field. Spence (1959), for example, perceived classroom learning as much too complex to permit the discovery of general laws of learning, and advocated a straightforward application to the classroom situation of the laws of learning discovered in the laboratory; he saw very little scope, however, for applying the latter laws to problems of educational practice. Melton (1959) and E. R. Hilgrad (1964) take a more eclectic position. They would search for basic-science laws of learning in both laboratory and classroom contexts, and would leave to the educational technologist the task of conducting the research necessary for implementing these laws in actual classroom practice.

My position, in other words, is that the principles governing the nature and conditions of school learning can be discovered only through an applied or engineering type of research that actually takes into account both the kinds of learning that occur in the classroom as well as salient characteristics of the learner. We cannot merely extrapolate to classroom learning general basic-science laws that are derived from the laboratory study of qualitatively different and vastly simpler instances of learning. Most attempts to do so, as, for example, Mandler's (1962) attempt to explain complex cognitive functioning in terms of the laws of association, or Sheffield's (1961) recent explanation of the hierarchical learning of sequentially organized materials in terms of the principle of contiguous conditioning, are extremely tortuous.

Laws of classroom learning at an applied level are needed by the educational technologist before he can hope to conduct the research preparatory to effecting scientific changes in teaching practices. He can be aided further by general principles of teaching which are intermediate, in level of generality and prescriptiveness, between laws of classroom learning and the technological problems that confront him. Contrary to Spence's (1959) contention, the greater complexity and number of determining variables involved in classroom learning does not preclude the possibility of discovering precise laws with wide generality from one educational situation to another. It simply means that such research demands experimental ingenuity and sophisticated use of modern techniques of research design.

Basic Science versus Applied Approach

Three different kinds of research orientations have been adopted by those who are concerned with scientific progress in applied disciplines such as medicine and education: (a) basic-science research, (b) extrapolated research in the basic sciences, and (c) research at an applied level (Ausubel, 1953).

The basic-science research approach is predicated on the very defensible proposition that applied sciences are *ultimately* related to knowledge in the underlying sciences on which they are based. It can be demonstrated convincingly, for example, that progress in medicine is intimately related to progress in general biochemistry and bacteriology; that progress in engineering is intimately related to progress in physics and chemistry; and that progress in education is similarly dependent upon advances in general psychology, statistics, and sociology. However, two important qualifications have to be placed on the value of basic-science research for the applied sciences: qualifications of purpose or relevance and qualifications of level of applicability.

By definition, basic-science research is concerned with the discovery of general laws of physical, biological, psychological, and sociological phenomenology as an end in itself. Researchers in these fields have no objection, of course, if their findings are applied to practical problems which have social value; in fact, there is reason to believe that they are motivated to some extent by this consideration. But the design of basic-science research bears no *intended* relation whatsoever to problems in the applied disciplines, the aim being solely to advance knowledge. Ultimately, of course, such knowledge is applicable in a very broad sense to practical problems; but since the research design is not oriented to the solution of these problems, this applicability is apt to be quite indirect and unsystematic, and relevant only over a time span which is too long to be meaningful in terms of the short-range needs of the applied disciplines.

The second qualification has to do with the level at which findings in the basic sciences can be applied once their relevance has been established. It should be self-evident that such findings exhibit a much higher level of generality than the problems to which they can be applied. At the applied level, specific ends and conditions are added which demand *additional* research to indicate the precise way in which the general law operates in the specific case. That is, the applicability of general principles to specific problems is *not given* in the statement of the general principle, but must be explicitly worked out for each individual problem. Knowledge about nuclear fission, for example, does not tell us how to make an atomic bomb or an atomic-powered airplane.

In fields such as education, the problem of generality is further complicated by the fact that practical problems often exist at higher levels of complexity with respect to the order of phenomenology involved than do the basic-science findings requiring application. That is, new variables are added which may *qualitatively* alter the general principles from the basic science to such an extent that at the applied level they have substrate validity but lack explanatory or predictive value. For example, antibiotic reactions that take place in test tubes do not necessarily take place in living systems, and methods of learning that children employ in rotely mastering lists of nonsense syllables in the laboratory do not necessarily correspond to methods of learning children use in classrooms to acquire a meaningful grasp of subject matter.

The basic-science approach in educational research, therefore, is subject to many serious disadvantages. Its relevance is too remote and indirect because it is not oriented toward solving educational problems; and its findings, if relevant, are applicable only if much additional research is performed to translate general principles into the more specific form they have to assume in the task-specialized and more complex contexts of pedagogy.

These limitations would not be so serious if they were perceived. In the latter event, it would be defensible for educational institutions to set aside a *small* portion of their research funds for basic-science research as a long-term investment. But since the limitations of this approach are *not* generally appreciated, some bureaus of educational research confidently invest their major resources in such programs, and then complacently expect that the research findings which emerge will be both relevant and applicable in their original form to the problems of education.

Naïvete with respect to the second premise, that is, of immediate applicability, is especially rampant and has led to very serious distortions in our knowledge of those aspects of the psychology of learning that are relevant for pedagogy. The psychology of learning that teachers study is based on findings in general psychology which have been borrowed wholesale without much attempt to test their applicability to the kinds of learning situations that exist in classrooms. It would be a shocking situation indeed if a comparable procedure were practiced in medicine, that is, if physicians employed therapeutic techniques validated only *in vitro* or by animal experimentation.

The second general research approach in the applied disciplines is "extrapolated basic-science research." Unlike pure basic-science research, it is oriented toward the solution of practical or applied problems. It starts out by identifying significant problems in the applied field, and designs experiments pointed toward their solution on an analogous but highly simplified basic-science level. In this way it satisfies the important criterion of relevance, but must still contend with the problem of level of applicability. The rationale of this approach is that many practical problems are so complex that they must be reduced to simpler terms and patterned after simpler models before one can develop fruitful hypotheses leading to their solution. Once the problems are simplified, control and measurement become more manageable.

Depending on the nature of the problem under investigation, this approach may have genuine merit provided that the resulting research findings are regarded only as "leads" or hypotheses to be tested in the applied situation rather than as definitive answers *per se* to problems in pedagogy. As already noted, however, educational researchers have a tendency to extrapolate basic-science findings to pedagogical problems without conducting the additional research necessary to bridge the gap between the two levels of generality involved.

The third approach to educational research, research at the applied level, is the most relevant and direct of the three, yet paradoxically is utilized least of all by professional research workers in the field. When research is performed in relation to the actual problems of education, at the level of complexity at which they exist, that is, *in situ* (under the conditions in which they are to be found in practice), the problems of relevance and extrapolation do not arise. Most rigorous research in applied disciplines other than education is conducted at this level. The research program of a hospital or medical school would be regarded as seriously unbalanced if most of its funds and efforts went into pure biochemical or bacteriological research instead of into applied and clinical research. The major responsibility for furthering research in the former areas belongs to graduate departments of chemistry and bacteriology. On the other hand, unless medical schools undertake to solve their own applied and clinical problems who else will? And the same analogy obviously holds for education as well.

Although applied research presents greater difficulties with respect to research design, control, and measurement, the rewards are correspondingly greater when these problems are solved. Certainly such problems cannot be solved when they are deliberately avoided. If other applied disciplines have been able to evolve satisfactory research methodologies, there is no reason why education cannot also do so. In fact, if any applied discipline with unique and distinctive problems of its own is to survive as a science it has no choice in the matter—it is obliged to do so.

Many of the better-known generalizations in educational psychology—the principle of readiness, the effects of overlearning, the concrete to abstract trend in conceptualizing the environment—illustrate the pitfalls of the basic-science approach to educational research. They are interesting and potentially useful ideas to curriculum specialists and educational technologists, but have little utility in educational practice until they are *particularized* at an applied level of operations. The prevailing lack of practical particularization damages the "image" of educational psychology insofar as it induces many beginning teachers to nurture unrealistic expectations about the current usefulness of these principles. Subsequently, after undergoing acute disillusionment, they may lose whatever original confidence they may have felt in the value of a psychological approach to educational problems.

The need for applied research in these areas is well illustrated by the principles of readiness. At the present time we can only speculate what curriculum sequences might conceivably look like if they took into account precise and detailed (but currently unavailable) research findings on the emergence of readiness for different subject-matter areas, for different subareas and levels of difficulty within an area, and for different methods of teaching the same material. Because of the unpredictable specificity of readiness as shown, for example, by the fact that four- and five-year-olds can profit from training in pitch but not in rhythm (Jerslid and Bienstock, 1931, 1935), valid answers to questions, such as those of readiness, cannot be derived from logical extrapolation; they require meticulous empirical research in a school setting. The next step involves the development of teaching methods and materials appropriate for taking optimal advantage of existing degrees of readiness, and for increasing readiness wherever necessary and desirable. But since we generally do not have this research data available, except perhaps in the field of reading, we can pay only lip service to principles of readiness in curriculum planning.

The basic-science-extrapolation approach, of course, offers several very attractive methodological advantages in verbal learning experiments. First, by using nonsense syllables of equal meaningfulness, it is possible to work with additive units of equal difficulty. Second, by using relatively meaningless learning tasks, such as equated nonsense syllables, it is possible to eliminate, for the most part, the indeterminable influence of meaningful antecedent experience, which naturally varies from one individual to another. But it is precisely this interaction of new learning tasks with existing knowledge in the learner that is the distinctive feature of meaningful learning.

Thus, although the use of nonsense syllables adds undoubted methodological rigor to the study of learning, the very nature of the material limits the applicability of experimental findings to a type of short-term, discrete learning that is rare both in everyday situations and in the classroom. Nevertheless, even though there are no *a priori* grounds for supposing that meaningful and nonmeaningful learning and retention occur in the same way, the findings from rote-learning experiments have been commonly extrapolated to meaningful learning situations. One cannot have one's cake and eat it too. If one chooses the particular kind of methodological rigor associated with the use of rote materials, one must also be satisfied with applying the findings from such experiments to only rote learning tasks.

In conclusion, therefore, educational psychology is unequivocally an applied discipline, but it is *not* general psychology applied to educational problems—no more so than mechanical engineering is general physics applied to problems of designing machinery or medicine is general biology applied to problems of diagnosing, curing, and preventing human diseases. In these latter applied disciplines, general laws from the parent discipline are not applied to a domain of practical problems; rather, separate bodies of applied theory exist that are just as basic as the theory undergirding the parent disciplines, but are stated at a lower level of generality and have more direct relevance for and applicability to the applied problems in their respective fields.

The time-bound and particular properties of knowledge in the applied sciences has also been exaggerated. Such knowledge involves more than technological applications of basic science generalizations to current practical problems. Although less generalizable than the basic sciences, they are also disciplines *in their own right,* with distinctive and relatively enduring bodies of theory and methodology that cannot simply be derived or extrapolated from the basic sciences to which they are related. It is simply not true that only basic-science knowledge can be related to and organized around general principles. Each of the applied biological sciences (e.g., medicine, agronomy) possesses an *independent* body of general principles underlying the detailed knowledge in its field, in addition to being related in a still more general way to basic principles in biology.

Theories of Learning versus Theories of Teaching

Disillusionment regarding the relevance and usefulness of learning theory for educational practice has been responsible, in part, for the recent emergence of "theories of teaching" that are avowedly independent of theories of learning. The justification for such theories has been advanced on both historical and logical grounds.

The Historical Argument Gage (1964) cites the historical record to argue that theories of learning have had very little applicability to and influence on educational practice, whether in educational psychology textbooks, in courses devoted to teaching methods, or in the everyday operations of classroom teaching. He argues further that theories of learning are *inherently irrelevant* for problems of instruction, and should therefore be replaced by theories of teaching in dealing with such problems. For example, he states that:

> while theories of learning deal with the ways an organism learns, theories of teaching deal with the ways in which a person influences an organism to learn . . . . To satisfy the practical demands of education, theories of learning must be 'stood on their head' so as to yield theories of teaching (pp. 268–269).

Actually, however, *both* of these arguments are based essentially on the *historical* failure of learning theory to provide a *psychologically* relevant basis for pedagogic practice. For this undeniable shortcoming of learning theory to date is by no means a necessary or *inherent* limitation in the applicability of such theory to education; it is merely characteristic of the *prevailing* brand of school learning theory which, in general, does not deal with the kind of learning that occurs in the classroom but, rather, has, for the most part, been uncritically extrapolated from the main body of laboratory learning theory. A truly realistic and scientifically viable theory of classroom learning, in contrast, would be primarily concerned with *complex* and *meaningful* types of verbal and symbolic learning that takes place in school and similar learning environments, and would also give a prominent place to those *manipulable* factors that affect it. There is, in other words, a very close relationship between knowing how a pupil learns and the manipulable variables influencing learning, on the one hand, and knowing what to do to help him learn better, on the other. By teaching we mean primarily the deliberate guidance of learning processes along lines suggested by relevant classroom learning theory. It would seem reasonable, therefore, to suppose that the discovery of the most effective methods of teaching would be inherently dependent upon and related to the status of learning theory.

Of course, only *general* principles of deliberately facilitating school learning could be considered part of classroom learning theory. The more applied and prescriptive aspects of pedagogy that are derived from these principles (that is, those aspects that take account of the many complexities of the classroom teaching process, both generally and for particular age groups and subject matters) would constitute a theory of instruction and would continue to be taught in methods courses that are comparable to the clinical phase of a medical student's training.

The Logical Argument In contrast to Gage's historical argument which focuses on the *de facto* failure of learning theory to prove relevant to educational practice, B. O. Smith (1960) presents a strictly logical rationale for formulating theories of teaching that are wholly independent of, rather than complementary to, theories of learning. He bases his case on the propositions that learning and teaching are neither coextensive nor inextricable from each other, and that a theory of learning cannot tell us how to teach.

First, Smith's insistence that learning and teaching are different and separately identifiable phenomena admittedly does more than belabor the obvious. It clears up some widely prevalent semantic confusion—since, in his own words, it is frequently implied that "if the child has not learned, the teacher has not taught," or else has taught incompetently. Teaching and learning are not coextensive, for teaching is only one of the conditions, and not a necessary or sufficient one at that, which may influence learning. Thus pupils can learn without being taught, that is, by teaching themselves; and even if teaching is manifestly competent, it does not necessarily lead to learning if the pupils concerned are inattentive, unmotivated, or cognitively unprepared.

Nevertheless, once these unwarranted inferences about the coextensiveness of learning and teaching are discarded, it is useful, practically, to focus on those aspects of teaching and learning that *are* reciprocally related to each other. These reciprocal relationships include the purposes, the effects, and the evaluation of teaching. Thus, although it is true that teaching is logically distinct from learning, and can be analyzed independently of what pupils learn, what would be the practical advantage of so doing? The facilitation of learning is the only proper end of teaching. We do not teach as an end in itself but only that pupils may learn; and even though the failure of pupils to learn does not necessarily indict the competence of the teacher, learning is still the only feasible measure of teaching merit. Further, as was just pointed out, teaching itself is effective only to the extent that it manipulates effectively those psychological variables that govern learning.

Second, even though a valid theory of learning cannot tell us how to teach in a prescriptive sense, it does offer us the most feasible point of departure for discovering general principles of teaching that can be formulated in terms of both intervening psychological processes and cause-effect relationships. It is largely from a theory of learning that we can develop defensible notions of how crucial factors in the learning-teaching situation can be most effectively manipulated. The only other possible approaches are to vary teaching factors at random or to rely on intuition. The latter approaches not only are more time-consuming, but can also yield only purely empirical laws that cannot be formulated in general terms with respect to the psychological conditions and relevant cognitive processes involved.

It is realized, of course, that an adequate theory of learning is a necessary but not a sufficient condition for the improvement of instruction. Valid principles of teaching are necessarily based on relevant principles of learning, but, as pointed out above, are not simple and direct applications of these principles. Laws of classroom learning merely provide *general* direction for discovering effective teaching principles; they do not indicate *per se* what these principles are. The formulation of teaching principles requires much supplementary research that takes account of practical problems and new instructional variables not implicit in the learning principles themselves. In other words, one can consider basic principles of teaching as applied derivatives of school learning theory; they are products of an engineering type of research and are based on such modifications of learning theory as are necessitated by the practical difficulties or the additional new variables involved in the task of teaching.

As B. O. Smith (1960) asserts, simply by knowing "the cause of a phenomenon," one does not thereby acquire control of it "for practical ends." Thus, for example, we can know the cause of a disease without knowing how to treat it, and we can treat a disease successfully without knowing its cause. It is undeniable that many practical and useful inventions are made accidentally without any understanding of how or why they work, that is, of the explanatory principles and relevant variables involved. But who would advocate this as a deliberate research strategy? Ordinarily, scientists search for practical methods of control that can be related to general statements of relationship among the relevant variables involved. The superiority of this approach inheres in the fact that methods of control that are relatable to general principles not only are understandable and interpretable, but also are more widely transferable to other practical problems. We could, for example, discover as an empirical fact that using teaching method X facilitates learning. But the practical value of such knowledge is quite limited. Would it not be preferable to formulate the research problem so that we could ascertain in what ways method X influences relevant psychological variables and intervening cognitive states in the course of facilitating learning, retention or problem-solving? It is extremely wasteful of time and effort to search for more efficient methods of teaching that can be described only in terms of descriptive characteristics of the teaching act and cannot be related to laws of learning. Even when scientists do stumble accidentally on useful empirical laws, they immediately launch new hypothesis-oriented research to explain in more general terms the underlying basis of the accidental discovery.

Finally, although knowledge of causation does not imply immediate discovery of control procedures, it does constitute a tremendous advantage in discovering such procedures. For one thing, it narrows the field; for another, it enables one to try procedures that have proven successful in controlling related conditions. Knowing that tuberculosis was caused by a microorganism, for example, did not provide us immediately with a cure or a preventative. But it enabled us to try such approaches as vaccines, immune sera, antisepsis, quarantine, and chemotherapy that had been used successfully in treating other infectious diseases. In the same sense, knowledge of the cause of cancer would help immeasurably in discovering a cure, and knowledge of the nature and relevant variables involved in concept acquisition would be of invaluable assistance in devising effective methods of teaching concepts.

The Decline of Classroom Learning Theory

The serious decline in knowledge and theorizing about school learning that has taken place over the past half century, accompanied by the steady retreat of educational psychologists from the classroom, has not been without adequate cause. Much of this deliberate avoidance can be attributed to the scientific disrepute into which studies of school learning fell as a result of both (a) glaring deficiencies in conceptualization and research design, and (b) excessive concern with the improvement of particular narrowly conceived academic skills and techniques of instruction rather than with the discovery of more general principles affecting the improvement of classroom learning and instruction in *any* subject-matter field. The vast majority of studies in the field of school learning, after all, have been conducted by teachers and other non-professional research workers in education. In contrast, laboratory studies of simple learning tasks were invested with the growing glamour and prestige of the experimental sciences, and also made possible the investigation of general learning variables under rigorously controlled conditions.

Thus the more *scientifically* conducted research in learning theory has been undertaken largely by psychologists unconnected with the educational enterprise, who have investigated problems quite remote from the type of learning that goes on in the classroom. The focus has been on animal learning or on short-term and fragmentary rote or nonverbal forms of human learning, rather than on the learning and retention of organized bodies of meaningful material. Experimental psychologists, of course, can hardly be criticized if laboratory studies of nonverbal and rote verbal learning have had little applicability to the classroom. Like all pure research efforts in the basic sciences, these studies were designed to yield only general scientific laws as ends in themselves, quite apart from any practical utility. The blame, if any is to be assigned, must certainly fall upon educational psychologists who, in general, have failed to conduct the necessary applied research and have succumbed to the temptation of extrapolating the theories and findings of their experimental colleagues to problems of classroom learning.

Finally, for the past three decades, educational psychologists have been preoccupied with measurement and evaluation, personality development, mental hygiene, group dynamics, and counseling. Despite the self-evident centrality of classroom learning and cognitive development for the psychological aspects of education, these areas were ignored, both theoretically and empirically (Ausubel, 1963).

Although the withdrawal of educational psychologists from problems of meaningful classroom learning was temporarily expedient, it was, in the long run, highly unfortunate on both theoretical and research grounds. In the first place, rotely and meaningfully learned materials are represented and organized quite differently in the student's psychological structure of knowledge (cognitive structure), and hence conform to quite different principles of learning and retention. Not only are the respective learning processes very dissimilar, but the significant variables involved in the two processes are also markedly different, and, where similar, have very different effects. Second, it is evident that a distinction must be made between learning tasks involving the short-term acquisition of single, somewhat contrived concepts, the solution of artificial problems, or the learning of arbitrary associations—in a laboratory setting—and long-term acquisition and retention of the complex network of interrelated ideas characterizing an organized body of knowledge that is presented to the learner for active incorporation into his cognitive structure.

Hence the extrapolation of rote learning theory and evidence to school learning problems has had many disastrous consequences. It perpetuated erroneous conceptions about the nature and conditions of classroom learning, led educational psychologists to neglect research on factors influencing meaningful learning, and hence delayed the discovery of more effective techniques of verbal exposition. And, finally, it convinced some educators to question the relevance of learning theory for the educational enterprise, and to formulate theories of teaching that attempt to conceptualize the nature, purposes, and effects of instruction independently of its relationship to learning.

Still another reason for the decline in classroom learning theory can be found by examining its historical development during the twentieth century. First, E. L. Thorndike initiated a movement that separated school learning theory from its relevant concern with the acquisition of large bodies of organized knowledge (as represented by the scholastic and humanistic philosophers and by such educational theorists as Herbart), and focused theoretical attention on a mechanistic and reductionistic concern with explaining the rote acquisition of discrete units of such knowledge. This concern was reinforced later by behaviorism, neobehaviorism, Pavlovian psychology, a revival of associationism, the functionalism of the Twenties and Thirties, and Skinnerian psychology and the teaching machine movement it spawned. Second, the immediate theoretical reaction to connectionism, associationism, and behaviorism, namely, Gestalt and field theory approaches, failed to provide a viable theoretical alternative for educational psychology. Their doctrinaire overemphasis on a perceptual model of learning and retention led to a vastly oversimplified interpretation of the actual learning task involved in the acquisition of subject matter, an overvaluation of the role of stimulus properties and stimulus organization and a corresponding undervaluation of the role of existing cognitive structure in school learning, an emphasis on nativistic explanatory principles that was quite alien to the very spirit of education, and an unrealistic preoccupation with discovery learning and problem solving that diverted attention from the more basic reception aspects of classroom learning. Lastly, John Dewey and the Progressive Education movement derogated expository teaching, verbal learning, structured learning experience, and the importance of practice and testing, and also placed undue emphasis on direct, nonverbal, concrete-empirical experience and on learning by discovery.

Prerequisites for a Discipline of Educational Psychology

The foregoing historical considerations and substantive propositions regarding the definition of the field of educational psychology, its relationships to general psychology, and its status as an applied discipline lead to the conclusion that a minimum number of crucial prerequisites must first be met before educational psychology can emerge as a viable and flourishing discipline. First the acquisition of certain basic intellectual skills, the learning and retention of subject-matter knowledge, and the development of problem-solving capabilities must be regarded as the principal practical concerns toward which theory and research in this area of inquiry are directed. Second, the attainment of these objectives must be conceptualized as products of meaningful verbal or symbolical learning and retention, and a cogent theory of such learning and retention must be formulated in terms of manipulable independent variables. Third, the elaboration of this theory implies the delineation of unambiguous distinctions between meaningful learning, on the one hand, and such other forms of learning as classical and operant conditioning, rote verbal and instrumental learning, perceptual-motor and simple discrimination learning, on the other, as well as clear distinctions between such varieties of meaningful verbal learning as representational or vocabulary learning, concept learning, and propositional learning, and between reception and discovery learning. Finally, meaningful verbal learning must be studied in the form in which it actually occurs in classrooms, that is, as the guided, long-term, structured learning in a social context of large bodies of logically organized and interrelated concepts, facts, and principles rather than as the short-term and fragmented learning of discrete and granulated items of information such as is represented by short-frame and small-step-size teaching machine programs.

Predicted New Look in Educational Psychology

It is obviously difficult to separate the objective delineation of future research trends in educational psychology from a statement of personal values and preferences in this area. Nevertheless, although frankly conceding this serious limitation at the very outset, I still venture to predict the emergence of four major trends in the coming decade. First, I am confident that educational psychologists will return to the classroom to study the kinds of learning processes that are involved in the meaningful acquisition of subject-matter knowledge, instead of continuing to extrapolate to such processes theories and evidence derived from highly simplified instances of nonverbal or rote verbal learning in laboratory situations. Second, I think we will shortly cease pretending that meaningful classroom learning consists merely of a designated series of problem-solving tasks, and will also make a serious attempt to study the learning of ideas and information presented by teachers and textual materials. Third, I feel reasonably certain that we will devise appropriate methods of investigating the effects of general variables influencing meaningful learning, both singly and in combination, instead of vainly seeking to speculate about these effects from the results of particular curriculum improvement projects (e.g., the PSSC, the UICSM) in which an indeterminate number of variables are manipulated in uncontrolled and indeterminate fashion. Lastly, I am hopeful that we will focus our attention increasingly on the long-term learning and retention of large bodies of sequentially organized subject matter rather than on short-term mastery of fragmentary learning tasks.

What about the product of this research activity, that is, the future shape of the discipline? I am hopeful that the educational psychology of tomorrow will be primarily concerned with the nature, conditions, outcomes, and evaluation of classroom learning, and will cease being an unstable and eclectic amalgam of rote learning theory, developmental and social psychology, the psychology of adjustment, mental hygiene, measurement, and client-centered counseling. Thus, hopefully, the new discipline will not consider such topics as child development, adolescent psychology, the psychology of adjustment, mental hygiene, personality, and group dynamics as ends in themselves but only insofar as they bear on and are *directly* relevant to classroom learning. It will confine itself only to such psychological theory, evidence, problems, and issues that are of *direct* concern either to the serious student of education or to the future teacher in his role as facilitator of school learning. It will also eliminate *entirely* many normally covered topics in educational psychology courses which are typically drawn from general and developmental psychology and which bear little or no relation to classroom learning. Examples of such topics include the nature and development of needs, general determinants of behavior, general reactions to frustration, developmental tasks, mechanisms of adjustment, parent-child relationships, noncognitive development during infancy and the pre-school years, and physical development. It is true, for example, that physical development during childhood affects motor coordination, writing, and popularity in the peer group, and that physical changes in adolescence affect the self-concept, emotional stability, peer relations, and athletic skills. But an educational psychology course cannot cover everything. Prospective elementary-school teachers will presumably have a course in child development, and prospective secondary-school teachers will presumably have a course in adolescent psychology. Similarly, certain aspects of motivation *are* obviously relevant for classroom learning, but a general discussion of needs, their nature, function, development, and classification, such as would be appropriate in a course in general psychology, hardly seems necessary.

One might reasonably anticipate that the new discipline of educational psychology will be principally concerned with the kinds of learning that take place in the classroom, that is, with meaningful symbolic learning—both reception and discovery. Some kinds of learning, such as rote learning and motor learning are so inconsequential a part of school learning as to warrant no systematic treatment in a course on educational psychology. Other kinds of learning, for example, the learning of values and attitudes, are not indigenous to the primary or distinctive function of the school, and should be considered only insofar as they affect or are part of the learning of subject matter; their more general aspects may be left to such courses as general and social psychology. And still other kinds of learning, for example, animal learning, conditioning, instrumental learning, and simple discrimination learning, are wholly irrelevant for most learning tasks in school, despite the fact that wildly extrapolated findings in these areas quite commonly pad the learning chapters of many educational psychology textbooks. The new discipline, also, will hopefully not be eclectic in theoretical orientation, but will proceed from a consistent theoretical framework or point of view based on a cognitive theory of meaningful verbal learning. Greater stress would be placed on cognitive development than was true in the past, and this material would be integrated more closely with related aspects of cognitive functioning.

Finally, an effort should be made to employ a level of discourse in teaching educational psychology that is appropriate for prospective teachers and mature students of education, that is, to avoid oversimplified explanations, language, and presentation of ideas. Educational psychology is a complex rather than a simple subject. Hence to oversimplify it is to render the beginning student a serious disservice. Clarity and incisiveness of presentation, also, do not require reversion to a kindergarten level of writing and illustration. In fact, it is the writer's firm conviction that much of the thinly disguised contempt of many prospective teachers for courses in pedagogy and educational psychology stems from the indefensible attempt to expose them to watered-down, repetitive content and to an unnecessarily elementary level of vocabulary, sentence structure, illustration, example, and pedagogic device.

It is true, of course, that if educational psychologists limit their coverage of learning to meaningful verbal learning, the unfortunate paucity of experimental evidence in this area becomes painfully evident. This situation is a reflection of the prevailing tendency, over the past three or more decades, for educational psychologists to extrapolate findings from animal, rote, and perceptual-motor learning experiments rather than to conduct research on meaningful verbal learning. In my opinion, presenting certain significant theoretical propositions to students without definitive empirical support for the time being would be preferable to leaving large gaps in theory or filling them by means of unwarranted extrapolation.

Organization of the New Discipline

How will the subject matter of the new discipline of educational psychology be organized? Inasmuch as classroom instruction involves the manipulation of those variables influencing learning, a rational classification of learning variables can be of considerable value in clarifying both the nature of the learning process and the conditions that affect it. Such a classification also provides, in a sense, an organizational framework for the field, since any course in educational psychology must, of necessity, be organized largely around the different kinds of factors influencing classroom learning.

One obvious way of classifying learning variables is to divide them into *intrapersonal* (factors within the learner) and *situational* (factors in the learning situation) categories. The *intrapersonal* category includes:

a) *cognitive structure* variables—substantive and organizational properties of previously acquired knowledge in a particular subject-matter field that are relevant for the assimilation of another learning task in the same field. Since subject-matter knowledge tends to be organized in sequential and hierarchical fashion, what one already knows in a given field, and how well one knows it, obviously influence one's readiness for related new learnings;
b) *developmental readiness*—the particular kind of readiness that reflects the learner's stage of intellectual development and the intellectual capacities and modes of intellectual functioning charac-

teristic of that stage. The cognitive equipment of the fifteeen-year-old learner self-evidently makes him ready for different kinds of learning tasks than does that of the six- or ten-year-old learner;

c) *intellectual ability*—the individual's relative degree of general scholastic aptitude (general intelligence or brightness level), and his relative standing with respect to particular more differentiated or specialized cognitive abilities.

How well a pupil learns subject matter in science, mathematics, or literature obviously depends on his general intelligence, verbal and quantitative abilities, on his problem-solving ability, and on his cognitive style;

d) *motivational and attitudinal factors*—desire for knowledge, need for achievement and self-enhancement, and ego-involvement (interest) in a particular kind of subject matter. These general variables affect such relevant conditions of learning as alertness, attentiveness, level of effort, persistence, and concentration;

e) *personality factors*—individual differences in level and kind of motivation, in personal adjustment, in other personality characteristics, and in level of anxiety. Subjective factors such as these have profound effects on quantitative and qualitative aspects of the learning process.

The *situational* category of learning variables includes:

a) *practice*—its frequency, distribution, method, and general conditions (including feedback or knowledge of results)
b) the arrangement of *instructional materials*—in terms of amount, difficulty, step size, underlying logic, sequence, pacing, and the use of instructional aids
c) such *group and social* factors as classroom climate, cooperation and competition, social-class stratification, cultural deprivation, and racial segregation
d) *characteristics of the teacher*—his cognitive abilities, knowledge of subject matter, pedagogic competence, personality, and behavior

Intrapersonal and situational variables "undoubtedly have interactive effects upon learning. . . . The external variables cannot exert their effects without the presence in the learner of certain states derived from motivation and prior learning and development. Nor can the internal capabilities of themselves generate learning without the stimulation provided by external events. . . . As a problem for research, the learning problem is one of finding the necessary relationships which must obtain among internal and external variables in order for a change in capability to take place. Instruction may be thought of as the institution and arrangement of the *external* conditions of learning in ways which will optimally interact with internal capabilities of the learner, so as to bring about a change in these capabilities" (Gagné, 1967).

Another equally meaningful and useful way of classifying the same set of learning variables is to group them into *cognitive* and *affective-social* categories. The former group includes the relatively objective intellectual factors, whereas the latter group includes the subjective and interpersonal determinants of learning. This scheme of categorization is perhaps somewhat more convenient for the researcher, and is also more familiar to the classroom teacher than is the intrapersonal-situational scheme.

References

Ausubel, D. P. The nature of educational research. *Educational Theory,* 1953, *3,* 314–320.

———, *The psychology of meaningful verbal learning.* New York: Grune & Stratton, 1963.

Gage, N. L. Theories of teaching. In *Theories of learning and instruction.* 63rd Yearbook, *Nat. Soc. Stud. Educ.,* Part I. Chicago: Univer. Chicago Press, 1964, pp. 268–285.

Gagné, R. M. Instructions and the conditions of learning. In *Instruction; Some contemporary viewpoints* (L. Siegel, Ed.). San Francisco: Chandler, 1967, pp. 291–313.

Hilgard, E. R. A perspective on the relationship between learning theory and educational practices. In *Theories of learning and instruction.* 63rd Yearbook, *Nat. Soc. Stud. Educ.,* Part I. Chicago: Univer. Chicago Press, 1964, pp. 402–415.

Jersild, A. T., and S. F. Bienstock. The influence of training on the vocal ability of three-year-old children. *Child Development,* 1931, *2,* 277–291.

——, Development of rhythm in young children. *Child Development Monographs,* 1935, No. 22.

Mandler, G. From association to structure. *Psychological Review,* 1962, *69,* 415–426.

Melton, A. W. The science of learning and the technology of educational methods. *Harvard Educational Review,* 1959, *29,* 96–106.

Sheffield, F. D. Theoretical considerations in the learning of complex sequential tasks from demonstration and practice. In *Student response in programmed instruction* (A. A. Lumsdaine, Ed.). Washington, D.C., National Academy of Sciences, National Research Council, 1961, pp. 13–32.

Smith, B. O. Critical thinking. In *Recent research developments and their implications for teacher education,* Thirteenth Yearbook, *Amer. Ass. Coll. Teacher Educ.* Washington, D.C.: The association, 1960, pp. 84–96.

Spence, K. W. The relation of learning theory to the technology of education. *Harvard Educational Review,* 1959, *29,* 84–95.

2 The Contribution of Educational Psychology to Teacher Training*

Floyd G. Robinson

In the limited time at my disposal I want to look at the following four questions:

a) What is the intent of educational psychology?
b) To what extent is this intent realized in current textbooks?
c) What might be done to improve the content of educational psychology?
d) What experiences should be planned for the teacher in training which go beyond subjecting him to improved content?

Before turning to these major questions, I should like to raise some preliminary issues, mainly in the hope of establishing an appropriate mental set for the conference. To begin with, I think we should keep in mind that the problem of introducing an ap-

**From a speech presented at a conference on the role of psychology in education, sponsored by the Ontario Institute for Studies in Education, April 1968.*

propriate educational psychology component into teacher training is part of the much larger task of bringing psychological knowledge to bear upon educational decision making in general. I believe that two unfortunate consequences will follow any attempt to isolate the problem of teacher training. The lesser evil is that we tend to pad our courses with information the classroom teacher cannot use, because the action proposed lies for the most part outside his domain of decision making. For example, theories of cognitive development might deal with when a child is ready to learn particular concepts and thus with how curriculum content should be spaced out over the grade structure, but the decision as to which concepts should be taught at which grade level is generally made by the curriculum developer rather than by the teacher. Similarly, while educational psychology has many useful things to say about practice, the existing degrees of freedom for constructing practice schedules are almost determined by the author of the reading text, the arithmetic text, or spelling text. It might be interesting, in fact, to speculate upon the extent to which such devices as programmed instruction, educational television, and the explicit teaching procedures derived from task analysis either eliminate independent teacher behavior altogether or enmesh him so tightly in a network of specific procedural directions that the teacher's knowledge of educational psychology could hardly be a significant variable affecting student learning.

The fact that we give teachers knowledge which is relatively useless to them may be of no great importance. The second consequence of treating teacher education in isolation, however, is that we easily forget that the failure of both psychology and educational psychology to make an impact at those levels of decision making where the real character and substance of public education is decided will mean that our intervention in teacher education may have only a peripheral effect; indeed, I will conclude my paper by arguing that until some substantial changes are made in the expectations that exist at these higher decision-making levels, the defeat of whatever inventive methodology might be devised with the help of educational psychology is fairly assured in advance.

Some documentation of our failure to influence high-level decision making can be had by looking at the field of mathematics education. More than a decade ago when the first wave of the mathematics revolution rocked our traditional viewpoint, it was hoped that an opportunity had arisen to inject psychological insights into educational practice via the new curricula. Many efforts were made to bring psychologists and mathematicians together to achieve that end; the results, however, were disastrous as far as psychology was concerned, for mathematicians rapidly concluded that psychologists had little to tell them. In my opinion the current attitude of mathematicians and mathematics methodologists toward the likely contribution of educational psychology is best epitomized by the prestigious Cambridge Report on *Goals for School Mathematics,* which dismissed Piaget with the simple assertion that his theoretical and experimental work had no relevance for the major reform of mathematics education which they were proposing.

Mathematicians, then, have proceeded to take matters into their own hands, have completely dominated the thinking that lies behind new programs in secondary school mathematics, and in many cases are even exercising critical influence on the programs designed for *elementary school* children. In pontificating on the appropriateness of different levels of abstraction at different ages, on the proper sequencing of ideas, and on appropriate methods of presentation, the mathematicians have become the acting educational psychologists in the mathematics field. Moreover, since mathematicians and other university subject-matter specialists have the upper hand in instituting curriculum reform and in influencing the educational hierarchy, their active disdain for the educational psychologist is likely to have important implications for teacher training. For example, while many of the proposed reforms of educational psychology call for an expansion of its offerings in teacher-training programs, I suggest it would be more realistic to believe that while opportunities in that direction may be created by increasing the length of teacher-training programs, the additional time made available will be usurped by subject-matter specialists, who are determined that teachers in training will receive more instruction in their substantive fields. As an example of the trend in local events I would point out that in Ontario, a province blessed by both strong psychology and educational psychology communities, we have recently established a Master of Arts in Teaching (MAT) degree in mathematics, the precursor of general developments in this field. In the midst of talk of expanding educational psychology offerings it is interesting to note that the typical course pattern for the MAT consists of four courses in graduate-level mathematics and one course in educational theory, and that the latter requirement need not be educational psychology or any of its near relatives (measurement, curriculum development, research, and the like). It is clear then that the prestigious elements of the mathematics education community conceive of the master teacher as a person who has no need for the insights of educational psychology. The major implication I draw from the preceding observations, aside from the need to tone down our expectations, is that any plan for the reform of educational psychology in teacher education must take into account the existing power structure in educational decision making. I will return later in my paper to this question.

The Intent of Educational Psychology Programs in Teacher-Training Institutions

What is it that educational psychology is trying to do? Judging from the textbooks and writings of those who express themselves coherently on the subject, I believe it is the intention that educational psychology should attempt to create a kind of input-output model. According to this conception, the "output" would be a class of variables comprising those outcomes which are considered to be the school's responsibility. The "inputs" represent a class of psychological variables—or variables linked to mediating psychological variables—known to be causally linked to the desired behavioral outcomes, and whose manipulation or accommodation lies within the school's power. While this abbreviated statement leaves a few "tag-ends," such an input-output conception is clearly visible in our writing efforts. Thus, we explicitly categorize behavioral outcomes in such terms as concept learning, generalization learning, problem solving, creativity, and the like. Moreover, the bulk of our text is concerned with empirical evidence and logical argument linking a great variety of cognitive, affective, social, situational, and task variables to these outcomes. And to varying degrees, different authors attempt to formulate a set of unifying ideas that allow some economy in predicting, explaining, or simply organizing the vast multitude of potential relationships.

When we intervene in teacher training we assume that the teacher will be able to superimpose this input-output mesh upon his classroom decision making and that, as a result, decisions will be reached which—as the common wording goes—"will optimize or maximize the product," the latter being some function of output variables. I think it unfortunate that this rather facile assumption has never been scrutinized by detailed analysis. It seems to me that we must possess an infinite amount of uncertainty as to what the optimum program might be, or even what the optimum individual choice will be, in a particular situation; and that the application of any empirically derived generalization—which is capable of reducing uncertainty by a finite amount—will still leave us mightily uncertain. The only conclusion I can come to in this respect is that we had best cease speaking of the maximum or the optimum when referring to procedures that might be concocted for classroom use on the basis of educational psychology. More realistically, one could probably demonstrate that the assignment of the values of input variables on the basis of an empirically derived generalization will produce a positive probability of increasing the value of some well-defined output function over that produced by the assignment of the values normally made by a teacher whose intuitive generalizations disagreed with empirically derived ones.

I am, then, prepared to believe—on purely logical grounds—that educational psychology *can* have some positive influence on decision making, although I cannot accept the facetious platitudes on the benefits to be derived from our field which are advanced—largely by questionable analogy—by our spokesmen and textbook writers. But even my more modest formulation of the benefits to be conferrred requires that the essence of our discipline, the propositions or generalizations that we formulate, must meet certain requirements. My list of requirements is as follows:

a) The generalization has to be incorporable into the cognitive structure that is activated by the teacher while operating in the classroom. In other words, the concepts and variables contained in it must have meaning for the teacher to the point where their values or exemplars can be unequivocally identified.
b) The generalization has to suggest manipulations of input variables or methods of accommodating input variables over which the teacher has some control.
c) The generalization has to suggest manipulations that the teacher would not ordinarily arrive at by simple inspection of the situation or by more profound intuition.
d) The generalization has to be valid, that is, has to possess some uncertainty-reducing potential in an objective sense.

From this point on I shall refer to generalizations meeting these criteria simply as being "potentially useful" generalizations.

The Educational Psychology Literature

Given that our intent is to create an input-output system with the hope that it will improve educational decision making, and having laid down certain conditions for generalizations which might be useful in this respect, we must next ask to what extent this intent is realized in our current textbooks. Since I should not want any particular author to take umbrage at my remarks, let me state that the quotations I shall be citing are not from authors present at this meeting; moreover, to avoid embarrassment in other quarters I have paraphrased liberally. Perhaps it would make everyone feel better if I were to say that the deficiencies I will report are those I first discovered in my own recent attempts to write an educational psychology textbook; as a matter of honesty, however, I must record that comparative reading suggests that these faults are fairly widespread.

Undoubtedly part of our difficulty in formulating useful generalizations in educational psychology can be traced to the fact that while we borrow many of our concepts from academic psychology, we exhibit a curious approach-avoidance tendency toward that discipline. On the one hand, we are attracted by its power to confer respectability upon our work; on the other hand, we are anxious to take our audience somewhat into account. The typical compromise reached in dealing with the concepts of psychology is to dilute their definitions into language thought more congenial to the teacher's ear. The result is that even the most rigorously defined concepts acquire a gratuitous aura of ambiguity in the translation. For example, the common definition of a positive reinforcer as "a stimulus whose presentation strengthens the response which it follows" remains ambiguous because the word "strengthens" is undefined and exceedingly misleading. Not many would attempt to improve on this definition by defining "strengthen" in terms of the probability of a response and by indicating how this probability is to be measured. If we begin this far from the accurate definition of a concept that is capable of clarity, it is understandable that as we engage intrinsically vaguer terms like "motivation," "personality," "need," "problem," or "ability," the informality of our language increases to the point where it is difficult to see how the student can emerge with a clear concept. Such beginnings augur an unfortunate ending, for from fuzzy concepts one can surely generate only chaotic generalizations.

The substance of the generalization itself introduces a second problem. I think the typical approach of the educational psychology textbook writer might be described as an eclectic one, in that he grasps hold of established psychological theory or hypotheses resulting from laboratory studies and uses these as the basis of hypotheses or inferences as to what will happen in what he regards as an analogous educational situation. No doubt this approach will keep educational psychology abreast with the advance of psychological knowledge in general and has the further advantages that it is both interesting and comfortable for the writer and lecturer. I think, for example, that it is attractive to many minimally qualified instructors because a one-lecture-stand on Berlyne's theory of transformational thinking or on operant conditioning, in addition to generating the interest that accrues to any plausible idea on first encounter, does not allow time for perceptive students to collect their thoughts sufficiently to ask embarrassing questions.

However the eclectic-translative approach suffers from what appear to be sizeable weaknesses. The most dangerous one is that at least some of the extrapolations appear to be *invalid* because the assumed analogous situations in the classroom are simply not analogous. We all *say* that the phenomena of the classroom are of a different order of complexity than the phenomena of the psychological laboratory and that one cannot indiscriminately extrapolate from the simple to the complex. Yet, apparently our conviction does not travel with this assertion. For we seem to persist in citing the interference theory of forgetting with its implications of the inevitability of retroactive inhibition, the operant conditioning view that explicit reinforcements ought to be built into instructional materials, or the Thorndike-Skinner view that aversive stimulation is generally ineffective and should be avoided as a classroom motivational device. Yet the tenability of such generalizations when examined in terms of the actual complexity of the learning of an organized body of knowledge and of the sophisticated motivations operating in the school setting, seem highly questionable and can hardly be thought to have a positive influence on classroom decision making.

Another tendency inherent in the loose structure of an eclectic approach is that of our backing ourselves into elaborate tautologies. For example, many writers—during the rapid review of learning theory—define a positive reinforcer as the stimulus that strengthens the response it follows. Fifty pages later, in the discussion of motivation, these writers can be found advising teachers that if they want a particular behavior to recur they should make sure that an appropriate positive reinforcement follows the desired response. Putting these statements together, the teacher has now been informed that to make behavior recur he must provide something which will strengthen it, that is, make it more likely to recur. Somehow this does not seem very helpful.

Typically, our writing is not sufficiently sustained to carry us all the way to complex tautology, and we stop at mere meaningless generalization. For example, we say that "authoritarian teachers tend to depress pupils' creativity"—and we leave both "authoritarian" and "creativity" undefined. These faults of tautology and meaninglessness cannot, of course, be entirely attributed to the eclectic-translative approach. We are in danger of them whenever, starting off in a great conceptual confusion, we inch toward generalization with little more than syntax as a restraining influence, coming back at last upon ourselves in the dense verbal fog.

Not all our generalizations are fuzzy, however; many are clear enough but stand at a great distance from any suggested or implied action. Such, for example, are detailed data—including graphs and charts—on the relative height and broad-jumping abilities of boys and girls at various ages, on the distribution of socioeconomic classes in particular towns, on the improvement of maze learning with practice, or on the forgetting of nonsense syllables over varying periods of time. I suppose one might argue that by understanding such relationships the teacher acquires a firmer grasp of the phenomena of education; and yet, no manipulable variable being in evidence, I find it difficult to believe that any of these statements would figure very prominently in the improvement of the educational product.

Of course it would be unfair to assert that *all* educational psychology consists of nothing more than erroneous, tautologous, vague, or inconsequential generalizations. In fact, a good part of the writing is merely descriptive and when this is done accurately—as for example in elaborating a system of behavioral outcomes or describing a particularly relevant experiment—the product can have some value. Moreover, some of the generalizations offered do seem to meet the criteria of potential usefulness cited in an earlier section. And yet I feel that my bland descriptions have not really captured the "unreal" impression of the prose in this field. To do this, one must make two excursions: first by sampling intact sections of writing rather than isolated generalizations, and second by proceeding to those remarkable statements which conclude our labors.

As to the first excursion, the stringing together of a series of undefined terms and vague generalizations of the type previously described reaches its most ludicrous extreme in the numerous five-page summaries of Piaget's theory, the last part of which typically begins in somewhat the following fashion:

> In the stage of "formal" operations, beginning somewhere in the 11–15 age group, the child acquires the ability to undertake "combinatorial," "hypothetical deductive," and "if-then" thinking. At this stage the child is no longer bounded by the "empirical givens" but can hypothesize and is capable of "thinking about thinking." . . .

This account is typically larded with further undefined terms (curiously set in quotation marks as if this practice somehow explained their meaning) and several incomprehensible passages from Piaget himself. Such small snatches as I have been able to understand strike me as being extremely misleading and I find it difficult to believe that the teacher can profit much from them.

Our second excursion is to travel to the back of the chapter where, having now defined concepts and formulated generalizations, the textbook writer must take the last desperate step and attempt to offer the teacher some straightforward advice on how to manipulate input variables. Here I feel educational psychology sinks to levels of banality unmatched in any other scientific or professional writing. "The teacher," we announce with a straight face, "must keep in mind that her pupils are individuals, each with his own unique pattern of abilities." Other good advice is that the teacher should remember that "not all pupils are motivated toward school work," and that "the child should move at the pace determined by his abilities." Frankly, I think this is as patronizing and insulting as it would be to inform a neophyte physicist that "objects generally fall downward, other things being equal," or the medical student that "patients are not always as sick as they think they are."

In summary, it seems to me that educational psychology, as represented by the texts we put into the hands of teachers in training, moves through the progressive errors of defining its concepts poorly, fashioning generalizations by an uninhibited translation of psychological theory into the educational situation, and abstracting from these generalizations some pitiful caricature of good advice. By the time we have finished one of these wretched essays I think we know in that region of our soul not contaminated by the poisons of rationalization that, having written at enormous length, we have said very little of any real value to the teacher. The impression that experienced teachers take from our writing, if I might cite a response from a course evaluation, is that "after a bold initial sally in which educational psychologists cite the importance of a particular topic, they retreat from the phenomenon as it is found in the classroom with frightening acceleration, resorting in the final stages to covering their tracks with desperately spiraling verbal gymnastics."

Reforming the Educational Psychology Text

I believe it will be worthwhile to attempt to reform the educational psychology text because, aside from what may happen in a few advanced experimental programs—and despite the fanciful speculations that we shall no doubt hear during the next two days—what the typical teacher is likely to know about our discipline for a considerable period in the future will be what is contained between the covers of a text, coupled with such folksy elaborations as may be offered by a none-too-well-qualified instructor. Such reform will not be an easy task, since texts are oriented toward a large commercial market that seems to impose its own conditions for approval. Surely, only a belief that the market place demands complete coverage could induce us to range so widely over the cognitive, affective, and motor domains; to add to this, miniature courses in statistics and evaluation; and, finally, to season the work well with liberal extractions from learning theory, developmental psychology, and personality theory.

We seem terribly fearful of leaving anything out; yet common sense indicates that coverage must be narrowed if our writing is to acquire any depth. And with less coverage perhaps we can make some inroads on the problem of vague terminology. No writer can emerge with a universally accepted and for-all-times definition of "problem solving," but he should be expected to be consistent in the use of this term throughout his tome and to distinguish it from "creativity" or "discovery" if he uses the last two terms.

But a bigger step forward will come, in my opinion, when we are able to wean ourselves from the eclectic-translative approach that characterizes contemporary educational psychology. Although it can be interesting, its net effect is like shining a number of small colored lights on a vast dark object: there are points of brilliance here and there, but the total structure of the object and the relationship of its parts remain invisible. It would be preferable, I believe, if we started by setting out the categories of behaviors we are interested in producing in public education, and by adhering doggedly to the phenomena defined by these categories as they exist in the classroom. For example, believing that problem solving is an appropriate educational goal, let us analyze the characteristics of problems as they exist in the context of complex bodies of knowledge taught in school; let us define some reasonable criteria for setting off problems from lower orders of behavioral outcomes; and let us exemplify how strategies can be devised to lead students to independent solution of classes of such problems. By all means let us draw upon laboratory psychology where it is appropriate, but an immense difference in utility results from making the classroom phenomena the focal point of our discussion or from wandering vaguely through *Einstellung* effects, the two-pendulum problem, "after-the-fact" habit family analyses of problem solving, Dewey's five stages, and a host of other miscellanea.

And where, as is usually the case, definitive empirical evidence is lacking, I would not hesitate to speculate on the basis of analysis and deduction from a set of theoretical constructs; such approaches are, after all, luxuries unavailable to the harried teacher, and their application may well cast a good deal of light on classroom learning. Of several instances that might be cited, I would think that much of the impressive success of task analysis in recent years can be attributed to the power of reasoning unfettered by psychological dogma. Thus Piaget's theory argues that children will not ferret out the cause-effect relationships in natural phenomena until their mental operations form the complex structure characteristic of the formal stage of thinking; task analysis, abetted by straightforward reasoning, suggests that Piaget has read too much into the problem and that the child can, given a small amount of training, produce acceptable solutions at much younger ages. Although no hard data appear to be available, I think that the task analysis conclusion should be entered as a relevant educational hypothesis and guide to the teacher's action.

BEYOND THE TEXTBOOK

One might thus envisage an educational psychology text of the future which would contain a number of useful generalizations, either empirically derived or speculative, bearing on classroom learning and organized around the central concepts of the nature of the learner and the learning process. Since I might be challenged to produce such entities, I would say that generalizations concerning the efficacy of advance organizers, or the distinctive kinds of stimulus support (dependence upon empirical props) required by children at different stages of cognitive development, or the differential relationship of arousal—manifested by drive level, emotion or anxiety—to performance of simple, as opposed to complex, tasks all satisfy my criterion of potential usefulness and can be incorporated into a larger ideational structure.

The preceding are *potentially* useful generalizations, but they are not likely to be used by the individual classroom teacher. The difficulty is that they are *indeed* generalizations across tasks, personality types, motivational states and—most important—subject-matter areas. They are not ready for incorporation into the teacher's decision-making structure without further working down, at least to the level of his particular subject-matter field. One can understand well enough the general principle of organizers, but it takes a good deal of further initiative and invention actually to construct an organizer for an algebra passage, or to discern the proper placement, level of generality, and method of incorporation of a series of organizers into an algebra course.

Now, while we intimate in our educational psychology textbooks that the teacher ought to do this working down—or do "applied research" as we say—we cannot realistically expect this to happen. The teacher will not do it even if he has the time, because the teacher's decision-making schema are completely pre-empted by the ultraspecific procedural rules of the methodologist who, not content to speak of trends, general relationships, or suggestions, tells the teacher which book to buy, how to teach specific lessons, how much homework to assign, how to take it up, what to write on the board, what to put on the bulletin board, and so on. Moreover, these specific procedural rules are reinforced by observation, practice teaching, and written examinations. It is not surprising, then, that these strictures tend to be prepotent from the moment a teacher steps into the class and that the teacher finds they will work well enough—at least up to whatever ambiguous standard he may be able to fashion, given no training in evaluation. Furthermore the teacher—particularly in his early years—is in a high-anxiety situation, a state which does not lend itself to that more extended reflection that draws upon remote rules and peripheral knowledge. Thus an initial prepotency, energized by a high-drive level and lack of opportunity for critical assessment, causes the methodological rules to congeal rapidly into fixed habits, while the airy generalizations of educational psychology travel the way of all unused ideas.

The previous paragraphs suggest the direction of my proposed solution. In view of the prevailing power structure in education, and for the reasons previously cited, it seems to me that during the next few years the "enlightened" methodologist will provide the best hope for educational psychology to make an impact through teacher training (as opposed to contributions at higher levels). It is in the framework of inventive methodology that the potentially useful generalizations of educational psychology, mixed with other ingredients, jell into detailed procedural rules for developing specific kinds of behavior in the school setting. This is not to say that methodology will ever be a derivative of psychology, for the former is still largely an inventive process and seems likely to remain so. How educational psychology contributes to the process of methodological invention will vary from case to case; sometimes it may suggest a procedure directly; more often, however, it may merely act as a set of logical and empirical constraints upon otherwise freewheeling hypothesizing about procedures.

Perhaps my view of the ultimate relationship between educational psychology and methodology is too much colored by personal experience. For some years (as a classroom teacher) I labored to no great avail to inculcate in my students the ability to solve the kinds of geometry problems to which we were all subjected in our high-school days. Even though I was unsuccessful, I expect I would have gone on for thirty years with the procedural rules taught in the methodology courses, had I not been diverted by the enticements of graduate study. Anyway, I came back to the problem many years later and worked out a strategy that seems to allow much younger children to cope with these logical exercises, even to the point of handling "originals" (that is, problems they have not seen before). When embroiled in the kind of discussion which underlies this conference, I have often reflected on the contribution of educational psychology to this small personal triumph in methodological invention. For the most part, this success was largely a matter of having time to analyze what appeared to be the component tasks in the class of problems and to ask myself in respect to each task, "How can I get around the difficulties that kids seem to have here?" I had no conscious experience of the generalizations of educational psychology suggesting a solution, but possibly these generalizations were active in whatever internal-combustion chamber creative fires burn. And when ideas came forth, such principles frequently allowed a rapid assessment of practical potential. "Perhaps I should have the children explicitly verbalize a rule for proceeding from a fact to be proved to a class of propositions which would establish this fact," I would say to myself. "Ah yes," I would answer, "this is consistent with the general efficacy of verbal rules in steering the child's mental operation through tasks with a higher order of perceptual complexity." And so the internal conversation went, some internal process (possibly aided by psychological principles) throwing up suggestions; a critical faculty dissecting and evaluating them in the light of known relationships.

My proposal that we should make our move through the methodologist is at considerable odds with such solutions as:

a) Core courses in academic psychology surrounded by satellite courses stressing application;
b) Educational psychologists combining in team fashion to acquaint teachers with their basic research interests;
c) Educational psychologists attempting to make the application to subject-matter areas themselves.

The first two approaches seem appropriate to graduate instruction in educational psychology, but I would reject all three for teacher-training programs because, in general, neither psychologists nor educational psychologists are prepared to keep up with the rapid changes underway in the substantive fields now taught in our schools—and therefore they are not in a position to make imaginative applications. On the other hand, I think we can safely assume that the methodologist, if he so wished, is quite capable of assimilating in relatively short order the essential substance of our discipline.

An alliance with methodologists is just the beginning step, however. I agree with proposals that the teacher in training needs some kind of behavioral laboratory experience, my reasoning being that the procedural rules obtained from inventive methodology need strengthening through practice until they are at operational strength prior to the time the teacher enters the classroom. No doubt the practice-teaching experience—now largely an exercise in observing and practicing specific methodological rules—could be used to better advantage. For example, if the instructor in the educational psychology course is talking about categories of behavioral outcomes and the methodologist is illustrating these in the teacher's substantive field, then the teacher himself should be instructed to identify and classify those activities observed in an ongoing lesson. Again, if the educational psychologist explains the theory of organizers and the methodologist examines their application to a subject-matter field, then the teacher should be required to design and use one in his actual teaching. Much can be done in that way to give the teacher some experience in applying educational psychology principles.

However I would also advocate exercises in behavioral change which employ much smaller groups of children, perhaps even one child. The typical classroom teacher is so harried, and so far removed from the possibility of close observation and the precise control of the child's behavior, that he actually learns little about learning from his experience. For this and other reasons he is susceptible to the many myths about learning which permeate professional thinking, one of the most pernicious being that the present limitations on what the child learns in school can be safely attributed to the operation of some kind of natural law of development. Every teacher should have the experience of identifying some behavioral goal presently thought difficult or impossible for a child to attain, of performing a task analysis to reveal component skills, of attempting to teach these skills, and of evaluating the results; if the outcome were successful—as it would be with careful selection—the teacher would go into the classroom with a healthy respect for the potential of the child and a valuable impatience with the limitations of mass education.

Not all such "lab" experiences need be of this dramatic kind. I have found that requiring experienced teachers to teach a concept to children of different age levels, while carefully observing both the kind and quality of props required to do so, fixed the essential attributes of stages of cognitive development in their minds far more precisely and permanently than reams of printed discourse. I would add, too, that the results of these exercises in attempting to produce specified behavioral goals should figure prominently in the training institution's decision as to when the neophyte should be allowed to assume independent status in the classroom. I expect that the suggestion that the teacher should not be granted a certificate until he demonstrates he can *change behavior* will sound abrasive in the ears of more genteel teacher educators, but it seems reasonable counsel nonetheless.

Effecting a liaison with inventive methodologists will not be an easy task, but not for the reason that they are a breed limited in number, nor even because they presently despise us. The chief obstacle is that there is little incentive at the moment to improve methodology—other than changing the content with which it deals—because the present methodology is quite capable of accomplishing the low-level behavioral goals we have set in education. By way of analogy, I would think that the typical group of children in today's schools could be compared to a group of runners jogging around a track who are required merely to keep pace with a slow-moving mechanical rabbit. If the trainer's methods are 20 percent less efficient than they might be, then the student may have to expend roughly 20 percent more effort, but he will have no trouble keeping up to the modest standard. The point is that efficient methodology becomes critical (insofar as achievement is concerned) only at the point of maximum effort, and we are far away from this point at the moment.

What I have just said may be thought a negative view. Let me, then, express the ultranegative view. For some time a private hypothesis has been pressing inward upon my consciousness—supported by personal observation—that certain attitudes are so ingrained in educators that the methodologist will be subjected to ridicule, scorn, and abuse in direct proportion to his inventiveness, that is, in direct proportion to his ability to produce behavioral change over and above that now produced by the school. Although I am tempted to speak of other people's experience here, certain matters of delicacy do not permit it, so that I will continue my account of my own limited personal experience. Having worked out a method for getting children aged eight to ten to solve problems that most students in the age group 14–16 found difficult, thus making a methodological improvement of the order of approximately 200 percent on my scale, I was naturally ready to accept the plaudits and homage of teachers who were, I supposed, awaiting this beneficence. Alas, no commendation was forthcoming, but rather—if I might appeal to literary sources—curses, both loud and deep. Typical reactions of teachers when told of these results were: "I think it is monstrous to force logical thinking on immature minds;" "All you will succeed in doing is warping the child's mind;" and this—which particularly grieves me—"What right have you to play God?" It is easy to single out the romantic naturalists, the embryological model theorists, the humanistic psychologists, or the Summerhillians as the official spokesmen for such viewpoints, but I think there is a kind of ambivalence in most of us about the desirability of producing, via external control, dramatic changes in the behavior of a normal child.

At long last I have come back, not entirely in circular fashion I hope, to the point from which I started. In my view, until we are able to change the expectation of senior educational decision makers and significant elements of the public, to enlist not only their support but also their *demand* for our inventive methodologies, the creator of such methodology must be prepared to be something of a martyr. Some may be willing to do this, but although I once felt I might have made some modest contribution to mathematics instruction, I am too thin-skinned to endure sustained criticism, or even the interminable hassle that invariably arises from conferences of this kind between those who believe that inventive methodology means, in the final analysis, that one must be prepared to shape the child's behavior toward well-defined goals and those who would have few external controls, permitting the child to develop according to his own "needs" and "nature." Thus, frustrated in the public sphere, I have retreated into retirement where at least I can try out my methods on my own children, imbibe the fermented juices of Niagara District grapes, and write parodies on educational practices and personalities. And if all attempts at honest employment fail, I can always make my living as a professor of educational psychology.

PART II
MEANINGFUL VERBAL LEARNING THEORY

Much of the experimentally supported theoretical distinction between *meaningful* retention and forgetting on the one hand, and *rote* retention and forgetting on the other, rests on the nature and direction of induced change in the amount of material retained when similar and confusable material is introduced before (proactively) or after (retroactively) a given learning task. In rote learning, the introduction of such material proactively or retroactively typically results in a retention decrement because of its associative interference with corresponding elements of the learning task. In meaningful material, however, where new concepts and propositions are nonarbitrarily and substantively related (anchored) to existing ideas in cognitive structure, the newly learned material is protected by such anchorage from the automatic interfering effects of the proactively or retroactively introduced material.

Whether increment (facilitation), decrement (interference), or neither increment or decrement results, depends on the net facilitating or interfering effects of such material on the stability, clarity, and discriminability of the learning task.

In the two experiments on retroactive and proactive effects in meaningful learning and retention reported in this unit, interference fails to occur, a situation different from that observed in studies of rote learning and retention. The reported outcome of facilitation in the first case, or of interference in the second, depends on whether various specified facilitating factors prevail or are counterbalanced by stipulated interfering factors.

The two concluding articles in Part II involve applications of meaningful verbal learning to interpretations of learning how to read and of second-language learning. In both instances the initial mediating function of an already acquired system of symbols (the spoken native language and the spoken or written first language) in acquiring a new set of equivalent symbols (reading and second-language learning) is stressed. Logical considerations derived from meaningful verbal learning theory favor the phonetic over the "look-say" approach to reading and challenge some widely accepted principles of the audio-lingual approach to second-language learning.

3 Retroactive Facilitation in Meaningful Verbal Learning*

David P. Ausubel
Mary Stager
A. J. H. Gaite

The phenomenon of retroactive interference in verbal learning has been clearly demonstrated in many studies which have used nonmeaningful and unconnected materials, chiefly nonsense syllables. However, there is much doubt as to whether retroactive interference occurs when connected material is meaningfully learned (i.e., when it interacts on a nonarbitrary, substantive basis with established ideas in cognitive structure).

In general, those studies with connected material which demonstrated the occurrence of retroactive interference have demanded *verbatim* recall of material (e.g., Jenkins and Sparks, 1940; King and Cofer, 1960; Slamecka, 1959, 1960a, 1960b, 1962). Further, Mehler, and Miller (1964) obtained retroactive

Reprinted from the article of the same title,* Journal of Educational Psychology, *1968,* **59, *250–255. By permission of the authors and The American Psychological Association, Inc.*

interference for the syntactic, but not for the semantic, aspects of potentially meaningful sentences, and Newman (1939) demonstrated retroactive interference for nonessential, but not for essential, details of a narrative.

The majority of studies (Ausubel, Robbins, and Blake, 1957; Hall, 1955; McGeoch and McKinney, 1934; Mehler and Miller, 1964; Newman, 1939) requiring substantive (as opposed to verbatim) recall of connected verbal material have failed to demonstrate clearly the operation of retroactive interference. Two of these studies (Ausubel *et al.*, 1957; Mehler and Miller, 1964), in fact, found that material similar to the original material and interpolated between original learning and the tests for retention of such learning led to retroactive *facilitation*. But a recent study by Entwisle and Huggins (1964) indicated that, when engineering students were tested on a set of principles in electrical circuit th3ory, the interpolation of a highly similar set of principles before testing produced significant retroactive interference. It is debatable, however, whether the type of learning involved was nonarbitrary and substantive in nature; it is quite possible that the students may have learned the material, which was essentially mathematical (formulae, etc.) rather than verbal, by rote. Hence, it is concluded that there has been no definitive demonstration of the retroactive interference phenomenon in studies requiring the meaningful (nonarbitrary and substantive) learning and retention of connected verbal material.

Traditionally, retroactive interference has been explained in behavioristic terms: specific responses (from the originally learned material) are lost (forgotten) because they are superseded by competing associative tendencies (from the interpolated material) with greater relative strength. A major variable found to determine the amount of forgetting is the similarity of responses in interpolated and original activities (Osgood, 1953). In studies of rote learning, which employ nonmeaningful material or require the verbatim recall of potentially meaningful connected material (e.g., Slamecka, 1959, 1960b), this relationship has been experimentally verified: increased similarity, short of identity, of original and interpolated material, leads to increased interference.

However, in situations involving the substantive retention of potentially meaningful material, the effect of similarity of material is uncertain, and the applicability of the behavioristic explanation is questionable. Interpolated material that was substantively similar to originally learned material was reported to result in interference in only one study (Entwisle and Huggins, 1964) and, in this case, as was noted before, the material was perhaps learned by rote. Aside from this one exception, similar interpolated material led either to no interference (Hall, 1955) or to facilitation (Ausubel *et al.*, 1957; Mehler and Miller, 1964). Ausubel *et al.* found that an interpolated passage, which compared Buddhism and Christianity and which was substantively similar to the Buddhism passage that was tested, induced retroactive facilitation.

These findings suggested the interpretation that in the case of meaningful learning, where new concepts and propositions are nonarbitrarily and substantively related (anchored) to existing ideas in cognitive structure, the newly learned material is protected, by virtue of such anchorage, from the interfering effects of subsequently encountered competing stimuli and responses (Ausubel *et al.*, 1957). More important than the similarity variable for learning and retention in these circumstances, it was hypothesized, are such variables as the availability of relevant anchoring ideas in cognitive structure, their stability and clarity, and their discriminability from the learning material.

These authors proposed therefore that the influence of interpolated learning on retention is not necessarily a function of similarity of original and interpolated materials; instead it depends on whether or not the interpolated passage increases or decreases the discriminability of the original passage from its anchoring concepts in cognitive structure and hence counteracts or promotes irreversible reduction (forgetting), i.e., the process whereby the originally learned material is reduced to a least common denominator of and thus is no longer dissociable (retrievable) from the ideational system in which it is embedded.

The present study was designed to discover whether retroactive interference could be demonstrated in a learning situation that involved the substantive retention of potentially meaningful material and that was more analogous both to the Entwisle and Huggins study and to experiments demonstrating retroactive interference with verbatim recall than was the Ausubel *et al.* (1957) study. To satisfy these conditions, both original and interpolated materials had to be both unfamiliar and sufficiently similar to each other to engender confusion and conflict. Thus, the interpolated passage, a discussion of Buddhism, was highly similar to and conflicted with basic concepts in the originally learned passage (which dealt with Zen Buddhism), and both passages were generally unfamiliar to the experimental sample.

The present-study also investigated the operation of another variable whose effect on retroactive interference with the retention of nonmeaningful material and with the verbatim recall of connected material (Slamecka, 1959, 1960a) is well established. It is generally accepted (Slamecka and Ceraso, 1960) that susceptibility to retroactive interference after rote learning is inversely related to the level of verbatim acquisition of the original material. To investigate the effect of overlearning on retroactive interference or facilitation in a meaningful learning context, this experiment was designed so that certain subjects reread the original Zen Buddhism passage.

METHOD

Subjects

The experimental sample consisted of 156 students (91 male and 65 female). The subjects were drawn from the total membership of all of the Grade 13 classes in two suburban high schools and consisted of those students who were present for all four sessions of the experiment. These sessions, given once at each school on the same day, took a maximum of 40 minutes and were conducted during regular school hours over a period of one week.

Learning Passages and Measuring Instrument

The material used to investigate retroactive interference consisted of two passages that on the basis of content analysis were thought to be highly similar and conflicting. The first (original) passage (approximately 2200 words in length) was concerned with the history, sacred literature, doctrine, and ethical teachings of Zen Buddhism. The second (interpolated) passage (approximately 2100 words in length) dealt with similar topics in the Buddhist faith.

A third passage (approximately 1500 words in length), which dealt with the causes and types of drug addiction, was presented instead of the Buddhism passage to control group subjects. Because of its totally different content, it was presumed that this passage would not interfere with the Zen Buddhism passage.

The material in all three passages was selected on the basis of its unfamiliarity to almost any high school student. Hence the interpolated material (the Buddhism and drug addiction passages) differed for the experimental and control groups only in degree of similarity to the original (Zen Buddhism) passage and not, presumably, in familiarity. Empirical confirmation of the unfamiliarity of these passages was obtained when naive *S*s who had not studied the material in question made scores on the respective tests that were not significantly better than chance.

A 35-item multiple-choice test on Zen Buddhism was used to measure the learning performance of all *S*s. Before the data were analyzed, it was decided to eliminate four items from the test. These were items on which the experimental sample did more poorly than chance. In addition, two of these items had negative indices of discrimination, i.e., the subjects in the bottom quartile (as determined from total test scores) performed better on these two items than did the subjects in the top quartile. The corrected split-half reliability of this shortened (31-item) version of the test was .73. Scores showed a satisfactory range of variability and their distribution did not deviate significantly from the normal curve.

Procedure

At the beginning of each 40-minute session, *S*s spent approximately 5 minutes reading instructions. The balance of the session was available for reading the passages and, in the final session, for taking the test of Zen Buddhism; no subjects appeared to have difficulty in completing either type of task.

In the first session of the experiment, all subjects studied the Zen Buddhism passage. They were told, with this passage and with the Buddhism and drug addiction passages, that they were to read at their customary speed, that they were not to turn back once they had completed reading a page, and that they would be examined on the material at a later time by means of a multiple-choice test. (They were not actually tested on any material other than the Zen Buddhism passage, but the anticipation of a test on each passage was thought necessary to sustain and equate motivation in all conditions).

After the first session, *S*s were assigned to one of four groups, according to a 2 × 2 factorial design. Groups A and D were to receive the "overlearning" treatment, whereby they restudied the Zen Buddhism passage during the second session. Groups A and B were to receive the "interpolated learning" treatment, studying the Buddhism material in the third session.

Two stipulations were made in assigning subjects to treatment groups. First, because high school girls have been found to have higher verbal ability than high school boys (e.g., superior performance on the verbal portion of the School and College Ability Test, as shown by Ausubel and Fitzgerald, 1962), *S*s were assigned to groups in such a way that the ratio of girls to boys in each group was equal. (A chi-square test showed that, after eliminating those subjects who were not present for all four sessions, the male:female ratio in each treatment group did not depart significantly from equality). Second, because of possible differences in ability between the populations of the two schools, equal proportions of students from each school were assigned to each treatment group. (A chi-square test showed that, with the 156 subjects present during the entire experiment, the proportion of *S*s from each school in each group was not significantly different). Aside from these two restrictions, assignment of subjects to groups was made on a random basis.

The second session took place two days after the first. Groups A and D studied the Zen Buddhism passage a second time; Groups B and C studied the unrelated drug addiction passage.

In the third session, two days later, Groups A and B studied the potentially interfering Buddhism passage, and Groups C and D studied the unrelated drug addiction passage.

During the final session, which took place three days after the third, and one week after the initial session, all subjects were tested on the Zen Buddhism passage. They were instructed to answer all questions, and not to turn back once a page was completed.

Results and Discussion

Effect of Interpolated Learning on Retention

A comparison of the means (Table 1) on the 31-item test of Zen Buddhism indicates that the interpolated Buddhism passage, when compared with the irrelevant drug addiction passage, did not interfere with, but in fact facilitated, retention of the original Zen Buddhism passage.

TABLE 1

Mean Scores, Cell Variances and Frequencies of Four Treatment Groups on Test of Zen Buddhism

TREATMENT	TREATMENT	
	OVERLEARNING OF ZEN BUDDHISM PASSAGE	
Interpolated Buddhism Passage	Present	Absent
Present	Group A	Group B
Mean	16.08	11.36
S^2	19.41	14.31
n	38	39
Absent	Group D	Group C
Mean	14.55	9.89
S^2	16.61	16.46
n	42	37

Analysis of variance, following Winer's (1962) method for dealing with unequal cell frequencies when cell variances are homogeneous, shows (Table 2) that the overall facilitating effect of the interpolated passage is significant at the .05 level. The nonsignificant interaction term indicates that the interpolated Buddhism material affected retention in the same way regardless of degree of original learning.

TABLE 2

Analysis of Variance of Zen Buddhism Scores

SOURCE	*Ss*	*df*	*MS*	*F*
Interpolated learning	87.55	1	87.55	5.10*
Overlearning	855.87	1	855.87	49.90**
Interaction	.04	1	.04	.002
Error	2607.00	152	17.15	

*$p<.05$
**$p<.01$

The evidence is clear, therefore, that in this meaningful learning situation, retroactive interference did not occur when a connected and potentially meaningful passage was interpolated between material to which it was highly similar and a test for substantive retention of such material. Indeed, the interpolated passage appears to have had an effect that was small but reliably facilitating in comparison to that produced by a dissimilar and nonconflicting alternative passage. Thus it is suggested that the learning of the Buddhism passage may have served as a review and clarification of the Zen Buddhism material, thereby increasing both its stability and clarity and its discriminability from its anchoring concepts (presumably, related aspects of Judaism and Christianity) in cognitive structure.

The interpolation of similar and conflicting material between the meaningful learning of a Zen Buddhism passage and a later test of its retention may have had a facilitating effect on the retention of the Zen Buddhism material because it induced *S*s to compare, on their own, the two sets of material, and thus (a) to delineate those similarities between them that define their common differences from those established ideas in cognitive structure to which both were related in the course of learning, and (b) to delineate the differences between them. Both of these comparative operations conceivably could have facilitated retention of the original learning material by clarifying and sharpening its distinctive features and by increasing its discriminability from anchoring ideas in cognitive structure. In addition, these comparative operations may have further enhanced retention of the Zen Buddhism material because they necessarily required rehearsal of this material, which rehearsal, in turn, increased its stability, clarity, and discriminability.

To the extent that both the interpolated material and the original learning material share certain common ideas that are differentiable on the same basis from their common anchoring concepts in cognitive structure, later exposure to the interpolated material may increase the possibility that basic differences between the original material and the anchoring ideas will be cognized. In other words, if learning passages B and C are conflicting (similar but not identical), and thus necessarily share certain common differences relative to their common anchoring concepts (A), exposure to passage C makes possible the delineation of a common set of differences between the learning passages (B and C) and A, and may thereby make B more discriminable from A than if later exposure to C had not taken place. On the other hand, comparative efforts aimed at delineating the more specific kinds of differences between original and interpolated materials presumably help to sharpen the distinctive features of the original material, and may thus indirectly increase its discriminability from anchoring ideas in cognitive structure.

Furthermore, in the process of identifying and clarifying simple differences between original and interpolated learning passages, as well as more generic differences which differentiate both learning passages from relevant anchoring ideas in cognitive structure, *S*s must necessarily rehearse (i.e., activate or attempt to retrieve from storage) the original learning material. Such rehearsal may facilitate later retention in two ways. First, the very activation or retrieval of partially forgotten material

(material in the process of undergoing obliterative reduction) serves as a partial review of this material, and may thus enhance its stability and clarity in cognitive structure (thereby directly increasing its availability or retrievability at the time of later testing). Second, the greater clarity and stability of the original material resulting from rehearsal may indirectly increase its later retrievability by enhancing its discriminability from those established ideational systems in cognitive structure to which it is anchored.

These findings, if replicated and given greater generality, would have far-reaching implications for classroom teaching practice. Instead of suggesting (as do the classical retroactive interference findings in the case of rote learning and retention) that teachers scrupulously avoid introducing similar and conflicting material after a typical lesson involving meaningful learning, they imply that such material should be introduced deliberately. This recommendation would be based on the expectation that conflicting interpolated material would encourage the learner to compare related ideas in the original and interpolated sets of material, and thus facilitate retention of the original material through the influence of such intervening variables as rehearsal and clarification.

Effect of Overlearning on Retention

It is evident from Table 1 that a second session of studying the Zen Buddhism passage improved the retention of this passage relative to the groups who studied it only once. The analysis of variance in Table 2 indicates that this facilitating effect is significant at the .01 level. This finding is consistent with the results of previous studies (Ausubel and Youssef, 1965; Reynolds and Glaser, 1964) which demonstrated that review facilitates the retention of meaningfully learned material. It presumably does so through mechanisms similar to but by no means identical with those postulated above to account for the effects of rehearsal. For one thing, since overlearning of the original material involves both more complete and more explicit repetition than that involved in rehearsal, the facilitating effect of overlearning is accordingly much more pronounced (see Tables 1 and 2).

The absence of any interaction effect, however, indicates that the interpolation of conflicting material in this experiment did not differentially affect retention of the original material for the groups which overlearned the latter material and the groups which did not. That is, the facilitating effect of interpolation was neither greater nor less when it was preceded by overlearning of the original material than when it was not so preceded, and hence cannot be attributed in any way to the effect of such prior overlearning.

Although this finding contrasts markedly with the comparable, previously discussed situation in regard to rote learning, where overlearning of the original material has been invariably found to diminish subsequent susceptibility to retroactive interference, it is nonetheless readily understandable. When, as in the case of rote learning, interpolation has an interfering effect on the retention of the original material, any factor (e.g., overlearning) that increases the associative strength of such material quite naturally tends to lessen the interfering potential of competing associative tendencies. But since the interpolation of conflicting material facilitates rather than interferes with the retention of meaningfully learned original material, one cannot expect overlearning of the latter material to interact with the very different effects of interpolation in the same way as in the case of rote learning. However, the fact that the facilitating effect of interpolation is as great in a context of prior overlearning as in the absence of such a context, permits the inference that the mechanisms underlying the facilitating influence of interpolation are different than those underlying the facilitating influence of overlearning, and hence that the occurrence of the prior facilitating effect of overlearning does not preclude the later facilitating effect of interpolation.

Summary and Conclusions

In order to ascertain whether retroactive interference occurs in meaningful verbal learning and retention, the experimental conditions favoring such interference were maximized by using both unfamiliar and conflicting original and interpolated learning materials. The effects of interpolated learning (Buddhism) and of overlearning of the original material (Zen Buddhism) were tested in a 2 × 2 factorial design, using 156 12th grade pupils. Both independent variables significantly facilitated the retention of the original material (overlearning: $p < .01$; interpolation: $p < .05$). The facilitating influence of interpolated learning was attributed to the rehearsal and clarification of the original material which it presumably induced. The absence of a significant interaction term indicated that prior overlearning did not differentially affect the later facilitating effect of interpolation.

References

Ausubel, D. P., and D. Fitzgerald. Organizer, general background, and antecedent learning variables in sequential verbal learning. *J. educ. Psychol.*, 1962, *53*, 243–249.

Ausubel, D. P., and M. Youssef. The effect of spaced repetition on meaningful learning. *J. gen. Psychol.*, 1965, *73*, 147–150.

Ausubel, D. P., Lillian C. Robbins, and E. Blake. Retroactive inhibition and facilitation in the learning of school materials. *J. educ. Psychol.*, 1957, *48*, 334–343.

Entwisle, Doris R., and W. H. Huggins. Interference in meaningful learning. *J. educ. Psychol.*, 1964, *55*, 75–78.

Hall, J. F. Retroactive inhibition in meaningful material. *J. educ. Psychol.*, 1955, *46*, 47–52.

Jenkins, J. G., and W. M. Sparks. Retroactive inhibition in foreign language study. *Psychol. Bull.*, 1940, *37*, 470 (abstract).

King, D. J., and C. N. Cofer. Retroactive interference in meaningful material as a function of the degree of contextual constraint in the original and interpolated learning. *J. gen. Psychol.*, 1960, *63*, 145–158.

McGeoch, J. A., and F. McKinney. The susceptibility of prose to retroactive inhibition. *Amer. J. Psychol.*, 1934, *46*, 429–436.

Mehler, J., and G. A. Miller. Retroactive interference in the recall of simple sentences. *Brit. J. Psychol.*, 1964, *55*, 295–301.

Newman, E. B. Forgetting of meaningful material during sleep and waking. *Amer. J. Psychol.*, 1939, *52*, 65–71.

Osgood, C. E. *Method and theory in experimental psychology.* New York: Oxford University Press, 1953.

Reynolds, J. H., and R. Glaser. Effects of repetition and spaced review upon retention of a complex learning task. *J. educ. Psychol.*, 1964, *55*, 297–308.

Slamecka, N. J. Studies of retention of connected discourse. *Amer. J. Psychol.*, 1959, *72*, 409–416.

_____, Retroactive inhibition of connected discourse as a function of practice level. *J. exp. Psychol.*, 1960, *59*, 104–108(a).

_____, Retroactive inhibition of connected discourse as a function of similarity of topic. *J. exp. Psychol.*, 1960, *60*, 245–249(b).

_____, Retention of connected discourse as a function of duration of interpolated learning. *J. exp. Psychol.*, 1962, *63*, 480–486.

Slamecka, N. J., and J. Ceraso. Retroactive and proactive inhibition of verbal learning. *Psychol. Bull.*, 1960, *57*, 449–475.

Winer, B. J. *Statistical principles in experimental design.* New York: McGraw-Hill, 1962.

4 Proactive Effects in Meaningful Verbal Learning and Retention*

David P. Ausubel
Mary Stager
A. J. H. Gaite

In attempting to account for the nature of meaningful retention, it has been hypothesized that meaningfully learned materials, i.e., materials that have been nonarbitrarily and substantively related (anchored) to relevant established ideas in cognitive structure are protected, by virtue of such anchorage, from the interfering effects of similar previously learned, concurrently experienced, or subsequently encountered associations or ideas (Ausubel 1963; Ausubel, Robbins, and Blake, 1957; Ausubel, Stager, and Gaite, 1968). When material is meaningfully learned, according to this hypothesis, its subsequent availability (retrievability) does not depend on its resistance to interference

**Reprinted from the article of the same title,* Journal of Educational Psychology, *1969, in press. By permission of the authors and The American Psychological Association, Inc.*

from other similar associations or ideas, but, rather, on its *dissociability* from the established ideas in cognitive structure to which it is anchored and in relation to which it acquires its meaning. Thus, much more important for its retention than this kind of interference are such variables as the availability in cognitive structure of proximately and specifically relevant ideas, their stability and clarity, and their discriminability from the learning material. These latter variables affect the dissociability strength of the newly learned meanings and hence determine their availability. Whether previously learned or subsequently encountered meaningfully learned ideas facilitate or inhibit the retention of other meaningfully learned material depends, therefore, on their effects on the stability, clarity, and discriminability of the learning task and of the established ideas in cognitive structure to which the learning task is related.

A recent experiment (Ausubel, Stager, and Gaite, 1968) supported this theoretical view of meaningful retention, and confirmed the general finding in the literature that the *retroactive* interpolation of similar material does not inhibit the retention of *meaningfully* (as opposed to *rotely*) learned material. It was shown that the interpolation of learning material (Buddhism) between the learning of and a test of the retention of a similar, previously learned passage (Zen Buddhism), when both passages were relatively unfamiliar and unestablished, facilitated rather than inhibited the retention of the Zen Buddhism passage. This facilitating effect of the Buddhism passage was attributed to an increase in the stability, clarity, and discriminability of the remembered Zen Buddhism material which it (the Buddhism passage) presumably induced through retroactive rehearsal of the Zen ideas and comparison of them with corresponding Buddhist ideas.

The principal problem in the present experiment was to ascertain whether, in accordance with this same theoretical formulation of meaningful learning and retention, similar ideational material introduced *proactively* (rather than retroactively) has a facilitating, or at least a neutral, transfer effect on *meaningful* retention, in contrast to the uniformly negative effect which similar materials have been shown to have on the retention of *rotely* learned serial and paired associate learning tasks (Atwater, 1953; Mandler, 1954; Siipola and Israel, 1933; Underwood, 1949; Young and Underwood, 1954). To parallel further the chief variables investigated in rote retention, the transfer effect of overlearning of the proactively learned material on the retention of the meaningfully-learned learning task was also ascertained. Moreover, as was also true for the prior retroactive interference-facilitation study (Ausubel, Stager, and Gaite, 1968), experimental conditions maximizing the possibility of interference were imposed; that is, both the learning task and the proactive task consisted of unfamiliar and unestablished materials that were sufficiently similar and conflicting to be confusable with each other.

In a recent experiment, Suppes and Ginsberg (1963) found evidence of negative transfer (proactive interference) when an experimental group of first-graders learned the concept of identity of ordered sets after previously learning the concept of identity of unordered sets. The possibility of proactive interference was enhanced for the *S*s in this group because the proactive material (the concept of identity of unordered sets), which actually constituted the anchoring ideas for the second set of materials (the concept of identity of ordered sets), was unfamiliar, relatively unestablished in cognitive structure, and confusably similar to the first set of materials. This state of affairs is in sharp contrast to the situation confronting the *control* group both in the Suppes-Ginsberg experiment and in the present experiment where the learner relates the new learning task (e.g., Zen Buddhism) to a less relevant but *more highly established* set of ideas in cognitive structure (e.g., analogous Judeo-Christian ideas). The latter situation was also true for both control and experimental groups in the retroactive inhibition-facilitation study (Ausubel, Stager, and Gaite, 1968); that is, both groups learned the Zen Buddhism material first and related it to established Judeo-Christian concepts, and the experimental group was *subsequently* exposed to the Buddhism material.

It is quite possible, however, that the Suppes-Ginsberg findings are attributable, at least in part, to the *rote* learning of the mathematical relationships involved in their materials. Entwisle and Huggins (1964) similarly obtained evidence of retroactive interference in the learning of similar passages dealing with electrical circuit theory—a finding that was not replicated by Ausubel, Stager, and Gaite (1968) when purely verbal materials were used. Thus there is good reason to believe that the use of these same verbal materials in the present study provides a more adequate test of proactive interference-facilitation in meaningful learning and retention.

Regarding the second problem in this study—the influence of overlearning on proactive effects—it has been found that in rote, instrumental, and discrimination learning, overlearning generally increases positive transfer and decreases negative transfer. Bruce (1953) reported that increased practice on the training task tends to increase positive transfer in serial and paired-associate rote learning under conditions comparable to stimulus generalization. Under conditions typically associated with negative transfer, on the other hand, increased prior training tends to reduce and even reverse the direction of negative transfer (Atwater, 1953; Mandler, 1954; Siipola and Israel, 1933; Underwood, 1949; Young and Underwood, 1954; Yarcozower, 1959). Presentation of heterogeneous stimulus material that does not provide sufficient repetition to allow for mastery does not facilitate the learning of a reversal principle during the transfer period (Sassenrath, 1959). Reversal learning in rats and nursery-school children is facilitated when the first of two discrimination problems is overlearned (Bruner, Mandler, O'Dowd, and Wallach, 1958; Marsh, 1964; Pubols, 1957; Reed, 1953). In all of the above learning situations, overlearning was effective because it apparently established the particular relevance of specific elements for specific instances while, at the same time, permitting the positive transfer of general factors.

Insofar as *meaningful verbal* learning is concerned, the evidence similarly indicates that the stability and clarity of the anchoring ideas are positively related to the learning and retention of similar material. The greater the subject's knowledge of Christianity, for example, the more readily he is able to learn a passage on Buddhism, holding verbal ability constant (Ausubel and Fitzgerald, 1961; Ausubel and Youssef, 1963); similarly, the greater his knowledge of Buddhism, the better able he is to learn a passage on Zen Buddhism. This is presumably the case because an increase in the stability and clarity of the anchoring ideas obviously enhances their discriminability from similar, conflicting, and even confusable new learning tasks.

In the retroactive interference-facilitation paradigm with meaningful learning, the facilitating effect of the interpolated material was not found to be differentially greater or less when the original material was first overlearned (Ausubel, Stager, and Gaite, 1968). When interpolation has an inhibitory effect, however, as in the case of rote learning, susceptibility to retroactive interference is inversely related to degree of overlearning of the original material (Entwisle and Huggins, 1964; McGeoch, 1929; Slamecka, 1960; Slamecka and Ceraso, 1960). It should be noted, however, that in the proactive interference-facilitation paradigm, it is the proactive task (Buddhism), rather than the learning task (Zen Buddhism) that is overlearned.

The foregoing considerations led to the following hypotheses: (1) that learning of the Buddhism passage would facilitate, or at least not inhibit, the learning and retention of the Zen Buddhism passage; (2) that the degree of facilitation would be greater with two readings of the Buddhism passage than with one; and (3) that in each instance the effect of the independent variable would be significantly greater on the retention than on learning of the Zen Buddhism material.

METHOD

Subjects

The experimental sample consisted of 143 students (79 male and 64 female). The subjects were drawn from the total membership of all of the grade 13 classes in two suburban high schools and consisted of those students who were present for all four experimental sessions. These sessions were conducted during regular school hours, and took a maximum of 80 minutes.

Learning Passages and Measuring Instrument

The material used to investigate proactive effects consisted of two passages that, on the basis of content analysis, were judged to be highly similar and conflicting. The learning task consisted of a 2200-word passage concerning the history, sacred literature, doctrine, and ethical teachings of Zen Buddhism. The proactive task consisted of a 2100-word passage which dealt with similar topics in the Buddhist faith. A 1500-word passage concerning the causes and types of drug addiction was presented as control material when the Buddhism passage was not used for inducing either the proactive or the overlearning effects.

The material in all three passages was selected on the basis of its unfamiliarity, as measured by empirical test, to most high school students. (Naive *S*s who did not read the passages did not score significantly better than chance on multiple-choice tests on same.) Hence the Buddhism and drug addiction passages differed from each other only in degree of similarity and relevance to the Zen Buddhism passage and not, presumably, in familiarity to the subjects.

A 31-item multiple-choice test on the Zen Buddhism material was used to test immediate and delayed retention of the Zen passage. This test had been previously subjected to item analysis (so that all nondiscriminating items were excluded), and had been found to have a corrected split-half reliability of .73. Scores on the test showed a satisfactory range of variability, and their distribution did not deviate significantly from the normal curve.

Procedure

At the outset of the experiment, *S*s were assigned to one of three groups. The Overlearning-Proactive (O-P) Group studied the proactive Buddhism passage twice, the Proactive (P) Group studied the proactive Buddhism passage once, and the Control (C) Group was not exposed to the Buddhism passage.

Two stipulations were made in assigning *S*s to treatment groups. First, because high-school girls have been found to have higher verbal ability than high-school boys (e.g., to exhibit superior performance on the verbal portion of the School and College Ability Test, as shown by Ausubel and Fitzgerald, 1962), *S*s were assigned to groups in such a way that the ratio of girls to boys in each group was equal. (A chi-square test showed that after eliminating those *S*s who were not present for all four sessions, the male:female ratio in each treatment group did not depart significantly from equality). Second, because of possible differences in ability between the populations of the two schools, equal proportions of students from each school were assigned to each of the three treatment groups. (A chi-square test showed that, with the 143 *S*s present during the entire experiment, the proportion of *S*s from each school in each group was not significantly different.) Aside from these two restrictions, assignment of *S*s was made on a random basis.

In the first session of the experiment (Day 1), Group O-P studied the Buddhism passage, and Groups P and C studied the irrelevant drug addiction passage. All *S*s were told, when studying these passages and the Zen Buddhism passage, that they were to read at their customary speed, that they were not to turn back once they had completed reading a page, and that they would be examined on the material at a later time by means of a multiple-choice test. (They were not actually tested on any material other than the Zen Buddhism passage, but the anticipation of a test on each passage was thought necessary to sustain and equate motivation in all conditions.)

In the second session, two days after the first (i.e., Day 3), Groups O-P and P read the Buddhism passage, and Group C again read the drug addiction passage.

In the third session, two days after the second (i.e., Day 5), all groups studied the Zen Buddhism material, and all were then tested immediately on the Zen Buddhism passage. *S*s were instructed to answer all questions, and not to turn back once a page was completed.

In the fourth session, seven days after the third (i.e., Day 12), all *S*s took the delayed test on retention of the Zen Buddhism material. This test was identical with the immediate test of learning of this material.

In the first, second, and fourth experimental sessions, *S*s spent the first five minutes of the 40-minute period receiving instructions and the balance of the period reading a passage or taking the test. In the third session, which was 80 minutes long, the *S*s spent 5 minutes receiving instructions, 35 minutes reading the Zen Buddhism passage, 5 minutes receiving test instructions, and 35 minutes taking the test. No *S* ever appeared to have difficulty in completing any of these tasks within the allotted time.

RESULTS AND DISCUSSION

A comparison of the means on the 31-item immediate and delayed tests of Zen Buddhism indicates that the Buddhism passage, when compared to the irrelevant drug addiction passage, induced neither proactive interference nor proactive facilitation. A 3×2 analysis of variance was performed, with one variable being the treatment received (O-P vs. P vs. C), and the other variable (with repeated measures on the same *S*s) being the time at which the Zen Buddhism test was administered (immediate vs. delayed); Winer's (1962) method for dealing with unequal cell frequencies when cell variances are homogeneous was followed. It showed that the overall effect of the Buddhism passage, on the learning and retention of the Zen Buddhism material for both learning and overlearning treatments, was not significant, $F(2,140) = .74, p > .10$. A nonsignificant interaction term, $F(2,140) = .58$, $p > .10$, indicates that the proactive effect of the Buddhism passage was not differentially greater for retention than for learning. The assumption regarding homogeneity of variance was tested by Hartley's method and found to be tenable.

Individual comparisons of the means (O-P vs. C, P vs. C, and O-P vs. P) were made following analysis of variance, using the Newman-Keuls procedure (Winer, 1962). None of these comparisons was significant, thus confirming further that neither the learning nor the overlearning of the Buddhism passage had significant proactive interfering or facilitating effects on the learning and retention of the Zen Buddhism material. Immediate retention was significantly superior to delayed (7-day) retention, $F(1,140) = 19.66, p < .01$), but the actual decrement in absolute terms was relatively small for a 7-day period, as is typically the case for meaningful retention.

How can one explain the fact that confusably similar material did not induce proactive interference in this meaningful learning and retention experiment, in contrast to the usual finding in rote learning situations, and also did not induce facilitation as in the previously described study (Ausubel, Stager, and Gaite, 1968) of retroactive effects under meaningful learning conditions? On the

TABLE 1

Mean Scores, Cell Variances, and Frequencies of Four Treatment Groups on Test of Zen Buddhism

Treatment Group	Time: Immediate Test	Time: Delayed Test
Overlearning–Proactive		
Mean	14.07	13.33
S^2	23.31	26.89
N	43	43
Proactive		
Mean	14.73	13.88
S^2	26.77	25.66
N	51	51
Control		
Mean	15.51	14.24
S^2	17.19	18.86
N	49	49

positive side (making for facilitation), in comparison to rote learning situations, the Buddhism material is obviously more nonarbitrarily and substantively relatable to, and accordingly provides greater anchorage for, Zen Buddhist ideas than one serial learning or paired-associate task provides for another corresponding task. Also, in comparison to the control group in this experiment, proactive exposure to Buddhist concepts and principles furnishes apter and more proximately relevant anchorage for the Zen Buddhism material in the experimental (O-P and P) groups than do established and Judeo-Christian ideas for the same material in the control *S*s.

Second, the experimental groups presumably derive greater benefit from comparison of the Buddhism and Zen Buddhism ideas than the control group derives from corresponding comparison of the Zen Buddhism and established Judeo-Christian ideas. This is so because the contrasting materials are both more comparable and more recently and explicitly available in the case of the experimental groups. Thus, as was also presumably true in the retroactive facilitation study (Ausubel, Stager, and Gaite, 1968), similarities between Buddhism and Zen Buddhism should highlight their common differences from corresponding Judeo-Christian ideas, and differences between the two varieties of Buddhism should clarify and sharpen the distinctive features of Zen. The net result of these differences in the potential value of such comparison should be reflected in a greater gain for the experimental groups on this basis in the clarity and discriminability of the Zen Buddhism ideas.

Finally, more rehearsal of the Zen Buddhism material, subsequent to learning, can be anticipated in the experimental groups than in the control group because of the greater comparability of, and more recent and explicit exposure to, the contrast material.

On the negative side, counteracting proactive facilitation, are two factors making for proactive inhibition: (a) the negative transfer effect of anchoring the learning task (the Zen Buddhism material) to the proactively presented Buddhism material that is relatively much less stable and familiar than the long-established Judeo-Christian ideas serving as the anchoring material for the control group; and (b) the inherently less *initial* discriminability that prevails between the Buddhism and Zen Buddhism materials in the case of the experimental groups than between the Judeo-Christian and Zen Buddhism ideas in the case of the control group. These two factors apparently counterbalance the aptness and proximateness of relevance and other advantages listed above for the experimental groups. The net effect of these opposing sets of influences is that the facilitation found in the retroactive experimental paradigm does not appear in this experiment. In addition, less rehearsal effect can be anticipated in the proactive than in the retroactive situation, since the retroactive introduction of Buddhism material tends to elicit reproduction of the partially forgotten Zen ideas. In the proactive paradigm, on the other hand, traces of the Zen ideas obviously cannot be reproduced when *S*s in the experimental groups are first exposed to the Buddhism material; whatever rehearsal of the partially forgotten Zen material occurs in the experimental groups must take place *spontaneously* after the learning of this material (i.e., apart from the experimental arrangements).

Although overlearning of the proactive Buddhism material might have been expected to increase the stability and clarity of the anchoring ideas in the experimental group, and, hence, indirectly to enhance their discriminability from the Zen Buddhism material, by the same token it presumably decreased discriminability equally in more direct fashion by increasing the strength and thereby the capability of confusably similar material to interfere with the learning task.

Summary and Conclusions

Contrary to the typical proactive interference finding in rote verbal learning, proactive learning of Buddhism material by grade 13 students induced neither interference nor facilitation in the *meaningful* learning and retention of a Zen Buddhism passage. Overlearning of the Buddhism passage also had no significant effect on the meaningful learning and retention of the Zen Buddhism material, and there was no significant interaction between either proactive variable (learning or overlearning) and the length of the retention interval (immediate versus 7 days).

References

Atwater, S. K. Proactive inhibition and associative facilitation as affected by degree of prior learning. *Journal of experimental Psychology,* 1953, *46,* 400–404.

Ausubel, D. P. *The psychology of meaningful verbal learning.* New York: Grune & Stratton, 1963.

Ausubel, D. P., and D. Fitzgerald. The role of discriminability in meaningful verbal learning. *Journal of educational Psychology,* 1961, *52,* 266–274.

———, Organizer, general background, and antecedent learning variables in sequential verbal learning. *Journal of educational Psychology,* 1962, *53,* 243–249.

Ausubel, D. P., Lillian C. Robbins, and E. Blake. Retroactive inhibition and facilitation in the learning of school materials. *Journal of educational Psychology*, 1957, *48*, 334–343.

Ausubel, D. P., and M. Youssef. The role of discriminability in meaningful parallel learning. *Journal of educational Psychology*, 1963, *54*, 331–336.

Ausubel, D. P., Mary Stager, and A. J. H. Gaite. Retroactive facilitation in meaningful verbal learning. *Journal of educational Psychology*, 1968, *59*,

Bruce, R. W. Conditions of transfer of training. *Journal of experimental Psychology*, 1933, *16*, 343–361.

Bruner, J. S., J. M. Mandler, D. O'Dowd, and M. A. Wallach. The role of overlearning and drive level in reversal learning. *Journal of comparative and physiological Psychology*, 1958, *51*, 607–613.

Entwisle, Doris R., and W. H. Huggins. Interference in meaningful learning. *Journal of educational Psychology*, 1964, *55*, 75–78.

McGeoch, J. A. Influence of degree of learning upon retroactive inhibition. *American Journal of Psychology*, 1929, *41*, 252–262.

Mandler, G. Transfer of training as a function of degree of response overlearning. *Journal of experimental Psychology*, 1954, *47*, 411–417.

Marsh, G. Effect of overtraining on reversal and nonreversal shifts in nursery school children. *Child Development*. 1964, *35*, 1367–1372.

Pubols, B. H. Successive discrimination learning in the white rat: a comparison of two procedures. *Journal of comparative and physiological Psychology*, 1957, *50*, 319–332.

Reed, L. S. The development of non-continuity behavior through continuity learning. *Journal of experimental Psychology*, 1953, *46*, 107–112.

Sassenrath, J. M. Learning without awareness and transfer of learning sets. *Journal of educational Psychology*, 1959, *50*, 205–211.

Siipola, E. M., and H. E. Israel. Habit-interference as dependent upon stage of training. *American Journal of Psychology*, 1933, *43*, 205–207.

Slamecka, N. J. Retroactive inhibition of connected discourse as a function of practice level. *Journal of experimental Psychology*, 1960, *59*, 104–108.

Slamecka, N. J., and J. Ceraso. Retroactive and proactive inhibition of verbal learning. *Psychological Bulletin*, 1960, *57*, 449–475.

Suppes, P., and Rose Ginsberg. A fundamental property of all-or-none models, binomial distribution of responses prior to conditioning, with application to concept formation in children. *Psychological Review*, 1963, *70*, 139–161.

Underwood, B. J. Proactive inhibition as a function of time and degree of prior learning. *Journal of experimental Psychology*, 1949, *39*, 24–34.

Winer, B. J. *Statistical principles in experimental design*. New York: McGraw-Hill, 1962.

Yarcozower, M. Conditioning test of stimulus predifferentiation. *American Journal of Psychology*, 1959, *72*, 572–576.

Young, R. K. and B. J. Underwood. Transfer in verbal materials with dissimilar stimuli and response similarity varied. *Journal of experimental Psychology*, 1954, *47*, 153–159.

5 Cognitive Structure: Learning to Read*

David P. Ausubel

Cognitive structure is centrally involved whenever meanings emerge or are acquired, as, for example, in comprehending any message, in learning to understand one's native language, in learning to read, or in learning a second language. Meaning emerges when a message or learning task is nonarbitrarily and substantively related to the learner's existing structure of knowledge, that is, to meaningful ideas, symbols, or images in his cognitive structure. This presupposes (a) that the learner manifest a *meaningful learning* set, i.e., a set to relate the new learning task nonarbitrarily and substantively to what he already knows, and (b) that the learning task itself is *potentially*

**Reprinted from the July 1967 issue of* Education. *Copyright 1967 by the Bobbs-Merrill Company, Inc., Indianapolis, Indiana. By permission.*

meaningful to him, namely, relatable to his structure of knowledge on a nonarbitrary and nonverbatim basis.

Whether new material is potentially meaningful or nonarbitrarily and substantively relatable to a given learner's structure of knowledge is a somewhat more complex matter than meaningful learning set. It obviously depends on the two factors involved in establishing this kind of relationship—that is, on the nature of the material to be learned and on the availability of relevant content in the *particular* learner's cognitive structure. Turning first to the nature of the material, its properties must be such that it could be related on a nonarbitrary and substantive basis to *any* hypothetical cognitive structure exhibiting the necessary ideational background and intellectual maturity. Second, since meaningful learning or the acquisition of meanings takes place in *particular* human beings, for meaningful learning to occur in fact, it is not sufficient that the new material simply be relatable to relevant ideas in the abstract sense of the term. It is also necessary that the cognitive structure of the *particular* learner include the relevant ideational content and the requisite intellectual abilities.

Inasmuch as meaningful learning or the acquisition of meanings requires that the learner nonarbitrarily and substantively relate a new message to his existing structure of knowledge, it is a cognitive rather than a perceptual process. However, for an individual who already understands the meanings and syntactical functions of the component words comprising the message, the initial aspect of this process is perceptual in nature, that is, it involves an *immediate* content of awareness. A child who understands spoken language, for example, *perceives* the potential meaning of a sentence, as conveyed by the meanings and syntactical functions of its component words, and then relates this perceived potential meaning to his cognitive structure to grasp its propositional meaning. On the other hand, if the message is written and he does not yet know how to read, comprehension of the meanings and syntactical functions of the component words of the written message is a cognitive rather than a perceptual task, until the ability to read is acquired.

Learning to Read

Learning to read is essentially a matter of learning to perceive the potential meaning in *written* messages and then relating the perceived potential meaning to cognitive structure so as to comprehend it. The beginning reader who is already able to perceive the potential meaning in spoken messages must now acquire the same ability in relation to written messages. Because the denotative meanings and syntactic functions of the component words he will encounter are already known to him in their corresponding spoken forms, learning to read obviously constitutes a less significant cognitive accomplishment than the original learning of the spoken language. In other words, the beginning reader is not really learning a completely new symbolic code, but rather a written equivalent of a familiar spoken code whose basic vocabulary and syntax he has already mastered.

The most salient psychological characteristic of learning to read, therefore, is the dependence of the learning process on the previously acquired mastery of the spoken language and on the use of this mastery as a medium for perceiving the potential meaning in written messages. In fact, the child learns to read his native language by reconstructing written into spoken messages. He tries to establish representational equivalence between new written words and their already meaningful spoken counterparts. In view of this important mediating function of the spoken language in learning to decipher the meaning of written messages, it is theoretically indefensible to teach reading by seeking to establish direct equivalences between the new visual symbols and their significates (objects or pictures).

Learning to reconstruct written into spoken messages involves at least two major component steps. First, there is the problem of converting written words into spoken words. This problem is rendered less difficult, however, by the alphabetic basis of structuring most written languages. Thus, written words are not just configurations of visual symbols that arbitrarily represent their auditory counterparts. Rather, there is a more or less lawful relationship between the combination of distinguishable sounds (phonemes) constituting the spoken word and the analogous combination of letters (graphemes) constituting the corresponding written word. The beginning reader must, therefore, learn how to convert graphemes and combinations of graphemes into their phonemic equivalents, and then learn how to coalesce several graphemic combinations and reconstruct them into spoken words. In this latter process of word recognition he is aided by such cues as knowledge of commonly occurring graphemic combinations (e.g., prefixes and suffixes) and awareness of the wider context in which the written message is presented.

The second step in reconstructing the written message is learning how to combine and convert groups of written words into spoken phrases and sentences. In this way knowledge of the syntactic code of the spoken language can be utilized in perceiving the potential meaning of the written message. The beginning reader, in other words, is unable to apprehend directly the syntactic functions of the words in the written message; in order to perceive its potential propositional meaning, therefore, he reconstructs it into a spoken message and relies on his intuitive knowledge of the syntax of the spoken language.

However, once a certain facility in reading is acquired, it seems reasonable to suppose that the spoken language no longer plays a mediating role in the perception of potential meaning from written messages. It is therefore unlikely, as Carroll (1964) contends, that even in skilled silent reading, "the reader does not respond solely to visual symbols . . . [but] also to some sort of reconstruction of a spoken message which he derives from the written message" (p. 338). The skilled reader, rather, perceives *directly* both the denotative meanings of words in a sentence and their syntactic functions without any prior need for reconstructing words or phrases into their spoken counterparts; once the reconstructive process is dispensed with, these meanings emerge as an immediate (perceptual) content of awareness. Thus, *current* skilled reading capability becomes functionally autonomous of its previous association with the spoken language. It goes without saying, however, that the directly perceived denotative and syntactic meanings first have to be related to relevant ideas in cognitive structure before they yield actual propositional meaning.

We can compare the acquisition of the ability to perceive denotative and syntactic meanings directly from the written message to the ability which an experienced student of a foreign language eventually acquires to speak and understand that language without first translating it into his native tongue. In both instances, dependence on the mediating function of an already meaningful code is restricted to the learning phase of the new language capability. In short, a cognitive process characterizing the acquisition of a new ability does not necessarily apply to the exercise of that ability after it is acquired.

Actually, although native readers of a language typically go through the stage of reconstructing written into spoken messages, this reconstructive stage is not absolutely necessary in learning to read. Deaf mutes, for example, can learn to read without being able to use or understand the spoken language. One can also learn to read a second language—without first learning to speak or understand it—simply by converting foreign language written words and phrases into their native-language equivalents. This does not mean, of course, that one should not take advantage of the normal child's mastery of the spoken language in teaching him to read his native tongue. By the same token, however, after he already knows how to read there is no point in insisting that he is *currently* dependent on the mediating function of the spoken language.

Phonetic versus Wholistic Methods of Teaching Reading

In terms of the foregoing analysis of the cognitive processes involved in learning to read, the so-called phonetic or phonic method of teaching reading (that is, prior emphasis on letter recognition and grapheme-phoneme correspondences before actual reading practice) makes more psychological sense than teaching children to recognize words as wholes from the outset (the "look-say" method). The phonetic approach makes the problem of word recognition less arbitrary by giving the child a lawful code with which to reconstruct currently meaningless written words into their already meaningful spoken equivalents. Word recognition thus becomes more a matter of rational problem-solving than of random guessing; that is, it becomes a process of lawfully decoding the unknown written word by applying existing knowledge of grapheme-phoneme correspondences with the aid of such additional cues as context. The "look-say" method, on the other hand, renders written English, based for the most part on regular and learnable correspondences between graphemes and phonemes, into a pictorial, non-alphabetic written language like Chinese. It is true, of course, that children who learn to read by the "look-say" method tend spontaneously to develop some impressions about grapheme-phoneme correspondence and to use these impressions in deciphering unfamiliar words. But this haphazard, incidental, and unguided discovery learning of grapheme-phoneme correspondences can hardly be considered a defensible instructional procedure when such knowledge can be transmitted much more efficiently on a systematic, suitably programmed, and guided reception basis.

The use of an augmented Roman alphabet in teaching reading (Pitman, 1961), now in the experimental try-out stage, represents a further attempt to capitalize on grapheme-phoneme correspondences in helping children to derive meaning from written messages. This method seeks to overcome the ambiguities and inconsistencies inherent in the fact that some English graphemes, particularly vowels, have several phonemic equivalents. It accomplishes this aim by using instructional materials based on an alphabet of 46 graphemes, one for each recognizable phoneme in the English language. Yet, once children acquire initial facility in reading materials written in the augmented alphabet, they apparently experience little difficulty in reading text employing the conventional alphabet. This is not so surprising, however, when one considers that the use of supplementary cues to simplify the learning process during early stages of acquiring a new cognitive skill does not necessarily create dependence on these same cues after the skill is partially acquired. The beginning reader is much better equipped to cope with irregularities in grapheme-phoneme correspondence after mastering the regularities and acquiring a basic vocabulary of written words.

The learning of grapheme-phoneme correspondences does not imply that pupils must learn a set of formal rules. This would hardly be practicable at the age of initial reading instruction. Rather, it means providing guided practice in responding phonically to the more frequently encountered letter combinations in words so that the child acquires an intuitive grasp of grapheme-phoneme correspondence. He thus becomes capable of responding automatically with the correct phonemic equivalents of the different graphemes and graphemic combinations.

Wholistic methods of teaching reading are sometimes defended on the grounds that mature readers perceive whole words and even phrases at a time rather than individual letters or syllables. This, of course, is true but totally irrelevant to the point at issue. What applies to skilled readers does not necessarily apply to pupils who are first learning to read. The techniques employed by an expert in performing a complex skill can hardly be recommended as suitable practice exercise for the novice. The beginning student of Morse code, for example, thinks in terms of letter units, not in terms of the larger word and phrase units characterizing the transmitting and receiving operations of the skilled telegraphist.

Finally, it is important to bear in mind that phonetic and wholistic approaches need not be mutually exclusive procedures, either in theory or in practice. Advocates of the phonetic method ordinarily teach whole-word recognition of some of the more common words as a means of making possible earlier reading of a simple meaningful text, and of thereby enhancing the beginning reader's interest, self-confidence, and motivation; and "look-say" advocates typically introduce varying degrees of phonic analysis *after* their pupils acquire some reading fluency. The difference between the two schools of thought today is largely one of timing and relative emphasis. Nevertheless, this difference is still important both theoretically and practically; and although definitive empirical evidence is still lacking, the arguments of the phonetic school, in our opinion, rest on theoretically more tenable ground.

References

Carroll, J. B. The analysis of reading instruction: perspectives from psychology and linguistics. In *Theories of Learning and Instruction,* 63rd Yearbook, *Nat. Soc. Stud. Educ.,* Part I. Chicago: Univer. Chicago Press, 1964. pp. 336–353.

Pitman, I. J. Learning to read. *J. roy. Soc. Arts,* 1961, *109,* 149–180.

6 Adults versus Children in Second-Language Learning: Psychological Considerations*

David P. Ausubel

The great popularity of audiolingual methods in second-language teaching today is more than just an overreaction to previous pedagogic techniques that concentrated almost exclusively on reading, translation, and composition skills, and neglected oral comprehension and speaking ability. In large part, it is also a reflection of the widespread cultural belief that children learn languages much more readily than adults do. Hence, the argument runs, if children achieve such spectacular success by means of an audiolingual approach, it must obviously be the most effective way of learning foreign languages, and adults should follow their example.

Reprinted from the article of the same title, Modern Language Journal, *1964,* **48,** *420–424. By permission of the author and the* Modern Language Journal.

This line of argument, in my opinion, is vulnerable on two counts. In the first place, on either research or theoretical grounds, it is difficult to substantiate the thesis that children are in fact superior to adults in learning languages. Second, even if this were the case, there would still be no good reason for believing that methods which yield satisfactory results with children must necessarily be appropriate for adults. These latter methods are used, after all, not because they are demonstrably more efficacious under all conditions, but because children's cognitive immaturity and lack of certain intellectual skills preclude many approaches that are feasible for older age groups. Naturalness is a slippery argument because what is natural for one age group is not necessarily natural for another.

In this article, therefore, I propose to do two things. First, I will argue that adults can acquire new languages more readily than can children. Second, I will take the position that certain features of the audiolingual approach are psychologically incompatible with effective learning processes in adults. These features include (1) the rote learning of phrases; (2) inductive rather than deductive learning of grammatical generalizations; (3) avoidance of the mediational role of the native language; (4) presentation of the spoken form of the language before the written form; and (5) insistence on exposing the beginner to the "natural speed rendition" of the spoken language.

Relative Language Learning Ability of Children and Adults

To begin with, we must appreciate the fact that the child does not learn his native language with phenomenal ease and rapidity. Quite the contrary! His acquisition of his native tongue is a long, slow, and arduous process—despite prolonged and continuous exposure, and despite exceedingly strong motivation to learn so that he can communicate with adults and peers. Typically, he is four years old before his use of syntax even begins to approximate the conventional standards of his language.

In natural settings (e.g., home, neighborhood, school) where children are completely or partially immersed in a second language environment, it is true that they appear to learn the language more readily than adults do under similar circumstances. Actually, however, the two situations are hardly comparable. Children receive much more practice in the new language since they are less able to maintain contact with spoken and written sources of their native language. Their motivation is also usually higher because mastery of the second language is more essential for communication, peer relationships, and school progress. Furthermore, they are typically less self-conscious than adults in attempting to speak the new language.

Objective research evidence regarding the relative learning ability of children and adults is sparse but offers little comfort to those who maintain the child superiority thesis. Although children are probably superior to adults in acquiring an acceptable accent in a new language, E. L. Thorndike[1] found many years ago that they make less rapid progress than adults in other aspects of foreign language learning when learning time is held constant for the two age groups.

In addition to the pronunciation or mimicry factor, children probably have some other intrinsic advantages over adults in foreign language learning. Their intellectual capacities are less differentiated along particular lines, and they are more venturesome and less rigid in undertaking new learning tasks. As a result of fewer past frustrating experiences in academic work, they are also less likely to manifest strong emotional blocks in particular subject-matter areas.

The disadvantages of adults in these latter respects, however, are more than counterbalanced by two overwhelming advantages which they enjoy. First, they have a much larger native-language vocabulary than children, particularly with regard to abstract concepts. Hence in learning a foreign language, unlike children, they need not acquire thousands of new concepts but merely the new verbal symbols representing these concepts. Second, in learning the structure of a new language—both in comprehending oral and written materials and in speaking—they can

[1] E. L. Thorndike *et al.*, *Adult Learning*. New York: Macmillan, 1925.

make conscious and deliberate use of grammatical generalizations and can explicitly apply them to suitable exemplars. Young children, on the other hand, are limited to the much less efficient approach of discovering syntactical rules through repetitious exposure to models and corrective feedback. Largely because of these two factors, certain characteristic features of the audiolingual method are pedagogically inappropriate for adults.

Rote Learning of Phrases

Because young children are explicitly unaware of syntactic functions and categories, it is often assumed that their language capability consists of rote verbal habits. Actually, however, the ability to understand and generate sentences implies, even in children, a meaningful process in which there is at least some implicit awareness of the lexical and syntactic contribution of component words to the total meaning of the sentence. In adults this awareness, particularly in second-language learning, exists on a much more explicit and abstract basis, and hence meaningfulness in such learning is an even more important consideration than in children.

The audiolingual approach, however, tends to assume that second-language learning, both in children and adults, is largely a process of rote verbal learning. Both in pattern practice drills and memorized dialogue practice, there is either no awareness of phrase meaning whatsoever or, at the very best, awareness of *total* phrase meaning. Thus the learner understands neither the syntactic functions of the component words nor the lexical and syntactic contributions of the individual words to the total meaning of the phrase. A purely arbitrary (rote) rather than lawful or meaningful relationship prevails between phrase meaning and component elements of the phrase.

Under these circumstances it is hardly surprising that particular grammatical patterns can be emitted perfectly in a familiar and structurally limited context, or that simple substitutions, transformations and elaborations can be made, but that new words in a wider, unfamiliar context cannot be fitted into the learned pattern, or that the same words and syntactic categories cannot be recombined in different patterns to express different ideas. The principal transferable element in pattern practice is precise knowledge of the syntactic function of each word and its semantic contribution to total phrase meaning. When the learner manifests this knowledge, it is possible for him (a) to construct a structurally comparable phrase expressive of an entirely different idea, in which each component word bears a syntactic relationship to total phrase meaning that is analogous to the set of relationships prevailing between component words and total phrase meaning in the learned model phrase; and (b) to recombine familiar words and known syntactic functions in the learning of new patterns.

The remedy, of course, is not to eliminate pattern drills but to make them more meaningful. Second-language learning obviously requires overlearning of the basic and characteristic structural patterns of the language. But unless the learner appreciates the precise relationship between the verbal manipulations he practices and the changes in meaning that he induces by such manipulation, the practice is not very transferable.

Inductive Learning of Grammatical Rules

Pattern practice drills seek to duplicate in second-language learning the process whereby children attain syntactic mastery of their native language. What is primarily striven for is a functional, intuitive grasp of syntax after inducing much manipulative experience with the major structural patterns of the language. Grammatical generalizations are provided, if at all, only after the principles in question are acquired on an inductive, intuitive basis and are rendered virtually automatic.

Young children, of course, have to learn syntactic rules through an inductive process of discovering various linguistic regularities in the multiform language patterns to which they are repetitively exposed. Grammatical generalizations would make absolutely no sense whatsoever to them, since they are manifestly incapable of understanding complex relationships between abstractions. This type of discovery learning, however, is exceedingly wasteful and unnecessary when we deal with older learners who are perfectly capable of comprehending abstract syntactic propositions. It takes a long time to discover grammatical rules autonomously and inductively; and until the correct discovery is made, practice is not transferable. Furthermore, as long as these rules are known only intuitively and implicitly, their transferability to comparable situations is restricted to what is analogically quite similar and obvious.

Deductive use of grammatical generalizations, on the other hand, is decidedly more efficient in second-language learning. No time is wasted in discovery, and both the generalization and the experience of applying it to appropriate exemplars are transferable from the very beginning of practice. As a precisely, explicitly, and abstractly stated proposition, it also has more general transferability to new situations.

Avoidance of the Native Language

The audiolingual method seeks in all possible ways to avoid the mediating role of the native language in second-language learning. It attempts to accomplish this objective through the rote learning of phrases and through the inductive learning of syntactic rules; through direct association of second-language words and phrases with objects, pictures, and situations rather than with native language words; by giving second-language instruction in the target language itself; and by proscribing translation practice.

Avoidance of the mediating function of the student's native language in second-language learning is customarily justified on two grounds. First, it is argued that children do not learn their native language through the mediation of another language. This argument, however, is no more relevant when applied to adults than the previously cited argument that children do not learn syntax from grammatical generalizations. Second, it is pointed out that the bilingual individual thinks directly in the second language rather than translates from his native tongue. It must be realized, however, that although this latter state of affairs is generally true, it is a reflection of a terminal state of second-language proficiency and does not describe the learning situation when the bilingual individual is a beginning student.

Actually, it is both unrealistic and inefficient for the older student to attempt to circumvent the mediating role of his native language when learning a second language. As we have already observed, the rote learning of phrases and the inductive learning of syntactic rules detracts greatly from the transferability of pattern practice drills. In addition, numerous aspects of first-language knowledge (i.e., the meanings of many concepts, the understanding of syntactic categories and functions, facility in using many structural patterns that are nearly identical in the two languages) are directly transferable to second-language learning. Lastly, it is developmentally anachronistic and artificial for the older individual to learn a new set of second-language terms for familiar concepts by associating them directly with their referents (objects, pictures, situations). Customarily, after early childhood, new terms for familiar concepts in the native language (synonyms) are learned indirectly through association with the first-learned set of terms for the objects and situations in question.

Prior Presentation of Materials in Spoken Form

A cardinal principle of the audiolingual approach is that instructional materials should be presented in their spoken form before they are presented in their written form, and that listening and speaking skills should be acquired before reading and writing skills.

The major rationale offered for this order of skill acquisition is that it is the "natural" order in which children learn their native language. But because a child has to learn how to speak and understand his native tongue before he can read it, it does not necessarily follow that once he knows how to read, he has to observe the same sequence of events in learning a second language. Once any new skill such as reading is learned, it can obviously be used as a tool in acquiring new knowledge. It is unnatural to expect that after an individual becomes literate, he will learn in the same way as when he was illiterate.

A second reason for advocating this order of learning is the belief that it can lead to "direct reading" in the second language. It is maintained that if various items of second-language material can be understood and spoken, they can also be read without any explicit practice in reading as such. This would have the additional presumed advantage of avoiding any tendency to translate the material as it was being read. The available research evidence[2] indicates, however, that audiolingual and reading skills are separate and independently developed abilities. Although practice in one is partly transferable to the other, especially at higher levels of proficiency, considerable specific training in each skill is required for the acquisition of competence.

Still a third reason for advocating prior presentation of materials in spoken form is the possibility that the written form of the second language will generate phonological interference from the native language in which the same written letters often have different phonological values. On the other hand, it can be plausibly argued that the individual sooner or later has to learn to associate letters in the second language with their phonological equivalents, and that he may as well confront this first-language interference and learn to overcome it from the very beginning.

Turning now to the other side of the argument, two defensible reasons can be advanced for presenting written and spoken materials in the second language both alternately and concomitantly. First, in our culture, adolescents and adults are habituated to learning most new ideas and subject matter by reading rather than by listening. Thus a pure audiolingual approach deprives the older learner of his principal learning tool and of the instructional medium in which he feels most comfortable and confident. This is particularly unfortunate during the early phases of instruction when learning stresses tend to be greatest.

[2] F. B. Agard and H. B. Dunkel, *An Investigation of Second-Language Teaching*. Boston: Ginn, 1948.

Second, prior familiarization with and simultaneous exposure to the written form of the material can serve as helpful props in the early stages of acquiring oral comprehension skills. Because of unfamiliarity with new sounds, with typical sequences of sounds, and with the characteristic word order and syntactic patterns of the second language, it is very difficult for the beginner to distinguish individual words, inflectional forms, and groups of words from listening alone. Hence he often fails not only to grasp the meaning of the spoken material, but also to appreciate its syntactic structure well enough for purposes of transfer. Simultaneous reading support can furnish the necessary cues for meaning and grasp of syntactic structure while listening skills are being developed, and can be withdrawn gradually, both generally and for particular passages, as oral comprehension increases.

"Natural Speed Rendition" of the Spoken Language

In the audiolingual approach, beginners are typically exposed to the "natural speed rendition" of the spoken language—presumably to accustom them to the "natural rhythm" of the language. It is pointed out that children eventually learn to understand their native tongue under comparable circumstances. In terms of gain per unit of learning time, however, it should be self-evident that practice in listening improves oral comprehension ability primarily insofar as what is heard is also understood. Thus, if the sample of speech to which the learner listens is too rapid for him to understand, it does little to enhance his ability to comprehend the spoken language. Furthermore, even if he is able to understand the material in a general way, he may still not be able to distinguish the major structural patterns well enough to transfer them to speaking and other listening situations.

Hence, since learning to comprehend the spoken language is a very gradual process, it should undoubtedly be assisted in the beginning by means of a slower rate of speech that is progressively accelerated as oral comprehension improves. Artificial simplification is always justifiable during the early stages of any learning process. When any given passage of material is presented to the beginner, he can, of course, be exposed first to a slowed-down version and then to a normal speed rendition.

PART III COGNITIVE FACTORS IN LEARNING

Cognitive factors influencing school learning have been categorized under five headings: cognitive-structure variables, developmental considerations, intellectual ability, practice, and instructional material variables. In contrast to the affective-social factors considered in Part V, they are relatively objective determinants of meaningful verbal learning which can directly affect the availability (retrievability) of the assimilated learning task at any stage of the learning or retention process and also affect both original learning and later retention in the same way.

Of all the cognitive factors, cognitive structure variables—the availability of relevant ideas in the learner's structure of knowledge in any given subject-matter area, and their stability, clarity, and discriminability—are perhaps the most important. In selections 8 and 10 it is shown that what a learner already knows in any designated area of knowledge, and how well he knows it, has a powerful effect on how well he can learn related ideas in that same area. Selections 7, 8, and 10 are also concerned with the facilitating effect of organizers on meaningful verbal learning; that is, they are concerned with the effect of introductory materials at a high level of abstraction, generality, and inclusiveness, materials that attempt either to provide relevant ideational scaffolding for the more differentiated learning task or to increase the discriminability of the latter from related ideas in existing cognitive structure. These same selections also suggest that organizers have a differentially greater facilitating effect in learners with either less verbal ability or less clear and stable existing knowledge in related areas.

Selection 9 attempts to apply the concept of cognitive structure variables to the important problem of curriculum transfer in medical education. Particular emphasis is placed on such pedagogic applications of these variables as the principles of progressive differentiation and integrative reconciliation. The problem of transfer in medical education is of special significance to teachers because of its striking parallel to teacher education and other varieties of professional education.

Developmental factors have a self-evidently important influence on school-learning outcomes. The level of cognitive maturity not only limits the depth and complexity of the learning task which can be successfully handled, but also determines the *mode* of cognitive functioning—particularly in the degree of dependence on concrete-empirical props in acquiring concepts, understanding propositions, and solving problems. Hence cognitive maturity also limits the extent to which abstract verbal learning is possible. Selections 12 and 13 characterize the distinctive features of cognitive functioning and development during the elementary and secondary school periods, respectively, and bring out their implications for pedagogic practice. These same selections also explore such theoretical issues in cognitive development as Piaget's concept of stages of cognitive development, qualitative versus quantitative aspects of intellectual development, the distinction between general and specific aspects of cognitive development, the determinants of intellectual development, and the possibility of accelerating the rate of cognitive development.

Selection 11 presents a critical evaluation of the currently fashionable proposition that children can not only learn anything that adolescents and adults can, but can also do so more efficiently.

Intellectual ability was one of the earliest cognitive factors recognized as influencing school learning. Selection 14 examines the impact of environmental deprivation on intellectual development. The issue of whether the effects of such deprivation are partly irreversible, and through what mechanisms the irreversibility might be mediated, is discussed in considerable detail.

Practice is one of the most significant and manipulable cognitive factors affecting school learning. Little permanent learning occurs in school without repetition or review. Selection 15 considers some classical objections to structured practice or drill, and Selection 16 considers the respective mechanisms through which early and delayed review enhance meaningful learning and retention.

Instructional material variables are tactically important factors in the school-learning situation, since they constitute pedagogic applications of cognitive-structure variables to the magnitude, difficulty, organization, logical meaningfulness, and communicability of school-learning tasks. And inasmuch as the cumulative influence of these instructional materials variables eventually determines the fabric of cognitive structure itself, they have long-term as well as short-term effects on subject-matter learning.

It is evident that most of the currently flourishing curriculum-reform movements in mathematics and the natural sciences are based on the latter assumptions. However, as Selection 17 points out, there is always the danger that by placing undue emphasis on valid, up-to-date, and highly sophisticated subject-matter content and on the quantitative-experimental aspects of science, these reformed curricula fail to render the new instructional materials potentially meaningful to beginning pupils. Such pupils lack the background in science necessary for making such instructional materials nonarbitrarily and substantively relatable to their cognitive structures.

7 The Use of Advance Organizers in the Learning and Retention of Meaningful Verbal Material*

David P. Ausubel

The purpose of this study is to test the hypothesis that the learning and retention of unfamiliar but meaningful verbal material can be facilitated by the advance introduction of relevant subsuming concepts (organizers). This hypothesis is based on the assumption that cognitive structure is hierarchically organized in terms of highly inclusive concepts under which are subsumed less inclusive sub-concepts and informational data (Ausubel, 1957). If this organizational principle of progressive differentiation of an internalized sphere of knowledge does in fact prevail, it is reasonable to suppose that new meaningful material becomes incorporated into cognitive

Reprinted from the article of the same title,* Journal of Educational Psychology, *1960,* **51, *267–272. By permission of the author and The American Psychological Association, Inc.*

structure in so far as it is subsumable under relevant existing concepts. It follows, therefore, that the availability in cognitive structure of appropriate and stable subsumers should enhance the incorporability of such material. If it is also true that "meaningful forgetting" reflects a process of memorial reduction, in which the identity of new learning material is assimilated by the more inclusive meaning of its subsumers (Ausubel, 1957), the same availability should also enhance retention by decelerating the rate of obliterative subsumption.

In the present study, appropriate and relevant subsuming concepts (organizers) are deliberately introduced prior to the learning of unfamiliar academic material, in order to ascertain whether learning and retention are enhanced thereby in accordance with the theoretical premises advanced above.

METHOD

Subjects

The experimental population consisted of 110 senior undergraduate students (78 women and 32 men) in four sections of an educational psychology course at the University of Illinois. All *S*s were enrolled in one of eight teacher education curricula at the secondary school level. Students specializing in industrial education and in vocational agriculture were excluded from the study, since they had received specific instruction in the topic covered by the learning passage. The experiment was conducted separately in each section as a required laboratory exercise and was performed during regularly scheduled class hours. In order to maximize ego-involvement, *S*s were informed that after the data were processed their individual scores, as well as the class results, would be reported to them.

Learning Passage and Test of Retention

The learning material used in this study was a specially prepared 2500 word passage dealing with the metallurgical properties of plain carbon steel. Emphasis was placed on such basic principles as the relationship between metallic grain structure, on the one hand, and temperature, carbon content, and rate of cooling, on the other. Important factual information (e.g., critical temperatures), however, was also included, and basic principles were also applied to such technological processes as heat treatment and tempering.

The metallurgical topic was chosen on the basis of being generally unfamiliar to undergraduates in liberal arts and sciences (i.e., not ordinarily included in chemistry courses), but still sufficiently elementary to be both comprehensible and interesting to novices with no prior background in the field. The criterion of unfamiliarity was especially crucial because the purpose of the study was to ascertain whether advance organizers could facilitate retention in areas of knowledge *new* to learners. By using unfamiliar material it was also possible to ensure that all *S*s started from approximately the same baseline in learning the material. Empirical proof of unfamiliarity was sought, therefore, by administering the retention test on the steel passage to a comparable group of naïve subjects who had *not* studied the material; but although this latter group of subjects made scores which, on the average, were only slightly and not significantly better than chance, it was evident from later analysis of the experimental data that scores earned by *S*s who *had* studied the passage were related to both sex and field of specialization. Male students and majors in science and art were better able to learn and retain the steel material than were female students and majors in English, foreign languages, music, and the social sciences. Hence, the criterion of unfamiliarity was not completely satisfied, in as much as these differences undoubtedly reflected, in part, variability in relevant incidental experience influencing the learnability of the material.

Knowledge of the steel passage was tested by a 36-item multiple-choice examination with a corrected split-half reliability of .79. Test questions covered principles, facts, and applications, and were selected by an item analysis procedure from a larger population of items. Scores on the test showed a satisfactory range of variability and were distributed normally. Since it was intended as a power test, no time limit was imposed.

Procedure

It was first necessary to equate experimental and control groups on the basis of ability to learn an unfamiliar scientific passage of comparable difficulty. The passage used for this purpose was concerned with the endocrinology of human pubescence and was approximately 1800 words long. Subjects were given twenty minutes to read and study this material, and were tested immediately thereafter by a 26-item multiple-choice test with a corrected split-half reliability of .78. (The unfamiliarity of the material had been previously ascertained by administering the test to a comparable group of naïve subjects who had not studied the passage, and obtaining a mean score only slightly and not significantly greater than chance.) Scores on the pubescence test were normally distributed and correlated .64 on a product-moment basis with the steel scores. *F* tests were performed on the variance ratios of the pubescence scores for all possible combinations of the four sections, and none approached significance at the .05 level of confidence. It was considered justifiable, therefore, to treat the steel retention scores of experimental and control groups as if derived respectively from one large class rather than from four separate sections.

Subjects in each of the four sections were matched on the basis of pubescence scores and assigned to experimental and control groups. Experimental and control treatments were then administered simultaneously to experimental and control *S*s respectively within each section. This procedure was possible because the two treatments consisted of studying identical appearing introductory passages differing only in content. The use of this procedure also provided the important methodological advantage of holding instructor, class, and situational variables constant for both groups. Each introductory passage of approximately five hundred words was studied twice, five minutes each time, by the appropriate group of *S*s. The two occasions were 48 hours and immediately before exposure to the main learning passage.

The experimental introductory passage contained background material for the learning passage which was presented at a much higher level of abstraction, generality, and inclusiveness than the latter passage itself. It was designed to serve as an organizing or anchoring focus for the steel material and to relate it to existing cognitive structure, but not to contain information that would provide a direct advantage in answering any of the questions on the steel test. This latter criterion was tested empirically and shown to be warranted when a comparable group of subjects made only a slightly better than chance mean score on the steel test after studying the introductory passage alone. The control introductory passage consisted of historically relevant background material. It was methodologically necessary to provide this control treatment in order that any obtained difference between experimental and control groups could be attributed to the particular nature of the experimental introductory passage (i.e., to its organizing properties) rather than its presence per se.

Both groups studied the steel passage for 35 minutes and took the multiple-choice steel test three days later. Since it was evident from a comparison of pubescence and steel scores that scores on the steel test were related to *S*s' sex and major field, it was necessary to hold these latter factors (as well as pubescence test scores) constant. Hence it was no longer possible to use the originally matched pairs of subjects within each section. Sufficient subjects were also not available to rematch individual pairs of subjects on all three variables. By matching experimental and control *S*s across sections, however, it was possible to equate two groups of forty subjects each for sex, pubescence scores, and field of specialization. The crossing of sectional lines in this rematching procedure was justifiable in view of the intersectional homogeneity of variance.

Results and Discussion

The distribution of steel test scores for both experimental and control groups did not deviate significantly from the normal. The mean steel score of the experimental group was 16.7, as compared to 14.1 for the control group and a mean chance score of 7.2 (one-fifth of 36). The standard deviations of the two groups were 5.8 and 5.4 respectively, and the respective variances were 34.1 and 29.6. The difference between the means of the two groups divided by its standard error[1] yielded a *t* value of 2.353, which for a one-tailed test and 77 df was significant beyond the .01 level of confidence.

The obtained difference in retention between experimental and control groups, although statistically significant, would undoubtedly have been even greater if *S*s could have been matched on an individual basis, and if the learning passage used for matching purposes had been in the same subject-matter field as the steel material (i.e., if the relationship between the two sets of scores were higher than that indicated by the correlation of .64 between the steel and pubescence scores). Another experimental condition probably detracting from the difference between the two groups was the fact that the steel material was not completely unfamiliar to many *S*s. Because of some prior general familiarity with the contents of the steel passage, many *S*s already possessed relevant and stable subsuming concepts. These obviously rendered less significant the potential learning advantages conferable by advance organizers.

It could be argued, of course, that exposure to the experimental introduction constituted in effect a partial substantive equivalent of an additional learning trial. Actually, however, any substantive repetition was at most very indirect, since the introductory passage consisted of much more inclusive and general background material than was contained in the learning task itself, and also provided no direct advantage in answering the test items. Furthermore, according to behavioristic (interference) theory, prior exposure to similar but not identical learning material induces proactive inhibition rather than facilitation.

Advance organizers probably facilitate the incorporability and longevity of meaningful verbal material in two different ways. First, they explicitly draw upon and mobilize whatever relevant subsuming concepts are already established in the learner's cognitive structure and make them part of the subsuming entity. Thus, not only is the new material rendered more familiar and meaningful, but the most relevant ideational antecedents are also selected and utilized in integrated fashion. Second, advance or-

[1] The standard error of the difference for equated groups was calculated according to a method described by Edwards (1954, pp. 282–288).

ganizers at an appropriate level of inclusiveness provide optimal anchorage. This promotes both initial incorporation and later resistance to obliterative subsumption.

The appropriate level of inclusiveness may be defined as that level which is as proximate as possible to the degree of conceptualization of the learning task—relative, of course, to the existing degree of differentiation of the subject as a whole in the learner's cognitive background. Thus, the more unfamiliar the learning material (i.e., the more undifferentiated the learner's background of relevant concepts), the more inclusive or highly generalized the subsumers must be in order to be proximate. If appropriately relevant and proximate subsuming concepts are not available, the learner tends to use the most proximate and relevant ones that are. But since it is highly improbable, however, that we can count on the spontaneous availability of the most relevant and proximate subsuming concepts, the most dependable way of facilitating retention is to introduce the appropriate subsumers and make them part of cognitive structure prior to the actual presentation of the learning task. The introduced subsumers thus become advance organizers or anchoring foci for the reception of new material.

Even though this principle seems rather self-evident it is rarely followed in actual teaching procedures or in the organization of most textbooks. The more typical practice is to segregate topically homogeneous materials into separate chapters, and to present them throughout at a uniform level of conceptualization in accordance with a logical outline of subject-matter organization. This practice, of course, although logically sound is psychologically incongruous with the postulated process whereby meaningful learning occurs, i.e., with the hierarchical organization of cognitive structure in terms of progressive gradations of inclusiveness, and with the mechanism of accretion through a process of progressive differentiation of an undifferentiated field. Thus, in most instances, students are required to learn the details of new and unfamiliar disciplines before they have acquired an adequate body of relevant subsumers at an appropriate level of inclusiveness.

As a result, students and teachers are coerced into treating meaningful materials as if they were rote in character, and consequently experience unnecessary difficulty and little success in both learning and retention. The teaching of mathematics and science, for example, still relies heavily on rote learning of formulas and procedural steps, on recognition of stereotyped "type problems," and on mechanical manipulation of symbols. In the absence of clear and stable concepts which can serve as anchoring points and organizing foci for the incorporation of new meaningful material, students are trapped in a morass of confusion and have little choice but to rotely memorize learning tasks for examination purposes.

The pedagogic value of advance organizers obviously depends in part upon how well organized the learning material itself is. If it contains built-in organizers and proceeds from regions of lesser to greater differentiation (higher to lower inclusiveness), rather than in the manner of the typical textbook or lecture presentation, much of the potential benefit derivable from advance organizers will not be actualized. Regardless of how well organized learning material is, however, it is hypothesized that learning and retention can still be facilitated by the use of advance organizers at an appropriate level of inclusiveness. Such organizers are available from the very beginning of the learning task, and their integrative properties are also much more salient than when introduced concurrently with the learning material.

Summary and Conclusions

An empirical test was made of the hypothesis that the learning and retention of unfamiliar but meaningful verbal material could be facilitated by the advance introduction of relevant subsuming concepts (organizers). Experimental and control groups of forty undergraduate *S*s each were equated on the basis of sex, field of specialization, and ability to learn unfamiliar scientific material. The learning task consisted of a 2500 word passage of empirically demonstrated unfamiliarity, dealing with the metallurgical properties of steel. On two separate occasions, 48 hours and immediately prior to contact with the learning task, experimental *S*s studied a 500 word introductory passage containing background material presented at a much higher level of generality, abstraction and inclusiveness than the steel material itself. This passage was empirically shown to contain no information that could be directly helpful in answering the test items on the steel passage. Control *S*s similarly studied a relevant historical introduction of identical length. Retention of the learning material was tested three days later by means of a multiple-choice test. Comparison of the mean retention scores of the experimental and control groups unequivocably supported the hypothesis.

The facilitating influence of advance organizers on the incorporability and longevity of meaningful learning material was attributed to two factors: (a) the selective mobilization of the most relevant existing concepts in the learner's cognitive structure for integrative use as part of the subsuming focus for the new learning task, thereby increasing the latter's familiarity and meaningfulness; and (b) the provision of optimal anchorage for the learning material in the form of relevant and appropriate subsuming concepts at a proximate level of inclusiveness.

The suggestion was offered that the greater use of appropriate advance organizers in the teaching of meaningful verbal material could lead to more effective retention. This procedure would also render unnecessary much of the rote memorization to which students resort because they are required to learn the details of a discipline before having available a sufficient number of key subsuming concepts.

References

Ausubel, D. P., Lillian C. Robbins, and Elias Blake, Jr. Retroactive inhibition and facilitation in the learning of school materials. *J. educ. Psychol.*, 1957, *48*, 334–343.

Edwards, A. L. *Statistical Methods for the Behavioral Sciences.* New York: Holt, Rinehart and Winston, 1954.

8 The Role of Discriminability in Meaningful Verbal Learning and Retention*

David P. Ausubel

In a recent study (Ausubel, 1960), it was shown that introductory material at a high level of abstraction, generality, and inclusiveness (advance organizers) facilitates meaningful verbal learning and retention. By deliberately introducing relevant and appropriately inclusive subsuming concepts into cognitive structure, one provides helpful ideational scaffolding which enhances the incorporability and longevity of the more detailed material in the learning passage.

Advance organizers, however, ordinarily have two distinct functions that correspond in turn to two different aspects of the unfamiliarity of meaningful learning material. Sometimes, as in the above-mentioned experiment, the new material is almost completely unfamiliar in the sense that cognitive structure is

*Reprinted from the article of the same title, Journal of Educational Psychology, 1961, **52**, 266–274. By permission of the author and The American Psychological Association, Inc.

barren of even generally related concepts. Under these circumstances the purpose of the organizer is simply to provide ideational anchorage or scaffolding. More typically, however, the new learning material (e.g., Buddhist doctrines) is a variant of related, previously learned concepts (Christian doctrines) already established in cognitive structure. Here the role of the organizer is not only to provide optimal anchorage at an optimal level of inclusiveness, but also to increase the discriminability of the learning passage from analogous and often conflicting ideas in the learner's cognitive structure.

This second role of organizers is predicated on the assumption that if the distinguishing features of the new learning passage are not originally salient or readily discriminable from established ideas in cognitive structure, they can be adequately represented by the latter for memorial purposes, and hence would not persist as separately identifiable memories in their own right. It is assumed, in other words, that only discriminable categorical variants of previously learned concepts have long-term retention potentialities. Thus, if a *comparative* type of organizer could first delineate clearly, precisely, and explicitly the principal similarities and differences between the new learning passage (Buddhism) and existing, related concepts in cognitive structure (Christianity), it seems reasonable to suppose that the more detailed Buddhist ideas would be grasped later with fewer ambiguities, fewer competing meanings, and fewer misconceptions suggested by the learner's knowledge of Christianity; and that as these clearer, less confused Buddhist meanings interact with analogous Christianity meanings during the retention interval, they would be more likely to retain their identity. In this experiment, therefore, the value of a comparative organizer was tested by contrasting its effects on the retention of a Buddhism learning passage with both those of a nonideational (*historical*) introduction and those of a simple *expository* organizer.

It is hypothesized, first, that to the extent that the organizer is rendered discriminable from related concepts (Christianity) established in cognitive structure, and hence to the extent that it increases the discriminability of the Buddhism learning passage from these Christianity concepts, it facilitates the learning and retention of the new Buddhist ideas. In addition, it is hypothesized, for analogous reasons, that the discriminability (and hence the learning and retention) of the Buddhism passage varies as a function of the clarity and stability of the learner's existing knowledge of Christianity, and that *S*s with relatively unclear and unstable concepts of Christianity derive relatively more benefit from the organizers than do *S*s with clear and stable concepts in this area of knowledge.

These hypotheses were suggested by the findings of a previous experiment (Ausubel and Blake, 1958) in which the learning and retention of a comparative Buddhism passage were contrasted with that of an expository Buddhism passage. However, for the following reasons, the organizer approach was adopted in this experiment, in preference to manipulating the learning material itself: First, organizers provide advance ideational scaffolding. Second, they provide the learner with a generalized overview of *all* of the major similarities and differences between the two bodies of ideas *before* he encounters the new concepts individually in more detailed and particularized form. Finally, they create an advance set in the learner to perceive similarities and differences, and, by avoiding overly explicit specification, encourage him *actively* to make his own differentiations in terms of his own particular sources of confusion.

The hypotheses advanced in this study apply only to meaningful learning material which, although unfamiliar to *S*s, is relatable to long-established and relatively stable concepts in cognitive structure. They do not apply to rote learning, to completely unfamiliar learning material, or to learning tasks that can only be related to unstable or recently learned concepts. The organizers, furthermore, must consist of ideational material (both similarities and differences) at a high level of abstraction, generality, and inclusiveness, rather than constitute a simple summary or a mere listing of specific comparative points.

METHOD

Subjects

The experimental population consisted of predominantly senior undergraduate students (94 women and 61 men) in six sections of an educational psychology course at the University of Illinois. All *S*s were enrolled in one of ten teacher education curricula at the secondary school level. The experiment was conducted separately in each section as a required laboratory exercise, and was performed during regularly scheduled class hours. In order to maximize ego-involvement, *S*s were informed that after the data were processed their individual scores, as well as the class results, would be reported to them.

Learning Passages, Organizers, and Measuring Instruments

The learning material used in this study was a specially prepared 2500 word passage dealing with Buddhist concepts of God, immortality, soul, faith, salvation, morality and responsibility. These concepts were elaborated in considerable detail. The passage only presented the significant *ideas* of Buddhism and ignored material on the life of Buddha, the history and geographical distribution of Buddhism, schools of Buddhism, and Buddhist ritual. Flesch analysis of the passage yielded an abstractness score of 19.19 (highly abstract) and a readability score of 42.46 (difficult).

The topic of Buddhism was chosen both because it was explicitly unfamiliar to undergraduate students, and because it dealt with variants of previously learned concepts (i.e., Christian doctrines) generally familiar to all of our *S*s and, presumably, reasonably well-established in the cognitive structure of most of them. Both criteria were important since the main purpose of the study was to ascertain whether advance organizers could facilitate the learning and retention of *unfamiliar* meaningful material by increasing the discriminability between the new material and *related* concepts already established in cognitive structure. The use of unfamiliar learning material also made it possible for all *S*s to start from approximately the same baseline in learning the passage. Empirical confirmation of the unfamiliarity of the Buddhism material was obtained when a group of comparable *S*s, who had not studied the learning passage, made scores which, on the average, were only slightly and not significantly better than chance.

Still another advantage of the Buddhism material inhered in the fact that its learnability was relatively uninfluenced in our population by such factors as sex, field of specialization, and variability in relevant incidental experience. It is true that women *S*s made significantly higher scores than men *S*s on both the Buddhism and Christianity tests. This superiority, however, was not a function of differential background, interest, or motivation related to sex per se, but reflected significantly superior academic aptitude as measured by verbal score on the *School and College Ability Test* (SCAT).

Knowledge of the Buddhism material was tested three and ten days after learning, by equivalent forms of a 45-item multiple-choice test with corrected split-half reliabilities of .80 and .79 respectively. The correlation of the three-and ten-day retention scores was .79. This latter figure indicated both relatively high stability over time, in view of the different (three-versus ten-day) retention abilities involved, as well as a high degree of relationship between the two retention abilities. Test questions covered principles, facts, and applications, and were selected by an item analysis procedure from a larger population of items. Scores on both tests showed a satisfactory range of variability and were distributed normally. Since they were intended as power tests, no time limit was imposed.

Three types of introductory passages were used in this experiment, each about 500 words in length. The *comparative* organizer pointed out explicitly the principal similarities and differences between Buddhist and Christian doctrines. This comparison was presented at a much higher level of abstraction, generality, and inclusiveness than the Buddhism passage itself, and was deliberately designed to increase discriminability between the two sets of concepts. The *expository* organizer, on the other hand, merely presented the principal Buddhist doctrines at a high level of abstraction, generality, and inclusiveness, without making any reference whatsoever to Christianity. It was not explicitly designed to increase discriminability between the two religions, but merely to provide some general ideational scaffolding for the detailed Buddhist material. The *historical* introduction was intended solely as a control treatment. It contained interesting historical and human interest material about Buddha and

Buddhism, but neither provided any ideational scaffolding nor attempted to compare Buddhism and Christianity. No information was included in any of the introductory passages that could constitute a direct advantage in answering questions on the Buddhism test.

It was methodologically important to provide an historical introduction for the control group in order that any obtained differences in retention outcomes between experimental (comparative) and control (historical) groups could be attributed to the particular nature of the comparative organizer (i.e., to its enhancing effects on discriminability) rather than to its presence per se. The purpose of exposing another group of subjects to an expository introduction was to determine whether the comparative organizer could increase the discriminability of the learning passage over and above that which could be attributed to the influence of a simple organizer (i.e., to the mere provision of advance ideational scaffolding).

A 36-item multiple-choice test on Christianity was used to measure variability among our *S*s with respect to the stability and clarity of those existing (Christianity) concepts within cognitive structure which were analogous to the Buddhism learning material, and hence potentially interfering. Test items were noncontroversial, dealing with Old and New Testaments, church history, and denominational beliefs and differences. The scores on this test were normally distributed and the corrected split-half reliability was .84.

Scores on the verbal portion of the SCAT were available for 65 *S*s. This test had been previously administered as part of a battery of entrance examinations for incoming University freshmen.

Procedure

On the first day of experimentation, all *S*s took the Christianity test and then (after assignment to a treatment group) studied one of the three kinds of introductions for eight minutes. Membership in a treatment group (comparative, expository, or historical) was determined by random assignment. The population of each of the three treatment groups was also stratified by sex so that the proportion of men to women *S*s would be the same in each group. This was necessary because of the women's significantly higher verbal SCAT scores. It was possible to administer all three treatments simultaneously because they consisted of identical appearing introductory passages (with identical sets of directions), differing only in content.

To equalize the possible effects of prior extended exposure to the Buddhism material, those few subjects (5 percent of the total) who had taken a course in comparative religion were equally distributed in random fashion, among the three treatment groups. It had also been assumed that random assignment of *S*s would render the different treatment groups equivalent with respect to such factors as learning ability and knowledge of Christianity. This assumption was confirmed empirically by the finding that differences between these groups on SCAT and Christianity test scores were negligible.

In order to control for the effects of different instructor, situational, and classroom climate variables in the six sections, students *within each* section were equally divided among the three treatment groups. Since analysis of the data showed that homogeneity of variance prevailed, both on an intersectional as well as on an intergroup basis, for both the Christianity test scores and the two sets of Buddhism test scores, it was considered justifiable to treat the scores of the three treatment groups on each of these instruments as comparable random samples from the same population.

Two days after studying their designated introductions, all *S*s read and studied the same Buddhism passage for 35 minutes. One form of the Buddhism test was administered to all *S*s three days later, and an equivalent form of the same test was administered one week after the first test, or ten days after the learning passage.

A special randomly assigned control group of *S*s was constituted out of the six sections, along the same lines described above for the three treatment groups. The procedure followed with this special group was identical with that used for the comparative group except that *S*s studied an 1800-word passage on the endocrinology of human pubescence instead of the Buddhism passage. The purpose of this procedure was to ascertain to what extent mere knowledge of the comparative organizer (without any exposure to the Buddhism learning passage itself) could increase scores on the Buddhism tests beyond chance expectancy.

Results and Discussion

Comparison of corresponding three-and ten-day means of total treatment groups shows that retention loss during this interval was relatively slight. The loss was greatest in the historical group ($p = .05$), least in the expository group, and intermediate in the comparative group ($p < .10$). This low degree of retention loss is probably attributable both to the negatively accelerated shape of most retention curves, particularly in the case of meaningful material, and to the "rehearsal effect" of the three-day Buddhism test on the subsequent test of retention. The retention scores of our *S*s over the two intervals were highly correlated ($r = .79$).

Effect of Organizers on Retention

On a three-day basis, only the comparative organizer was effective in facilitating retention of the Buddhism material. Table 1 shows that the mean retention score of the total comparative group was significantly superior to both that of the historical group ($p = .05$) and that of the expository group ($p = .05$). However, practically all of this obtained difference between the comparative group, on the one hand, and the expository and historical groups, on the other, was derived from the below-median subgroups on the Christianity test. Within these below-median subgroups the differences between the means in question were much greater than the corresponding differences between total treatment groups, and their level of significance was also correspondingly higher ($p = .02$; $p = .005$).

It is apparent, therefore, that although provision of ideational scaffolding in the form of an expository organizer did not enhance retention of the Buddhism passage over a three-day interval, the combined scaffolding and explicit discriminability ef-

TABLE 1

Mean Retention Test Scores of Experimental and Control Groups on Buddhism Passage

Knowledge of Christianity	Treatment Groups: Comparative Organizer	Expository Organizer	Control (Historical)
Three-day Retention			
Above-Median	23.50	22.50	23.42
Below-Median	20.50	17.32	16.52
Total	21.83	19.91	19.97
Ten-day Retention			
Above-Median	21.79	22.27	20.87
Below-Median	19.21	17.02	14.40
Total	20.31	19.65	17.63

NOTE—Chance score on the multiple-choice test of 45 items is 9.0.

fects induced by the comparative organizer did significantly improve retention. The short-term retention loss in the control group was evidently small enough to preclude the possibility of a significant difference in retention attributable to the facilitating effects of a simple expository organizer. It is true that an expository type of organizer significantly increased three-day retention in an earlier experiment (Ausubel, 1960); but the learning passage used then was more unfamiliar to *S*s, and the latter also had the benefit of studying the organizer on two separate occasions.

As hypothesized, *S*s with relatively superior knowledge of Christianity derived considerably less benefit from the comparative organizer than did *S*s whose knowledge of Christianity was less impressive. This finding was consistent with the self-evident proposition that if the discriminability of a learning passage is already high because of endogenous factors within cognitive structure (i.e., because of the clarity and stability of related established knowledge), less scope exists for the potentially facilitating influence of exogenously manipulated factors (i.e., organizers) designed to promote discriminability.

On a ten-day basis, both the comparative and expository total groups were significantly superior to the historical total group in retaining the Buddhism material ($p = .02$; $p = .05$), but the difference between the comparative and expository groups was negligible (see Table 1). As was true of the three-day scores, however, most of the difference between organizer and control groups was derived from the below-median subgroups on the Christianity test. When the means of just these below-median subgroups were compared, the significance level of the comparative-historical and expository-historical differences was enhanced ($p = .0025$; $p < .05$), and the difference between the comparative and expository groups was significant at the .10 level.

In comparing the ten-to the three-day retention data, it appears first, that only over the longer time interval was the natural retention loss sufficiently great to provide scope for the limited facilitating influence of the scaffolding effects available from the expository organizer. Second, although the comparative organizer was not significantly more effective than the expository organizer over the longer interval when the results of all *S*s in these groups were considered, there was a suggestive trend in this direction among the below-median *S*s.

One explanation of the relatively small difference in ten-day retention attributable to the influence of explicit comparison per se, is the possibility that confronting the learner in advance with the major principles of Buddhism in a detail-free context (the expository organizer) *implicitly* increased the discriminability of his Buddhism ideas by enabling him to make his own comparisons with Christianity. Another plausible explanation is that by enhancing retention generally, the rehearsal effect induced by the three-day Buddhism test had a leveling influence on the relative degree of facilitation that might have been expected from the two kinds of organizers. This interpretation is supported by the erosion of the significant retention difference between the comparative and expository groups from the third to the tenth day.

The tendency noted above in the three-day results—for only the below- as opposed to the above-median subgroups on the Christianity test to derive appreciable benefit from the organizers—also appeared in the ten-day data. Thus, in the learning and retention of unfamiliar ideational material that is relatable to established concepts in the learner's cognitive structure, both comparative and expository organizers appear to be effective only in those instances where existing (endogenously determined) discriminability between the two sets of ideas is inadequate as a consequence of the instability or ambiguity of the established concepts.

The special control group which only studied the comparative organizer (without any exposure to the Buddhism passage itself) made a mean score of 13.20 on the three-day Buddhism test and a mean score of 13.45 on the ten-day test. These scores were significantly greater than the scores of a comparable naïve group (which took the Buddhism tests without being exposed to either organizer or learning passage), but were substantially below those of the historical and two organizer groups.

It is quite unlikely, however, that the organizers per se directly furnished pertinent information enabling *S*s to obtain higher scores on the Buddhism tests. In the first place, a deliberate effort was made to avoid providing such information in the two organizers. Second, if the organizers themselves had furnished useful information in answering test items, it would be difficult to explain why *S*s in the expository group did not make higher scores than *S*s in the historical group on the three-day Buddhism test. Much more credible, therefore, is the explanation that exposure to the comparative organizer merely increased the general sophistication of *S*s in the special control group about Buddhist concepts, and thereby helped them to eliminate misleads in the multiple-choice test questions. Thus, they were able to obtain better than chance scores without studying the learning passage itself. But when the learning passage was available (i.e., in the historical and two organizer groups), *S*s were neither benefited by the general sophistication they obtained from an ideational organizer, nor handicapped by not possessing such sophistication.

Effect of Knowledge of Christianity on Retention

The data clearly support the hypothesis that the discriminability of the Buddhism learning material varies as a function of the clarity and stability of the established concepts to which it is related (i.e., Christianity), and hence that Buddhism retention scores are positively correlated with knowledge of Christianity. Table 1 shows that within each treatment group the mean retention score of the above-median group was significantly greater than the mean retention score of the below-mediar group. For the historical, expository, and comparative groups, these differences were significant at the .0005, .001, and .02 levels, respectively, on the three-day Buddhism test, and at the .0005, .0005, and .10 levels, respectively, on the ten-day Buddhism test. The same trends are shown by the positive correlations between scores on the Buddhism and Christianity tests (see Table 2).

It is evident, therefore, that the clearer and more stable *S*s' knowledge of Christianity was, the more discriminable this knowledge was from Buddhism concepts, and hence the higher the Buddhism retention scores were. And conversely, the less clear and more unstable *S*s' knowledge of Christianity was, the less discriminable it was from Buddhism concepts, and the lower the Buddhism retention scores were.

The data also confirm the hypothesis that organizers (by virtue of their leveling effect on the endogenous discriminability advantage inherent in a clear and stable knowledge of Christianity) reduce the relationship between Christianity knowledge and Buddhism retention scores in proportion to their facilitating effect on retention. The leveling effect of the organizers (particularly the comparative) can be seen in Table 1 by comparing the relative magnitude of the differences between above-median and

TABLE 2

Correlations of Buddhism Retention Scores and Other Measures

Other Measures	Buddhism Retention Scores: Comparative Group		Expository Group		Historical Group	
	3-day	10-day	3-day	10-day	3-day	10-day
Christianity Scores	.37*	.21	.57**	.42**	.55**	.56**
Verbal Ability Scores	.62**	.60**	.75**	.79**	.58**	.52*
Christianity Scores with Verbal Ability Eliminated	.06	.07	.40**	.14	.40**	.43**

* Significant at .05 level
**Significant at .01 level

below-median subgroups in the various treatment groups. For historical, expository and comparative groups the respective t values of these differences were 4.86, 3.43, and 2.24 for the three-day Buddhism scores, and 4.72, 3.99, and 1.59 for the ten-day Buddhism scores. Correlations between the Buddhism and Christianity scores show the same trend (see Table 2). The correlation between the Christianity and Buddhism scores was higher in the historical than in the comparative group for both the three-day ($p = .12$) and ten-day ($p = .04$) retention intervals. The almost identical correlations, on the other hand, between Christianity and three-day Buddhism scores in the expository and historical groups, reflected the ineffectiveness of the expository organizer in facilitating retention over the three-day interval.

Because of the positive correlation of .44 ($p < .01$) between Christianity and SCAT scores, however, it was necessary to check the alternative hypothesis that the significantly higher retention scores of *S*s in the above-median groups reflect superior verbal ability rather than superior knowledge of Christianity per se (endogenous discriminability). But since the availability of only 65 SCAT scores made it impossible to match for verbal ability those *S*s within each treatment group who were above and below the median score on the Christianity test it was necessary to resort to partial correlation.

The partial correlations between the Buddhism and Christianity scores, with the effect of verbal ability eliminated, are shown for all three groups in Table 2. For the historical group the partial correlations of .40 and .43 (for the three-and ten-day scores, respectively), although lower than the corresponding simple correlations of .55 and .56 were still significant at the .01 level. Three of the four other partial correlations, however, were negligible and nonsignificant, indicating that the corresponding simple correlations largely reflected the positive relationship between verbal ability and Buddhism retention scores. The intrinsic residual relationship between knowledge of Christianity and retention of the Buddhism material, after the effect of verbal ability was eliminated, was actually close to zero in these instances because of the leveling influence of the organizers on the endogenous discriminability advantage conferred by superior knowledge of Christianity. The partial correlation between the Christianity and three-day Buddhism scores remained significant at the .01 level in the expository group, in as much as the expository organizer did not facilitate retention over the three-day interval.

Intergroup comparison of the partial correlations in Table 2 shows, even more clearly than does corresponding comparison of the simple correlations between Buddhism and Christianity scores, that the organizers (in proportion to their facilitating effect on retention) reduced the significant relationship between knowledge of Christianity and retention of Buddhism material. With the influence of verbal ability eliminated, the partial correlation between Christianity and three-day Buddhism scores in both the historical and expository groups was significantly higher than in the comparative group ($p = .05$; $p = .05$). The partial correlation between Christianity and ten-day Buddhism scores in the historical group was higher than the corresponding partial correlations in the expository ($p = .08$) and comparative ($p = .01$) groups. In effect, then, by being provided with a given type of discriminability aid (organizer), *S*s possessing relatively little knowledge of Christianity (and hence little endogenous discriminability) were placed on approximately the same footing with respect to the discriminability variable and its effect on retention, as *S*s possessing greater knowledge of Christianity (and greater endogenous discriminability).

Table 2 also shows that the correlation between verbal ability and Buddhism retention scores in the historical group (where the relationship was not influenced by interaction with organizer effects) was approximately the same as that between Christianity and Buddhism scores. But unlike the latter relationship, which was attenuated by interaction with the organizers, the correlation between verbal ability and Buddhism scores was slightly higher in the comparative than in the historical group, and suggestively but not significantly higher in the expository than in the historical group ($p = .17$; $p = .07$). At the very least, therefore, it is definite that neither organizer detracted from the strong positive relationship between verbal ability and the retention of the Buddhism material; and there was a suggestive tendency for verbal ability to have an even greater impact on the retention of the Buddhism passage when *S*s were given the benefit of an expository organizer.

Summary and Conclusions

This experiment was concerned with the role of endogenous and externally manipulated discriminability in the learning and retention of unfamiliar ideational material (Buddhism) that was relatable to previously learned concepts (Christianity) already established in cognitive structure. Endogenous discriminability was defined in terms of the relative clarity and stability of these latter established concepts in cognitive structure (as measured by performance on a test of Christianity); and discriminability was manipulated externally by means of advance introductory passages (organizers).

The learning task consisted of a 2500-word passage of empirically demonstrated unfamiliarity, dealing with the principles of Buddhism. Two days before studying this learning passage, one experimental group studied a 500-word *comparative* organizer that explicitly compared the major ideas of Buddhism and Christianity at a high level of generality, abstraction, and inclusiveness. Another experimental group studied an *expository* organizer presenting in similar fashion the basic doctrines of Buddhism, but without making any reference whatsoever to Christianity. The comparative organizer was designed explicitly to increase discriminability between Buddhist and Christian doctrines, and implicitly to provide ideational scaffolding for the unfamiliar new Buddhism material. The expository organizer, on the other hand, was designed explicitly to provide ideational scaffolding, and only implicitly to enhance discriminability. A control group studied a non-ideational (*historical*) introduction, dealing with the life of Buddha and the history of Buddhism rather than with Buddhist concepts as such. Retention of the Buddhism material was tested three and ten days after the learning session, by means of equivalent forms of a 45-item multiple-choice test. The experimental population consisted of undergraduate students in an educational psychology course. *S*s were randomly assigned to these three treatment groups.

On a three-day basis, only the comparative organizer was significantly effective in facilitating the retention of the Buddhism material, but over the ten-day interval both comparative and expository organizers were significantly effective. However, the facilitating influence of the comparative organizer was only suggestively greater than that of the expository organizer over the longer retention interval. The latter finding was attributed both to the implicit discriminability effect of the expository organizer and to the rehearsal (and hence leveling) effect of the three-day Buddhism test on subsequent retention.

The above-noted effects of the organizers on retention outcomes only applied to the below-median subgroups of the different treatment groups. Thus, in the learning and retention of unfamiliar ideational material that is relatable to established concepts in the learner's cognitive structure, both comparative and expository organizers appear to be effective only in those instances where existing discriminability between the two sets of ideas is inadequate as a consequence of the instability or ambiguity of the established concepts. When the discriminability of unfamiliar new ideas is already high because of endogenous factors within cognitive structure (i.e., because of the clarity and stability of related established knowledge), less scope exists for the potentially facilitating influence of externally manipulated factors (organizers) designed to promote discriminability. Organizers, therefore, exert a leveling effect on the positive relationship between endogenously determined discriminability and meaningful learning and retention: By differentially benefiting *S*s possessing relatively unclear and unstable backgrounds (and hence little endogenous discriminability), they place them on approximately the same footing with respect to the discriminability variable as *S*s possessing clearer and more stable backgrounds (and greater endogenous discriminability).

The data also clearly support the hypothesis that the learning and retention of unfamiliar verbal material varies positively with its discriminability from related, previously learned concepts established in cognitive structure. Hence *S*s with greater knowledge of Christianity made significantly higher scores on the Buddhism retention tests than did *S*s with less knowledge of Christianity. This significantly positive relationship between Christianity and Buddhism test scores held up even when the effect of verbal ability was partialled out.

Verbal ability was positively correlated both with knowledge of Christianity and with the retention of the Buddhism material. Unlike the relationship between Christianity and Buddhism test scores, however, the correlation between verbal ability and Buddhism test scores was not reduced by organizer effects. There was even a suggestive tendency for the expository organizer to enhance the facilitating influence of verbal ability on the retention of the Buddhism passage.

The following implications for teaching seem warranted: First, because of the importance of the clarity and stability of related, previously learned knowledge in cognitive structure (i.e., endogenous discriminability) for the meaningful learning and retention of unfamiliar verbal material, teachers should be particularly concerned with clarifying and stabilizing relevant background knowledge before introducing new subject-matter. Second, comparative organizers can be used most effectively in enhancing the discriminability and, hence, in facilitating the learning of unfamiliar new subject-matter, in the case of those students whose relevant background knowledge is weakest. Still to be explored is the possibility that comparative organizers can be used to increase the clarity and stability of the very background knowledge which determines the endogenous discriminability of unfamiliar but relatable new subject-matter.

References

Ausubel, D. P. The use of advance organizers in the learning and retention of meaningful verbal material. *J. educ. Psychol.*, 1960, *51*, 267–272.

Ausubel, D. P., and E. Blake, Jr. Proactive inhibition in the forgetting of meaningful school material. *J. educ. Res.*, 1958. *52*, 145–149.

9 A Transfer of Training Approach to Improving the Functional Retention of Medical Knowledge*

David P. Ausubel

Perhaps the most distinctive feature of medicine as a profession is the unusually large volume of relevant background knowledge which a medical trainee must first acquire in usable form before he can hope to engage in the actual practice of medicine. A central problem of medical education, therefore, is to discover efficacious ways of transmitting this knowledge to students so that it can be retained over long periods of time in the viable and functional condition necessary for successful application to problems of clinical practice.

In this paper I propose, first, to conceptualize in transfer of training terms the problem of enhancing the functional retention

Reprinted from the article of the same title,* Journal of Medical Education, *1962,* **23, *647–655. By permission of the author and the Journal of Medical Education.*

of medical knowledge. I will then examine various approaches that seem feasible in attacking this problem, outline the underlying theory of a "cognitive structure" approach to transfer, and advance a pedagogic strategy of implementing this approach. Finally, by way of illustration, I will describe in some detail three research proposals based on this latter strategy.

The Problem of Transfer in Medical Education

Since a minimal fund of preclinical and clinical background information must be acquired before any serious exposure to clinical problem-solving experience is feasible, and since this is largely acquired during the two preclinical years and the first clinical year of medical school, the educational problem may be conceptualized as one of long-term transfer of training. How, for example, can the subject-matter of the preclinical years be best taught so that it can be retained in useable form, and hence be available both as a foundation for learning new bodies of clinical subject matter, and as a basis for clinical problem solving? Obviously, preclinical knowledge which is not retained at all, or which is retained in a disorganized, unclear, nonmeaningful (rote), unstable, or isolated fashion cannot be used effectively for these latter purposes.

Yet it is a well-known fact that many medical students, especially those with high levels of anxiety, cope with the problem of digesting the large volume of material with which they are confronted, by memorizing it rotely for examination purposes and by relying compulsively on their lecture notes which, often as not, are grossly inaccurate. Other students narrowly restrict their intellectual horizons to the prescribed textbooks, phobically avoiding supplementary readings, special lectures, and extra-curricular activities because they fear that additional information or other points of view will add to the already unmanageable burden of knowledge. Both adjustive techniques obviously tend to foster a closed-minded, uncritical attitude toward prevailing doctrines and practices in medicine.

Two Types of Transfer

Historically speaking, the major problem of transfer with which medical educators have grappled has been the best way of teaching preclinical subjects so that an adequate residue of relevant and viable knowledge is retained for later use in learning clinical subject matter. The most widely used approach to this problem of maximizing the transferability of preclinical medical knowledge to both clinical subject matter and problems of clinical practice involves the use of explicit transitional materials and devices. During the first preclinical year, for example, some anatomy is presented in the context of its explicit relevance for surgery, physical diagnosis, and clinical neurology; and some aspects of physiology and biochemistry are consisered in the context of pathological aberrations encountered in medical practice. During the second preclinical year, such courses as pathology, pharmacology, laboratory diagnosis, and physical diagnosis are partly designed so as to constitute a theoretical link between the first-year study of normal structure and function, on the one hand, and the clinical understanding and manipulation of pathological conditions, on the other. Some time is also devoted in the preclinical years to the demonstration and discussion of patients and to clinical-pathological conferences.

During the clinical years the articulation of preclinical and clinical background knowledge is approached from the opposite direction. Preceding the discussion of the diagnosis, prognosis, and treatment of clinical entities, some attempt is usually made to summarize the relevant anatomy, physiology, and pathology. In my opinion, efforts to achieve this type of articulation—in both directions—are extremely worthwhile, have demonstrably efficacious results, and should be extended.

Another important problem of transfer in medical education is concerned with the transfer of clinical *background* knowledge (third-year lecture courses) to the *particular* diagnostic and therapeutic issues posed by individual patients in clinic and hospital practice (senior-year clinical clerkships and fifth-year internship.) However, the problem of transfer here is somewhat different from that of making optimal use of *abstract preclinical* knowledge in the learning of *abstract clinical* subject matter. It involves, rather, the optimal utilization of *general* clinical knowledge in particular *problem-solving* situations.

This second problem of transfer, although no less real and important than the first, is, unfortunately somewhat less susceptible to educational manipulation. Transfer from one body of abstract knowledge to another is wholly a cognitive problem. That is, all that is involved in considering the influence of preclinical knowledge on success in learning clinical subject matter, are the actual content relationships between the disciplines in question, and the relationships between the quite analogous intellectual abilities needed in the two learning tasks. But the relationship between knowledge of clinical subject matter and success in clinical practice is much more complicated. In this instance, the two kinds of learning tasks (i.e., learning an abstract body of clinical knowledge and learning to solve the particular clinical problems of individual patients) are less closely related than in the case of the first transfer situation; and the abilities influencing success in the first task are similarly less related to the abilities influencing success in the second task than is true of the earlier described transfer situation.

Another way of contrasting these two types of transfer is to say that knowledge of clinical and preclinical subject matter is a necessary but not a sufficient condition for successful clinical problem solving. To solve problems of clinical practice successfully, one not only requires a sound background of relevant background knowledge, but also (a) an adequate amount of appropriately organized and supervised clinical experience, and (b) such problem-solving traits as resourcefulness, problem sensitivity, originality, perseverance, flexibility, improvising ability, and venturesomeness. And these latter traits are undoubtedly both more dependent on genic endowment and less teachable than either background knowledge or strategies of clinical problem solving.

It is apparent, therefore, that the problem of transfer from preclinical to clinical knowledge is simpler in terms of the variables involved than is the corresponding problem of transfer from relevant background knowledge (clinical and preclinical) to clinical problem solving. Furthermore, transfer is more predictable and educationally manipulable in the first situation than in the second. In the second situation we can enhance ultimate problem-solving (i.e., diagnostic and therapeutic) ability by both increasing the stability and usability of relevant background knowledge, and providing more adequate and better organized and supervised clinical experience. However, we have little control over and cannot materially influence by educational techniques those problem-solving traits that are so crucially important for success in any kind of problem solving.

Approaches to the Enhancement of Transfer

To summarize, three kinds of approaches seem feasible in attacking the transfer problem in medical education. First we can try to incorporate into the medical curriculum explicit transitional materials and experiences that bridge the gap between the structural and the functional; between the normal and the pathological; between basic science knowledge (both normal and pathological) and bodies of clinical knowledge; and between abstract subject matter (both basic science and clinical) and clinical problem solving. This is currently the most widely used approach in medical schools. Second, we can attempt both (a) to enhance the clarity, stability, and usability of preclinical subject-matter that is retained as a foundation for learning clinical subject matter, and (b) to enhance the clarity, stability, and usability of both preclinical and clinical knowledge that is available for application to clinical problem solving. This is the approach that is explored and advocated in this paper. Third, we can endeavor to improve the experiential content, organization, and supervision of the student's hospital and outpatient training, as well as to teach more effective strategies of diagnosis and therapeutic decision making.This type of supervised clincial problem-solving experience can be considered a special variant of the first approach, i.e., as a protracted, concentrated, but nevertheless transitional training device bridging the gap or facilitating transfer between abstract clinical knowledge, on the one hand, and *independent* clinical practice, on the other.

Bedside apprenticeship, case study review, and diagnostic problem-solving exercises are representative of the last-mentioned approach. When used intelligently and with full awareness of the realistic limitations involved, such techniques are very effective and enjoy an established place among the more promising methods of enhancing the clinical skills of medical trainees. One important limitation that must be accepted from the outset is the already emphasized fact that much of the ultimate variability in clinical problem-solving performance reflects genically determined variability in problem-solving traits that are not very susceptible to training measures. An equally important limitation involves recognition of the fact that clinical problem-solving techniques can only be used in conjunction with rather than as a substitute for didactic exposition of clinical subject matter. Training in particular problem-solving situations is much too time-consuming to constitute a feasible method of transmitting the vast array of abstract clinical knowledge medical students are required to know. As a matter of fact, if problem-solving techniques were misused for this latter purpose they would ultimately prove to be self-defeating, because in the absence of adequate background knowledge students could not possibly hope to solve clinical problems successfully, irrespective of the adequacy of their clinical training. Enhanced ability to solve clinical problems, in other words, can be regarded as both the major objective of expository clinical teaching and as a principal criterion of its adequacy; but problem-solving exercises cannot be considered a practical means of teaching the abstract content of clinical subject matter.

Despite these limitations, however, much scope obviously remains for methods designed to improve the adequacy of clinical training. My decision to adopt the second of the three approaches outlined above is largely a reflection both of personal preference and of the judgment that this approach, although exceedingly promising, is the most neglected of the three. It does not in any way imply a derogation of the other two approaches.

In my opinion, the most significant advances that have occurred in recent years in the teaching of such subjects as mathematics, chemistry, physics, and biology have been predicated on the assumption that efficient learning and functional retention of ideas and information are largely dependent upon the adequacy of cognitive structure, *i.e.*, upon the adequacy of an individual's existing organization, stability and clarity of knowledge in a particular subject-matter field. The acquisition of adequate cognitive structure, in turn, has been shown to depend upon two factors: (a) using for organizational and integrative purposes those substantive concepts and principles in a given discipline that have the widest explanatory power, inclusiveness, generalizability, and relatability to the subject-matter content of that discipline; and (b) employing those methods of presenting and ordering the sequence of subject matter that best enhance the clarity, stability and integratedness of cognitive structure for purposes of new learning and problem solving.

The "Cognitive Structure" Approach to Transfer

From the standpoint of the approach adopted herein to the transfer problem in medical education, the structure of a student's medical knowledge is regarded as the crucial variable influencing new learning, retention, and problem solving. Only in so far as it is possible to enhance the organizational strength of this structure, is it possible to increase the functional retention of medical knowledge so that both more preclinical subject matter is transferable to the learning of clinical subject matter, and that more abstract clinical knowledge is available for particular clinical problem solving. Cognitive structure itself, as indicated above, can be influenced substantively by the generality and integrative properties of the particular organizing and explanatory principles used in a given branch of medicine, and programmatically by methods of presenting, arranging, and ordering units of medical knowledge that impinge on the clarity, stability, and cohesiveness of that structure. We shall consider both of these factors below.

Substantive and Programmatic Factors Influencing Cognitive Structure

The task of identifying the particular organizing and explanatory principles in the various branches of medicine that manifest widest generality and integrative properties is obviously a formidable and long-range problem. Experience with other curriculum reform movements, however, indicates that it yields to sustained and resourceful inquiry, especially when it is possible to enlist the cooperative efforts of outstanding subject-matter specialists, talented teachers, and imaginative educational psychologists. Then, once the substantive organizational problem (*i.e.*, identifying the basic organizing concepts in a given discipline) is solved, attention can be directed to the programmatic organizational problems involved in the presentation and sequential arrangement of component units. Here, it is hypothesized, two principles concerned with the efficient programming of content are applicable, irrespective of the subject-matter field—the principle of progressive differentiation and the principle of integrative reconciliation.

Progressive Differentiation

When subject matter is programmed in accordance with the principle of progressive differentiation, the most general and inclusive ideas of the discipline are presented first, and are then progressively differentiated in terms of detail and specificity. This order of presentation demonstrably corresponds to the natural sequence of acquiring cognitive awareness and sophistication when human beings are exposed either to an entirely unfamiliar field of knowledge or to an unfamiliar branch of a familiar body of knowledge. It also corresponds to the postulated way in which this knowledge is represented, organized, and stored in the human nervous system. The assumption we are making here, in other words, is that an individual's organization of the content of a particular subject-matter discipline in his own mind, consists of a hierarchical structure in which the most inclusive concepts occupy a position at the apex of the structure and subsume progressively less inclusive and more highly differentiated subconcepts and factual data.

Now if the human nervous system as a data processing and storing mechanism is so constructed that both the acquisition of new knowledge and its organization in cognitive structure conform *naturally* to the principle of progressive differentiation, it seems reasonable to suppose that optimal learning and retention occur when teachers *deliberately* order the organization and sequential arrangement of subject matter along similar lines. A more explicit way of stating the same proposition is to say that new ideas and information can be efficiently learned and retained only to the extent that more inclusive and appropriately relevant concepts are already available in cognitive structure to serve a subsuming role or to furnish ideational anchorage. But:

> . . . even though this principle seems rather self-evident it is rarely followed in actual teaching procedures or in the organization of most textbooks. The more typical practice is to segregate topically homogeneous materials into separate chapters, and to present them throughout at a uniform level of conceptualization in accordance with a logical outline of subject-matter organization. This practice, of course, although logically sound is psychologically incongruous with the postulated process whereby meaningful learning occurs, i.e., with the hierarchical organization of cognitive structure in terms of progressive gradations of inclusiveness, and with the mechanism of accretion through a process of progressive differentiation of an undifferentiated field. Thus, in most instances, students are required to learn the details of new and unfamiliar disciplines before they have acquired an adequate body of relevant subsumers at an appropriate level of inclusiveness.[1]

One outstanding example of a textbook which is organized in accordance with the principle of progressive differentiation is Boyd's famous *Textbook of Pathology*. In this book Boyd parts company with most traditional treatises on pathology, which typically consist of about twenty chapters, each devoted to describing serially the major kinds of pathological processes occurring within the various organs or organ systems. Boyd, in contrast, reserves serial consideration of the pathology of separate organ systems to the second half of his text, and devotes the entire first half to such general organizing and integrative

[1] Ausubel, D. P. "The Use of Advance Organizers in the Learning and Retention of Meaningful Verbal Material, *J. educ. Psychol.*, 1960 (*51*: 267–272), p. 270.

topics as the different categories of pathological processes (e.g., inflammation, allergy, degeneration, neoplasm), and their principal causes and characteristics; the various kinds of etiological agents in disease; types of humoral and tissue resistance to disease; the interaction between genic and environmental factors in the development of pathological processes; and general relationships between pathological lesions and clinical symptoms.

Integrative Reconciliation

The principle of integrative reconciliation in programming instructional material can be best described as antithetical in spirit and approach to the ubiquitous practice among textbook writers of compartmentalizing and segregating particular ideas or topics within their respective chapters or subchapters.[2] Implicit in this latter practice is the assumption (perhaps logically valid, but certainly psychologically implausible) that pedagogic considerations are adequately served if overlapping topics are handled in self-contained fashion, so that each topic is presented in only one of the several possible places where treatment is relevant and warranted, i.e., the assumption that all necessary cross-referencing of related ideas can be satisfactorily performed (and customarily is) by students. Hence little serious effort is made explicitly to explore relationships between these ideas, to point out significant similarities and differences, and to reconcile real or apparent inconsistencies. Some of the undesirable consequences of this approach are that multiple terms are used to represent concepts which are intrinsically equivalent except for contextual reference, thereby generating incalculable cognitive strain and confusion, as well as encouraging rote learning; that artificial barriers are erected between related topics, obscuring important common features, and thus rendering impossible the acquisition of insights dependent on the perception of these commonalities; that adequate use is not made of relevant, previously learned ideas as a basis for subsuming and incorporating related new information; and that since significant differences between apparently

[2] The same practice is customarily followed in the lecture form of presentation.

similar concepts are not made clear and explicit, these concepts are often erroneously perceived and retained as identical.

The "Organizer" Technique of Didactic Exposition

In general, the pedagogic strategy proposed in this project for implementing the programming principles of progressive differentiation and integrative reconciliation involves the use of appropriately relevant and inclusive organizers that are maximally stable and discriminable from related conceptual systems in the learner's cognitive structure. These organizers are introduced in advance of the learning material itself, and are also presented at a higher level of abstractness, generality, and inclusiveness; and since the substantive content of a given organizer or series of organizers is selected on the basis of their suitability for explaining, integrating, and interrelating the material they precede (see above), this strategy simultaneously satisfies the substantive as well as the programming criteria specified above for enhancing the organizational strength of cognitive structure.

Progressive differentiation in the programming of subject matter is accomplished by using a hierarchical series of organizers (in descending order of inclusiveness), each organizer preceding its corresponding unit of detailed, differentiated material. In this way not only is an appropriately relevant and inclusive subsumer made available to provide ideational scaffolding for each component unit of differentiated subject matter, but the various units in relation to each other are also progressively differentiated, i.e., organized in descending order of inclusiveness.

The advantage of deliberately constructing a special organizer for each new unit of material is that only in this way can the learner enjoy the advantages of a subsumer which both (a) gives him a general overview of the more detailed material in *advance* of his actual confrontation with it, and (b) also provides organizing elements that are inclusive of and take into account most relevantly and efficiently the *particular content* contained in this material. Any existing subsumer in the learner's cognitive structure which he could independently employ for this purpose self-evidently lacks particularized relevance and inclusiveness for the new material, and would hardly be available in advance of initial contact with it. And although students might possibly be able to improvise a suitable subsumer for future learning efforts *after* they become familiar with the material, it is unlikely that they would be able to do so as efficiently as a person sophisticated in both subject-matter content and pedagogy.

Organizers are also expressly designed to further the principle of integrative reconciliation. They do this by explicitly pointing out in what ways previously learned, related concepts in cognitive structure are either basically similar to or essentially different from new ideas and information in the learning task. Hence, on the one hand, organizers explicitly draw upon and mobilize all available concepts in cognitive structure that are relevant for and can play a subsuming role in relation to the new learning material. This maneuver effects great economy of learning effort, avoids the isolation of essentially similar concepts in separate, noncommunicable compartments, and discourages the confusing proliferation of multiple terms to represent ostensibly different but essentially equivalent ideas. On the other hand, organizers increase the discriminability of genuine differences between the new learning materials and analogous but often conflicting ideas in the learner's cognitive structure. This second way in which organizers purportedly promote integrative reconciliation:

> . . . is predicated on the assumption that if the distinguishing features of the new learning task are not originally salient or readily discriminable from established ideas in cognitive structure, they can be adequately represented by the latter for memorial purposes, and hence would not persist as separately identifiable memories in their own right. It is assumed, in other words, that only discriminable categorical variants of previously learned concepts have long-term retention potentialities.[3]

Thus if an organizer can first delineate clearly, precisely, and explicitly the principal similarities and differences between the

[3] Ausubel, D. P. and D. Fitzgerald, "The Role of Discriminability in Meaningful Verbal Learning and Retention," *J. educ. Psychol.*, 1961, *52*, 266–274.

ideas in a new learning passage, on the one hand, and existing related concepts in cognitive structure, on the other, it seems reasonable to postulate that the more detailed ideas and information in the learning passage would be grasped later with fewer ambiguities, fewer competing meanings, and fewer misconceptions suggested by the learner's prior knowledge of the related concepts; and that as these clearer, less confused new meanings interact with analogous established meanings during the retention interval, they would be more likely to retain their identity.

10 Organizer, General Background, and Antecedent Learning Variables in Sequential Verbal Learning*

David P. Ausubel
Donald Fitzgerald

Typically in the course of meaningful school learning, the learner is introduced to new materials which are variants of and hence relatable to previously learned concepts already established in his cognitive structure. Ausubel and Fitzgerald (1961) have shown that under these circumstances the learner's ability to discriminate between the two sets of concepts has important implications for learning and retention. They demonstrated that such discriminability is partly a function of the clarity and stability of the previously learned concepts, and that when discriminability is low because of inadequate prior knowledge, learning and retention can be enhanced by the use of "comparative organizers."

Reprinted from the article of the same title,* Journal of Educational Psychology, *1962,* **53, *243–249. By permission of the authors and The American Psychological Association, Inc.*

A somewhat different learning situation, however, not uncommonly arises when, for various reasons, students are required to learn a new unit of sequentially organized material which cannot be related to previously learned concepts. No specific referents, either explicit or implicit, are therefore available for this material in cognitive structure. Organizers, under these conditions, obviously cannot be used to increase discriminability; they can at best furnish ideational anchorage.

This type of learning situation also provides an excellent model and test of the transfer of training paradigm in sequential meaningful learning. When subject matter is organized sequentially (so that Part II is built upon and presupposes knowledge of Part I) the student's grasp of the earlier appearing material becomes a crucial factor influencing his learning of the later appearing material. When materials are sequentially presented, therefore, the residue of the earlier appearing material in cognitive structure—i.e., its clarity, stability, and organization—constitutes the impact of the "antecedent condition" in the transfer of training paradigm. It becomes in effect the anchoring post or ideational scaffolding in cognitive structure for the learning of the later appearing material. If this ideational scaffolding is clear, stable, and well organized, it is reasonable to suppose that it provides better anchorage for new learning and retention than if it is unclear, unstable, and poorly organized.

In addition to furnishing a theoretical model for sequential meaningful learning in terms of the familiar transfer of training paradigm, an analysis of covariance design utilizing this type of learning situation makes possible a more explicit test of the proposition that the quality of Part I learning actually influences Part II learning outcomes when subject matter is sequentially organized. Typically this proposition is assumed to be axiomatically true in the absence of proof because of the difficulty of controlling such significant variables as relative learning ability (which accounts for much of the positive relationship between Part I and Part II learning outcomes), and the availability in cognitive structure of relevant concepts relatable to and influencing the learning of Part II materials which were introduced prior to the Part I materials. In this study the influence of learning ability is held constant by statistical means, and the

TABLE 5

Covariance Analysis of Second Pubescence Test Scores × Test I Levels, Adjusting for GET Scores

Source	Adjusted		
	df	*MS*	*F*
Treatment	1	7	.39
Test I levels	2	282	15.7**
Interaction	2	11	.61
Between	5	99	5.50*
Within	131	18	

*.01 level of significance.
**.001 level of significance.

TABLE 6

Covariance Analysis of Second Pubescence Test Scores × Test I Levels, Adjusting for SCAT Scores

Source	Adjusted		
	df	*MS*	*F*
Treatment	1	12	.67
Test I levels	2	171	9.50*
Interaction	2	6	.34
Between	5	73	4.06*
Within	131	18	

*.01 level of significance.

Nevertheless, the significant partial correlations in the experimental group both between GET and Test II scores ($p < .01$), with the influence of SCAT eliminated, and between GET and Test II scores ($p < .05$), with the influence of Test I eliminated, when contrasted with the nonsignificant corresponding correlations in the control group (Table 3), suggest the occurrence of a positive interaction between the effects of the organizer and of general background knowledge. The organizer apparently helped the subjects utilize their existing background knowledge more effectively in structuring the second pubescence passage.

In order for organizers to be really effective in enhancing sequential learning and retention, it would probably be necessary to use another organizer prior to the second passage. The second organizer would attempt both to provide specific ideational scaffolding for the second passage, and also to increase discriminability between confusable concepts in the two passages.

Effect of Initial Learning on Sequential Learning

As hypothesized, Part I retention scores (initial learning) had a significant facilitating effect on Part II retention scores (sequential learning). Both experimental and control subjects in the upper part of the distribution of scores on the first pubescence test made higher retention scores on the second pubescence test than did subjects in the lower part of the distribution of first pubescence test scores. This facilitating effect of antecedent learning ($p < .001$; $p < .01$) was manifested when either the influence of general background knowledge (Table 5) or of verbal ability (Table 6) was statistically controlled in a covariance design. Stability and clarity of knowledge of the first passage therefore constituted a significant limiting condition with respect to learning and retaining the material in the second passage.

Sequential organization of subject matter, therefore, can be very effective because each new increment of knowledge serves as an anchoring post for subsequent learning. This presupposes, of course, that the preceding step is always clear, stable, and well organized. If it is not, the learning of all subsequent steps is jeopardized. Hence new material in the sequence should never be introduced until all previous steps are thoroughly mastered. Perhaps the chief pedagogic advantage of the teaching machine lies in its ability to control this crucial variable in sequential learning.

Effect of General Background Knowledge on Initial Learning

The data clearly support the hypothesis that general background knoweldge in endocrinology facilitates the learning of unfamiliar material in the same subject matter field (i.e., pubescence). This facilitating effect was significant at the .05 level when verbal ability was statistically controlled in a covariance design (Table 7). Significant interaction ($p < .03$) also occurred between the

TABLE 7

Covariance Analysis of Second Pubescence Test Scores × GET Levels, Adjusting for SCAT Scores

Source	Adjusted		
	df	*MS*	*F*
Treatment	1	33	1.57
GET level	2	76	3.64*
Interaction	2	98	4.67*
Between	5	74	3.52**
Within	131	21	

*.05 level of significance.
**.01 level of significance.

organizer and general endocrinology knowledge. Reference to Table 8 shows that the interactional effect was positive for the subjects in the upper third and lower third subgroups of the distribution of GET scores and negative for subjects in the middle third subgroup. The overall interactional effect, however, was positive as shown by the contrast between the significant partial correlation ($p < .05$) in the experimental group between GET and initial retention scores, with SCAT held constant, and the nonsignificant corresponding correlation in the control group (Table 3). Similar positive correlations were reported above in relation to Test I scores.

TABLE 8

Adjusted Mean Retention Scores of Experimental and Control Groups on First Pubescence Passage Analyzed by GET LEVELS

General Endocrinology Knowledge	Treatment Group	
	Organizer	Control
Upper third	21.1	18.3
Middle third	18.4	20.8
Lower third	18.6	16.1
Total	19.4	18.4

General endocrinology knowledge was too distantly related to the pubescence material to provide relevant ideational anchorage. For the most part, it probably facilitated the learning and retention of the pubescence passage by increasing its general familiarity, and hence the subjects' self-confidence in handling it. However, the positive interaction between the effects of the organizer and of general background knowledge in endocrinology suggests that the organizer better enables the subjects to put their background knowledge to effective use in structuring the unfamiliar new material. This finding was consistent for both initial and sequential learning.

Summary and Conclusions

An analysis of covariance design was used with undergraduate students in studying the effects of an advance organizer, antecedent learning, and general background knowledge on the learning and retention of 2 unfamiliar sequential passages about endocrinology. The organizer, by providing relevant ideational anchorage, suggestively enhanced the learning of the material for those *S*s with relatively poor verbal ability. Knowledge of the 1st passage constituted a statistically significant limiting condition in learning the 2nd passage when the influence of both verbal ability and general endocrinological knowledge was statistically controlled. Finally, general background knowledge in endocrinology significantly facilitated the learning and retention of the 1st passage, presumably by increasing the familiarity of the new material.

Reference

Ausubel, D. P., and D. Fitzgerald. The role of discriminability in meaningful verbal learning and retention. *J. educ. Psychol.*, 1961, *52*, 266–274.

11 Can Children Learn Anything That Adults Can—and More Efficiently?*

David P. Ausubel

Two related and currently fashionable propositions in education are that elementary school children can not only learn any subject that can be taught to adolescent and adult students, but that they can also do so *more* efficiently. "Any subject," states Jerome Bruner (1960, p. 33), "can be taught effectively in some intellectually honest form to any child at any stage of development." And carrying this proposition one step further, David Page asserts:

> In teaching from kindergarten to graduate school, I have been amazed at the intellectual similarity of human beings at all ages, although children are perhaps more spontaneous, creative, and energetic than

Reprinted from the article of the same title, Elementary School Journal, *1962,* **62,** *270–272. By permission of the author and The University of Chicago Press.*

adults. As far as I am concerned, young children can learn almost anything *faster* than adults do if it can be given to them in terms they can understand. (quoted in Bruner 1960, pp. 39–40).

How plausible are these propositions? To what extent are they realistic statements of fact and to what extent are they mere wishful thinking? It is important that we at least reach some tentative conclusions because these issues are basic to much present-day thinking about the reorganization of the curriculum. A positive set of answers to these questions would obviously make for much greater curricular change than would a negative set of answers.

In my opinion, although both propositions are generally untrue and unsupportable, they are nevertheless valid in a very limited sense of the term. Even more important, however, they are, in many instances, partially true for reasons that are very different from those offered by their advocates.

The Bruner Proposition: Children Can Learn Anything that Adults Can

Bruner (1960, pp. 12, 13, 38) contends quite reasonably that many of "the basic ideas that lie at the heart of . . . mathematics, the sciences, the humanities, and the social sciences . . . are as simple as they are powerful." But although these ideas are completely beyond the reach of young children when "put in formalized terms as equations or elaborated verbal concepts" (p. 13), they can be grasped concretely and intuitively if presented in developmentally appropriate fashion and in terms children can understand. It is readily conceivable, therefore, that some topics such as "set theory" are not intrinsically difficult and can be adequately learned by fourth-grade children on an intuitive basis when recast in accordance with their characteristic ways of thinking and conceptualizing experience. In fact, one might even conclude that the grade placement of such topics has been erroneous all along when they were not included in the fourth-grade curriculum.

This hardly rules out the possibility, however, that many other ideas do exist that *are* intrinsically too difficult for elementary school children irrespective of how they are presented. Even assuming that all abstract-verbal concepts could be restructured on an intuitive basis, it would be unreasonable to expect that they could *all* be made comprehensible to children at *any* grade level. Although the intuitive comprehensibility of any given restructured idea is best determined empirically, it would surely be plausible on *a priori* grounds to expect that a certain proportion of these ideas could not be rendered comprehensible to typical pupils in some of the elementary grades.

The Page Proposition: Children Can Learn Everything More Efficiently than Adults Can

Many reasons exist for believing that under *certain* conditions young children *can* learn more efficiently than older and intellectually more mature persons. In the first place, older individuals, particularly if miseducated, must often first unlearn what they have previously been taught before they are ready for new learning. This is frequently the case when a student's knowledge is unclear, unstable, or disorganized because of a prior history of rote or nonmeaningful learning. Second, older individuals are more apt to have "emotional blocks" with respect to particular subject-matter areas. Finally, there is a marked falling off of intellectual enthusiasm as children climb the various rungs of the academic ladder.

Generally speaking, however, adolescents and adults have a tremendous advantage in learning any new subject-matter—even if they are just as unsophisticated as young children in that particular subject-matter. This advantage inheres in the fact that they are able to draw on various transferable elements of their *overall* ability to function at an abstract-verbal level of logical operations. Hence they are able to move through the concrete-intuitive phase of intellectual functioning very rapidly; and, unlike the comparably unsophisticated child, who is tied to this latter stage developmentally, they are soon able to dispense entirely with concrete-empirical props and with intuitive understandings. These facilitating transferable elements include the possession of transactional terms and higher-order concepts, as well as successful past experience in *directly* manipulating relationships between abstractions (i.e., without the benefit of concrete-empirical props).

But according to the advocates of the Page proposition, this more rapid shift on the part of the older learners from a concrete-intuitive to an abstract-verbal level of intellectual functioning in the unfamiliar new subject-matter area, results in *less* efficient learning processes and outcomes. Research findings, however, suggest precisely the opposite conclusion, namely, that as long as abstract-verbal understandings are meaningful rather than rote, they constitute a more complete, explicit, inclusive and transferable form of knowledge. For example, numerous experiments on the effects of verbalization on children's ability to solve transposition problems (e.g., Spiker and Terrell, 1955; Weir and Stevenson, 1959) demonstrate that verbal concepts are more manipulable and transferable than their subverbal equivalents. The availability of distinctive verbal responses has also been shown to facilitate rather than inhibit concept formation and conceptual transfer (Kendler and Karasik, 1958; Liublinskaya, 1957).

Advocates of the Page proposition also contend that the concrete-intuitive approach of young children is more creative than the abstract-verbal approach of older individuals, and is comparable to the creative type of intuitive thinking found among creative scholars and scientists. Actually, however, there is no necessary or intrinsic relationship between intuitive thinking and creativity—either among children or adults. The only existing relationship is a chronological one: if a given individual happens to be creative, whether he is a child or an adult, he will obviously first manifest his creativity during the intuitive phase, because this phase invariably precedes the abstract-verbal phase; and contrariwise, if he is not creative, either as a child or an adult, he will not manifest any creativity during either phase.

Hence there is a world of difference between the intuitive thinking of elementary school children and the intuitive thinking of creative scholars or scientists. The elementary school child, irrespective of whether or not he is creative, thinks intuitively about many abstract ideas because this is the best he can do at his particular stage of intellectual development. He is incapable of understanding relationships between complex abstractions in abstract-verbal terms and without the benefit of concrete-empirical props. The intuitive expressions of creative scholars or scientists, on the other hand, consist of tentative and roughly formulated "hunches" or exploratory germs of ideas which are merely preparatory to more rigorous thought. Thus they are reflective of a preliminary phase in a particular problem-solving sequence—when full information and precise ideas about the problem in question are not yet available—rather than of gross developmental limitations in level of intellectual functioning. Furthermore, although the hunches themselves are only make-shift approximations that are not precisely stated, they presuppose both a high level of abstract verbal ability as well as sophisticated knowledge of a particular discipline.

A final argument sometimes advanced for the Page proposition is that since there are allegedly optimal (i.e., "critical") periods of readiness for all kinds of developmental acquisitions, many intellectual skills can be acquired more easily by younger than by older pupils. But although this argument is supported by some aspects of motor, physical and perceptual development, it has still to be validated in the field of intellectual development. Of course, one would hardly attempt to justify the postponement of any subject-matter content on the grounds that older children generally learn more efficiently than younger children; the resulting waste of precious years in which reasonably economical learning could have taken place if attempted, would in this instance more than offset the waste attributable to less efficient learning. But by the same token this wasted opportunity cannot be used as an argument in support of the proposition that the occurrence of optimal periods of readiness renders the learning of younger pupils more efficient than that of older pupils in certain subject-matter areas.

References

Bruner, Jerome S. *The Process of Education*. Cambridge, Massachusetts: Harvard University Press, 1960.

Kendler, Howard H., and Alan D. Karasik. "Concept Formation as a Function of Competition between Response Produced Cues." *Journal of Experimental Psychology 55*: 278–83; March 1958.

Liublinskaya, A. A. "The Development of Children's Speech and Thought." *Psychology in the Soviet Union*. (Edited by Brian Simon.) Stanford, California: Stanford University Press, 1957. pp. 197–204.

Spiker, Charles C., and Glenn Terrell, Jr. "Factors Associated with Transposition Behavior of Preschool Children." *Journal of Genetic Psychology 86*: 143–58; March 1955.

Weir, Morton W., and Harold W. Stevenson. "The Effect of Verbalization in Children's Learning as a Function of Chronological Age." *Child Development 30*: 143–149; March 1959.

12 Stages of Intellectual Development and Their Implications for Early Childhood Education*

David P. Ausubel

Stages of Intellectual Development

Any discussion of stages of intellectual development must, of necessity, begin with Piaget's outstanding contributions to this problem, both theoretical and empirical. Piaget's delineation of qualitatively distinct stages of intellectual development has been a powerful stimulus to research in this area, as well as a perennial source of theoretical controversy. Despite the general cogency and heuristic promise of his formulations, however, the issue of stages remains, for a number of

Reprinted from the article of the same title,* Orientamenti Pedagogici, *1966,* **6, *47–60. By permission of the author and* Orientamenti Pedagogici.

reasons, unresolved. Some of these reasons, unfortunately, derive from Piaget's unsystematic and faulty methods of conducting his research and reporting his findings.

During the past few years the findings of other investigators (8, 15, 17, 18, 30, 31, 32, 34, 37, 51) have, on the whole, been in general agreement with Piaget's more recent formulations regarding stages of intellectual development. They differ from Piaget's findings less with regard to the developmental sequences involved than in specifying different age levels for particular stages, in exhibiting greater intra-stage variability, and in manifesting less intersituational and intertask generality (8, 15, 16, 30, 31, 32, 34, 37). Nevertheless, much more rigorous developmental data than have been presented to date, especially of a longitudinal nature, are required to substantiate Piaget's conclusions.

In the first place, he is almost totally indifferent to problems of sampling, reliability, and statistical significance. He fails to present adequate normative data on age level, sex, and IQ differences, to use uniform experimental procedures for all subjects, to designate unambiguous criteria for classifying the responses of his subjects, and to determine inter-rater reliability. In place of a statistical analysis of data and the customary tests of statistical significance, he offers confirmatory illustrations selectively culled from his protocols.

Second, he tends to ignore such obvious and crucial considerations as the extent of intersituational generality and the relative degrees of intra and interstage variability in delineating stages of development.

Third, the cross-sectional observations he uses to measure developmental change, i.e., observations on different age groups of children, are particularly ill-adapted for his purposes. The transitional stages and qualitative discontinuities that he purports to find can be convincingly demonstrated only by longitudinally extended studies of the same children. Logical inference is not an adequate substitute for empirical data in naturalistic investigation.

Finally, he refines, elaborates, and rationalizes the subdivision of his stages to a degree that goes far beyond his data. Hence, the psychological plausibility and freshness of the general outlines of his theory tend to become engulfed in a welter of logical gymnastics, prolix detail, tedious repetition, and abstruse, disorganized speculation.

CRITERIA OF DEVELOPMENTAL STAGES

Even more important than Piaget's own methodological shortcomings in impeding the resolution of disagreements with respect to stages of intellectual development, are the unwarranted and gratuitous assumptions made by his critics with regard to the criteria that any designated stage of development must meet.

Many American psychologists and educators, for example, have been sharply critical of Piaget's designation of stages for the concrete-abstract dimension of cognitive development. They argue that the transition between these stages takes place gradually, rather than abruptly or discontinuously; that variability exists, both between different cultures and within a given culture, with respect to the age at which the transition takes place; that fluctuations occur over time in the level of cognitive functioning manifested by a given child; that the transition to the abstract stage occurs at different ages both for different subject-matter fields, and for component subareas within a particular field; and that environmental as well as endogenous factors have a demonstrable influence on the rate of cognitive development. For all of these reasons, therefore, they deny the validity of Piaget's designated stages.

Actually, developmental stages imply nothing more than identifiable sequential phases in an orderly progression of development, which are qualitatively discriminable from adjacent phases and generally characteristic of most members of a broadly defined age range.

As long as a given stage occupies the same sequential position in all individuals and cultures no matter when it occurs, it is perfectly compatible with the existence of intra-individual, interindividual, and intercultural differences in the age levels of incidence and in subject-matter field. It reflects the influence of both genic and environmental determinants, and can occur either gradually or abruptly. Hence, all of the aforementioned arguments disputing the legitimacy of Piaget's stages of intellectual development seem to me to be quite irrelevant.

Although each stage of development is qualitatively discontinuous in process from both the preceding and the succeeding stage, there is no reason why its manner of achievement must necessarily be abrupt or saltatory. This is particularly true when the factors that bring it into being are operative over many years and cumulative in their impact. Unlike physical, emotional, and personality development, cognitive development is not marked by the sudden, dramatic appearance of discontinuously new determinants.

It is also unreasonable to insist that a given stage must always occur at the same age in every culture. Since rate of development is at least in part a function of environmental stimulation, the age range within which a stage occurs tends to vary from one culture to another. Thus, considering the marked differences between the Swiss and American school systems, it would be remarkable indeed if comparable stages of development took place in both at the same ages.

Similarly, within a given culture, a particular stage cannot be expected to occur at the same age for all individuals. When a particular age level is designated for a given stage, it obviously refers to a mean value and implies that a normal range of variability prevails around the mean. This variability reflects differences in intellectual endowment, experiential background, education, and personality. Thus a certain amount of overlapping among age groups is inevitable. A particular stage may be generally characteristic of five and six-year-olds, but may also typically include some four and seven-year-olds, and even some three and eight-year-olds.

Piaget's age levels, like Gesell's, are nothing more than average approximations set for purposes of convenience. Hence, to attack the concept of developmental stages on the grounds that a given stage includes children of varying ages, instead of taking place at some precise age designated by Piaget, is simply to demolish a straw man.

Also, one cannot expect complete consistency and generality of stage behavior within an individual from one week or month to another, or from one subject matter or level of difficulty to another. Some overlapping and specificity are inevitable whenever development is determined by multiple variable factors.

A particular twelve-year-old may use abstract logical operations in his science course in October, but he will revert for no apparent reason to a concrete level of cognitive functioning in November, or even several years later when he is confronted with an extremely difficult and unfamiliar problem in the same field. Furthermore, he may characteristically continue to function at a concrete level for another year or two in social studies and literature. Since transitions to new stages do not occur instantaneously, but over a period of time, fluctuations between stages are common until the newly emerging stage is consolidated.

In addition, because of intrinsic differences in level of subject-matter difficulty, and because of intra and interindividual differences in ability profiles and experiential background, it is hardly surprising that transitions from one stage to another do not occur simultaneously in all subject-matter areas and subareas.

Abstract thinking, for example, generally emerges earlier in science than in social studies because children have more experience manipulating ideas about mass, time, and space than about government, social institutions, and historical events. However, in some children, depending on their special abilities and experience, the reverse may be true. In any developmental process where experiential factors are crucial, age *per se* is generally less important than degree of relevant experience.

Finally, stages of development are always referable to a given range of difficulty and familiarity of the problem area. Beyond this range, individuals commonly revert (regress) to a former stage of development.

Nor is the concept of developmental stages invalidated by the demonstration that they are susceptible to environmental influence. It is erroneous to believe that stages of intellectual development are exclusively the products of "internal ripening," and hence that they reflect primarily the influence of endogenous factors.

Gesell's embryological model of development has little applicability to human development beyond the first year of life, at which time environmental factors become increasingly more important determinants of variability in developmental outcomes. In fact, as our own educational system improves, we can confidently look forward to an earlier mean emergence of the various stages of cognitive development.

Quantitative and Qualitative Changes in Intellectual Development

Still another reason for confusion and conflict about the problem of stages in intellectual development is the tendency to adopt an all-or-none position regarding such stages. Actually, the evidence suggests that some aspects or dimensions of intellectual development are characterized by quantitative or continuous change, whereas others are characterized by qualitative or discontinuous change. Hence, once the issue is no longer approached from the standpoint of an all-or-none proposition, much truth can be found on both sides.

Changes in learning ability, thought processes, and the approach to problem-solving appear as differences in degree, rather than in kind. No qualitative transitions in learning ability occur at any age; and the evidence indicates that the same kinds of logical operations and problem-solving techniques are employed at all age levels, differing principally in degree of complexity (10, 28, 29, 50).

As Munn (35) points out, the age-level differences are partly attributable to disparity in previous experience, motivation, and neuromuscular coordination. Perhaps an even more important source of these differences, however, is the child's growing ability to generalize and to use abstract symbols. Both trial-and-error and insightful problem-solving are found in preschool children, elementary school children, adolescents, and adults. The choice among these approaches depends on the inherent difficulty of the problem, the individual's prior background of experience, and the problem's amenability to logical analysis. It is true that insightful approaches tend to increase with age, but only because increasing ability to generalize and to use abstract symbols permits a more hypothesis-oriented approach.

Two dimensions of intellectual development that are characterized by gradually occurring qualitative change, on the other hand, are the transition from subjective to objective thought and the transition from concrete to abstract cognitive operations.

Acquisition of the ability to separate objective reality from subjective needs and preferences results in the gradual disappearance of autistic, animistic, anthropomorphic, magical, absolutistic, and nominalistic thinking (38, 39, 40).

Children seem to pass through gross qualitative stages of causal thinking (12, 13, 21, 45), rarely appreciating antecedent-consequent relationships, in the adult sense of the term, prior to the ages of eight to ten (11, 27).

Even Piaget's severest critics concede that there is gradual improvement with increasing age in the quality of children's causal explanations (12, 36). On the other hand, much overlapping prevails between age groups. All kinds of causal explanations are found at all age levels (14, 21, 36); some adolescents and adults even give responses characteristic of young children (13, 22, 36).

Furthermore, such changes tend to occur gradually, and the quality of causal thinking shows much specificity and dependence on particular relevant experience (12, 14, 36). None of these latter facts, however, is incompatible with the existence of stages in children's thinking, as defined above.

THE CONCRETE-ABSTRACT DIMENSION OF COGNITIVE DEVELOPMENT

The following description of this aspect of cognitive development is a modified version and perhaps somewhat idiosyncratic interpretation of the account given by Piaget and Inhelder (23, 41, 42, 43).

The concrete-abstract dimension of intellectual development may be divided into three qualitatively distinct developmental stages: the preoperational stage, the stage of concrete operations, and the stage of abstract operations. These occur respectively during the preschool, elementary-school, and adolescent-adult periods of development.

During the preoperational stage, although the child is capable of using language to represent objects and experiences, he is unable to manipulate or relate these verbal representations to each other meaningfully for the purpose of solving problems or comprehending new ideas. Lacking the ability to relate verbal symbols internally, he relies instead on the direct manipulation of objects, i.e., on overt trial and error. Thus what he manipulates are relations between objects *per se,* rather than relations between their symbolic representations. In the sense that the learning behavior of the preoperational child is thus largely regulated by overt action rather than verbal mediation, it is very similar to that manifested by infrahuman mammals (24, 25, 26, 33).

Because logical operations during this period are not internalized, and therefore lack the quality of reversibility that characterizes an internalized operation, the child in this developmental stage cannot grasp the concept of conservation of mass, i.e., the ideas that the mass of an object remains constant, even though the shape of the object changes.

This same inability to relate ideas internally to each other obviously precludes the *correlative* type of meaningful reception learning—the kind of learning that requires an individual to relate presented new ideas to existing concepts in his cognitive structure, in an elaborative, correlative, or qualifying sense—unless concurrent overt manipulation is possible.

The *derivative* type of meaningful reception learning, however, is entirely compatible with cognitive capacity during the preoperational stage, even in the absence of such manipulation. In this kind of learning, the new idea is simply a symbolic representation of an existing concrete image, or an illustration of an established concept or proposition in the cognitive structure.

The stage of concrete operations is inaugurated when behavior and learning finally come under predominantly verbal or symbolic control. During this stage, the child is able to manipulate relations between ideas internally—that is, without overt manipulation of the objects represented in the ideas.

In solving problems and in meaningful reception learning, he tends to work exclusively with ideational representations of ideas, and with the relations between them. Thus he is thoroughly capable both of solving problems, either by internal (covert) trial-and-error or by testing hypotheses, and of meaningfully understanding new ideas presented to him which imply correlative relationships with existing concepts in his cognitive structure.

It is also important to realize that logical operations, at this stage of intellectual development, are not really concrete, in the sense that concrete images of objects are relationally manipulated in problem-solving or in meaningful reception learning. The elementary-school child actually manipulates relations between the verbal representations of objects. The concreteness of the operations inheres in the fact that they are dependent upon current or recent concrete-empirical experience, and are to that extent constrained in their logical implications by the particularity of this experience.

The logical operations performed at this point of development are relational extensions of, and make explicit reference to, particular and tangible empirical data. Unlike the situation in the abstract stage, they cannot be considered logical transformations of hypothetical relationships between general abstract variables. Nevertheless, they constitute a significant advance over the preceding preoperational stage, in which correlative relations between ideas could not be handled at all in reception or discovery learning, even with the aid of concrete-empirical props, but required the direct manipulation of objects.

The elementary-school child is, of course, no more dependent on immediate concrete-empirical experience than is the preoperational child, in his understanding and manipulating simple abstractions, or ideas about objects and phenomena. It is true that the emergence of such ideas must always take place against an adequate background of direct, nonverbal experience with the use of the empirical data from which they are abstracted. But once their meaning has become firmly established, as the result of this background of past experience, the child can meaningfully comprehend and use them, without the necessity of reference to concrete-empirical data.

The meaningful understanding or manipulation of relationships between abstractions, or of *ideas about ideas*, on the other hand, is quite another matter. In this kind of operation, the elementary-school pupil is still dependent upon current or recent concrete-empirical experience. When such experience is not available, he finds abstract relational propositions unrelatable to his cognitive structure, and hence devoid of meaning.

This dependence upon concrete-empirical props obviously limits his ability meaningfully to grasp and manipulate relationships between abstractions, since he can only acquire those understandings and perform those logical operations which do not go beyond the concrete and particularized representation of reality implicit in his use of props. Thus, where complex relational propositions are involved, he is largely restricted to a subverbal, concrete, or intuitive level of cognitive functioning, a level that falls far short of the clarity, precision, explicitness, and generality associated with the more advance abstract stage of intellectual development.

Educational Implications of the Intuitive-Concrete Level

Intuitive cognitive functioning refers to an implicit, relatively unprecise and informal type of understanding or thought process, in which the individual is only vaguely aware of the parameters of a problem or its solution and of the logical operations involved. In contrast to formal abstract thought, it is nonanalytic and unsystematic in its approach, relies on immediate apprehension, and defies explicit formulation.

The principal difficulty with this concept is the failure on the part of those who use it to differentiate between four very different kinds of intuitive processes, i.e., developmental, unsophisticated, sophisticated, and creative, and their tendency instead to treat all four types as if they were identical. This obviously leads to incalculable semantic and pedagogic confusion.

Types of Intuitive Processes

The *developmental* type of intuitive process occurs in the child who is in the preoperational stage, or in the stage of concrete operations. The lack of explicitness and precision, and the unsystematic, nonanalytic approach in this case reflect the semi-abstract and relatively nonverbal character of the preschool or elementary-school child's cognitive functioning, the paucity of his higher-order concepts and transactional terms, as well as the particularity of his logical operations and their dependence on overt manipulation or concrete-empirical props. In addition, these cognitive attributes reflect a general lack of sophistication in all subject-matter fields. The *unsophisticated* type of intuitive process, on the other hand, occurs in the cognitively mature individual who happens to be a complete novice in a *particular* subject-matter field. It is phenomenologically similar to the developmental type, but it is a limited condition, lasting only until the individual has acquired some minimal sophistication in the area in question.

Intuitive processes also occur in *cognitively mature* individuals when they are confronted with a new and difficult problem in a subject-matter field in which they are already highly sophisticated. In fact, it is this very sophistication, and their thorough familiarity with the field as a whole, which enables them to explore the problem informally without systematic analysis of the data, to develop hunches, and to use short-cuts. Although the probings are unsystematic, and the formulations unprecise and lacking in explicitness, the logical operations, by contrast with those of the two previously described types of intuition, are conducted on an abstract and completely verbal level, and are not limited by the particularity of specific instances.

Sophisticated, intuitive processes become *creative* when they reflect notable degrees of perceptiveness, sensitivity, originality and insight, in addition to thorough familiarity with the subject-matter field.

Bruner (9) tends to treat the developmental and sophisticated kinds of intuitive process as if they were synonymous. Anderson (1) and Page (9, pp. 39–40) go even further. They contend that the concrete-intuitive approach of young children is more creative than the abstract-verbal approach of older individuals, and is comparable to the creative type of intuitive thinking found among scholars and scientists.

Actually, however, there is no necessary or intrinsic relationship between intuitive thinking and creativity, among either children or adults. The only relationship is a chronological one: If a given individual happens to be creative, whether he is a child or an adult, he will obviously first manifest his creativity during the intuitive phase, because that phase invariably precedes the abstract-verbal phase; contrariwise, if he is not creative, either as a child or an adult, he will not manifest any creativity during either phase.

Hence, there is a world of difference between the intuitive thinking of preschool or elementary-school children and the intuitive thinking of sophisticated scholars or scientists.

The preschool or elementary-school child, irrespective of whether or not he is creative, thinks intuitively about many abstract ideas, because that is the best he can do at his particular stage of intellectual development. He is incapable of understanding relationships between complex abstractions in abstract-verbal terms, and without the benefit of overt manipulation or concrete-empirical props.

The intuitive expressions of creative, or even of just ordinarily competent scholars or scientists, on the other hand, consist of tentative and roughly formulated hunches, or exploratory germs of ideas, which are merely preparatory to more rigorous thought. Thus, they represent a preliminary phase in a particular problem-solving sequence—a phase when full information and precise ideas about the problem in question are not yet available—rather than gross developmental limitations in the level of intellectual functioning. Furthermore, although these hunches are themselves only makeshift approximations and therefore not precisely stated, they presuppose a high level of abstract verbal ability, as well as sophisticated knowledge in a particular discipline.

Can Any Subject Be Taught Intuitively at Any Age Level?

It is readily conceivable that some topics, such as "set theory" verbal concepts, are more manipulable and transferable than their subverbal equivalents.

The availability of distinctive verbal responses has also been shown to facilitate rather than inhibit concept formation and conceptual transfer. We have already observed that there is no necessary or intrinsic relationship between intuitive thinking and creativity, and that the developmental type of intuitive process bears little relationship to the intuitive thinking of sophisticated or creative scholars.

A final argument sometimes advanced for the child superiority proposition is that since there are allegedly optimal, i.e., "critical," periods of readiness for all kind of developmental acquisitions, many intellectual skills can be acquired more easily by younger than by older pupils.

Although this argument is supported by some aspects of motor, physical, and perceptual development, it has yet to be validated in the field of intellectual development. Of course, one would hardly attempt to justify the postponement of any subject-matter content on the grounds that older children generally learn more efficiently than do younger children. The resulting waste of precious years in which reasonable economical learning could have taken place if it had been attempted, would in this instance more than offset the waste supposedly attributable to less efficient learning.

Nevertheless, by the same token, this wasted opportunity cannot be used as an argument in support of the proposition that the occurrence of optimal periods of readiness renders the learning of younger pupils more efficient than that of older pupils in certain subject-matter areas.

Acceleration of the Concrete Stage

Is it possible to accelerate children's progress through the preoperational stage, or the stage of concrete logical operations, by taking account of their characteristic cognitive limitations, and by providing suitable contrived experience, geared to their cognitive capacity and mode of functioning?

Can we, for example, train them, as Inhelder suggests (9), to focus on more than one aspect of a problem at a time, or to acquire a genuine appreciation of the concept of conservation of mass? If stages of development have any true meaning, the answer to this question can only be that, although some acceleration is possible, it is necessarily limited in extent.

Suitable training can undoubtedly accelerate to some extent the rate at which the various stages of intellectual development succeed each other. Inevitably, however, maturational considerations impose a limit on such acceleration. For example, training of children in the preoperational stage to appreciate the notion of conservation of mass tends to produce an unstable understanding of this principle, which is hardly equivalent to that acquired by older children (65).

Similarly, young children who receive laboratory training in learning the principle of a teeter-totter, i.e., that the longer side from the fulcrum falls when both ends are equally weighted, fail to acquire any resistance to learning a spurious causal relationship about the operation of a teeter-totter, i.e., that the color of the blocks placed at either end is the determining factor (6). Older children, on the other hand, who are both cognitively more mature, and have more incidental experience with teeter-totters, resist learning the spurious causal relationship (6).

In general, therefore, transitions from one stage of development to another presuppose the attainment of a critical threshold level of capacity that is reflective of extended and cumulative experience. This does not mean, obviously, that development occurs spontaneously, as the result of internal ripening. In addition to the operation of genic patterning factors, the necessary environmental stimulation must be forthcoming. Yet as children advance in age and in their cognitive capacity, teaching methods can place increasingly less reliance on concrete-empirical props. (Galperin (20) describes a method of teaching arithmetic to slow-learning pupils, in which concrete-empirical props are eliminated very gradually and replaced by abstract-verbal representations.)

Also, since rate of development is partly a function of the quantity and appropriateness of relevant experience, it is quite conceivable that suitable long-term training procedures may produce more *stable* developmental acceleration than is shown in the previous reported studies of short-term training.

Dependence on Nonverbal and Self-Discovery Teaching Methods

Lastly, although the preschool child is basically dependent on overt manipulation of objects and situations for the understanding of correlative relational propositions, it is not necessary that *all* teaching during this period be conducted on a nonverbal, problem-solving, or self-discovery basis in order to be meaningful.

Derivative propositions can be directly apprehended when they are presented verbally, and correlative propositions can be verbally presented and understood, so long as an opportunity exists for preliminary or concurrent overt manipulation. Self-discovery of the proposition to be learned may conceivablly enhance current learning, but it is certainly not indispensable for meaningful understanding. In fact, for most instances of preschool learning, the advantages of self-discovery are not sufficiently great to outweigh the inordinate time-cost involved. It still remains to be established, therefore, that primary reliance on such self-discovery methods is pedagogically defensible in preschool teaching.

References

1 Anderson, H. H.: Preface. In *Creativity and its Cultivation.* (H. H. Anderson, ed.) New York, Harper, 1959.

2 Ausubel, D. P.: *Theory and Problems of Child Development.* New York, Grune & Stratton, 1958.

3 ____ : Can children learn anything that adults can—and more efficiently? *Elem. Sch. J., 62*:270–72, 1962.

4 ____ : Implications of preadolescent and early adolescent cognitive development for secondary school teaching. *High Sch. J., 45*:268–75, 1962.

5 ____ : Some psychological considerations in the objectives and design of an elementary-school science program. *Science Educ.*, in press.

6 Ausubel, D. P., and H. M. Schiff: The effect of incidental and experimentally induced experience in the learning of relevant and irrelevant causal relationships by children. *J. Genet. Psychol., 84*:109–23, 1954.

7 Baer, C. J.: The school progress and adjustment of underage and overage students. *J. Educ. Psychol., 49*:17–19, 1958.

8 Braine, M. D. S.: The ontogeny of certain logical operations: Piaget's formulations examined by nonverbal methods. *Psychol. Monogr., 73*, No. 4 (Whole No. 475), 1959.

9 Bruner, J. S.: *The Process of Education.* Cambridge, Harvard University Press, 1960.

10 Burt, C.: The development of reasoning in children. *J. Exp. Pedag. 5*:68-77, 1919.

11 Cohen, J., and C. E. M. Hansel: The idea of independence. *Brit. J. Psychol., 46*:178–90, 1955.

12 Dennis, W.: Piaget's questions applied to a child of known environment. *J. Genet. Psychol., 60*:307–20, 1942.

13 ____ : Animism and related tendencies in Hopi children. *J. Abnorm. Soc. Psychol., 38*:21–36, 1943.

14 Deutsche, J. M.: *The Development of Children's Concepts of Causal Relationships.* Minneapolis, University of Minnesota Press, 1937.

15 Dodwell, P. C.: Children's understanding of number and related concepts. *Can. J. Psychol., 14*:191–205, 1960.

16 ____ : Children's understanding of number concepts: Characteristics of an individual and of a group test. *Can. J. Psychol., 15*:29–36, 1961.

17 Elkind, D.: The development of quantitative thinking: A systematic replication of Piaget's studies. *J. Genet. Psychol., 98*:37–48, 1961.
18 Ervin, Susan M.: Experimental procedures of children. *Child Develp., 31*:703–19, 1960.
19 Fast, I.: Kindergarten teaching and Grade I reading. *J. Educ. Psychol., 48*:52–57, 1957.
20 Galperin, P. Ya.: An experimental study in the formation of mental actions. In *Psychology in the Soviet Union*. (B. Simon, ed.) pp. 213–25, Stanford, Stanford University Press, 1957.
21 Grigsby, O. J.: An experimental study of the development of concepts of relationship in preschool children as evidenced by their expressive ability. *J. Exp. Educ., 1*:144–62, 1932.
22 Hazlitt, V.: Children's thinking. *Brit. J. Psychol., 20*:354–61, 1930.
23 Inhelder, Barbel, and Jean Piaget: *The Growth of Logical Thinking from Childhood to Adolescence*. New York, Basic Books, 1958.
24 Kendler, H. H.: Vertical and horizontal processes in problem solving. *Psychol. Rev., 69*:1–62, 1962.
25 Kendler, T. S., and H. H. Kendler: Reversal and nonreversal shifts in kindergarten children. *J. Exp. Psychol., 58*:56–60, 1959.
26 Kendler, T. S., H. H. Kendler, and D. Wells: Reversal and nonreversal shifts in nursery school children. *J. Comp. Physiol. Psychol., 52*:387–89, 1959.
27 Lacey, J. I., and K. M. Dallenbach: Acquisition by children of the cause-effect relationship. *Amer. J. Psychol., 53*:575–78, 1940.
28 Long, L., and L. Welch: The development of the ability to discriminate and match numbers. *J. Genet. Psychol., 59*:377–87, 1941.
29 ——: Influence of level of abstractness on reasoning ability. *J. Psychol., 13*:41–59, 1942.
30 Lovell, K.: A follow-up study of some aspects of the work of Piaget and Inhelder on the child's conception of space. *Brit. J. Educ. Psychol., 29*:104–17, 1959.
31 Lovell, K., and E. Ogilvie: A study of the conservation of substance in the junior school child. *Brit. J. Psychol., 30*:109–18, 1960.
32 Lunzer, E. A.: Some points of Piagetian theory in the light of experimental criticism. *Child Psychol. Psychiat., 1*:192–202, 1960.
33 Luria, A. R.: The role of language in the formation of temporary connections. In *Psychology in the Soviet Union*. (B. Simon, ed.) pp. 115–29, Stanford, Stanford University Press, 1957.
34 Mannix, J. B.: The number concepts of a group of E. S. N. children. *Brit. J. Educ. Psychol., 30*:180–81, 1960.
35 Munn, N. L.: Learning in Children. In *Manual of Child Psychology*. (L. Carmichael, ed.), ed. 2. pp. 374–458, New York, Wiley, 1954.

36 Oakes, M. E.: *Children's Explanations of Natural Phenomena*. New York, Bureau of Publications, Teachers College, Columbia University, 1946.

37 Peel, E. A.: Experimental examination of some of Piaget's schemata concerning children's perception and thinking and a discussion of their educational significance. *Brit. J. Educ. Psychol., 29*:89–103, 1959.

38 Piaget, J. *Judgment and Reasoning in the Child*. New York, Harcourt, 1928.

39 ____: *The Child's Conception of the World*. London, Routledge, 1929.

40 ____: *The Child's Conception of Physical Causality*. New York, Harcourt, 1932.

41 ____: *The Psychology of Intelligence*. New York, Harcourt, 1950.

42 ____: *Logic and Psychology*. Manchester, University of Manchester Press, 1953.

43 ____,: *The Construction of Reality in the Child*. New York, Basic Books, 1954.

44 Piaget, J., and Barbel Inhelder: *La Genese des Structures Logiques Elementaires: Classifications et Seriations*. Neuchatel, Editions Delachaux and Niestle, 1959.

45 Russell, R. W.: Studies in Animism. II. The development of animism. *J. Genet. Psychol., 56*:353–66, 1940.

46 Sax, G., and J. P. Ottina: The arithmetic reasoning of pupils differing in school experience. *Calif. J. Educ. Res., 9*:15–19, 1958.

47 Smedslund, J.: The acquisition of conservation of substance and weight in children. *J. Scan. Psychol., 2*:11–20; 71–87; 153–60; 203–10, 1961.

48 Spiker, C. C., and G. Terrell: Factors associated with transposition behavior of preschool children. *J. Genet. Psychol., 86*:143–58, 1955.

49 Weir, M. W., and H. W. Stevenson: The effect of verbalization in children's learning as a function of chronological age. *Child Develp., 30*:143–49, 1959.

50 Welch, L., and L. Long: Comparison of the reasoning ability of two age groups. *J. Genet. Psychol., 62*:63–76, 1943.

51 Wohlwill, J. F.: A study of the development of the number concept by scalogram analysis. *J. Genet. Psychol., 97*:345–77, 1961.

13 Cognitive Development in Adolescence*

David P. Ausubel
Pearl Ausubel

During the six-year interval since the appearance of the last issue on adolescence, theoretical and research activity with respect to cognitive development has increased tremendously. Unfortunately for our purposes, however, most of this activity has been directed toward the preschool and elementary-school periods. The few research studies and theoretical papers that did concern themselves with cognitive development during adolescence were stimulated by the pioneering work of Inhelder and Piaget (1958). Concurrently, during this same interval, interest in adolescent intelligence declined markedly.

Reprinted with the permission of the author and publisher from the article of the same title,* Review of Educational Research, *1966,* **36, 403–413.

The Transition from Concrete to Formal Operations

Inhelder and Piaget presented considerable evidence indicating that "formal" (abstract) operations appear slightly before the onset of adolescence. On the whole, their findings were corroborated by other investigators (Goldman, 1965; Jackson, 1965; Lovell, 1961; Yudin and Kates, 1963). Lovell's subjects attained this stage of development somewhat later than Inhelder and Piaget's, and Case and Collison's (1962) somewhat earlier. Both Goldman and Jackson reported greater age variability, and Jackson less intertask generality, than did Inhelder and Piaget in the development of formal thinking. None of these findings, however, detracted from the essential validity of Piaget's conclusion that for the first time the child entering this stage of cognitive development thinks in terms of all-inclusive hypothetical possibilities (instead of "the here and now") or in terms of propositional logic ("second-degree operations" or "operations on operations"). "Instead of just coordinating facts about the actual world, hypothetico-deductive reasoning draws out the implications of possible statements and thus gives rise to a unique synthesis of the possible and the necessary" (Piaget, 1957).

Beginning with the adolescent period children become increasingly less dependent upon the availability of concrete-empirical experience in meaningfully relating complex abstract propositions to cognitive structure. Eventually, after sufficient gradual change in this direction, a qualitatively new capacity emerges: the intellectually mature individual becomes capable of understanding and manipulating relationships between abstractions *directly*, that is, without any reference whatsoever to concrete, empirical reality. Instead of reasoning directly from a particular set of data, he uses indirect, second-order logical operations for structuring the data; and instead of merely grouping data into classes or arranging them serially in terms of a given variable, he formulates and tests hypotheses based on all possible combinations of variables. Since his logical operations are performed on verbal propositions, he can go beyond the operations that follow immediately from empirical reality (equivalence, distinctiveness, reversibility, and seriation), and deal with all possible or hypothetical relations between ideas. He can now transcend the preciously achieved level of intuitive thought and understanding, and formulate general laws relating general categories of variables that are divorced from the concrete-empirical data at hand. His concepts and generalizations, therefore, tend more to be second-order constructs derived from relationships between previously established verbal abstractions already one step removed from the data itself.

Careful analysis of the experiments performed by Inhelder and Piaget and by the other investigators cited above does not substantiate their view, as well as Lunzer's (1965), that the *distinctive* feature of formal or abstract (as opposed to concrete) operations is that the older child is able to deal operationally and verbally with ideas about ideas, to perform "second-order operations," or to go "beyond the framework of transformations bearing directly on empirical reality." The younger ("concrete operational") child can also do these things, as shown by the studies of Case and Collinson (1962) and Hill (1961). The latter demonstrated, for example, that most children aged six to eight can easily draw correct inferences from hypothetical premises involving second-order operations. It is rather the preadolescent's and adolescent's ability verbally to manipulate relationships between ideas ("second-order relations) *in the absence of recently prior or concurrently available concrete-empirical props* that is the distinctive attribute of formal operations. (Hill's subjects, after all, were given logical problems that were invariably stated in terms of particular instances). This new capability emerging at age eleven and beyond invests propositional thought with a genuinely abstract and nonintuitive quality. Ideas about ideas now achieve a truly general status that is freed from any dependence whatsoever on particular instances and concrete experience. It is for this reason that thinking becomes hypothetico-deductive in nature, i.e., refers to all possible relationships between variables rather than to relationships delineated by concrete manifestations of particular instances.

General and Specific Aspects of the Transition

It is apparent from the previous discussion that the transition from concrete to abstract cognitive functioning takes place specifically in each separate subject-matter area, and invariably presupposes a certain necessary amount of sophistication in each of the areas involved. This state of affairs follows directly from intra-individual differences in experience and component intellectual abilities. Inhelder and Piaget (1958) explicitly recognized that complete intersituational generality cannot be expected at any stage of development, referring to this phenomenon as "horizontal decalage." Many other investigators (Dodwell, 1960, 1961, 1962, 1963; Elkind, 1961; Jackson, 1965; Lovell and Slater, 1960) have also confirmed this prediction.

In the more general sense of the term, however, it is possible to designate the individual's *overall* developmental status as "concrete" or "abstract" on the basis of an estimate of his characteristic or predominant mode of cognitive functioning. This distinction is important for two reasons: First, the individual necessarily continues to undergo the same transition from concrete to abstract cognitive functioning in each *new* subject-matter area he encounters—even *after* he reaches the abstract stage of development on an overall basis. Second, once he attains this latter general stage, however, the transition to abstract cognitive functioning in unfamiliar new subject-matter areas takes place much more readily.

Thus, even though an individual characteristically functions at the abstract level of cognitive development, when he is first introduced to a wholly unfamiliar subject-matter field, he tends initially to function at a concrete-intuitive level. But since he is able to draw on various transferable elements of his more *general* ability to function abstractly, he passes through the concrete stage of functioning in this particular subject-matter area much more rapidly than would be the case were he still generally in the concrete stage of cognitive development. These facilitating transferable elements presumably include transactional terms, higher-order concepts, and experience in *directly* understanding and manipulating relationships between abstractions (i.e., without the benefit of props) which, although acquired in specific subject-matter contexts, are generally applicable to other learning situations.

Determinants of the Transition

It appears that the combined influence of three concomitant and mutually supportive developmental trends accounts for the transition from concrete to abstract cognitive functioning. In the first place, the developing individual gradually acquires a working vocabulary of transactional or mediating terms that makes possible the more efficient juxtaposition and combination of different relatable abstractions into potentially meaningful propositions. Second, he can relate these latter propositions more readily to cognitive structure, and hence render them more meaningful, in view of his growing fund of stable, higher-order concepts and principles encompassed by and made available within that structure. A sufficient body of abstract ideas that are clear and stable is obviously necessary before he can hope efficiently to manipulate relationships between them so as to develop meaningful general propositions. The possession of a working body of inclusive concepts also makes possible the formulation of more general statements of relationship that are less tied to specific instances; greater integration of related ideas and different aspects of the same problem; the elaboration of more precise distinctions and finer differentiations; and less dependence on complete concrete-empirical data in reaching warranted inferences. Finally, it seems reasonable to suppose that after many years of practice in meaningfully understanding and manipulating relationships *with* the aid of concrete-empirical props, he gradually develops greater facility in performing these operations, so that eventually (after acquiring the necessary transactional and higher-order concepts) he can perform the same operations just as effectively *without* relying on props. The same sequence of events is seen in acquiring many other neuromuscular and cognitive skills, e.g., walking without "holding on," bicycling "without hands," speaking a foreign language without internal translation from one's mother tongue, transmitting Morse code in sentences rather than in word or letter units.

Inhelder and Piaget (1958) have advanced a motivational explanation to account for the transition from concrete to abstract cognitive functioning, namely, cultural pressure and adolescent desire to assume adult roles, which, in turn, presuppose adult modes of thought. But even though motivation may conceivably energize and facilitate cognitive change, it cannot possibly explain either its occurrence or direction. No amount of motivation would suffice to effect the change in question in the absence of both the necessary genic potentialities and the supportive experience. Whatever facilitive influence motivational factors have is undoubtedly mediated through greater effort to seek out and participate in the kind of cognitive experiences that promote a shift from concrete to abstract functioning. It is also unconvincing to attribute the shift to "maturation of cerebral structures," by invoking the patently circular Gestalt argument that "lattice and group structures are probably isomorphic with neurological structures" (Inhelder and Piaget, 1958). No independent evidence of significant neuroanatomical or neurophysiological change at adolescence has yet been adduced.

Braham (1965) suggests that the negative sanctioning of intellectual achievement in adolescent peer groups, particularly among lower-class and culturally deprived youth, has a deterrent effect on cognitive development during adolescence. Such negative sanctioning of intellectual achievement has been reported for Maori adolescents (Ausubel, 1965).

Educational Implications of the Transition from Concrete to Abstract Cognitive Functioning

From the standpoint of the secondary-school teacher, the most significant development in cognitive functioning that occurs during the preadolescent and early adolescent years is the gradual transition from a predominantly concrete to a predominantly abstract mode of understanding and manipulating complex relational propositions. This developmental shift, in turn, has far-reaching implications for teaching methods and curricular practices in the secondary school.

Once the developing individual reaches the abstract stage of cognitive functioning, he becomes in large measure an abstract verbal learner. He now acquires most new concepts and learns most new propositions by *directly* apprehending verbally or symbolically stated relationships between previously learned abstractions. To do so meaningfully, he need no longer refer to firsthand, nonrepresentational experience, nor actually perform any of the abstracting or generalizing operations on the underlying empirical data. With his developmental dependence on concrete-empirical props removed, the only condition necessary for the meaningful understanding and manipulation of higher-order concepts and relational propositions is that their substantive import be nonarbitrarily relatable to his particular cognitive structure, and that he adopt a set to learn them in this fashion. Hence, on developmental grounds, he is ready at the secondary-school level for a new type of verbal expository teaching that uses concrete-empirical experience primarily for *illustrative* purposes, i.e., to clarify or dramatize truly abstract meanings rather than to generate intuitive meanings.

Many features of the activity program were based on the quite defensible premise that the elementary-school child perceives the world in relatively specific and concrete terms, and requires considerable firsthand experience with diverse concrete instances of a given set of relationships before he can abstract genuinely meaningful concepts and relate them meaningfully to cognitive structure. Thus, an attempt was made to teach factual information and intellectual skills in the "real-life" functional contexts in which they are customarily encountered, rather than through the medium of verbal exposition supplemented by artificially contrived drills and exercises. This approach has real merit provided that a fetish is not made of naturalism and incidental learning; that adequate use is made of appropriate expository teaching; that drills and exercises are provided in instances where opportunities for acquiring skills do not occur frequently and repetitively enough in more natural settings; and that deliberate or guided effort in most learning situations is not regarded as incompatible with incidental learning in others. Even more important, however, is the realization that in older children, once a sufficient number of basic concepts is consolidated, new concepts are primarily acquired from verbal rather than from concrete experience. Hence, in secondary school it may be desirable to reverse both the sequence and the relative balance between abstract concepts and supportive data. There is a good reason for believing, therefore, that much of the time presently spent in cookbook laboratory exercises in the sciences could be much more advantageously employed in formulating precise definitions, making explicit verbal distinctions between concepts, generalizing from hypothetical situations, etc.

It would be very misleading, however, to assert that secondary-school and even older students can *never* profit either from the use of concrete-empirical props to generate intuitive meanings, or from the use of inductive discovery and deductive problem-solving techniques to enhance such meanings. As previously suggested, generally mature students tend to function at a relatively concrete level when confronted with a particularly *new* subject-matter area in which they are as yet totally unsophisticated. But since abstract cognitive functioning in this new area is achieved with the attainment of a minimal degree of subject-matter sophistication, these special auxiliary techniques should be employed only for the aforementioned purposes during the early stages of instruction. Continued use for other purposes, however, (i.e., to improve problem-solving skills, to foster appreciation of scientific method, or to test verbal understanding) is quite another matter. It is one thing occasionally to use examples and analogies to clarify meanings of particularly difficult or unfamiliar concepts. It is quite another to use them routinely as an *invariably* necessary prop for the acquisition of all relational meanings.

The transition from concrete to abstract cognitive functioning also enables the secondary-school student to master a much greater volume of subject-matter knowledge. To begin with, the logistics of the learning situation become more favorable. His ability to understand abstract relational propositions directly (i.e., to dispense with the time-consuming operations of using both concrete-empirical props and discovery and problem-solving experience to generate and enhance intuitive insights) permits one to present much more subject matter in the same period of time. In addition, his qualitatively higher level of abstract understanding makes possible a more efficient means of organizing and integrating the materials that are presented. Because his higher-order concepts and relational propositions are no longer intuitive, but are meaningfully formulated in truly abstract and general terms, they become clearer, more stable, more precise, and sufficiently inclusive to subsume a wider array of differentiated facts and subconcepts.

In view of these latter developments and of the greater differentiation of his abilities and interests, the secondary-school student is prepared to cope with a greater depth as well as with a greater volume of subject matter. He is ready for more intensive and differentiated coverage of smaller areas of knowledge as opposed to more global and superficial coverage of larger areas. "Depth" in this context, however, implies greater substantive density of knowledge rather than greater degree of autonomy in discovering the principles and obtaining the information to be learned. If the secondary-school student is required to discover most principles autonomously, to obtain most subject-matter content from primary sources, and to design his own experiments, he only has time to acquire methodological sophistication. In terms of *substantive* depth, he has simply moved from previously superficial coverage of broad areas to comparably superficial coverage of more circumscribed areas. The aim of secondary-school and undergraduate education is not to produce substantively ignorant junior scholars and scientists, but to produce students who are knowledgeable both in breadth and depth of subject matter.

Intelligence in Adolescence

By intelligence we simply mean a measurement construct designating level of ability in performing a graded series of tasks implicating the component aspects of cognitive functioning at any given stage of intellectual development. For the most part, it is representative at adolescence and beyond of a general capacity for processing information and for utilizing abstract symbols in the solution of abstract problems. Intelligence tests, therefore, are valid to the extent that they measure this capacity. An intellectual ability, in other words, is really nothing more nor less than a functional manifestation of a distinct and identifiable cognitive process as expressed in a range of individual performance or capacity differences.

Ljung (1965) has recently described an "adolescent growth spurt" in mental development that is more marked in girls than in boys. This spurt undoubtedly reflects the adolescent's greater ability to process information and solve abstract problems more efficiently that results from the shift to abstract cognitive functioning. It is not typically reflected in conventional intelligence tests but was in Ljung's because the measures he used were more comparable to academic achievement tests. Both Meyer (1960) and Bradway and Thompson (1962) confirmed the fact that the predictive power of total intelligence test scales, as well as of primary ability scales, increases with age.

Cattell (1963) has reported the isolation of "fluid" and crystallized components of intelligence. As might be anticipated, the "crystallized" factor consists largely of "process" functions, presumably not much influenced by learning or educational experience, and reaches maturity at a relatively early age. The "fluid" factor, in contrast, consists more of "product" functions which are appreciably influenced by education and experience, and therefore reach maturity later in life. So-called culturally-deprived adolescents are naturally more deficient in the fluid than in the crystallized components of intelligence.

Evidence (Green and Berkowitz, 1964; Guilford, 1966; Heinonen, 1963; Ljung, 1965; Meyer, 1960) continues to accumulate that intellectual ability becomes more highly differentiated with increasing age. This trend exists despite the fact that the older individual, who has presumably undergone the shift from concrete to abstract logical operations in more subject-matter areas, is probably more homogeneous in his mode of cognitive functioning. Increased integration also occurs *within* the various component sub-abilities. Thus the more established differential aptitude batteries probably have greater predictive value for the *particular* kinds of subject-matter achievement for which they are relevant than do composite scores on tests of general intelligence or of general scholastic aptitude. However, the latter tests, as McNemar (1964) points out, are more useful for predicting complex criteria of academic achievement, involving the interaction among several abilities.

Bradway and Thompson (1962) confirmed the well-established fact that males show more IQ gain from adolescence to adulthood than do females. Differences in favor of girls were found in word fluency, rote memory, and reasoning, but boys were superior in spatial and quantitative ability (Carlsmith, 1964).

References

Ausubel, David P. *The Psychology of Meaningful Verbal Learning.* New York: Grune & Stratton, 1963. 255 pp.

——, *Maori Youth: A Psychoethnological Study of Cultural Deprivation.* New York: Holt, Rinehart and Winston, 1965. 221 pp.

Bradway, Katherine P., and Clare W. Thompson. "Intelligence at Adulthood: A Twenty-five Year Follow-Up." *Journal of Educational Psychology* 53: 1–14; February 1962.

Braham, Mark. "Peer Group Deterrents to Intellectual Development during Adolescence." *Educational Theory,* July 1965.

Carlsmith, Lyn. "Effect of Early Father Absence on Scholastic Aptitude." *Harvard Educational Review* 34: 3–21; Winter 1964.

Case, Duncan, and J. M. Collinson. "The Development of Formal Thinking in Verbal Comprehension." *The British Journal of Educational Psychology* 32: 103–111; June 1962.

Dodwell, P. C. "Children's Understanding of Number and Related Concepts." *Canadian Journal of Psychology* 14: 191–205; September 1960.

——, "Children's Understanding of Number Concepts: Characteristics of an Individual and a Group Test." *Canadian Journal of Psychology* 15: 29–36; March 1961.

——, "Relations Between the Understanding of the Logic of Classes and of Cardinal Number in Children." *Canadian Journal of Psychology* 16: 152–160; June 1962.

_____, "Children's Understanding of Spatial Concepts." *Canadian Journal of Psychology* 17: 141–161; March 1963.

Elkind, David, "Quantity Conceptions in Junior and Senior High School Students." *Child Development* 32:551–560; September 1961.

_____, "Quantity Conceptions in College Students." *The Journal of Social Psychology* 57: 459–465; August 1962.

Goldman, R. J. "The Application of Piaget's Schema of Operational Thinking to Religious Story Data by Means of the Guttman Scalogram." *The British Journal of Educational Psychology* 35: 158–170; June 1965.

Green, Russel F., and Bernard Berkowitz. "Changes in Intellect with Age: II. Factorial Analysis of Wechsler-Bellevue Scores." *Journal of Genetic Psychology* 104: 3–11; March 1964.

Guildford, J. P. "Intelligence: 1965 Model." *The American Psychologist* 21: 20–26; January 1966.

Heinonen, Veikko. *Differentiation of Primary Mental Abilities*. Jyvaskyld, Finland: Kustantajat Publishers, 1963. 76 pp.

Hill, Shirley A. A Study of the Logical Abilities of Children. Doctor's Thesis. Stanford, Calif.: Stanford Universitv, 1961. 121 pp. Abstract: *Dissertation Abstracts* 21: 3359; No. 11, 1961.

Inhelder, Bärbel, and Jean Piaget. *The Growth of Logical Thinking from Childhood to Adolescence*. New York: Basic Books, 1958. 356 pp.

Jackson, Stephen. "The Growth of Logical Thinking in Normal and Subnormal Children." *The British Journal of Educational Psychology* 35: 255–258; June 1965.

Ljung, Bengt-Olov. *The Adolescent Spurt in Mental Growth*. Stockholm Studies in Educational Psychology 8. Uppsala: Almquist and Wiksell, 1965. 350 pp.

Lovell, Kenneth, and A. Slater. "The Growth of the Concept of Time: A Comparative Study." *Journal of Child Psychology and Psychiatry* 1: 179–190; October 1960.

Lovell, Kenneth. "A Follow-Up Study of Inhelder and Piaget's 'The Growth of Logical Thinking.' " *The British Journal of Psychology* 52: 143–153; May 1961.

Lunzer, Eric. "Problems of Formal Reasoning in Test Situations." *Monographs of the Society for Research in Child Development* 30: 19–46; Number 2, 1965.

McNemar, Quinn. "Lost: Our Intelligence! Why?" *The American Psychologist* 19: 871–882; December 1964.

Meyer, William J. "The Stability of Patterns of Primary Mental Abilities Among Junior High and Senior High School Students." *Educational and Psychological Measurement* 20: 795–800; Winter 1960.

Piaget, Jean. *Logic and Philosophy*. New York: Basic Books, 1957. 48 pp.

Yudin, Lee, and Solis L. Kates. "Concept Attainment and Adolescent Development." *Journal of Educational Psychology* 54: 177–182; August 1963.

14 The Influence of Experience on the Development of Intelligence*

David P. Ausubel

In considering the impact of experience on the development of intelligence, two issues, in my opinion, are of paramount theoretical and practical significance. First, what effects does environmental deprivation have on intellectual development, and to what extent are these effects reversible? If some retardation is irreversible, through what kinds of mechanisms is such irreversibility mediated? Second, is it possible through a program of cognitive enrichment to accelerate both the rate of intellectual development as well as the rate of intellectual achievement?

**Reprinted from an article of the same title in H. J. Ascher and C. E. Bish (Eds.)* Productive Thinking in Education. *(2d ed., paperback, $3.00) Washington, D. C.: National Education Association, 1968. Pp. 45–62. By permission of the author, editors, and publisher.*

The Effects of Environmental Deprivation on the IQ

What theoretical grounds and relevant evidence do we have for believing that prolonged environmental deprivation induces retardation in intellectual development? It is reasonable to assume, in the first place, that whatever the individual's genic potentialities are, cognitive development occurs largely in response to a variable range of stimulation requiring incorporation, accommodation, adjustment, and reconciliation. The more variable the environment to which individuals are exposed, the higher is the resulting level of effective stimulation. Characteristic of the culturally deprived environment, however, is a restricted range and a less adequate and systematic ordering of stimulation sequences (13). The effects of this restricted environment include poor perceptual discrimination skills; inability to use adults as sources of information, correction, and reality testing, and as instruments for satisfying curiosity; an impoverished language-symbolic system; and a paucity of information, concepts, and relational propositions (13).

Both the animal and human evidence indicates that early environmental deprivation stunts the development of intelligence. Cage-reared rats (4, 20, 26) and dogs (57) who are deprived of visual and exploratory experience are significantly inferior to pet-reared control animals in later problem-solving ability; and the longer children remain in substandard environmental conditions, i.e., in foundling homes (16, 54, 55), in orphanages (12, 47, 48), or with mentally retarded mothers (53), the progressively lower their IQ's become in comparison with the IQ's of control children placed in more favorable environments. These findings are consistent with the reports of progressive decline in the intelligence test scores of isolated mountain and canal boat children who also grow up in unstimulating and nondemanding intellectual environments (2, 23, 44, 60); with the lower IQ's of rural than of urban children (2, 3, 8, 60); with the social class differential in IQ (5, 56); with the upgrading effect of urban residence on Negro children's IQ's (32); and with the high correlation between the intra-pair discrepancies in the IQ's of separated monozygotic twins and the discrepancies in their educational advantages (34). Evidence of depressed IQ, of special retardation in language skills and conceptualization, and of inability to concentrate is found as late as adolescence among children who spend the first three years of life in foundling homes (21).

Language Retardation

It is in the area of language development, and particularly with respect to the abstract dimension of verbal functioning that the culturally deprived child manifests the greatest degree of intellectual retardation. Many factors contribute to this unfortunate developmental outcome. The culturally deprived home, to begin with, lacks the large variety of objects, utensils, toys, pictures, etc., that require labeling and serve as referents for language acquisition in the middle-class home. The culturally deprived child is also not spoken to or read to very much by adults.[1] Hence his auditory discrimination tends to be poor and he receives little corrective feedback regarding his enunciation, pronunciation, and grammar (13). Furthermore, the syntactical model provided him by his parents is typically faulty. Later on, when new concepts and transactional terms are largely acquired verbally, i.e., by definition and context from speech and reading, rather than by abstraction from direct concrete experience, he suffers from the paucity of abstractions in the everyday vocabulary of his elders, from the rarity of stimulating conversation in the home, from the relative absence of books, magazines and newspapers, and from the lack of example of a reading adult in the family setting.

It is small wonder, therefore, that the abstract vocabulary of the culturally deprived child is deficient in range and precision, that his grammar and language usage are shoddy, that his atten-

[1] In this connection it is interesting to note that Anastasi and de Jesus (1) attribute the relative language superiority of Puerto Rican nursery school children over comparable white and Negro children in New York City slum areas—in the face of more severe socioeconomic handicaps—to the fact that they enjoy more contact with adults in the home.

tivity and memory are poorly developed, and that he is impoverished in such language-related knowledge as the number concepts, self-identity information, and understanding of the physical, geometric, and geographical environments (13). Social class differences in language and conceptual measures also tend to increase with increasing age (13), thus demonstrating the cumulative effects of both continued environmental deprivation and of intial deficit in language development.

The culturally deprived child's entire orientation to language is also different from that of the middle-class child. He responds more to the concrete, tangible, immediate, and particularized properties of objects and situations rather than to their abstract, categorical and relational properties (6, 7, 45). His speech is instigated more by the objects and actions he sees than by abstract ideas emanating from within, and he makes more ancillary use of nonverbal forms of communication (40). In short, the language of the culturally deprived child is more concrete, expressive, and informal than that of the middle-class child, showing signs of impoverishment mainly in its formal, abstract, and syntactical aspects (13).

However, the most important consequence of the culturally deprived child's language retardation is his slower and less complete transition from concrete to abstract modes of thought and understanding. This transition normally begins to occur in our culture during the junior high-school period. As a result, preadolescent and adolescent children are able to understand and manipulate relationships between abstractions directly, i.e., without the benefit of reference to current or immediately prior concrete-empirical experience (29). Thus they are no longer limited to semi-abstract, intuitive, and particularized thought, and can formulate more precise, abstract, and general propositions that embody all possible and hypothetical relationships between categorical variables. The transition takes place more slowly and less completely in culturally deprived children for two reasons. First, the culturally deprived child lacks the necessary repertoire of clear and stable abstractions and transactional terms that is obviously prerequisite for the direct manipulation and understanding of relationships between abstractions. Second, for lack of adequate practice, he has not acquired sufficient facility in relating abstractions to each other *with* the benefit of concrete-empirical props, so that he can later dispense with their assistance at the same age as his environmentally more favored contemporaries. Because concrete thought operations are necessarily more time-consuming than their abstract-verbal counterparts, and also because of his distractibility, unfamiliarity with formal language, impaired self-confidence, and unresponsiveness to time pressure, the culturally deprived child typically works more slowly than the middle-class child in an academic setting (40).

Preventing and Reversing Initial Intellectual Retardation

The modifiability of children's relative intellectual ability as measured by intelligence tests is no longer seriously in dispute. Once we grant that the IQ represents a multiply determined functional capacity in the development of which experiential and motivational factors play an important regulatory role, it is superfluous to inquire whether it can be modified by significant changes in such factors. The more relevant questions at this point are the extent of the modification that is possible and the conditions under which it occurs, that is, how late in the course of cultural deprivation appropriate experience can reverse intellectual retardation, and what the most suitable kind of experience is for this purpose.

The available evidence indicates that removal from a nonstimulating orphanage to a superior institutional environment (46) or to superior foster homes (15, 49, 50), and the provision of an enriched nursery school environment to orphanage children (38) tend to raise the IQ level. Intensive preschool training even improves the IQ's and educability of children who are mentally retarded on an endogenous basis (31). It is important to bear in mind, however, that in all of these instances enhancement of intellectual capacity was effected in relatively young children of preschool age. We still lack firm evidence concerning the influence of an optimal learning environment on the intellectual development of culturally deprived elementary-school and adolescent children, especially those who have been subjected for many years to the frustration and demoralization of inappropriate school experience.[2] This is an extremely urgent research problem that should engage our immediate attention. We need to investigate the effects of an optimal learning environment on both IQ scores and on the acquisition of school knowledge, making special efforts to eliminate errors of measurement associated with test content bias, test-taking skills, test rapport, and test motivation. On *a priori* grounds one might anticipate that school knowledge would be more ameliorable than intelligence level to the influence of environmental stimulation.

This discouraging picture of language retardation in the culturally deprived child can be counteracted in at least three different ways. In the first place, it seems credible that most of the language retardation and its grim consequences for school learning could be prevented by an enriched program of preschool education that would emphasize perceptual discrimination and language acquisition. In addition to the usual preschool activities, much time would be spent in reading and talking to children, in furnishing an acceptable model of speech, in supplying corrective feedback with respect to grammar and pronunciation, in developing listening, memory, and attentivity skills, and in providing appropriate reading readiness, reading, and writing instruction. Concomitantly, of course, an attempt could be made to raise the cultural and intellectual level of the home through a long-range program of involvement in adult education.

Within the regular classroom setting two kinds of ameliorative approaches are possible, especially for those children who have not had the benefit of preschool training. The first approach takes account of the culturally deprived child's slower and less complete transition to abstract modes of thought and understanding during the junior high-school period, and provides more concrete-empirical props and opportunities for direct physical

[2] Some tangential evidence concerning the ameliorative effect of school experience on intellectual development comes from studies showing that the resumption of regular schooling in Holland after World War II raised the mean IQ of children (10, 11), and that long-term improvement in substandard school conditions raised the mean IQ among Hawaiian (52) and East Tennessee mountain children (60).

manipulation of objects and situations in the presentation of abstract ideas and relational propositions. Such props, for example, might include audio-visual aids, Cuisenaire rods, the abacus, laboratory material, schematic models and diagrams, and role-playing activities; and in the teaching of mathematics and science, much reliance would be placed on applicability to common problems in the immediate environment and on illustrations drawn from everyday experience. It should be appreciated, however, that these techniques are merely ways of facilitating the transition to a more abstract level of cognitive functioning. We do not want to induce permanent dependence on concrete-empirical props or to be satisfied with this state of affairs as our ultimate objective. In fact, the pursuit of a vigorous program of relational thinking and understanding in the elementary school could help greatly in reducing the later delay in the transition from concrete to abstract thought.

The second needed change within the classroom setting is the long overdue introduction of more imaginative and effective ways of teaching the language arts. More emphasis, for example, needs to be placed on the mastery of the principal syntactical forms in spoken and written discourse, through repetitive practice with feedback, than on the pedantic and essentially trivial labeling and classifying of different varieties of grammatical structure. The culturally deprived child with his pragmatic and nonabstract approach to knowledge couldn't care less, after all, about the different parts of speech and the various esoteric names attached to the different uses of each; and for the most part he is correct insofar as the value or functional utility of such knowledge is concerned.

Mechanisms Mediating Irreversibility

The Critical Periods Hypothesis

An increasingly more popular explanation that has been advanced in recent years to account for the apparent irreversibility of certain kinds of behavioral development and developmental retardation is the "critical periods" hypothesis. According to this hypothesis, irreversibility of behavioral development is a function of extreme susceptibility to particular types of stimulation during those brief periods in ontogeny when certain types of behavior are shaped and molded for life. By the same token, if the organism is deprived of the necessary stimulation during the critical period, when he is maximally susceptible to it in terms of actualizing potential capacities or developing in new directions, it is held that some degree of permanent retardation is inevitable.

Numerous examples of the existence of critical periods can be found in the perceptual, motor, and social development of infrahuman mammals. Infant chimpanzees isolated from normal tactual stimulation exhibit defective kinaesthetic learning and cutaneous localization (35); and if reared in darkness fail to fixate or recognize familiar objects or to blink in response to a threatening object (39). Newly born domestic lambs reared on a bottle and isolated from sheep for ten days experience difficulty later in adjusting to the flock and tend to graze by themselves (42). Similarly, puppies isolated for nine weeks or more are unable to adapt socially to other dogs; and if not removed from the litter by three months of age, are extremely difficult to tame at a later date (43).

An implicit form of the "critical periods" hypothesis was applied to intellectual development many years ago by Montessori and her followers to justify the particular graded series of learning tasks which children are set in Montessori schools (37). More recently it has been invoked by advocates of the proposition that young children can learn many intellectual skills and kinds of subject matter more efficiently than adults can. The argument in both instances is that since there are allegedly optimal (i.e., critical) periods of readiness for all kinds of cognitive acquisitions, children who fail to learn the age-appropriate skills at the appropriate times are forever handicapped in acquiring them later.

Serious difficulties, however, lie in the path of extrapolating the "critical periods" hypothesis to human cognitive development. In the first place, it has been validated only for infant individuals in infrahuman species, and in relation to those kinds of rapidly developing perceptual, motor, and social traits that are largely regulated by genic factors. In human individuals, especially beyond the prenatal period and first year of life, environmental determinants of development are more important, and the rate of maturation is significantly slower. Second, it has never been empirically demonstrated that optimal readiness exists at particular age periods for specified kinds of intellectual activities, and that if adequate conditions for growth are not present during those periods, no future time is ever as advantageous, thereby causing irreparable developmental deficit.

Hence, if specific intellectual skills or subject-matter content are not acquired at the earliest appearance of readiness, this does not mean that they cannot be acquired later just as well or even better. The disadvantage of unnecessarily postponing such learnings inheres rather in the irreparable loss of precious years of opportunity when reasonably economical learning could have occurred if attempted, but did not. When this happens, the individual, in comparison with equally endowed peers, incurs a learning deficit which limits his current and future rate of intellectual development.

The Cumulative Nature of Intellectual Deficit

This brings us to a second, somewhat more credible explanation of the possible irreversibility in cognitive development that results from prolonged cultural deprivation. I refer to the tendency for existing developmental deficits to become cumulative in nature, since current and future rates of intellectual growth are always conditioned or limited by the attained level of development. The child who has an existing deficit in growth incurred from past deprivation is less able to profit developmentally from new and more advanced levels of environmental stimulation. Thus, irrespective of the adequacy of all other factors—both internal and external—his deficit tends to increase cumulatively and to lead to permanent retardation.

New growth, in other words, always proceeds from the existing phenotype, that is, from already actualized capacity, rather than from potentialities inherent in the genotype. It makes no difference in terms of this limiting influence whether the attained deficiency is attributable to inferior genic endowment or to inadequate environment. If, as a result of a consistently deprived environment during the early formative years, superior intellectual endowment is not actualized, the attained deficit in functional capacity significantly limits the extent to which later environmental stimulation, even if normal in quantity and quality, can increase the rate of cognitive growth. Hence, an individual's prior success or failure in developing his intellectual capacities tends to keep his future rate of growth relatively constant.

Differentiation of Intelligence

In addition to the limiting condition of attained level of development or of existing degree of deficiency, we must consider the further limiting factor of the organism's degree of plasticity or freedom to respond developmentally in a given direction in response to appropriate environmental stimulation.

Generally speaking, the plasticity of intelligence tends to decrease with increasing age. At first, intelligence is a relatively undifferentiated capacity that can develop in several different directions. But as children grow older, particularly during preadolescence and adolescence, it becomes increasingly more differentiated as shown by the decreasing intercorrelations among the subtests of a given intelligence scale (17). Another indication of the trend toward the progressive differentiation of abilities is the fact that ten-year-old boys of high socioeconomic status make higher scores than ten-year-old boys of low socioeconomic status on tests of both verbal *and* mechanical ability, but at age 16 are only superior on the verbal tests (25, 30). Furthermore, the verbal ability scores of boys who drop out of school at the age of 17 tend to decline whereas their scores on tests of mechanical aptitude continue to improve (59). Thus by the time an individual reaches adolescence, differential factors of interest, relative ability, specialization of training,[3] motivation, success

[3] Additional evidence of the effect of experience on the differentiation of intelligence comes from studies showing that the intelligence test scores of boys who continue longer in school tend to exceed, even twenty years later, the test scores of matched controls with less schooling (33), and that gains in IQ scores are much more common in college than in non-college populations (58).

and failure experience, and cultural expectation operate selectively to develop certain potential abilities and to leave others relatively undeveloped.

Once intelligence undergoes definite relative commitment in the various aforementioned channels, the individual is less responsive to stimulation in areas of minimal development than he was in the original undifferentiated state. Thus, for example, if because of inadequate stimulation during early and middle childhood, genic potentialities for verbal intelligence fail to be adequately actualized, other facets of intelligence (e.g., mechanical, social) which are more satisfactorily stimulated become differentially more highly developed. At this point, therefore, the development of the individual's verbal intelligence is not only limited by his existing deficiency in the verbal area, but also by the fact that his once undifferentiated intelligence has been definitely committed in other directions, and is hence less free to respond than previously to an enriched verbal environment. Hence it is evident that the possibility for complete reversibility of environmentally induced retardation in verbal intelligence decreases as children advance in age. This is not to say, of course, that later enrichment is entirely to no avail; but, in my opinion, some of this failure in developmental actualization is irreversible and cannot be compensated for later, irrespective of the amount of hyperstimulation that is applied.

The hypothesis of cumulative developmental deficit implicitly assumes the continued operation of a learning environment the stimulating value of which remains average or below average during the crucial formative years. Hence, despite the twin limiting effects of attained deficit in intellectual development and of increasing differentiation of intelligence on subsequent responsiveness to cognitive stimulation, it is completely consistent with our theoretical analysis to hypothesize that an *optimal* learning environment could arrest and reverse in part the existing degree of retardation. Such an environment must obviously be adequately stimulating, must be specially geared to the deprived individual's particular level of readiness in each subject-matter area and intellectual skill, as well as to his over-all level of cognitive sophistication, and presupposes much individualized attention and guided remedial effort. This, of course, is a far cry from the kind of learning environment that culturally deprived children typically enjoy. In actual practice their existing intellectual deficit is usually compounded by the fact that not only are they less able than their peers to profit from appropriate new experience, but they are also usually overwhelmed by exposure to learning tasks that exceed by far their prevailing level of cognitive readiness. Hence, since they do not possess the necessary background of knowledge or sophistication required for efficient learning, they typically fail, lose self-confidence in their ability to learn, become thoroughly demoralized in the school situation, and disinvolve themselves from it.

Are Intelligence Tests Unfair to Culturally Deprived Children?

Liberal educators often unwarrantedly castigate the intelligence test as being unfair to the culturally deprived child, both because it emphasizes verbal ability rather than the mechanical and social kinds of abilities in which lower-class children excel, and because the middle-class environment is more propitious than the lower-class environment for the development of verbal intelligence. Actually, however, the intelligence test is not really unfair to the culturally deprived child on either count. In the first place, it only purports to measure verbal ability and to predict school performance—not ability or performance in the mechanical and social areas. Second, any intelligence test can only hope to measure functional or operating capacity at a given point of development (i.e., degree of actualized genic potentiality) rather than innate potentiality per se. Adequacy of environmental stimulation is always a significant determinant of functional capacity and hence affects performance on an intelligence test. If the environment is inadequately stimulating, then functional capacity is naturally impaired. But this does not mean that our measuring instrument, the intelligence test, is unfair, since its function is merely to identify and measure impaired operating capacity irrespective of the origin of the impairment. The intelligence test, in other words, purports to measure functional capacity rather than to account for it. If the culturally deprived child scores low on an intelligence test because of the inadequacy of his environment, it is not the test which is unfair but the social order which permits him to develop under such conditions.

By the same token we would not say that the tuberculin test is unfair or invalid (a) because the lower-class child really does not have any greater genic susceptibility to tuberculosis but happens to live in an environment that predisposes him to this disease, and (b) because it measures exposure to a particular disease which happens to be related to lower social class status rather than to one which is not so related. In terms of operating functional capacity, an intelligence test is no less fair or valid because a low score is reflective of cultural deprivation than because it is reflective of low genic endowment. Furthermore, to argue that test scores are valid is not to claim that they are necessarily immutable irrespective of future environmental conditions, or to defend those aspects of the social system that give rise to the culturally deprived environment.

Traditional verbal intelligence tests *are* unfair to culturally deprived children in the sense that such children, in comparison with their middle-class agemates, have fewer test-taking skills, are less responsive to speed pressure, are less highly motivated in taking tests, have less rapport with the examiner, and are less familiar with the specific vocabulary and tasks that make up the content of the test. The tests are unfair in that they do not give the lower-class child a fair opportunity to demonstrate his true attained level of cognitive capacity. When these errors of measurement are eliminated, however, substantial social class differences in IQ still remain (9, 24). These may reflect both hereditary and environmental influences.

ACCELERATION THROUGH ENRICHED EXPERIENCE

To what extent can one accelerate the rate of intellectual development in normal or superior nondeprived children by providing enriched or optimal educational experience? If stages of development have any true meaning, the answer to this question can only be that although suitable long-term training could conceivably accelerate to some extent the rate at which the various stages of intellectual development succeed each other, maturational considerations inevitably impose a limit on such acceleration. Also, unlike its effect on children reared under substandard home or school conditions, a program of either preschool (22, 36, 61) or elementary-school (22) enrichment does *not* accelerate the growth of intelligence when provided to children who already enjoy reasonably stimulating home environments and school opportunities.

In general, transitions from one stage of development to another presuppose the attainment of a critical threshold level of capacity that is reflective of extended and cumulative experience which can only be reduced up to a point. Premature practice prior to the onset of readiness in such preschool activities as cube building and cutting with scissors does not hasten the emergence of these skills (19, 27, 28). In other instances, training beyond children's current state of developmental readiness, as for example, practice in extending their memory span for digits (18), results in unstable and transitory gains. It was also found that training children in the preoperational stage to appreciate the notion of conservation of mass tends to produce an unstable understanding of this principle which is hardly equivalent to that acquired by older children (51). Similarly, young children who receive laboratory training in learning the principle of a teeter-totter (i.e., that the longer side from the fulcrum falls when both ends are equally weighted) are able to learn the principle but fail to acquire any resistance to learning a spurious causal relationship about the operation of a teeter-totter (i.e., that the color of the blocks placed at either end is the determining factor (4).) Older children, on the other hand, who are both cognitively more mature and have more incidental experience with teeter-totters resist learning the spurious causal relationship (4).

But although the possibility of accelerating movement through the stages of intellectual development is at best highly limited, the acquisition of many intellectual achievements that lie within the intrinsic readiness of children can be accelerated by providing suitably contrived experience geared to their cognitive capacity and mode of functioning. Age of readiness for a given intellectual task, after all, is not an absolute, but is always relative, in part, to the method of instruction employed. By taking advantage of the preschool child's extensive reliance on overt manipulative activity in understanding and using symbols, both Montessori and O. K. Moore were able to advance considerably the typical age of reading and writing. Similarly, it is possible successfully to teach the elementary school child many ideas in science and mathematics that were previously thought much too difficult by presenting them at a purely intuitive level. However, one must balance against these possible advantages of early intuitive learning the excessive time cost involved in many instances. In certain cases it may be more feasible in the long run to postpone entirely the introduction of particular subject-matter fields until children are cognitively mature. The decision in each case must be based upon the findings of particularized research. In one progressive school, for example, children who learned no formal arithmetic until the fifth grade equalled matched controls in computation by the seventh grade, and surpassed them in arithmetic reasoning (41).

In conclusion, therefore, although prior intuitive understanding of many ideas during childhood may greatly extend the elementary-school child's horizon of useful knowledge and facilitate the learning and stabilize the retention of these same ideas when they are taught later at a more formal and abstract level, there is little warrant for believing that children can learn *everything* in this manner, or that this type of learning is more efficient than the verbal-abstract learning that succeeds it. The intellectual achievement of children can only be accelerated within the limits imposed by the prevailing stage of intellectual development. These limitations cannot be transcended through experience. One can, at best, take advantage of methods that are most appropriate and effective for exploiting the existing degree of readiness.

References

1 Anastasi, A., and C. de Jesus. Language development and non-verbal IQ of Puerto Rican preschool children in New York City. *J. abnorm. soc. Psychol.*, 1953, *48:* 357–66.

2 Asher, E. J. The inadequacy of current intelligence tests for testing Kentucky mountain children. *J. genet. Psychol.*, 1935, *46*: 480–86.

3 Ausubel, D. P. *Maori Youth.* Wellington, New Zealand: Price, Milburn, 1961.

4 Ausubel, D. P., and H. M. Schiff. The effect of incidental and experimentally induced experience in the learning of relevant and irrelevant causal relationships by children. *J. genet. Psychol.*, 1954, *84*: 109–23.

5 Bayley, N., and H. E. Jones. Environmental correlates of mental and motor development: a cumulative study from infancy to six years. *Child Develpm.*, 1937, *4*: 329–41.

6 Bernstein, B. Some sociological determinants of perception: an enquiry into subcultural differences. *Brit. J. Sociol.*, 1958, *9*: 159–74.

7 ——, Language and social class. *Brit. J. Psychol.*, 1960, *11*: 271–76.

8 Chapanis, A., and W. C. Williams. Results of a mental survey with the Kuhlmann-Anderson intelligence tests in Williamson County, Tennessee. *J. genet. Psychol.*, 1945, *67*: 27–55.

9 Coleman, W., and A. H. Ward. A comparison of Davis-Eells and Kuhlmann-Finch scores of children from high and low socio-economic status. *J. educ. Psychol.*, 1955, *46*: 465–69,

10 de Groot, A. D. The effects of war upon the intelligence of youth. *J. abnorm. soc. Psychol.*, 1948, *43*: 311–17.

11 ——, War and the intelligence of youth. *J. abnorm. soc. Psychol.*, 1951, *46*: 596–97.

12 Dennis, W., and P. Najarian. Infant development under environmental handicap. *Psychol. Monogr.*, 1957, *71* (Whole No. 436).

13 Deutsch, M. The disadvantaged child and the learning process: some social, psychological and developmental considerations. Paper presented to Work Conference on Curriculum and Teaching in Depressed Urban Areas, Teachers College, Columbia University, July 10, 1962.

14 Forgus, R. H. The effect of early perceptual learning on the behavioral organization of adult rats. *J. comp. physiol. Psychol.*, 1954, *47*: 331–36.

15 Freeman, F. N., K. J. Holzinger, and C. B. Mitchell. The influence of environment on the intelligence, school achievement, and conduct of foster children. *In Twenty-seventh Yearbook, Natl. Soc. Stud. Educ.*, 1928, Part I, pp. 103–217.

16 Freud, A., and D. Burlingham. *Infants Without Families.* New York: International Universities Press, 1944.

17 Garrett, H. F., A. I. Bryan, and R. E. Perl. The age factor in mental organization. *Arch. Psychol.*, 1935, (Whole No. 175).

18 Gates, A. I., and G. A. Taylor. An experimental study of the nature of improvement resulting from practice in a mental function. *J. educ. Psychol.*, 1925, *16*: 583–93.

19 Gesell, A., and H. Thompson. Learning and growth in identical twin infants. *Genet. Psychol. Monogr.*, 1929, *6*: 1–124.

20 Gibson, E. J. and R. D. Walk. The effect of prolonged exposure to visually presented pattern on learning to discriminate between them. *J. comp. physiol. Psychol.*, 1956, *49*: 239–42.

21 Goldfarb, W. Psychological privation in infancy and subsequent adjustment. *Amer. J. Orthopsychiat.*, 1945, 247–55.

22 Goodenough, F. L. New evidence on environmental influence on intelligence. In *Thirty-ninth Yearbook, Nat. Soc. Stud. Educ.*, Part I, 1940, pp. 307–365.

23 Gordon, H. Mental and scholastic tests among retarded children: an enquiry into the effects of schooling on the various tests. *Educ. Pamphlets, Bd. Educ.*, London, No. 44, 1923.

24 Haggard, E. A. Social status and intelligence: an experimental study of certain cultural determinants of measured intelligence. *Genet. Psychol. Monogr.*, 1954, *49*: 141–86.

25 Havighurst, R. J., and L. L. Janke. Relations between ability and social status in a Mid-Western community. I. Ten-year-old children. *J. educ. Psychol.*, 1944, *35*: 357–68.

26 Hebb, D. O. *The Organization of Behavior.* New York: Wiley, 1949.

27 Hilgard, J. R. Learning and maturation in preschool children. *J. genet. Psychol.*, 1932, *41*: 36–56.

28 ——, The effect of early and delayed practice on memory and motor performances studied by the method of co-twin control. *Genet. Psychol. Monogr.*, 1933, *14*: 493–567.

29 Inhelder, B., and J. Piaget. *The Growth of Logical Thinking from Childhood to Adolescence.* New York: Basic Books, 1958.

30 Janke, L. L., and R. J. Havighurst. Relations between ability and social status in a Mid-Western community. II. Sixteen-year-old boys and girls. *J. educ. Psychol.*, 1945, *36*: 499–509.

31 Kirk, S. A. *Early Education of the Retarded Child: An Experimental Study.* Urbana, Illinois: University of Illinois Press, 1958.

32 Klineberg, O. *Negro Intelligence and Selective Migration*: New York: Columbia University Press, 1935.

33 Lorge, I. Schooling makes a difference. *Teach. Coll. Rec.*, 1945, *46*: 483–92.

34 Newman, H. H., F. N. Freeman, and K. J. Holzinger. *Twins: A Study of Heredity and Environment.* Chicago: University of Chicago Press, 1937.

35 Nissen, H. W., K. L. Chow, and J. Semmes. Effects of restricted opportunity for tactual, kinaesthetic, and manipulative experience on the behavior of a chimpanzee. *Amer. J. Psychol.*, 1951, *64*: 485–507.

36 Olson, W. C., and B. O. Hughes. Subsequent growth of children with and without nursery school experience. In *Thirty-ninth Yearbook, Nat. Soc. Stud. Educ.*, Part I, 1940, pp. 237–44.

37 Rambusch, Nancy M. *Learning How to Learn: An American Approach to Montessori*. Baltimore: Helicon, 1962.

38 Reymert, M., and R. Hinton. The effect of change to a relatively superior environment upon the IQ's of one hundred children. In *Thirty-ninth Yearbook, Natl. Soc. Stud. Educ.*, 1940, Part 2, pp. 255–68.

39 Riesen, A. H. The development of visual preception in man and chimpanzee. *Science*, 1947, *106*: 107–108.

40 Riessman, F. *The Culturally Deprived Child*. New York: Harper, 1962.

41 Sax, G., and J. P. Otina. The arithmetic reasoning of pupils differing in school experience. *Calif. J. educ. Res.*, 1958, *9*: 15–19.

42 Scott, J. P., E. Fredericson, and J. L. Fuller. Experimental exploration of the critical period hypothesis. *J. Personal.*, 1951, *1*: 162–83.

43 Scott, J. P., and M. Marston. Critical periods affecting the development of normal and maladjustive social behavior of puppies. *J. genet. Psychol.*, 1950, *77*: 25–60.

44 Sherman, M., and C. B. Key. The intelligence of isolated mountain children. *Child Develpm.*, 1932, *3*: 279–90.

45 Siller, J. Socio-economic status and conceptual thinking. *J. abnorm. soc. Psychol.*, 1957, *55*: 365–71.

46 Skeels, H. M., and H. Dye. A study of the effects of differential stimulation in mentally retarded children. *Proc. Amer. Assoc. Ment. Defic.*, 1939, *44*: 114–36.

47 Skeels, H. M., and E. A. Fillmore. Mental development of children from underprivileged homes. *J. genet. Psychol.*, 1937, *50*: 427–39.

48 Skeels, H. M., R. Updegraff, B. L. Wellman, and H. M. Williams. A study of environmental stimulation: an orphanage preschool project. *Univ. Iowa Stud. Child Welf.*, No. 4, 1938.

49 Skodak, M. Children in foster homes: a study of mental development. *Univ. Iowa Stud. Child Welf.*, *16*, No. 1, 1939.

50 Skodak, M., and H. M. Skeels. A final follow-up of one hundred adopted children. *J. genet. Psychol.*, 1949, *75*: 85–125.

51 Smedslund, J. The acquisition of conservation of substance and weight in children. *J. Scan. Psychol.*, 1961, *2*: 11–20; 71–87; 153–60; 203–10.

52 Smith, S. Language and non-verbal test performance of racial groups in Honolulu before and after a fourteen-year interval. *J. gen. Psychol.*, 1942, *26*: 51–93.

53 Speer, G. S. The mental development of children of feeble-minded and normal mothers. In *Thirty-ninth Yearbook, Natl. Soc. Stud. Educ.*, 1940, Part 2, pp. 309–14.

54 Spitz, R. A. Hospitalism: an inquiry into the genesis of psychiatric conditions in early childhood. *Psychoanal. Stud. Child*, 1945, *1*: 53–74.

55 ——, The role of ecological factors in emotional development in infancy. *Child. Develpm.*, 1949, *20*: 145–55.

56 Terman, L. M., and M. A. Merrill. *Measuring Intelligence*. Boston: Houghton Mifflin, 1937.

57 Thompson, W. R., and W. Heron. The effects of restricting early experience on the problem-solving capacity of dogs. *Canad. J. Psychol.*, 1954, *8*: 17–31.

58 Thorndike, R. L. Growth of intelligence during adolescence. *J. genet. Psychol.*, 1948, *72*: 11–15.

59 Vernon, P. E. Changes in abilities from 14 to 20 years. *Adv. Sci.*, 1948, *5*: 138.

60 Wheeler, L. R. A comparative study of the intelligence of East Tennessee Mountain Children. *J. educ. Psychol.*, 1942, *33*: 321–34.

61 Wollman, B. L. IQ changes of preschool and nonpreschool groups during the preschool years: a summary of the literature. *J. Psychol.*, 1945, *20*: 347–68.

15 Is Drill Necessary? The Mythology of Incidental Learning*

David P. Ausubel

One of the strongest legacies of the Progressive Education movement and of Thorndikian educational psychology that still remains on the pedagogic scene is a confused and contradictory attitude toward structured practice or drill. On the one hand, we minimize the value of drill in educational theory, regarding it as rote, mechanical, passive, and old-fashioned, as psychologically unnecessary for the learning process, and as actually harmful for active, meaningful learning. On the other hand, as teachers, parents, coaches, and students, we still implicitly accept the old maxim that "practice makes perfect." The upshot of this conflict in our beliefs is that we still place considerable reliance on drill in actual classroom practice, but do so half-heartedly, apologetically, and in ways that detract from its effectiveness.

**Reprinted from the article of the same title,* Bulletin, National Association of Secondary School Principals, *1963*, 47, *44–50. By permission of the author and publisher.*

The progressivists, of course, did not entirely deny the value of practice. As a matter of fact, both their espousal of activity programs and their battle cry of "learning by doing" carried an implied endorsement of the importance of appropriate practice. But by appropriate practice they meant direct (concrete, manipulative), nondeliberate, and autonomous learning encounters with different examples of the same concept or principle in uncontrived, "real-life" situations. Their mistake lay in assuming that all structured practice (drill) is necessarily rote; that unstructured, unguided, and unintentional (incidental) practice is maximally effective for school learning tasks; and that "doing" necessarily leads to learning simply because it involves direct experience and occurs repeatedly in natural, problem-solving situations.

Actually, for practice to result in meaningful mastery of material, the only really essential conditions are that the learning task be potentially meaningful; that the learner exhibit a meaningful learning set and possess the necessary background concepts; and that the number, distribution, sequence, and organization of practice trials conform to empirically established principles of efficient learning and retention. Not only is the uncontrived or unstructured quality of practice an unessential condition of meaningful, effective learning, but it also often leads to no meaningful mastery whatsoever.

The fetish of naturalism and incidental learning embodied in the activity program movement emphasizes these five points: (1) unstructured and uncontrived learning situations; (2) direct kinds of experience, in a concrete, manipulative sense; (3) unintentional or nondeliberate learning effort; (4) learning by autonomous, unguided discovery; and (5) exposure to diversified rather than repetitive experience.

Learning in Natural Settings

How desirable is it that factual information and intellectual skills be acquired in the real-life, functional contexts in which they are customarily encountered, rather than through the medium of artificially contrived drills and exercises? It is true, of course, (providing that all other factors are equal) that learning is enhanced when the conditions of practice closely resemble the conditions under which the skill or knowledge in question will eventually be used. Wholly natural settings, however, rarely provide the practice conditions that are either necessary or optimal for efficient learning. Generally it is only during the latter stages of learning, *after* component aspects of the learning task have already been identified and mastered in structured practice sessions that naturalistic "dress rehearsals" become feasible.

This is so, in the first place, because unstructured learning settings typically fail to furnish examples that come along frequently, repetitively, and close enough together to make possible the learning of concepts and principles. Under these circumstances there is also inadequate opportunity for differential practice of particularly difficult components. Contrary to Thorndike's generally accepted but unwarranted inferences from his well-known experiments on the "law of frequency," the weight of the research evidence clearly indicates that repetition per se is typically necessary both for the learning and retention of associations and meanings. Second, unstructured practice does not receive the benefit of either skilled pedagogic selection, presentation, and organization of material or of careful sequencing, pacing, and gradation of difficulty.

Direct Experience

Many features of the activity program were based on the quite defensible premise that the elementary-school child perceives the world in relatively specific and concrete terms, and requires considerable first-hand experience with diverse concrete instances of a given set of relationships before he can acquire genuinely meaningful concepts and propositions. Thus, an attempt was made to teach factual information and intellectual skills through the medium of direct, manipulative experience in natural settings rather than through verbal exposition and drill.

In older pupils, however, once a sufficient number of basic concepts is consolidated, new concepts are primarily abstracted from verbal rather than concrete experience, and new propositions are comprehended without any direct reference to or manipulation of concrete props. Hence in secondary school it may be desirable to reverse both the sequence and relative balance between abstract concepts and supportive data. There is good reason for believing that much of the time presently spent in cookbook laboratory exercises in the sciences could be more advantageously employed in formulating precise definitions, making explicit verbal distinctions between concepts, generalizing from hypothetical situations, etc.

John Dewey correctly recognized that meaningful understanding of abstract concepts and principles in childhood must be built on a foundation of direct, empirical experience, and for this reason advocated the use of activity methods in the elementary school. But he also appreciated that once a firmly grounded first-story of abstract understandings was established, it was possible to organize secondary and higher education along more abstract and verbal lines. Unfortunately, however, some of Dewey's disciples blindly generalized over the entire life span the conditions that limit abstract verbal learning during childhood.

NONDELIBERATE LEARNING

Although individuals can acquire much miscellaneous information and some skills incidentally, deliberate effort is required for the efficient learning of most types of academic material. Countless experiments show that deliberate learning in response to explicit instructions is both more effective and more precise than is unintentional or implicitly instructed learning.

Especially for long-term meaningful learning of subject matter, doing per se is not sufficient in the absence of the felt needs and interests that give rise to deliberate intent. Inability to see any need for a subject is the reason students mention most frequently for losing interest in high-school studies. Doing, without being interested in what one is doing, results in relatively little permanent learning. Only that material can be meaningfully incorporated into an individual's structure of knowledge, on a long-term basis, which is relevant to areas of concern in his psychological field.

Learners who have little need to know and understand, quite naturally expend little learning effort and manifest an insufficiently meaningful learning set. They fail to develop precise meanings, to reconcile new material with existing concepts, and to reformulate new propositions in their own words. Finally, they do not devote enough time and effort to practice and review. Material is therefore never sufficiently consolidated to form an adequate foundation for sequential learning. Hence it is unrealistic to expect that school subjects can be effectively learned and retained until pupils develop a felt need to acquire knowledge as an *end in itself*—since much school learning can never be rationalized as necessary for meeting the demands of daily living.

Autonomous, Unguided Discovery

The unquestioning faith which advocates of incidental learning have in autonomous, unguided discovery is justified neither by logic nor by research evidence. In the first place, laboratory and problem-solving exercises are not inherently or necessarily meaningful. They may lead to little or no meaningful learning if a student's learning set is simply rotely to memorize type problems or techniques of manipulating reagents and symbols, and if he has inadequate background in or appreciation of the substantive and methodological principles underlying specific problem-solving or laboratory procedures.

Second, what is typically called "the discovery method" is really a contrived type of discovery that is a far cry from the truly autonomous discovery activities of the research scholar or scientist. Pure discovery techniques could lead only to utter chaos and waste of time in the classroom, inasmuch as immature students generally lack sufficient subject-matter sophistication both to formulate workable problems and to devise appropriate and relevant research methods. Before students can "discover" concepts reasonably efficiently, problems must be structured for them in such a way as to make ultimate discovery almost inevitable.

Third, numerous short-term studies have demonstrated that guided discovery is more efficacious for learning, retention, and transfer than is either completely autonomous discovery or the provision of complete guidance. Guidance under these circumstances sensitizes the learner to the salient aspects of the problem, orients him to the goal, and promotes economy of learning by preventing misdirected effort. However these findings do not necessarily indicate that guided discovery is more effective for teaching subject-matter content than is simple didactic exposition. For one thing, the solving by a naïve subject of a few novel problems in a laboratory setting is hardly comparable to the learning of a large body of sequentially organized material by a learner with varying degrees of subject-matter sophistication. For another, even contrived discovery techniques are incomparably more time-consuming than expository teaching.

Lastly, guidance in the form of prompting has been shown to be very helpful during the early stages of learning. At this point, in the learning process the learner has not mastered sufficient material to receive much practice benefit from unaided recitation. Further, the provision of prompts can prevent the learning of errors and thus obviate the necessity for costly unlearning.

Diversified Experience

Proponents of activity programs tend to favor task heterogeneity in practice. That is, they seek, in part, to escape the opprobrium associated with drill by stressing diversity both in the types of learning tasks and in the examples of each type that are presented to the learner. This approach undoubtedly has merit in that, other factors being equal, the defining attributes of a new concept are learned most readily when the concept is encountered in many different contexts. Such experience obviously enhances the generality of abstract knowledge and transferable skills. It also minimizes the possibility of boredom and of a rote and rigid approach to learning.

However, if diversity of learning task content is provided at the expense of attaining mastery of the particular component tasks which comprise it, its over-all effect on learning is detrimental. Positive transfer from one learning task to another requires that particular examples of a given type of task as well as particular types of tasks first be consolidated (i.e., mastered, overlearned) before new task content is introduced.

Many cases of disability in such academic skills as arithmetic, reading, spelling, and grammar can undoubtedly be attributed to overemphasis on the importance of diversified experience in unstructured learning situations. Failure to provide sufficient repetitive practice (drill) in antecedent learning tasks does not allow for the adequate mastery of these tasks that is essential if sequentially related tasks are to be successfully handled in the acquisition of concepts, generalizations and intellectual skills.

16 Early versus Delayed Review in Meaningful Learning*

David P. Ausubel

The role and significance of frequency are different for meaningful than for rote learning and retention, precisely because rote and meaningful learning processes themselves are so different from one another. Repeated encounters with the same array of stimulation presumably enhance rote learning and retention by increasing the strength of discrete, arbitrary, and verbatim associative linkages, i.e., their resistance to the short-term interfering effects of prior and subsequent stimulation. The same repetition, on the other hand, presumably enhances meaningful learning and retention by increasing the availability of learned instructional materials that have been nonarbitrarily and

Reprinted from the article of the same title,* Psychology in the Schools, *1966,* **3, *195–198. By permission of the author and* Psychology in the Schools.

substantively incorporated in relation to an existing concept or principle in cognitive structure, i.e., by facilitating the emergence of clear and stable meanings and their resistance to forgetting (Ausubel, 1963).

Thus it is reasonable to assume that *sheer* repetition would play a more significant role in the learning and short-term retention of discrete and arbitrary associations that are largely isolated from cognitive structure, than it would in the learning and longer-term retention of materials that can be meaningfully incorporated within that structure. In meaningful as opposed to rote learning situations, such other factors as the availability of clear and stable referents in cognitive structure, the discriminability between these subsumers and the learning task, and the internal logic and lucidity (the potential meaningfulness) of the learning task undoubtedly detract from the role played by repetition. Nevertheless, the influence of repetition is still considerable in the establishment and consolidation of meanings, and in the enhancement of their resistance to decremental processes. In any case, it cannot be dismissed as basically extrinsic to the process whereby increments in availability are effected.

From the standpoint of frequency, the chief practical implication of the differences between rote and meaningful learning for classroom teaching is that review can, and largely should, take the place of practice. Since meaningful learning occurs relatively quickly, and since the forgetting of meaningfully learned materials takes place relatively slowly, much of the potentially facilitating effects of frequency can be used more profitably for review than for original learning purposes. In terms of what is actually learned and retained, in other words, the relatively long interval between the initial learning and the review sessions, in the case of meaningful learning, is comparable to the short intertrial practice interval, in the case of advanced stages of rote learning. Thus, in teaching the meanings of a series of programmed scientific terms, Reynolds and Glaser (1964) recently found that "repetition had only transitory effects upon retention," whereas "spaced reviews produced a significant facilitation in retention of the reviewed material."

For purposes of meaningful learning and retention, should review be introduced shortly after original learning, when the material is still fresh in mind and relatively little has been forgotten, or would it be more effective to introduce review after an appreciable amount of material has been forgotten? This issue has significant implications for student study practices and for the programming of potentially meaningful instructional materials. It also has important theoretical implications for the psychology of meaningful learning and retention. Credible arguments can be adduced in support of each alternative, but the issue can obviously be decided only by empirical test.

The findings of two previous studies are particularly relevant for the problem at issue. Peterson, Ellis, Toohill, and Kloess (1935) reported no difference between the effects of a rereading review introduced one or nine days after original learning. Sones and Stroud (1940) found that there was a slight but nonsignificant tendency for a delayed rereading review to be more effective than an early rereading review. In both instances, however, these findings were somewhat equivocal because the criterion retention test was given an equal number of days from the original learning. Hence there was a greater time interval between the early review and the retention test than between the delayed review and the retention test, thereby tending to bias the results in favor of the latter condition. The present study, therefore, was designed to eliminate this methodological difficulty. The review session was administered on the *same* day for both early and delayed review groups and was followed by the retention test after an equal time interval for both groups. The same relearning of the material constituted early or delayed review for the two groups as a result of varying the interval between original learning and review.

Subjects The experimental population consisted of 97 students in a general psychology and a developmental psychology class at the Salesian University of Rome. Their average age was 26.9. For the most part, they were either priests or preparing to become priests. Within each class, *S*s were assigned randomly to the early and delayed review groups. The experiment was conducted separately in each class as a required laboratory exercise, and was performed during regularly scheduled class hours. In order to maximize ego-involvement, *S*s were informed that after the data were processed their individual scores, as well as the class results, would be reported to them.

Learning Passage and Test The learning material used in this study was a specially prepared, 2500-word passage dealing with Buddhist conceptions of God, immortality, soul, faith, salvation, morality, and responsibility. The topic of Buddhism was chosen because it was explicitly unfamiliar to the *S*s. Knowledge of the material was tested by a 45-item multiple-choice test that yielded a corrected split-half reliability of .73 for the retention scores. The distribution of the scores did not deviate significantly from the normal curve. Unfamiliarity of the material was established by administering the test to a comparable control group who did not study the passage; the immediate retention scores of the latter group were not significantly greater than chance.

As each group studied the Buddhism passage for the first time, the other group studied a passage of comparable length and difficulty on the causes and types of drug addiction. This made it possible to draw both groups from the same population, and to conduct the original learning in the same group setting. The topic of drug addiction was chosen because it is so dissimilar to the learning passage as to cause no retroactive interference.

All materials were written in the Italian language.

PROCEDURE

During the first session, seven days prior to review, the delayed review group studied the Buddhism passage, and the early review group studied the addiction passage. *S*s were requested to read the material only once; after finishing a given page they were not permitted to turn back. A time limit of 30 minutes, sufficient to accommodate the slowest reader, was imposed.

During the second session, one day prior to review, the delayed review group studied the addiction passage, and the early review group studied the Buddhism passage.

During the third or review session, both groups restudied the

Buddhism passage. The reading conditions were the same as during the first passage except for a time limit of 25 minutes.

During the fourth session, six days after review, both groups took the Buddhism test. A time limit of 45 minutes was imposed.

Results and Discussion

Confirming the findings of Peterson, *et al.*, (1935) and of Sones and Stroud (1940), there was a small and statistically nonsignificant difference between the mean retention scores of the early ($M = 19.14 \pm 5.21$) and delayed ($M = 17.87 \pm 5.77$) review groups. For a two-tailed *t*-test, this difference was significant at about the .30 level. Evidently, then, early and delayed review were not significantly different in enhancing the meaningful learning and retention of school material.

The results of this experiment can be best explained, in my opinion, by supposing that the respective advantages of early and delayed review counterbalance each other. The theoretical advantages of delayed review are perhaps more self-evident than those of early review. In the first place, after a longer retention interval, when more material is forgotten, the learner is more highly motivated to profit from the opportunity for review. He is less likely to regard this opportunity as unnecessary and superfluous, and is hence more disposed to take good advantage of it in terms of effort, attention, and concentration. Second, and even more important, prior forgetting presumably has a facilitating effect on meaningful learning and retention because, as a result of both trying and failing to remember material, the learner tends to become aware of negative factors in the learning and retention situations that promote forgetting, that is, of areas of instability, ambiguity, confusion, and lack of discriminability (Ausubel & Youssef, 1965). Thus forearmed, he can take the necessary steps during the relearning session to strengthen particularly weak components of the learning task, to resolve existing confusion and ambiguity, and to increase discriminability between previously learned ideas and related new propositions. Furthermore, greater potential benefit can always be anticipated from repetition when a larger proportion of the learning task is forgotten.

In what ways can early review conceivably counterbalance these evident advantages of delayed review? The most likely possibility is that repetition (review) has a specially potent consolidating effect on recently learned material while it is still appreciably above the threshold of availability, and that this consolidating effect decreases as the material becomes progressively less available. Obviously, another trial provides additional opportunity for the learner to interact cognitively with the learning material, and to relate the potential meaning it embodies to his existing structure of knowledge, thereby enabling actual or experienced meanings to eventuate and/or be consolidated. He has, in other words, another opportunity to acquire meanings potential in the material that he partially or completely missed on the first trial, as well as to consolidate meanings initially established at that time.

Another study trial also provides the learner with informational feedback in the form of textual reference, for testing the correctness of the knowledge he retained from the first trial. This testing confirms correct meanings, clarifies ambiguities, corrects misconceptions, and indicates areas of weakness requiring differential concentrated study. The net effect is consolidation of learning.

In addition to enhancing meaningful learning and retention in the two aforementioned direct ways, repetition also influences these processes in another indirect way through modifications in cognitive structure wrought by earlier trials. Not only do repeated presentations of the learning task determine and enhance cognitive content, but the newly acquired cognitive content also *reciprocally* induces changes in the *perceived* learning task which make it more learnable. That is, initial contact with the material *sensitizes* the learner to the meanings it contains when he encounters it again. Since he had previously derived meanings from the learning material on the first trial—by incorporating potential meanings into his cognitive structure—now the ideas as a whole, not merely the component words, immediately convey actual rather than merely potential meaning to him on second reading. Hence, on the second trial, actual rather than potential meanings interact with the residue of those recently acquired meanings in his cognitive structure which were established as a consequence of his first encounter with the material. This type of interaction particularly enhances consolidation of the previously established meanings, since this time the learner does not have to grasp meanings and can concentrate solely on trying to remember them. Moreover, establishment of gross meanings on the first trial sensitizes the learner to more refined meanings and subtle distinctions on the second trial. It stands to reason, therefore, that both the consolidation and "sensitizing effects" of repetition are greater earlier rather than later during the retention interval, when more of the learned material is still available.

In summary, then, the principal advantage of early review would appear to be its superior consolidating and "sensitizing" effects on more highly available material; whereas the principal advantage of delayed review probably inheres in superior relearning of forgotten material, both on motivational and cognitive grounds. Thus, since each kind of review has its own distinctive function and advantage, the two varieties are presumably complementary rather than redundant or mutually exclusive, and can thus be profitably combined.

References

Ausubel, D. P. *The psychology of meaningful verbal learning*. New York: Grune & Stratton, 1963.

Ausubel, D. P., and M. Youssef. The effect of spaced repetition on meaningful retention. *Journal of General Psychology*, 1965, *73*, 147–150.

Peterson, H. A., M. Ellis, H. Toohill, and P. Kloess. Some measurements of the effects of reviews. *Journal of Educational Psychology*, 1935, *26*, 65–72.

Reynolds, J. H., and R. Glaser. Effects of repetition and spaced review upon retention of a complex learning task. *Journal of Educational Psychology*, 1964, *55*, 297–308.

Sones, A. M., and J. B. Stroud. Review with special reference to temporal position. *Journal of Educational Psychology*, 1940, *31*, 665–676.

17 An Evaluation of the BSCS Approach to High School Biology*

David P. Ausubel

The principal objective of the BSCS program is to re-establish the close contact and congruence of high school biology with current conceptual and methodological developments in biological science, while still maintaining, and even increasing, its congruence with current psychological and pedagogical ideas about the learning-teaching process as they apply to tenth-grade students (Schwab, 1963) (1). According to Schwab, the content of high school biology, during the heyday of Progressive Education, "was no longer mainly determined by the state of knowledge in the scientific field," because of its excessive preoccupation with such matters as intellectual readiness, the learnability of material, and individual differences among

Reprinted from the article of the same title from* American Biology Teacher, *1966,* **28, *176–186. By permission of the author and* American Biology Teacher.

learners. The BSCS approach, in my opinion, has veered precisely toward the opposite extreme in trying to correct this unsatisfactory state of affairs: its three texts are reasonably congruent with the content and methods of modern biology, but, except for the Green Version, are psychologically and pedagogically unsound for the majority of tenth-graders.

Actually, of course, there is no *inherent* incompatibility between subject matter soundness, on the one hand, and pedagogic effectiveness, on the other. It is no more necessary to produce pedagogically inappropriate instructional materials in an attempt to make them reflective of the current state of knowledge in a given discipline, than it is necessary to present discredited concepts or inaccurate facts in order to make the subject matter more learnable. In practice, however, as the Yellow and Blue BSCS versions demonstrate, preoccupation with the recency of subject matter content, and with the completeness of conceptual, methodological, and historical coverage, can easily lead to the neglect of such basic pedagogic considerations as the educational appropriateness of course approach and objectives, the adequacy of the pupils' existing academic background for learning the content of the course, and the psychological tenability of the chosen ways of presenting, organizing, and sequencing materials. The inevitable outcome, under these circumstances, is the production of instructional materials that are admirably thorough, accurate, and up-to-date, but so ineffectively presented and organized, and so impossibly sophisticated for their intended audience, as to be intrinsically unlearnable on a long-term basis.

This latter assertion is defensible, I believe, despite evaluation data which show that the three BSCS versions are approximately as "learnable" as conventional textbooks. It was demonstrated, for example, that students using the BSCS texts score somewhat higher than students using conventional texts, on a final *Comprehensive BSCS Test*, and somewhat lower on a final *Cooperative Biology Test* (Wallace, 1963) (2). In the first place, it is questionable how well such final tests *really* measure the learnability of subject-matter content. Most reasonably bright students can "learn," for examination purposes, large quantities of overly sophisticated and poorly presented materials that they do not really understand; unfortunately, however, in such circumstances, little evidence of retention is present even a few days later. Second, one of the main objectives of any new, elaborately prepared curriculum program is presumably to exceed by far, rather than merely to approximate the level of academic achievement attained in conventionally taught courses.

Although the BSCS does not state explicitly its specific dissatisfactions with conventional high school biology textbooks, these dissatisfactions can be readily inferred from the content of its numerous publications: (1) Conventional texts abound in outmoded ideas and incorrect information, and ignore important contemporary developments in the biological sciences. (2) They are written at a largely descriptive level, and contain relatively few explanatory concepts; too much stress is placed on structural detail, useless terminological distinctions, and classification, thereby placing a premium on rote memory. (3) Their approach is too naturalistic, and insufficiently experimental, quantitative, and analytical. (4) They tend to focus excessively on the organ and tissue levels of biological organization, whereas recent biological progress has been greatest at the molecular (biophysical and biochemical), cellular, population, and community levels. (5) They are written at too low a level of sophistication and contain a profusion of elementary and self-evident generalizations. (6) Insufficient emphasis is placed on biology as a form of inquiry, as an experimental science, and as an ever-changing, open-ended discipline. (7) The biological ideas they contain are not presented in terms of their historical development and are not related to the social and technological contexts from which they arise. (8) They lack organizing and unifying themes, present a mass of disconnected facts, and fail to integrate related concepts and different levels of biological organization. (9) They place excessive emphasis on the application of biology to such areas as medicine, public health, agriculture, and conservation, and insufficient emphasis on basic biological principles as ends in themselves.

To what extent do the BSCS texts correct these perceived deficiencies, and to what extent do these corrections constitute improvements? In my opinion, they are most successful in their attempt to update the content of high school biology, and to make it more reflective of the actual state of knowledge in the field; but they are by no means unique in accomplishing this objective. More than most (but not all) conventional texts, they also contain more explanatory concepts and less factual data unrelated to theory. On the other hand, however, with the exception of the Green Version, they have greatly *overcorrected* the naturalistic and "applied" approach, the inadequate emphasis on the molecular and cellular levels of biological organization, the low level of intellectual sophistication, and the insufficient emphasis, both on biology as an experimental science and on the history of biological ideas, that characterize most traditional textbooks in high school biology.

Thus, the Yellow and Blue versions place inordinate emphasis on the experimental foundations and history of biology, and virtually ignore the naturalistic approach to and important applications of biological science. They introduce an absurd and unrealistic level of biochemical and biophysical sophistication for which the intended users lack any semblance of adequate background, and continue to overemphasize structural detail—not only at an organ and tissue, but also at a cellular level. In addition, the overall organization of these latter versions is chaotic; related concepts and different levels of biological organization are not integrated; unifying and organizing themes are not actually related in practice to subject-matter content; the sequence of topics proceeds from the unfamiliar to the familiar; and examples and illustrations tend to be overly sophisticated and used as ends in themselves, rather than to clarify ideas. Only the Green Version has a unifying theme, is free of the aforementioned overemphases, is reasonably well organized and integrated, and makes an original contribution to and introduces a new (i.e., ecological) approach in the teaching of high school biology. On balance, therefore, except for the Green Version, the BSCS textbooks do not, in my opinion, constitute much of an improvement over the better conventional texts, in terms of either conceptual content or congruence with contemporary thinking in and approach to biology; and, in some substantive and most pedagogic respects, they fall below the standard of the typical conventional text. The validity of this conclusion can be assessed only in relation to a more detailed examination of the approach, objectives, content, level of sophistication, theoretical biases, and organizational and pedagogic aspects of the three versions.

Approach and Objectives

In my opinion, introductory high school biology should continue to remain predominantly naturalistic and descriptive in approach rather than analytical and experimental. This does not imply emphasis on descriptive information or on disconnected facts unrelated to theory, but on *explanatory* concepts that are stated in relatively gross and descriptive language, instead of in the more technical, quantitative, and sophisticated terminology of biochemistry and biophysics. In short, high school biology should concentrate on those broad biological ideas that constitute part of *general* education—physiology, evolution, development, inheritance, uniformities and diversity in life, ecology, and man's place in nature—rather than on a detailed and technical analysis of the physical and chemical basis of biological phenomena or of the morphology and function of intracellular microstructures. This is particularly true for the substantial number of students who will receive no further instruction in biology.

Contrary to the strong and explicitly stated bias of the Blue and Yellow versions, there is still much room in introductory biology for the naturalistic approach. It is much more important for the *beginning* student in science to learn how to observe events in nature systematically and precisely, and how to formulate and test hypotheses on the basis of independent sets of naturally occurring antecedents and consequences, than to learn how to manipulate an experimental variable and control other relevant variables, by design, in a laboratory situation. The former approach not only takes precedence in the student's intellectual development, and is more consonant with his experiential background, but also has more transfer value for problem solving in future "real-life" contexts. To dogmatically equate scientific method with the experimental-analytical approach also excludes, rather summarily from the domain of science, such fields in biology as ecology, paleontology, and evolution, and such other disciplines as geology, astronomy, anthropology, and sociology.

The strong emphasis in the Yellow and Blue versions on "basic science" principles, and its relative lack of concern with applications to familiar or practical problems, is in accord with current fashionable trends in science education. However, the justification offered for this approach, namely, that only "basic science" knowledge can be related to and organized around general principles (Yellow Version, pp. 44–47) is theoretically untenable and misleading. Each of the applied biological sciences (e.g., medicine, agronomy) possesses an *independent* body of general principles underlying the detailed knowledge in its field, in addition to being related in a still more general way to basic principles in biology. Furthermore, physiological, genetic, and embryological applications of biology to many practical problems in public health, disease, sanitation, food technology, agriculture, etc., are not only familiar to and of intrinsic concern to high school students, but are also important components of general knowledge.

Retention of the naturalistic and descriptive emphasis, and of some applied content, in introductory high school biology is thus consistent with the fact that tenth-grade biology is the terminal course in science for many students. It is also more consistent than is the analytical-experimental approach with the tenth-grader's existing background of experience, his interests, his intellectual readiness, and his relative degree of sophistication in science. This proposed emphasis is also in no way inappropriate for those students who will subsequently take high school physics and chemistry, as well as more advanced biology courses. These latter students would be much better prepared, after taking such an introductory course, for a second course in biology, in the twelfth grade or in college, that takes a more quantitative and experimental-analytical approach, introduces more esoteric topics, and considers the biochemical and biophysical aspects of biological knowledge. By this time, they would also have the necessary mathematical sophistication and greater experience with experimental methodology.

Neglected and Inadequately Treated Topics

Many important aspects of organ system physiology that self-evidently belong in an introductory course are either ignored or treated inadequately in the BSCS textbooks. The Green Version attempts to cover the anatomy and physiology of all organ systems in a single chapter, and thus tells the student little that he has not learned previously in elementary or junior high school science. The Yellow and Blue versions present the sequential course of blood flow through the circulatory system in a very unclear and cursory fashion. The material on blood pressure is fragmentary, disjointed, and unclear; the various regulatory mechanisms involved in determining blood pressure level, the causes and effects of increased blood pressure, the inverse relationship between cardiac output and pulse rate, and the circulatory adjustments involved in physical exertion and oxygen lack are largely ignored. The important differences between the respective functions of glomerulus and tubule; the actual sequence of events beginning with the formation of the glomerular filtrate and ending with the selective reabsorption of water and various metabolites in the tubules; and the role of the renal tubules in maintaining homeostasis, are presented vaguely and unclearly. The nature of muscular fatigue and short-term and long-term muscular adaptation to physical exertion receive scant consideration.

Despite the inordinate attention given to the biochemistry of genetics, many important concepts and issues in descriptive genetics receive inadequate or no attention. These include the interaction between heredity and environment, and the different ways in which each variable actually influences phenotypic outcome; the difference between single-gene and polygenic mechanisms, and the relationship between each mechanism and intra-species uniformities, dichotomous variability, and continuous variability; the relative resistance of single-gene and polygenic effects to environmental influence, and how this affects phenotypic variability; the role of genes and the interaction between heredity and environment in resistance and susceptibility to disease; the varying contributions of heredity and environment to different *kinds* of traits; and the relationship between the relative influence of heredity and environment on the development of a given trait, on the one hand, and the degree of phenotypic variability in that trait, on the other. All three versions fail to relate molecular genetics to such obviously related topics as mitosis, meiosis, and descriptive genetics, and to emphasize sufficiently that classical Mendelian genetics cannot account for the commonest form of variability found in nature (i.e., normal, continuous variability). The important problem of intra-species uniformities and differences is not even mentioned. Genetics is not related to embryological development, and the relative influence of genic and environmental (gestational and intrafetal) factors in such development is not considered. The Mendelian principles of segregation and independent assortment are not related to meiosis in accounting for genotypic differences between parents and offspring. The difficulties involved in positive and negative eugenics, and the relative unfeasibility of eugenics, as compared to environmental manipulation, are not made adequately clear.

Certain important aspects of biological evolution are also not treated adequately. The contrast between the Darwinian and Lamarckian theories is not presented incisively enough in terms of the different roles attributed to the environment in each theory. The failure of Weismann's experiment really to test Lamarck's theory (i.e., that only traits acquired through prolonged acclimatization or adaptation are directly transmitted to offspring) is not pointed out. Except for the Green Version, the important relationships of evolutionary theory to ecology are neglected. Parallelisms between biological evolution and embryological development are summarily dismissed on the specious grounds that they are either not identical or have been exaggerated in some instances. It would be more edifying to explain why such parallelisms are only rough and approximate. Failure to consider continuity and modification in evolution concomitantly with the genic mechanisms responsible for each phenomenon makes it difficult to appreciate the concept of genetic continuity in evolution. The role of genes in the evolutionary process could also be made clearer if their common relationships to evolutionary and embryological development were pointed out, and if reference were made to the approximate sequential parallelisms between these two kinds of development.

Except for the Green Version, inadequate emphasis is placed on ecological concepts. In the Yellow Version, ecology is included somewhat as an afterthought, and the topic is treated on a nonconceptual basis (i.e., restricted to a detailed description of various kinds of ecological habitats). The Green Version, on the other hand, is conspicuously lacking in adequate detail regarding the different animal phyla and the anatomy and methods of plant reproduction.

The biological aspects of behavior, in general, are presented with insufficient incisiveness. Only the Green Version distinguishes clearly between innate and learned behavior, between instinctive and acquired social behavior, and between human and infra-human behavior; alone among the three versions, it indicates, as well, both the difficulty of making such distinctions, and the dangers of anthropomorphizing animal behavior and of attributing all specifically unlearned behavior to genic effects. The Yellow and Blue versions fail to relate behavioral adaptation to other kinds of adaptation; thus the "biological roots of behavior" (one of the nine main themes) are not made very salient. In none of the three versions is an adequate distinction made between animal and human communication, or between behavior that is motivated by the need to maintain homeostasis and behavior that is motivated by such drives as activity, curiosity, and exploration. None of the three versions points out the dependence of instincts on an adequate background of nonspecific experience, the absence of true instincts at the primate level, or the relationship between instincts and "imprinting." No distinction is drawn between the cyclic, hormonally-regulated sex behavior of sub-primate species (particularly among females) and the non-cyclic sex behavior of primate species (including man), which is partially independent of hormonal control, is stimulated, in part, by ideational and situational factors, and is both an end in itself and a means of expressing affection, submission, and dominance. Thus a legitimate opportunity for biology to contribute to the behavioral aspects of sex education is lost.

Consideration of the above inadequacies in the content of the BSCS textbooks leads to the conclusion that there is much significant but as yet unexploited *conceptual* content in introductory biology that can be treated in much more sophisticated terms at a *descriptive* level, without having to resort to the depth of biochemical and cellular detail given in the Yellow and Blue versions.

Level of Sophistication

In the Yellow and Blue versions, it appears as if little effort were made to discriminate between basic and highly sophisticated content—between what is appropriate and essential for an introductory high school course and what could be more profitably reserved for more advanced courses. These versions include topics, detail, and level of sophistication that vary in appropriateness from the tenth grade to graduate school. Only the Green Version gives the impression of being at an appropriate level of sophistication for a beginning course. And since the unsophisticated student cannot be expected to distinguish between more and less important material, he either throws up his hands in despair, learns nothing thoroughly in the effort to learn everything, or relies on rote memorization and "cramming" to get through examinations.

The Blue Version, especially, appears sufficiently sophisticated and challenging to constitute an introductory college course for students who *already* have an introductory biology course in high school as well as courses in chemistry and physics. It is true, of course, that subjects once thought too difficult for high school students (e.g., set theory, analytical geometry, and calculus) *can* be taught successfully to *bright* high school students with good quantitative ability. But in the latter instances, students are adequately prepared for these advanced subjects by virtue of taking the necessary preliminary, and sequentially antecedent courses in mathematics. The Blue Version, on the other hand, presents biological material of college-level difficulty and sophistication to students who do not have the necessary background in chemistry, physics, and elementary biology for learning it meaningfully. It should also be remembered that college-level mathematics is not considered appropriate for *all* high school students, but only for those brighter students with better-than-average aptitude in mathematics, who are college bound and intend to major in such fields as mathematics, science, engineering, and architecture.

An introductory high school course in any discipline should concentrate more on establishing a general ideational framework than in putting a great deal of flesh on the skeleton. Generally speaking, only the framework is retained anyway after a considerable retention interval; and if more time is spent on overlearning the framework, plus a minimum of detail, than in superficially learning a large mass of oversophisticated and poorly understood material, both more of the important ideas are retained in the case of students taking the subject terminally, and a better foundation is laid for students who intend to take more advanced courses later.

Oversophisticated detail is not only unnecessary and inappropriate for a beginning course, but also hinders learning and generates unfavorable attitudes toward the subject. The student "can't see the forest for the trees." The main conceptual themes get lost or become unidentifiable in a welter of detail. Both the average student, and the student not particularly interested in science, would tend to feel overwhelmed by the vast quantity and complexity of detail, terminology, methodology, and historical material in the Blue and Yellow versions. And a student who feels overwhelmed by a subject tends to develop an aversion toward it, and to resort to rote memorization for examination purposes.

In an introductory course, simplification of content—*without* teaching wrong ideas that have to be unlearned later—is always justifiable and indicated. This can be accomplished by simply presenting more general and less complete versions of much of the same material that can be presented subsequently in greater depth and at high levels of sophistication. Although the Green Version probably lacks sufficient detail, it is less damaging, in my opinion, to present inadequate historical detail and experimental evidence than to obscure the major concepts by providing excessive historical and experimental data. This book unquestionably stimulates the student to delve deeper on his own. In any case, the missing detail can always be furnished by the teacher or from other sources.

It is possible to present ideas relatively simply—yet correctly—by deleting a great deal of the dispensable terminological, methodological, and historical detail, as well as many of the intermediate steps in argumentation; by telescoping or condensing material; by eliminating tangential "asides" and less important qualifications; by limiting the scope of coverage; by omitting formulas, equations, and structural diagrams of complex molecules that are actually meaningless to unsophisticated students; by keeping the level of discourse general and simple; by writing lucidly, using terms precisely and consistently, and giving concise and familiar examples; by using schematically simplified models and diagrams; and by bearing in mind that a satiation point exists for any student. An atypically high level of sophistication may sometimes be employed simply to *illustrate* the complexity of a given topic; but in these instances students should be explicitly instructed not to master the details.

It is not necessary for a beginning student to be given so much sequential historical detail about the development of biological ideas, related experimental evidence from original sources, and pedantic information about *all* of the various misconceptions and twistings and turnings taken by these ideas before they evolve into their currently accepted form. As a result, the ideas themselves—which are really the important things to be learned—tend to be obscured and rendered less salient. This practice also places an unnecessary and unwarranted burden on learning and memory effort—effort that could be more profitably expended on learning the ideas themselves and the more significant aspects of their historical development.

To give students the flavor of biology as an evolving empirical science with a complex and often circuitous history, it would suffice to cite several *examples*. It is unnecessary to give the detailed ideational and experimental history of *every* biological concept and controversy. Unsophisticated students also tend to be confused by raw experimental data, and by the actual chronological and experimental history underlying the emergence of a biological law or theory—especially when long quotations are given from original sources that use archaic language, refer to obscure controversies, and report findings and inferences in an unfamiliar and discursive manner. It is sufficient (as the Green Version does) to review the historical background of biological concepts in a schematic, telescoped, simplified, and reconstructed fashion, deleting most of the detail, and disregarding the actual chronological order of the antecedent ideas and their related experiments.

Some examples of ideas discussed in excessive historical detail in the Yellow and Blue versions include Mendelian genetics, molecular genetics, Darwinian theory, photosynthesis, spontaneous generation, preformationism and epigenesis, and the cell theory. Many experiments, e.g., Beaumont's, Harvey's, Loewi's, Landis', Darwin's experiments on heliotropisms, the experiments on the determination of sex and on sex-linked genes, are discussed much too fully for an introductory text. Oversophisticated treatment is given to such topics as the factors regulating pulse rate; the origin of life; comparative digestion, excretion, neurology, and circulation; population genetics, meiosis, and plant reproduction; the origin of multicellular organisms; the evolution of roots and leaves; the micro-histology and physiology of the generalized cell; the regulatory functions of the thyroid gland; and hypothalamic-pituitary relationships. Many topics, such as coleoptiles, polyploid species, "what causes a cell to divide," and the microhistology and microphysiology of muscular contraction, could be profitably deleted altogether from a beginning high school course.

The Biochemical Aspects of Biology

In general, I believe that an introductory high school biology course should not include content that presupposes knowledge of chemistry. The essential and unavoidable biochemical aspects of such topics as genetics, photosynthesis, and protein synthesis can be presented at a purely verbal and descriptive explanatory level that requires no background in chemistry. More detailed and technical biochemical aspects of these topics can be considered in a second biology course after a student has learned the fundamentals of general chemistry.

The authors of the Blue and Yellow versions appear to have no conception of when degree of biochemical sophistication ceases being appropriate and verges on the absurd for a beginning high school course. Introductory sections are fairly general, but then details are piled on unmercifully, without any restraint or exercise of simple pedagogic judgment. Eventually, chemical structure and reactions are discussed which presuppose a high and nonexistent degree of sophistication in the physical-chemical nature of chemical bonds and in the structure of elements and molecules (both inorganic and organic).

All of the important concepts in physiology, metabolism, photosynthesis, and genetics, as well as consideration of the regulatory mechanisms (e.g., hormones, enzymes, vitamins) can be discussed meaningfully at a descriptive explanatory level that requires no detailed knowledge of chemical structure or reactions. In fact, the principal chemical knowledge that is needed could be summarized by the statement that molecules exist, that energy can be stored in these molecules, and that energy can be transformed or transferred when molecules interact. For example, ATP can be considered as a "general currency of energy exchange" (for metabolic reactions requiring the expenditure of energy) that is itself converted, in such reactions, to ADP; and that for ADP to be reconverted into energy-releasing ATP again, some other source of energy is required, such as that released from the oxidation of glucose. All of this can be expressed meaningfully without going into the chemical structure of ATP, ADP, and glucose. This is the level of sophistication at which the topic is treated in the Green Version.

Even DNA replication and the DNA code can be discussed, without introducing meaningless chemical structures to chemically unsophisticated students, by relating these concepts to the gross aspects of meiosis and Mendelian genetics; but the Yellow and Blue versions, despite a very sophisticated treatment of molecular genetics, fails to delineate these basic relationships. The same applies to the Green Version, even though it has little to say about the chemistry of genetics.

A great excess of chemical terminology and detail is used to express chemical concepts that could be explained in very simple terms to the beginning student. For example, instead of elaborating the mechanisms of protein synthesis step by step, it is only necessary to explain why protein synthesis must take place, to indicate the problems in such synthesis, and to use the DNA code as an example of a mechanism that enables cells to store and convey the necessary information required for protein synthesis. Even less defensible is such material as the law of conservation of mass, and the detailed history of the phlogiston-oxidation controversy.

If biochemical content is included, however, it is probably better to provide a minimal background in chemistry and to consider biochemical topics at a somewhat lower level of sophistication (Yellow Version), than to provide almost no background in chemistry and to consider biochemical topics at a very high level of sophistication (Blue Version). Nevertheless, it still seems unfair and irrational to require students in an introductory biology course to master a watered-down version of the basic principles in chemistry, so that they can acquire the necessary background for understanding an unnecessarily detailed presentation of the biochemistry of biology. This is really asking them to learn two courses in one; for most students there are already a sufficient number of new biological concepts to master. It constitutes a difficult and regrettable diversion from the principal objectives of the course. Why not reserve the more detailed biochemical material for a second course in biology after the student has had an opportunity to study chemistry as an end in itself?

Theoretical Bias

In my opinion, only the Green Version is adequately free of the strong theoretical bias and "axe-grinding" that are inappropriate for an introductory text. Only in this version does one generally get the impression that all theoretical issues are not yet finally resolved, that many different points of view are still theoretically tenable, and that the final word still has not been (and never will be) spoken. An introductory text in biology should be free of theoretical dogmatism and polemicism. This desirable degree of theoretical tolerance and open-endedness is found only in the Green Version. For example, the mechanistic bias in the other two versions is excessively and unabashedly polemical. Such topics as the biochemistry and synthesis of organic compounds and digestion *in vitro* are unwarrantedly discussed in the context of discrediting vitalism. It is strongly implied that differences between lower and higher levels of organization (e.g., molecular, cellular, organ and tissue, the individual, populations, etc.) are differences in degree rather than in kind, and that phenomena at the higher levels will *ultimately* be explainable by laws that apply at the molecular level. Although it is legitimate to express this type of reductionistic bias in the philosophy of science, it should at least be stated as a bias; and *current* alternative positions should also be fairly presented. The classical vitalistic position is no longer seriously advanced today, and hence constitutes a "straw man" alternative.

Such philosophical indoctrination is also indefensible when students are too unsophisticated to evaluate the merits of a given theoretical orientation. Until they are sufficiently mature to form independent judgments, it is important that they be permitted to retain an open mind on controversial issues in the philosophy of science.

The Green Version is more disposed to concede that very little is known about some topics, that some concepts are based on relatively little solid evidence, that the same evidence is subject to different interpretations, and that contemporary biologists do not always agree with each other. It also stresses, more than the other versions do, that biological knowledge is not immutable, and that it changes both as new facts and techniques are discovered and as new theories are proposed. It gives more explicit recognition to the fact that the transition between different forms of life is often not abrupt, and that it is therefore difficult and somewhat arbitrary to decide where one species, family, or phylum ends and another begins. Similarly, its policy of not defining such terms as "life," "health," "science," and "disease," that are highly controversial, is, in my opinion, wise at this level; it avoids arbitrariness and dogmatism. The topics themselves can be discussed adequately without being formally defined.

Finally, the Green Version suggests more explicitly than the other versions do that biological concepts and classifications are *man-made* attempts to interpret, organize, and simplify our understanding of natural phenomena; and that such concepts and categories are neither coextensive with the data from which they are derived, nor represent the *only* ways of conceptualizing the same data. This distinction between an abstraction and empirical reality is important for beginning students, who frequently tend to think of concepts and categories in absolute and axiomatic terms, as if given in reality itself and possessing the same reality status as data.

Presentation and Organization

Generally speaking, it makes good organizational sense if the presentation of more detailed or specific information is preceded by a more general or inclusive principle to which it can be related or under which it can be subsumed. This not only enables the student to anchor more easily forgotten specifics to more easily remembered generalizations, but also integrates related facts under a common principle under which they can all be subsumed. Thus, for example, the general characteristics of *all* regulatory or cybernetic systems should be presented before considering any *particular* regulatory or cybernetic system. The latter, in turn, should be explicitly related to the more general principles, showing how they exemplify them. This makes for some redundancy; but such redundancy greatly reinforces the general principles. Of course, the general principles themselves must be stated in terms and concepts that are already familiar to the learner. None of the three versions makes adequate use of this organizational device, but the Blue Version is particularly guilty of introducing complex and detailed information for which no adequate foundation has been laid in terms of organizing, unifying, or explanatory principles.

Thus a substantive introductory statement of the principal new ideas to be considered in a given chapter, stated at a high level of generality and inclusiveness, to which the more detailed information in the chapter can be related, could be very helpful in learning the latter information. For example, a brief overview of the chief propositions underlying Darwin's theory of evolution would be of greater functional utility in learning the more detailed mechanisms through which evolution operates, or the different kinds of evidence for evolution, than the kinds of introductions provided in the three BSCS versions (i.e., much folksy biographical information about Darwin or anecdotal material about how he arrived at his theory). It is not only desirable for the material in each chapter to become progressively more differentiated (i.e., to proceed from ideas of greater to lesser inclusiveness), but for the book as a whole (i.e., from one chapter to another) to follow the same organizational plan. In general, however, only the Green Version attempts both this latter kind of organization and the spiral kind of organization in which the *same* topics are treated at progressively higher levels of sophistication in successive sections.

Good organizational advantage can be taken of pervasive or recurrent themes that can integrate or interrelate many different topics or general ideas. The Green Version, for example, uses the beginning chapters on the "web of life" as an integrative device throught the entire book. None of the three versions, however, makes adequate use of Darwinian theory as a pervasive organizing principle. Evolutionary theory can be related to such varied concepts as uniformity and diversity in nature; genetic continuity; the complementarity of organism and environment, and of structure and function; the classification of and interrelationships between organisms; population genetics; the role of sexual reproduction in producing diversity; the geography of life; and the need for a self-replicating mechanism as well as the biological significance of mistakes in self-replication. It is obviously necessary for pervasive themes to be introduced early in a book if they are to serve an integrative function. But in the Yellow and Blue versions such themes (e.g., regulatory mechanisms, homeostasis, the cybernetic principle, the relationship of theory to data) often do not appear until late in the game.

The nine basic substantive themes of the three texts are not *organically* related to the actual content of the Yellow and Blue versions. In the Yellow Version, after being listed formally in the first chapter, they are presumably forgotten and are no longer identifiable in the content itself. The same is true of the Blue Version except that the themes are distributed quite randomly on separate pages scattered throughout the text. In the Green Version, on the other hand, the themes emerge naturally from and are organically related to the content of each section.

The Green Version's policy of treating function first, and then showing how function is served by complementary structure, rather than adopting the opposite sequence of presentation, is very appropriate for the beginning student. Functions can typically be remembered longer than structures. Thus, if function is stressed, more can be retained from which its complement can later be reconstructed, if forgotten, than if structure is emphasized. It is also easier to reconstruct forgotten structure from remembered function than vice versa. Nothing is forgotten more readily than the details and nomenclature of morphology.

In instances where new concepts are introduced that are similar or related to, but not identical, and hence confusable, with previously learned concepts (e.g., instinct and imprinting; fermentation and respiration; spontaneous generation and preformationism; elimination and excretion; behavioral versus physiological or morphological adaptation; variation as both a cause and product of evolution), it is advisable to point out *explicitly* the similarities and differences between them and to make this connection in *both* contexts. This practice integrates knowledge by making relationships between concepts explicit; by preventing artificial compartmentalization and the proliferation of separate terms for concepts that are basically the same except for contexual usage; and by differentiating between ostensibly similar but actually different concepts. Ignoring such relationships between later-appearing and previously learned content assumes, rather unrealistically, that students will independently perform the necessary cross-referencing by themselves. Only the Green Version makes even a beginning attempt at this type of cross-referencing. Its policy of placing a given category of organisms in relationship to the totality of life, before discussing it in detail, also helps to place it in perspective.

The Green Version explicitly accepts the widely accepted pedagogic principle that one proceeds from the familiar to the unfamiliar, using previously acquired knowledge and experience both as a foundation for understanding, interpreting, and remembering related new material that is less familiar, and as a means of rendering the latter less threatening. Thus it considers mammals before simpler animals, and flowering plants before simple plants. The other two versions consistently determine order of presentation on the basis of level of biological organization ("from molecule to man") or level of phyletic complexity. Thus the student must first contend with the most difficult material in the field, i.e., molecular and cellular biology, before he ever encounters the more familiar, descriptive, and intrinsically easier material in mammalian physiology, ecology, evolution, genetics, etc. This latter principle of organization may conform to some abstract canon of scientific logic, but it violates everything we know about the psychology of learning, and runs counter to the intuitive judgment of anyone who has ever done any classroom teaching. In ascertaining what is more or less familiar, or more or less difficult, psychological knowledge of learning and of intellectual development is a more relevant and reliable guideline than the wholly gratuitous assumption that level of phenomenological complexity in science necessarily parallels level of learning difficulty. The rationale given in the Yellow Version (p. 337) for discussing the plant kingdom before the animal kingdom, namely, that without plants there could be no animals, is an extremely gross *non sequitor,* both logically and pedagogically, for a textbook prepared with the assistance of professional educators and classroom teachers. The same kind of logic was apparently used in deciding to discuss the early forms of man in the order of their paleontological *discovery,* instead of in the chronological order of their appearance in evolutionary history.

Topical organization in the Yellow and Blue versions appears to be arbitrary and random. The sequencing of topics seems to follow no rational design. Such basic concepts as evolution, Mendelian genetics, embryology, reproduction, molecular genetics, and ecology are treated as if they were completely independent and unrelated topics; no attempt whatsoever is made to integrate them.

From a pedagogic standpoint, examples and illustrations are handled very poorly in the Yellow and Blue versions. Examples are often so detailed, esoteric, and complex that they become ends in themselves and serve to obscure rather than clarify the ideas they exemplify. Similarly, structural diagrams of nucleic acid, DNA, and chlorophyll molecules are meaningless to chemically unsophisticated students. In the Green Version, on the other hand, illustrations are generally pertinent to and either enhance or explain the text. One seldom feels that they are superfluous, serve as padding, or are intended to generate a spurious aura of scientific authenticity.

Lastly, the writing in the Yellow and Blue versions is dull and pedestrian in comparison to that in the Green Version. No great effort seems to have been made to arouse interest, or to achieve lucidity of expression. One topic does not lead naturally into another. There are too many tangential "asides" and digressions of dubious value. Both books lack the incisiveness of the Green Version in making conceptual distinctions. Their flavor is also highly pedantic. The many long quotations from original sources, in which style, vocabulary, methods of reporting (and even typography) are archaic, serve no useful purpose. In the Green Version, on the other hand, the writing style in the early chapters is so simple that it appears to "talk down" to students. But the style as well as the content become progressively more complex. This policy is deliberate and makes good pedagogic sense. It is based on the self-evident principle that a new subject is always most difficult in the beginning, and should therefore be presented most simply at first, with the level of difficulty increasing progressively as the student's level of sophistication increases.

References

1 Schwab, J. J. (Supervisor) 1963. *Biology Teachers' Handbook*. John Wiley & Sons, Inc., New York.

2 Wallace, W. W. 1963. The BSCS 1961–62 evaluation program—a statistical report. *BSCS Newsletter 19: 22–24*.

PART IV | LEARNING BY DISCOVERY

Most school learning involves meaningful verbal learning, and most instruction in a school setting is conveyed by means of meaningful verbal exposition. Yet few educational practices in our time have been repudiated quite as thoroughly by educational theorists as verbal learning and its instructional counterpart. Selection 18 attempts to show that much of the rationale behind this view is based on a failure to appreciate the distinction between the reception-discovery and rote-meaningful dimensions of learning and on the consequent assertion that reception learning is invariably rote and that discovery learning is invariably meaningful. Other arguments in support of the discovery learning thesis which are examined in selections 18 and 19 include the assertions that the developmental limitations applying to verbal reception during childhood are applicable to such learning during the entire life span; that the enhancement of problem-solving ability, critical-thinking ability, and creativity is the principal function of education; that discovery learning should be the primary means of transmitting subject-matter content; that learning the "heuristics of discovery" is more important than learning the substantive content of the various disciplines; and that the essence of insight, generalization and transfer inheres in subverbal awareness and is vitiated by verbalization.

Selection 20 is concerned with psychological aspects of problem solving involved in causal thinking. It is shown that the improvement with age in the quality of causal thinking, accompanying increased incidental learning and subject-matter sophistication, largely involves the ability to distinguish between the significant and the irrelevant. The methodology used in this study also anticipates the "extinction" technique used in later "conservation" studies which measures the stability or genuineness of a "nonconserving" child's concept of conservation, acquired through training procedures, by testing his resistance to spurious disconfirming experience.

Much of the uncritical enthusiasm today about "teaching for creativity" stems from ambiguity regarding the true nature of creativity and how it can be validly measured. Selection 21 attempts to resolve some of this conceptual confusion by distinguishing 1) between creativity as a normally distributed trait and the creativity of a person manifesting a singularly unique degree of this trait, and 2) between creativity as a substantive capacity in a recognized field of human achievement and the various general or content-free creative abilities that merely enhance the expression of this capacity.

18 In Defense of Verbal Learning*

David P. Ausubel

Few pedagogic devices in our time have been repudiated more unequivocally by educational theorists than the method of verbal instruction. It is fashionable in many quarters to characterize verbal learning as parrot-like recitation and rote memorization of isolated facts, and to dismiss it disdainfully as an archaic remnant of discredited educational tradition. In fact, quite apart from whatever intrinsic value they may possess, many educational innovations and movements of the past quarter-century—activity programs, project and discussion methods, various ways of maximizing non-verbal and manipulative experience in the classroom, emphasis on "self-discovery" and on learning for and by *problem-solving*—owe their origins and popularity to widespread dissatisfaction with the techniques

Reprinted from the article of the same title,* Educational Theory, *1961,* **11, *15–25. By permission of the author and* Educational Theory.

of verbal instruction. It is commonly accepted today, for example, (at least in the realm of educational theory) (a) that meaningful generalizations cannot be presented or "given" to the learner, but can only be acquired as a product of problem-solving activity (1); and (b) that all attempts to master verbal concepts and propositions are forms of empty verbalism unless the learner has recent prior experience with the realities to which these verbal constructs refer (1, 2).

Excellent reasons, of course, exist for the general disrepute into which verbal learning has fallen. The most obvious of these is that notwithstanding repeated policy declarations of educational organizations to the contrary, meaningful subject-matter is still presented to pupils in preponderantly rote fashion. Another less obvious but equally important reason stems from two serious shortcomings in modern learning theory. First, psychologists have tended to subsume many qualitatively different kinds of learning processes under a single explanatory model. As a result it has not always been sufficiently clear, for example, that such categorically different types of learning as problem-solving and the understanding of meaningfully presented verbal material have different objectives, and that conditions and instructional techniques facilitating one of these learning processes are not necessarily relevant or maximally efficient for the other. Second, in the absence of an appropriate theory of cognitive organization and of long-term learning and retention of large bodies of meaningful subject-matter, various explanatory principles (e.g., retroactive inhibition, stimulus generalization, response competition) have been uncritically extrapolated from laboratory findings on nonverbal or on short-term, fragmentary, and rote verbal learning. It is small wonder, therefore, that teachers nurtured on such theoretical fare have tended to perceive meaningful verbal materials as necessarily rote in character, and, in consequence, have either felt justified in using rote practices, or have summarily rejected verbal techniques as unsuitable for classroom instruction.

The present paper is concerned with the first of the two theoretical difficulties specified above. An attempt will be made to distinguish between "reception" and "discovery" learning, to sharpen the existing distinction between rote and meaningful learning, and to consider the distinctive role and relative importance of each of these types of learning in the total educational enterprise. It should then be clear that verbal learning *can* be genuinely meaningful without prior "discovery" or problem-solving activity, and that the weaknesses attributed to the method of verbal instruction do not inhere in the method itself, but are derived from either premature use of verbal techniques with cognitively immature pupils or from other serious misapplications. In another paper[1] I deal with the second theoretical problem, and propose a comprehensive theory of cognitive organization and classroom learning that has grown out of research on cognitive variables influencing the learning and retention of meaningfully presented verbal materials.

Reception versus Discovery Learning

From the standpoint of promoting intellectual development, no theoretical concern is more relevant or pressing in the present state of our knowledge than the need for distinguishing clearly among the principal kinds of cognitive learning (i.e., rote and meaningful verbal learning, concept formation, and verbal and nonverbal problem-solving) that take place in the classroom. One significant way of differentiating among the latter types of classroom learning is to make two crucial process distinctions that cut across all of them—distinctions between reception and discovery learning and between rote and meaningful learning. The first distinction is especially important because most of the understandings that learners acquire both in and out of school are presented rather than discovered. And since most learning material is presented verbally, it is equally important to appreciate that verbal reception learning is not necessarily rote in character and can be meaningful without prior nonverbal or problem-solving experience.

In reception learning (rote or meaningful) the entire content of what is to be learned is presented to the learner in final form. The learning task does not involve any independent discovery on

[1] See D. P. Ausubel, "A Subsumption Theory of Meaningful Verbal Learning and Retention," *J. gen. psychol.*, 1962, *66*, 213–224.

his part. He is only required to "internalize" the material (e.g., a list of nonsense syllables or paired associates; a poem or geometrical theorem) that is presented to him, i.e., make it available and functionally reproducible for future use. The essential feature of discovery learning (e.g., concept formation, rote or meaningful problem-solving), on the other hand, is that the principal content of what is to be learned is not given but must be independently discovered by the learner before he can internalize it. The distinctive and prior learning task, in other words, is to discover something—which of two maze alleys leads to the goal, the precise nature of a relationship between two variables, the common attributes of a number of diverse instances, etc. The first phase of discovery learning, therefore, involves a process quite different from that of reception learning. The learner must rearrange a given array of information, integrate it with existing cognitive structure,[2] and reorganize or transform the integrated combination in such a way as to create a desired end product or discover a missing means-end relationship. After this phase is completed, the discovered content is internalized just as in reception learning.

The foregoing distinction, of course, is by no means absolute. Rote reception learning requires little or no discovery. Meaningful reception learning, however (see below), often involves more than the simple cataloguing of ready-made concepts or propositions within existing cognitive structure. Because of the variable nature of learners' backgrounds, presented ideas can seldom be apprehended in a completely meaningful fashion without some reconciliation with existing concepts and translation into a personal frame of reference. In a sense, therefore, the resulting meanings may be said to be "discovered." But since the substance of the actual learning task (e.g., the nature of a given relationship, the defining attributes of a concept) is presented rather than discovered, the extent of the discovery activity involved is limited to that required in integrating the new material into existing cognitive structure. This is naturally of a qualitatively different order than that involved in independent dis-

[2] By "cognitive structure" is simply meant a given individual's organization of knowledge.

covery. Theoretically also discovery could be reduced to practically zero in meaningful reception learning if the presented material were appropriately programmed to fit each learner's experiential background and level of readiness.

An obvious corollary of the distinction between reception and discovery learning is that in the former instance repeated encounters with the learning material (apart from some possible changes in degree and precision of meaning) primarily increase the future availability of the material (i.e., the degree and duration of retention), whereas in the latter instance this same repetition gives rise to successive stages in a discovery process. Thus, the distinction between learning and forgetting is not nearly as great in reception as in discovery learning. Forgetting (i.e., a loss of availability) in reception learning merely constitutes a subsequent negative aspect of an original learning process which in essence required the learner to do little more than internalize and make material more available. In discovery learning, however, the later decrease in availability (forgetting) although also constituting a negative aspect of that terminal phase of the learning process during which availability is established and enhanced, has little in common with the prior and more distinctive phase of discovery.

It should be clear up to this point that reception and discovery learning are two quite different kinds of processes, and that much ideational material (e.g., concepts and generalizations) can be internalized and made available without prior independent discovery in the broader sense of the term. In the next section it will be shown that such generic verbal material may not only be meaningful without prior discovery (or nonverbal) experience, but may also be transferable and applicable to the solution of particular problems.

ROTE AND MEANINGFUL LEARNING

The distinction between rote and meaningful learning is frequently confused with the reception-discovery distinction discussed above. This confusion is partly responsible for the widespread but unwarranted belief that reception learning is invariably rote and that discovery learning is invariably meaningful. Actually, each distinction constitutes an entirely independent dimension of learning. Hence, both reception and discovery learning can each be rote or meaningful depending on the conditions under which learning occurs.

By "meaningful learning" we also refer primarily to a distinctive kind of learning process, and only secondarily to a meaningful learning outcome—attainment of meaning—that necessarily reflects the completion of such a process. Meaningful learning as a process presupposes, in turn, *both* that the learner employs a meaningful learning set and that the material he learns is potentially meaningful to him. Thus, regardless of how much potential meaning may inhere in a given proposition, if the learner's intention is to memorize it verbatim, i.e., as a series of arbitrarily related words, both the learning process and the learning outcome must necessarily be rote and meaningless. And conversely, no matter how meaningful the learner's set may be, neither the process nor outcome of learning can possibly be meaningful if the learning task itself is devoid of potential meaning.

Meaningful Learning Set

In meaningful learning the learner has a set to relate substantive (as opposed to verbatim) aspects of new concepts, information or situations to relevant components of existing cognitive structure in various ways that make possible the incorporation of derivative, elaborative, descriptive, supportive, qualifying or representational relationships. Depending on the nature of the learning task (i.e., reception or discovery) the set may be either to discover or merely to apprehend and incorporate such relationships. In rote learning, on the other hand, the learner's set is to discover a solution to a problem, or to internalize material verbatim, as a discrete and isolated end in itself. Such learning obviously does not occur in a cognitive vacuum. The material *is* related to cognitive structure, but not in a substantive, nonarbitrary fashion permitting incorporation of one of the relationships specified above. Where discovery learning is involved the distinction between rote and meaningful learning corresponds to that between "trial and error" and insightful problem solving.

Potentially Meaningful Material

A meaningful set or approach to learning, as already pointed out, only eventuates in a meaningful learning process and outcome provided that the learning material (task) itself is *potentially* meaningful. Insistence on the qualifying adjective "potential" in this instance is more than mere academic hair-splitting. If the learning material were simply considered meaningful, the learning process (apprehending the meaning and making it functionally more available) would be completely superfluous; the objective of learning would obviously be already accomplished, by definition, before any learning was ever attempted and irrespective of the type of learning set employed. It is true that certain component elements of a current learning task as, for example, the individual words of a new geometrical theorem, may already be meaningful to the learner; but it is the meaning of the relational proposition as a whole which is the object of learning in this situation—not the individual meanings of its component elements. Thus, although the term "meaningful learning" necessarily implies the use of potentially meaningful learning tasks, it does not imply that the learning of meaningful as opposed to rote material is the distinctive feature of meaningful learning. Meaningful material may be perceived and reacted to meaningfully, but cannot possibly constitute a learning task in as much as the very term "meaningful" connotes that the object of learning was previously consummated.

Two important criteria determine whether new learning material is potentially meaningful. The first criterion—nonarbitrary relatability to relevant concepts in cognitive structure, in the various ways specified above—is a property of the material itself. New material is *not* potentially meaningful if either the total learning task (e.g., a particular order of nonsense syllables, a particular sequence of paired adjectives, a scrambled sentence) or the basic unit of the learning task (a particular pair of adjectives) is only relatable to such concepts on a purely arbitrary basis. This criterion of potential meaningfulness applies solely to the current learning task itself—not to any of its structural elements which may already be meaningful, such as the component letters of a nonsense syllable,[3] each member of an adjective pair, or the component words of a scrambled sentence. The presence of meaningful component words, for example, no more detracts from the lack of potential meaningfulness in the task of learning the correct sequence of jumbled words in a scrambled sentence than it adds to potential meaningfulness in the task of learning the meaning of a geometrical theorem. In both instances the meaningful components, although structurally part of the learning material, do not constitute part of the learning task in a functional sense.[4]

Arbitrariness, of course, is a relative term. It is true, for example, that most verbal symbols represent the objects and concepts to which they refer on a purely arbitrary basis. Nevertheless, since such symbols are relatable to and incorporable by their referents as representational equivalents, the association of new words with concrete images or abstract concepts in cognitive structure meets our definition of a potentially meaningful learning task. The newly established relationship of representational equivalence in cognitive structure is predicated on a much less arbitrary basis than sequential associations among a randomly arranged list of words, numbers, nonsense syllables, or paired adjectives. The type of cognitive process involved in rep-

[3] A particular nonsense syllable as a whole may also be more or less meaningful apart from its component letters in so far as it resembles and hence evokes associations with actual words. This is a type of derived meaning based on linguistic similarity.

[4] The fact that meaningful components do not constitute the object of learning or a criterion of potential meaningfulness does not mean that they have no influence whatsoever on the current learning task. It is much easier, for example, to learn arbitrary (rote) sequential associations between a series of meaningful words or relatively "meaningful" nonsense syllables than between a series of relatively "meaningless" nonsense syllables. It is also obvious that before one can learn the meaning of a geometrical theorem, one must first know the meanings of its component words. The only point that is being made here is that nonarbitrary relatability of the actual learning task to cognitive structure rather than the presence of meaningful components is the determining factor in deciding whether learning material is or is not potentially meaningful.

resentational learning is basic to the acquisition of language or of any system of symbols. In fact it is only by combining these simple representational meanings in various ways that it is possible to obtain less arbitrary relational propositions which possess greater potential meaningfulness.[5]

The second important criterion determining whether learning material is potentially meaningful—its relatability to the *particular* cognitive structure of a particular learner—is more properly a characteristic of the learner than of the material per se. Phenomenologically, meaningfulness is an individual matter. Hence for meaningful learning to occur in fact, it is not sufficient that the new material simply be relatable to relevant ideas in the abstract sense of the term. The cognitive structure of the particular learner must include the requisite intellectual capacities, ideational content, and experiential background. It is on this basis that the potential meaningfulness of learning material varies with such factors as age, intelligence, occupation, cultural membership, etc.

The concept of meaningfulness implied here (i.e., the outcome of a learning process in which the learner attempts to relate nonarbitrarily to his cognitive structure a learning task which is potentially relatable in this fashion) departs from such classical behavioristic criteria of meaningfulness as the familiarity of a word or nonsense syllable and the number of associations it evokes. These criteria are regarded as correlates of the *degree* of meaningfulness rather than as distinguishing characteristics of meaningfulness per se. The strength of the association between a representational symbol and the object or concept to which it refers (and hence the availability of the symbol and its degree of meaningfulness) are functions of the frequency and variety of contexts in which the symbol is used or encountered. A highly meaningful symbol, therefore, tends both to be subjectively more familiar and to evoke more associations than a less meaningful symbol.

[5] On the grounds of both the verbatim character of the learning task and the relative arbitrariness of the latter's relatability to cognitive structure, the learning of representational equivalents may be considered the simplest type of meaningful learning. It is intermediate in process between rote learning and the more complex types of meaningful learning.

As long as the set and content conditions of meaningful learning are satisfied, the outcome should be meaningful and the advantages of meaningful learning (economy of learning effort, more stable retention and greater transferability) should accrue irrespective of whether the content to be internalized is presented or discovered, verbal or nonverbal. It now remains to be considered to what extent the potential meaningfulness of learning material in these various forms is influenced by developmental factors.

Developmental Considerations

In the absence of prior discovery and nonverbal experience, children approximately below the age of twelve [6] tend to find directly presented verbal constructs of any complexity unrelatable to existing cognitive structure, and hence devoid of potential meaning (6, 7, 8). Until they consolidate a sufficiently large working body of key verbal concepts based on appropriate experience, and until they become capable of directly interrelating abstract propositions without reference to specific instances, children are closely restricted to basic empirical data in the kinds of logical operations they can relate to cognitive structure. Thus in performing "class inclusive and relational operations," they generally require direct experience with the actual diverse instances underlying a concept or generalization as well as proximate, nonverbal (rather than representational) contact with the objects or situations involved (5). During the

[6] The designation of age level here is solely for purposes of convenience, and is not meant to imply that the change is abrupt or that overlapping of learning processes does not occur between children in adjacent age groups. Nor does it imply that the transition is reflective of "internal ripening" and hence takes place invariably at this age. The precise age *around* which the transition occurs depends on the nature of the child's prior experience and education and on such individual differences as IQ. The only necessary assumption, therefore, is that a gradual qualitative transition in mode of learning takes place as children reach a certain level of cognitive sophistication, and that the age at which this change is most salient varies with both individual capacity and experience.

elementary school years directly presented and verbal materials are too distantly removed from empirical experience to be relatable to cognitive structure.

This does not necessarily mean, however, that actual discovery is required before meaningfulness is possible. As long as direct, nonverbal contact with the data is an integral part of the learning situation, derivative verbal concepts and generalizations may be meaningfully apprehended even though they are presented rather than discovered. But since discovery probably enhances both retention and transferability (and also constitutes in this instance a built-in test of understanding), and since the time-consuming empirical aspect of the learning must take place anyway, it is usually preferable in these circumstances to encourage pupils independently to complete the final step of drawing inferences from data.

Beginning in the junior high school period, however, and becoming increasingly more true thereafter, prior empirical and nonverbal experience is no longer essential before concepts and generalizations become potentially meaningful. It is true, of course, that the pupil's established verbal concepts must have been preceded sometime in the past by direct, nonverbal experience with the data from which they were abstracted; but once these concepts are sufficiently well consolidated and the pupil is able to manipulate and interrelate them adequately on a purely abstract basis, new learning material is logically relatable to cognitive structure without any direct or nonverbal *current* reference to empirical data. The adolescent, unlike the typical elementary school child is capable of performing logical operations on verbal propositions (5). His concepts and generalizations, therefore, tend more to be second-order constructs derived from relationships between previously established verbal abstractions already one step removed from the data itself (5). And since he is freed from dependence on direct, nonverbal contact with data in independently discovering meaningful new concepts and generalizations, he is obviously also liberated from this same dependence in the much less rigorous task of merely apprehending these constructs meaningfully when they are verbally presented to him.

Reception versus Discovery Learning in Classroom Instruction

Formal education has two principal objectives with respect to the cognitive development of the individual: (a) the long-term acquisition and retention of stable, organized, and extensive bodies of meaningful, generalizable knowledge, and (b) growth in the ability to use this knowledge in the solution of particular problems, including those problems which, when solved, augment the learner's original store of knowledge. These objectives, therefore, although related and mutually supportive, do not overlap completely. In the first place, quite apart from its usefulness in problem-solving, the acquisition of knowledge is a legitimate objective in its own right. Second, the goal of most kinds and instances of problem-solving activity is to facilitate everyday living and decision-making—not to discover knowledge that is of sufficient general significance to merit permanent incorporation into cognitive structure. The inductive derivation of concepts and generalizations from diverse instances is an exception to this statement, but is only a conspicuous feature of concept attainment during childhood (before a really large quantity of subject matter is incorporated). For the most part, in the formal education of the individual, the educating agency merely transmits ready-made concepts, categorical schemata and relational propositions.

Many educators contend, however, that the use of problem-solving techniques beyond the elementary school years should neither be limited to the application of knowledge to particular problems of transitory significance, nor constitute the exclusive methodological prerogative of scientists and scholars engaged in pushing forward the frontiers of knowledge. They maintain that these techniques should be used generally, in preference to verbal reception learning, in acquiring the substantive *content* of subject-matter—in much the same manner as the method of inductive derivation of concepts and generalizations during childhood. Their reasoning is essentially based on the following premises: (a) that abstract propositions are forms of glib verbalism unless the learner constructs them directly out of his own nonverbal, empirical experience (1, p.112); that "generalizations are products of problem-solving . . . and are attainable in no other way" (1, p. 119); and (b) that discovery methods enhance the learning, retention, and transferability of principles.

It has already been shown, however, that although the first premise (apart from the gratuitous assumption about the indispensability of independent problem-solving for generalization) is warranted during the elementary school years, it does not validly apply to learning that takes place during and after adolescence. Students do not independently have to solve the intellectual problems they perceive in the content of learning materials in order for the solutions to have meaning and transferability for them. The deference to authority implied in accepting already discovered relationships has been condemned out of all reason. If students were required independently to validate every proposition presented by their instructors before accepting it, they would never progress beyond the rudiments of any discipline. We can only ask that established knowledge be presented to them as rationally and non-arbitrarily as possible, and that they accept it tentatively and critically as only the best available approximation of the "truth".

The second premise regarding the superior learning, retention, and transferability of material learned by the discovery method needs to be examined more closely. Although experimental findings tend to be inconclusive because of the confounding of variables (e.g., failure to hold constant the rote-meaningful and the inductive-deductive dimensions while varying the reception-discovery factor), it is plausible to suppose that the greater effort and vividness associated with independent discovery lead to somewhat greater learning and retention. One might expect the advantages conferred by discovery techniques to be even greater with respect to transferability, since the experience gained in formulating a generalization from diverse instances, for example, obviously facilitates the solution of problems involving this generalization. None of these advantages, however, seems sufficiently impressive to compensate for the unalterable fact that empirical problem-solving methods of instruction are incomparably more time-consuming than the method of verbal presentation. Problem-solving, manipulative, nonverbal, and inductive procedures undoubtedly have their place in promoting and reinforcing particular understandings that are difficult to grasp on a purely verbal basis (especially in fields such as mathematics with its own distinctive language), and in testing for the meaningfulness of verbal reception learning. Feasibility as a *primary* technique for transmitting the substantive content of an intellectual or scientific discipline, however, is quite another matter.

The development of problem-solving ability is, of course, a legitimate and significant educational objective in its own right. Hence it is highly defensible to utilize a certain proportion of classroom time in developing appreciation of and facility in the use of scientific methods of inquiry and of other empirical, inductive and deductive problem-solving procedures. But this is a far cry from advocating (a) that the presentation of scientific and other subject-matter should be organized in whole or part along the lines of inductive discovery, and should require nonverbal understanding and application of principles before the latter are introduced verbally (3, 4); and (b) that the enhancement of problem-solving ability is the major function of the school. To acquire facility in problem-solving and scientific method it is not necessary for learners to rediscover every principle in the syllabus. Since problem-solving ability, is itself transferable, at least within a given subject-matter field, facility gained in independently formulating and applying one generalization is transferable to other problem areas in the same discipline. Furthermore, overemphasis on developing problem-solving ability would ultimately defeat its own ends. It would leave students with insufficient time in which to learn the content of a discipline; and hence, despite their adeptness at problem-solving, they would be unable to solve simple problems involving the application of such content.

Aptitude in problem-solving also involves a much different pattern of abilities than those required for understanding and retaining abstract ideas. The ability to solve problems calls for qualities (e.g., flexibility, resourcefulness, improvising skill, originality, problem sensitivity, venturesomeness) that are less generously distributed in the population of learners than the ability to comprehend verbally presented materials. Many of these qualities also cannot be taught effectively. Although appropriate pedagogic procedures can improve problem-solving ability, relatively few good problem-solvers can be trained in comparison with the number of persons who can acquire a meaningful grasp of various subject-matter fields. Thus, to ignore the latter individuals and concentrate solely on producing talented problem-solvers would be educationally indefensible. Because of the different pattern of abilities involved, we also cannot assume that the learner who is unable to solve a given set of problems *necessarily* does not understand but has merely memorized the principles tested by these problems. Unfortunately, however, there is no other feasible way of testing for meaningfulness.

The method of verbal presentation does not necessarily constitute a deductive approach to instruction. For one thing it is entirely possible to follow an inductive order of presentation. But even when principles are presented first, the deductive designation is often inappropriate since much of the following material is correlative rather than supportive or illustrative in nature, and provides as much of a basis for deriving more inclusive new generalizations as for deriving subsidiary principles and solving subsidiary problems.

Misuses of the method of verbal learning are so well-known that only the following more flagrant practices need be mentioned: premature use of verbal techniques with cognitively immature pupils; arbitrary, cook book presentation of unrelated facts without any organizing or explanatory principles; failure to integrate new learning tasks with previously presented materials; and the use of evaluation procedures that merely measure ability to recognize discrete facts or to reproduce ideas in the same words or in the identical context as originally encountered. Although it is entirely proper to caution teachers against these frequent misuses of verbal learning, it is not legitimate to represent them as inherent in the method itself. An approach to instruction which on logical and psychological grounds appears appropriate and efficient should not be discarded as unworkable simply because it is subject to misuse. It would seem more reasonable to guard against the more common misapplications, and to relate the method to relevant theoretical principles and research findings that actually deal with long-term learning and retention of large bodies of meaningful, verbally presented materials. The latter research, of course, still remains to be conducted. But until it is, the efficient programming of verbal learning is impossible, and devices such as "teaching machines" can do no better than present automatically, with somewhat more immediate reinforcement, the same materials currently presented by teachers.

Summary and Conclusions

Much of the opprobrium currently attached to verbal learning stems from failure to distinguish between "reception" and "discovery" learning and to appreciate the underlying basis of meaningfulness. It is widely accepted, for example, that verbal learning is invariably rote (glib verbalism) unless preceded by recent nonverbal problem-solving experience.

Most classroom instruction is organized along the lines of reception learning. Independent discovery of what is to be learned is not required: the content of the learning task is typically presented, and only has to be internalized and made available (functionally reproducible) for future use. This learning is meaningful provided that the learner has a set to relate the learning material to cognitive structure, and that the material is in fact logically (non-arbitrarily) relatable thereto. Only approximately before the age of twelve is direct empirical and nonverbal contact with data necessary for relatability to cognitive structure (i.e., for potential meaningfulness). At no stage does the learner have to discover principles independently in order to be able to understand and use them meaningfully.

Thus, after the elementary school years, verbal reception learning constitutes the most efficient method of meaningfully assimilating the substantive content of a discipline. Problem-solving methods are too time-consuming to accomplish this objective efficiently, but are useful for communicating certain insights and for measuring the meaningfulness of reception learning. The promotion of problem-solving ability, however, is a legitimate educational objective in its own right as long as it is not overemphasized.

The method of verbal reception learning will be restored to its rightful place in classroom instruction only when it is related to relevant but still-to-be-conducted research on the nature and conditions of long-term meaningful learning of large bodies of verbally presented material.

References

1 Brownell, W. A., and G. Hendrickson. How children learn information, concepts and generalizations. In *Learning and instruction. Yearb. Nat. Soc. Stud. Educ.*, 1950, *49*, Part I, pp. 92–128.

2 Brownell, W. A. and V. M. Sims. The nature of understanding. In *The Measurement of understanding. Yearb. Nat. Soc. Stud. Educ.*, 1946, *45*, Part I, pp. 27–43.

3 Easley, J. A., Jr. Is the teaching of scientific method a significant educational objective? In I. Scheffler (Ed.), *Philosophy and Education.* (Boston: Allyn & Bacon, 1958).

4 ——, The Physical Science Study Committee and educational theory. *Harvard Educ. Rev.*, 1959, *29*, pp. 4–11.

5 Inhelder, Bärbel, and J. Piaget. *The growth of logical thinking from childhood to adolescence.* (New York: Basic Books, 1958).

6 Piaget, J. *The psychology of intelligence.* (New York: Harcourt, Brace, 1950).

7 ——, *The construction of reality in the child.* (New York: Basic Books, 1954).

8 Serra, M. C. A study of fourth grade children's comprehension of certain verbal abstractions. *J. exper. Educ.*, 1953, *22*, pp. 103–118.

19 Some Psychological and Educational Limitations of Learning by Discovery*

David P. Ausubel

Learning by discovery has its proper place among the repertoire of accepted techniques available to teachers. For certain purposes and under certain conditions it has a defensible rationale and undoubted advantages. Hence the issue is not whether it should or should not be used in the classroom, but rather for what purposes and under what conditions. As in the case of many other pedagogic devices, however, some of its proponents have tended to elevate it into a panacea. Thus, because many educators are tempted unwarrantedly to extrapolate the advantages of this technique to all age levels, to all levels of subject-matter sophistication, to all kinds of educational

* *Reprinted from the article of the same title,* The Arithmetic Teacher, *1964,* **11,** *290–302. By permission of the author and* The Arithmetic Teacher.

objectives, and to all kinds of learning tasks, it is important to consider its psychological and educational limitations. What doesn't learning by discovery do? What kinds of objectives can't we hope to accomplish by using it? When isn't its use appropriate or feasible? For what age levels or levels of sophistication isn't it suitable?

Problem-solving Is Not Necessarily Meaningful

The first psychological qualification I wish to propose disputes the widely accepted twin beliefs that, by definition, all problem-solving and laboratory experience is *inherently* and *necessarily* meaningful, and all expository verbal learning consists of rotely memorized glib verbalisms. Both assumptions, of course, are related to the long-standing doctrine that the only knowledge one *really* possesses and understands is knowledge that one discovers by oneself. A much more defensible proposition, I think, is that *both* expository *and* problem-solving techniques can be either rote *or* meaningful depending on the conditions under which learning occurs. In both instances meaningful learning takes place if the learning task can be related in nonarbitrary, substantive fashion to what the learner already knows, and if the learner adopts a corresponding learning set to do so.

It is true that by these criteria much potentially meaningful knowledge taught by verbal exposition results in rotely learned verbalisms. However, this rote outcome is not inherent in the expository method per se, but rather in such abuses of this method as fail to satisfy the criteria of meaningfulness. Some of the more commonly practiced and flagrantly inept of these abuses include "premature use of verbal techniques with cognitively immature pupils; arbitrary presentation of unrelated facts without any organizing or explanatory principles; failure to integrate new learning tasks with previously presented materials; and the use of evaluation procedures that merely measure ability to recognize discrete facts and to reproduce ideas in the same words or in the identical context as originally encountered."[1, pp. 23-24.]

Actually, a moment's reflection should convince anyone that most of what he *really* knows and meaningfully understands, consists of insights discovered by *others* which have been communicated to him in meaningful fashion.

Quite apart from its lack of face validity, the proposition that every man must discover for himself every bit of knowledge that he really wishes to possess is, in essence, a repudiation of the very concept of culture. For perhaps the most unique attribute of human culture, which distinguishes it from every other kind of social organization in the animal kingdom, is precisely the fact that the accumulated discoveries of millennia can be transmitted to each succeeding generation in the course of childhood and youth, and need not be discovered anew by each generation. This miracle of culture is made possible only because it is so much less time-consuming to communicate and explain an idea meaningfully to others than to require them to re-discover it by themselves.

There is much greater reluctance, on the other hand, to acknowledge that the aforementioned preconditions for meaningfulness also apply to problem-solving and laboratory methods. It should seem rather self-evident that performing laboratory experiments in cookbook fashion, without understanding the underlying substantive and methodological principles involved, confers precious little meaningful understanding, and that many students studying mathematics and science find it relatively simple to discover correct answers to problems without really understanding what they are doing. They accomplish the latter feat merely by rotely memorizing "type problems" and procedures for manipulating symbols. Nevertheless it is still not generally appreciated that laboratory work and problem-solving are not genuinely meaningful experiences unless they are built on a foundation of clearly understood concepts and principles, and unless the constituent operations are themselves meaningful.

Two related strands of the Progressive Education movement—emphasis on the child's direct experience and spontaneous interests, and insistence on autonomously achieved insight free of all directive manipulation of the learning environment—set the stage for the subsequent deification of problem-solving, laboratory work, and naïve emulation of the scientific method. Many mathematics and science teachers were rendered self-conscious about systematically presenting and explaining to their students the basic concepts and principles of their fields, because it was held that this procedure would promote glib verbalism and rote memorization. It was felt that if students worked enough problems and were kept busy pouring reagents into a sufficient number of test tubes, they would somehow spontaneously discover in a meaningful way all of the important concepts and generalizations they needed to know in the fields they were studying.

Of course, one had to take pains to discourage students from rotely memorizing formulas, and then mechanically substituting for the general terms in these formulas the particular values of specified variables in given problems. This would naturally be no less rote than formal didactic exposition. Hence, in accordance with the new emphasis on "meaningful" problem-solving, students ceased memorizing formulas, memorizing instead type problems. They learned how to work exemplars of all of the kinds of problems they were responsible for, and then rotely memorized both the form of each type and its solution. Thus equipped, it was comparatively easy to sort the problems with which they were confronted into their respective categories, and "spontaneously proceed to discover meaningful solutions"—provided, of course, that the teacher played fair and presented recognizable exemplars of the various types.

Similarly, as the terms "laboratory" and "scientific method" became sacrosanct in American high schools and universities, students were coerced into mimicking the externally conspicuous but inherently trivial aspects of scientific method. They wasted many valuable hours collecting empirical data which, at the very worst, belabored the obvious, and at the very best, helped them re-discover or exemplify principles which the teacher could have presented verbally and demonstrated visually in a matter of minutes. Actually, they learned precious little subject matter and even less scientific method from this procedure. The unsophisticated scientific mind is only confused by the natural complexities of raw, unsystematized empirical data, and learns much more from schematic models and diagrams; and following laboratory manuals in cookbook fashion, without adequate knowledge of the relevant methodological and substantive principles involved, confers about as much genuine appreciation of scientific method as putting on a white "lab" coat and doing a TV commercial for "Roll-Aids."

Partly as a result of the superstitious faith of educators in the magical efficacy of problem-solving and laboratory methods, we have produced in the past four decades millions of high school and college graduates who *never* had the foggiest notion of the meaning of a variable, of a function, of an exponent, of calculus, of molecular structure, or of electricity, but who have done all of the prescribed laboratory work, and have successfully solved an acceptable percentage of the required problems in differential and integral calculus, in logarithms, in molar and normal solutions, and in Ohm's Law. It is not at all uncommon, for example, to find students who have successfully completed a problem-solving course in plane geometry who believe that the descriptive adjective "plane" identifies the course as "ordinary" or "not fancy" rather than dealing with two-dimensional figures.

One basic lesson that some modern proponents of the discovery method have drawn from the educational disaster is that problem-solving per se is not conducive to meaningful discovery. Problem-solving can be just as deadening, just as formalistic, just as mechanical, just as passive, and just as rote as the worst form of verbal exposition. The type of learning outcomes that emerges is largely a function of the substance, the organization, and the spirit of the problem-solving experiences one provides. However, an equally important lesson which these same proponents of the discovery method refuse to draw, is that because of the educational logistics involved, even the best program of problem-solving experience is no substitute for a minimally necessary amount of appropriate didactic exposition. But this minimum will never be made available as long as we adhere to the standard university formula of devoting one hour of exposition to every four hours of laboratory work and paper-and-pencil problem-solving.

Developmental Limitations

A second psychological limitation of the discovery method is that on developmental grounds this technique is generally unnecessary and inappropriate for teaching subject-matter content, except when pupils are in the concrete stage of cognitive development. During the concrete stage, roughly covering the elementary-school period, children are restricted by their dependence on concrete-empirical experience to a semi-abstract, intuitive understanding of abstract propositions. Furthermore, even during these years, the act of discovery is not indispensable for intuitive understanding, and need not constitute a routine part of pedagogic technique. The only essential condition for learning relational concepts during this period is the ready availability of concrete-empirical experience. Thus, for teaching simple and relatively familiar new ideas, either verbal exposition accompanied by concrete-empirical props, or a semi-autonomous type of discovery, accelerated by the judicious use of prompts and hints, is adequate enough. When the new ideas to be learned are more difficult and unfamiliar, however, it is quite conceivable that autonomous, inductive discovery enhances intuitive understanding. It presumably does this by bringing the student into more intimate contact both with the necessary concrete experience and with the actual operations of abstracting and generalizing from empirical data.

During the abstract stage of cognitive development, however, the psychological rationale for using discovery methods to teach subject-matter content is highly questionable. Students now form most new concepts and learn most new propositions by directly grasping higher-order relationships between abstractions. To do so meaningfully, they need no longer depend on current or recently prior concrete-empirical experience, and hence are able to by-pass completely the intuitive type of understanding reflective of such dependence. Through proper expository teaching they can proceed directly to a level of abstract understanding that is qualitatively superior to the intuitive level in terms of generality, clarity, precision, and explicitness. At this stage of development, therefore, it seems pointless to enhance intuitive understanding by using discovery techniques.

It is true, of course, that secondary-school and older students can also profit sometimes from the use of concrete-empirical props and from discovery techniques in learning subject-matter content on an intuitive basis. This is so because even generally mature students still tend to function at a relatively concrete level when confronted with a new subject-matter area in which they are as yet totally unsophisticated. But since abstract cognitive functioning in this new area is rapidly achieved with the attainment of a minimal degree of subject-matter sophistication, this approach to the teaching of course content need only be employed in the early stages of instruction.

Even when discovery techniques are helpful in teaching subject-matter content, we must realize that they involve a "contrived" type of discovery that is a far cry from the truly autonomous discovery activities of the research scholar and scientist. As a matter of fact, *pure* discovery techniques, as employed by scholars and scientists, could lead only to utter chaos in the classroom. Put a young physics student into a bathtub, and he is just as likely to concentrate on the soap bubbles and on the refraction of light as on the displacement principle that he is supposed to discover. In the UICSM* program, therefore, students are given a prearranged sequence of suitable exemplars, and from these they "spontaneously self-discover" the appropriate generalization. Under these conditions pupils are engaging in "true," autonomous discovery in the same sense that a detective independently "solves" a crime after a benevolent Providence kindly gathers together all of the clues and arranges them in the correct sequence.

Nevertheless, if we wish to be pedagogically realistic about discovery techniques, we must concede in advance that before students can "discover" concepts and generalizations reasonably efficiently, problems must be structured for them, and the necessary data and available procedures must be skillfully "arranged" by others, that is, simplified, selectively schematized, and sequentially organized in such a way as to make ultimate

* University of Illinois Committee on School Mathematics.

discovery almost inevitable. No research scholar or scientist has it quite this easy.

Subverbal Awareness and Discovery

In attempting to provide a sophisticated and systematic pedagogic rationale for the discovery method, Gertrude Hendrix has placed much emphasis on the importance of subverbal awareness. According to her, the achievement of subverbal awareness constitutes the essence of understanding, insight, transfer, and generalization, as well as the basic element of the discovery process; verbalization, on the other hand, is necessary only for the labeling and communication of subverbally achieved insights. Hendrix (1961) denies that verbal

> generalizing is the primary generator of transfer power. . . . As far as transfer power [is] concerned the whole thing [is] there as soon as the nonverbal awareness [dawns]. . . . The separation of discovery phenomena from the process of composing sentences which express those discoveries is the big new breakthrough in pedagogical theory [7, pp. 292, 290].

The "key to transfer," Hendrix [5, p. 200] states, is a "subverbal internal process—something which must happen to the organism before it has any knowledge to verbalize." Verbalization, she asserts further, is not only unnecessary for the generation and transfer of ideas and understanding, but is also positively harmful when used for these purposes. Language only enters the picture because of the need to attach a symbol or label to the emerging subverbal insight so that it can be recorded, verified, classified, and communicated to others; but the entire substance of the idea inheres in the subverbal insight itself. The resulting problem then, according to Hendrix [7, p. 292], becomes one of how to plan and execute teaching so that language can be used for these necessary secondary functions "*without* damage to the dynamic quality of the learning itself."

How plausible is this proposition? Let us grant at the outset that a subverbal type of awareness or insight exists, and that this type of insight is displayed by rats, monkeys, and chimpanzees in experimental learning situations, and by household pets, saddle horses, barnyard animals, wild beasts, children, and adults in a wide variety of everyday problem-solving situations. But is it because of this type of insight that human beings have evolved a culture, and have achieved some progress in such fields as philosophy, chemistry, physics, biology, and mathematics, quite beyond anything yet approached by horses, chickens, or apes? Or is it because of the qualitatively superior transfer power of verbal or symbolic generalization?

The principal fallacy in Gertrude Hendrix's line of argument, in my opinion, lies in her failure to distinguish between the labeling and process functions of language in thought. She writes:

> We have been a long time realizing that subverbal awareness of a class, or a property, or a relation had to be in *some*one's mind before anyone could have thought of inventing a word for it anyway. In the natural order of events, the abstraction forms first, and *then* a name for it is invented [6, p. 335].

Now what Hendrix is referring to here is simply the labeling or naming function of language in thought. The choice of a particular arbitrary symbol to represent a *new* abstraction obviously comes *after* the *process* of abstraction, and is not organically related to it. But this is not the *only* role of language in the abstraction process, nor is it the *first* time that it is used in this process. Verbalization, I submit, does more than verbally gild the lily of subverbal insight; it does more than just attach a symbolic handle to an idea so that one can record, verify, classify, and communicate it more readily. It constitutes, rather, an integral part of the very process of abstraction itself. When an individual uses language to express an idea, he is not merely encoding subverbal insight into words. On the contrary, he is engaged in a process of generating a higher level of insight that transcends by far—in clarity, precision, generality and inclusiveness—the previously achieved stage of subverbal awareness.

The old philosophical notion that words merely mirror thought or clothe it in outer garments, is charmingly poetic but has little functional utility or explanatory value in the modern science of psycholinguistics. Even the seemingly simple act of making a choice of words in developing an idea, involves complex processes of categorization, differentiation, abstraction and generalization; the rejection of alternative possibilities; and the exclusion of less precise or over-inclusive meanings. All of these processes contribute to and help account for the qualitatively superior transfer power of symbolic generalization.

Although the transfer power of symbolic generalization operates at many different levels of complexity and sophistication, even the simplest level transcends the kind of transfer that can be achieved with subverbal insight. Consider, for example, the transfer power of the word "house," which most preschool children can use correctly. Obviously, before the child ever uses this word, he has some unverbalized notion of what a house is. But I submit that once he attains and can meaningfully use the verbal concept of "house," he possesses an emergent new idea that he never possessed before—an idea that is sharper, clearer, more precise, more inclusive, more transferable, and more manipulable for purposes of thinking and comprehension than its crude subverbal precursor. He can now talk about the idea of "house" in the abstract, devoid of all particularity, and can combine this idea with concepts of form, size, color, number, function, etc., to formulate relational propositions that could hitherto be formulated with only the greatest difficulty. That verbal concepts of this nature are more transferable and more manipulable than subverbal insights, is demonstrated by numerous experiments on the effects of verbalization on children's ability to solve transposition problems. Knowledge of underlying verbal principles also enhances the learning of relevant motor performance; and the availability of distinctive verbal responses facilitates rather than inhibits concept formation and conceptual transfer.

Not all ideas, however, are acquired quite as easily as the concept of house. As he enters school the child encounters other concepts of much greater abstractness and complexity, e.g., concepts of addition, multiplication, government, society, force, velocity, digestion, that transcend his immediate experience and language ability. Before he can hope to acquire a meaningful grasp of such abstractions directly, that is, through direct verbal exposition, he must first acquire a minimal level of sophistication in the particular subject-matter area, as well as graduate into the next higher level of intellectual development, i.e., the stage of formal logical operations. In the meantime he is limited to an intuitive, subverbal kind of understanding of these concepts; and even though convincing empirical evidence is still lacking, it is reasonable to suppose that preliminary acquisition and utilization of this subverbal level of insight both facilitates learning and transferability, and promotes the eventual emergence of *full* verbal understanding. (Gertrude Hendrix, of course, would say that *full* understanding was already attained in the subverbal phase, and that verbalization merely attaches words to sub-verbal insight.)

Now, assuming for the moment that Hendrix' experimental findings are valid, how can we explain the fact that immediate verbalization of newly acquired subverbal insight renders that insight less transferable than when verbalization is not attempted [5]? First, it seems likely that verbalization of nonverbal insight, before such insight is adequately consolidated by extensive use, may interfere with consolidation at this level, as well as encourage rote memorization of the ineptly stated verbal proposition. Even more important, however, is the likelihood that a verbally expressed idea—when ambiguous, unprecise, ineptly formulated, and only marginally competent—possesses less functional utility and transferability than the ordinarily more primitive and less transferable subverbal insight. This is particularly true in the case of children, because of their limited linguistic facility and their relative incompetence in formal propositional logic.

Drawing these various strands of argument together, what can we legitimately conclude at this point? First, verbalization does more than just encode subverbal insight into words. It is part of the very process of thought which makes possible a qualitatively higher level of understanding with greatly enhanced transfer power. Second, direct acquisition of ideas from verbally presented propositions, presupposes both that the learner has attained the stage of formal logical operations, and that he possesses minimal sophistication in the particular subject matter in question. The typical elementary-school child, therefore, tends to be limited to an intuitive, subverbal awareness of difficult abstractions. The older, cognitively mature individual, however, who is also unsophisticated in a particular subject-matter area, is able to dispense with the subverbal phase of awareness rather quickly, i.e., as soon as he attains the necessary degree of sophistication; and once he attains it, he probably short-circuits the subverbal phase completely. Lastly, immediate verbalization of a nonverbal insight, when this latter insight is newly acquired and inadequately consolidated, probably decreases its transferability. This phenomenon can be explained by means of the general developmental principle, that an ordinarily higher and more efficient stake of development, while still embryonic and only marginally competent, is less functional than an ordinarily more primitive and less efficient phase of development. Running, for example, is eventually more efficient than creeping, but if a one-year-old infant had to run for his life, he would make better progress creeping.

Gertrude Hendrix, however, comes out with somewhat different and more sweeping conclusions from the same set of data. First, she regards non-verbal awareness as containing within itself the entire essence of an emerging idea, and insists that language merely adds a convenient symbolic handle to this idea. Second, she generalizes children's dependence on a preliminary subverbal stage of awareness, to all age levels, to all degrees of subject-matter sophistication, and to all levels of ideational difficulty. Actually, this subverbal stage is highly abbreviated, both for young children learning less difficult kinds of abstractions, and for older, cognitively mature individuals working in a particular subject-matter area in which they happen to be unsophisticated; and it is by-passed completely when this latter sophistication is attained. Finally, she interprets her experimental findings regarding the inhibitory effects of immediate verbalization on the transferability of subverbal insight, as providing empirical *proof* of her thesis that both the substance of an idea and the essential basis of its transfer power are present in their entirety as soon as nonverbal awareness emerges. In my opinion, these findings do nothing of the kind. They merely show that a relatively clear subverbal insight, even when only partially consolidated, is more functional and transferable than an ambiguous, inept, and marginally competent verbally expressed idea.

Unlike Gertrude Hendrix, therefore, I would conclude that secondary school and college students, who already possess a sound, meaningful grasp of the rudiments of a discipline like mathematics, can be taught this subject meaningfully and with maximal efficiency, through the method of verbal exposition, supplemented by appropriate problem-solving experience; and that the use of the discovery method in these circumstances is inordinately time-consuming, wasteful, and rarely warranted. Why then do discovery techniques seem to work so well in programs such as the one devised by the University of Illinois Committee on School Mathematics? For one thing, the students entering the program, being victims of conventional arithmetic teaching in the elementary schools, do *not* have a sound, meaningful grasp of the rudiments of mathematics, and have to be reeducated, so to speak, from scratch. For another, I have a very strong impression that as the program develops, the discovery element becomes progressively attenuated, until eventually it is accorded only token recognition. Lastly, stripped of its quite limited discovery aspects, the UICSM approach is a much more systematic, highly organized, self-consistent, carefully programmed, abstractly verbal system of verbal exposition than anything we have known to date in secondary-school mathematics. If it proves anything, the success of this program is a testimonial to the feasibility and value of a good program of didactic verbal exposition in secondary school mathematics, which program is taught by able and enthusiastic instructors, and in its early stages, makes judicious use of inductive and discovery techniques.

Time-Cost Considerations

From a practical standpoint it is impossible to consider the pedagogic feasibility of learning by discovery as a primary means of teaching subject-matter content without taking into account the inordinate time-cost involved. This disadvantage is not only applicable to the type of discovery where the learner is thrown entirely on his own resources, but also applies in lesser degree to the "contrived" or "arranged" type of discovery. Considerations of time-cost are particularly pertinent in view of our aforementioned developmental conclusions, that the discovery approach offers no indispensable learning advantages, except in the very limited case of the more difficult learning task when the learner is either in the concrete stage of cognitive development, or, if generally in the abstract stage, happens to lack minimal sophistication in a particular subject-matter field. Also, once students reach secondary school and university, the time-cost disadvantage can no longer be defended on the dual grounds that the time-consuming concrete-empirical aspects of learning must take place anyway, and that in any case elementary school pupils can't be expected to cover a great deal of subject matter. Thus, simply on a time-cost basis, if secondary-school and university students were obliged to discover for themselves every concept and principle in the syllabus, they would never get much beyond the rudiments of any discipline.

Some discovery enthusiasts (Bruner [2]; Suchman [9]) grudgingly admit that there is not sufficient time for pupils to discover everything they need to know in the various disciplines, and hence concede that there is also room for good expository teaching in the schools. In practice, however, this concession counts for little, because in the very next breath they claim the acquisition of actual knowledge is less important than the acquisition of ability to discover knowledge autonomously, and propose that pedagogy and the curriculum be reorganized accordingly. Thus, in spite of the formal bow they make to didactic exposition, it is clear that they regard the acquisition of problem-solving ability as more basic than the acquisition of subject matter. There is, after all, only so much time in a school day. If the school accepts as its principal function the development of discovery and inquiry skills, even with the best intention in the world, how much time could possibly remain for the teaching of subject-matter content?

Another disadvantage of using a discovery approach for the transmission of subject-matter content is the fact that children are notoriously subjective in their evaluation of external events, and tend to jump to conclusions, to generalize on the basis of limited experience, and to consider only one aspect of a problem at a time. These tendencies increase further the time-cost of discovery learning in the transmission of knowledge. Moreover, children tend to interpret empirical experience in the light of prevailing folklore conceptions that are at variance with modern scientific theories. Lastly, one might reasonably ask how many students are sufficiently brilliant to discover everything they need to know. Most students of average ability can acquire a meaningful grasp of the theory of evolution and gravitation, but how many students can discover these ideas autonomously?

Training in the "Heuristics of Discovery"

Some advocates of the discovery method favor a type of guided practice in the "heuristics of discovery" that is reminiscent of the faculty psychology approach to improving overall critical thinking ability through instruction in the general principles of logic. For example, once the heuristics of discovery are mastered, they constitute, according to Bruner [3, p. 31], "a style of problem-solving or inquiry that serves for any kind of task one may encounter." In fact, one of the more fashionable movements in curriculum theory today is the attempt to enhance the critical thinking ability of pupils apart from any systematic consideration of subject-matter content. An entire course of study is pursued in which pupils perform or consider an unrelated series of experiments in depth, and then concentrate solely on the inquiry process itself rather than on this process as it is related to the acquisition of an organized body of knowledge.

One principal difficulty with this approach, apart from the fact that it fails to promote the orderly, sequential growth of knowledge is that critical thinking ability can only be enhanced within the context of a specific discipline. Grand strategies of discovery do not seem to be transferable across disciplinary lines—either when acquired within a given discipline, or when learned in a more general form apart from specific subject-matter content. This principle has been confirmed by countless studies, and is illustrated by the laughable errors of logic and judgment committed by distinguished scientists and scholars who wander outside their own disciplines. From a purely theoretical standpoint alone, it hardly seems plausible that a strategy of inquiry, which must necessarily be broad enough to be applicable to a wide range of disciplines and problems, can ever have, at the same time, sufficient particular relevance to be helpful in the solution of the specific problem at hand.

A second significant difficulty with this approach is that its proponents tend to confuse the goals of the scientist with the goals of the science student. They assert that these objectives are identical, and hence that students can learn science most effectively by enacting the role of junior scientist. The underlying rationale is that all intellectual activity regardless of level is of one piece, and that both creative scientists and elementary-school children rely heavily on intuitive thinking. Bruner [2, p. 14] is an eloquent spokesman for this point of view. According to him,

> . . . intellectual activity anywhere is the same, whether at the frontier of knowledge or in a third-grade classroom. . . . The difference is in degree, not in kind. The school-boy learning physics *is* a physicist, and it is easier for him to learn physics behaving like a physicist than doing something else.

It is also proposed that the ultimate goal of the Inquiry Training Program is for children to discover and formulate explanations which strive for the same universality and unification of concepts achieved by scientists (Suchman [9]).

First, I cannot agree that the goals of the research scientist and of the science student are identical. The scientist is engaged in a full-time search for new general or applied principles in his field. The student, on the other hand, is primarily engaged in an effort to learn the same basic subject matter in this field which the scientist had learned in his student days, and also to learn something of the method and spirit of scientific inquiry. Thus, while it makes perfectly good sense for the scientists to work full-time formulating and testing new hypotheses, it is quite indefensible, in my opinion, for the student to be doing the same thing—either for real, or in the sense of rediscovery. Most of the student's time should be taken up with appropriate expository learning, and the remainder devoted to sampling the flavor and techniques of scientific method. It is the scientist's business to formulate unifying explanatory principles in science. It is the student's business to learn these principles as meaningfully and critically as possible, and *then*, after his background is adequate, to try to improve on them if he can. If he is ever to discover, he must first learn; and he cannot learn adequately by pretending he is a junior scientist.

Second, there is, in my opinion, a world of difference between the intuitive thinking of elementary-school children and the intuitive thinking of scholars and scientists. The elementary school child thinks intuitively or subverbally about many complex, abstract problems, not because he is creative, but because this is the *best he can do* at his particular stage of intellectual development. The intuitive thinking of scientists, on the other hand, consists of tentative and roughly formulated "hunches" which are merely preparatory to more rigorous thought. Furthermore, although the hunches themselves are only make-shift approximations which are not very precisely stated, they presuppose both a high level of abstract verbal ability, as well as sophisticated knowledge of a particular discipline.

Development of Problem-solving Ability as the Primary Goal of Education

In the realm of educational theory, if not in actual practice, exaggerated emphasis on problem-solving still continues to disturb the natural balance between the "transmission of the culture" and the problem-solving objectives of education. Enthusiastic proponents of the discovery method (e.g., Suchman [9]) still assert that

> more basic than the attainment of concepts is the ability to inquire and discover them autonomously. . . . The schools must have a new pedagogy with a new set of goals which subordinates retention to thinking. . . . Instead of devoting their efforts to storing information and recalling it on demand, they would be developing cognitive functions needed to seek out and organize information in a way that would be most productive of new concepts.

The development of problem-solving ability, is of course, a legitimate and significant educational objective in its own right. Hence it is highly defensible to utilize a certain proportion of classroom time in developing appreciation of and facility in the use of scientific methods of inquiry and of other empirical, inductive, and deductive problem-solving precedures. But this is a far cry from advocating that the enhancement of problem-solving ability is the *major* function of the school. To acquire facility in problem-solving and scientific method it is also unnecessary for learners to rediscover *every* principle in the syllabus. Since problem-solving ability is itself transferable, at least within a given subject-matter field, facility gained in independently formulating and applying one generalization is transferable to other problem areas in the same discipline. Furthermore, overemphasis on developing problem-solving ability would ultimately defeat its own ends. Because of its time-consuming proclivities, it would leave students with insufficient time in which to learn the content of a discipline; and hence, despite their adeptness at problem-solving they would be unable to solve simple problems involving the application of such content.

Discovery as a Unique Generator of Motivation and Self-confidence

Bruner [3, 4] and other discovery enthusiasts (Hendrix [7]; Suchman [9] perceive learning by discovery as a unique and unexcelled generator of self-confidence, of intellectual excitement, and of motivation for sustained problem-solving and creative thinking. It is undeniable that discovery techniques are valuable for acquiring desirable attitudes toward inquiry, as well as firm convictions about the existence and discoverability of orderliness in the universe. It is also reasonable to suppose that successful discovery experience enhances both these attitudes and convictions, and the individual's feeling of confidence in his own abilities. On the other hand, there is no reason to believe that discovery methods are unique or alone in their ability to effect these outcomes.

As every student who has been exposed to competent teaching knows, the skillful exposition of ideas can also generate considerable intellectual excitement and motivation for genuine inquiry, although admittedly not quite as much perhaps as discovery. Few physics students who learn the principle of displacement through didactic exposition will run half-naked through the streets shrieking, "Eureka." But then again, how many students of Archimedes' ability are enrolled in the typical physics or mathematics class? How comparable to the excitement of Archimedes' purely autonomous and original discovery, is the excitement generated by discovering a general formula for finding the number of diagonals in an *n*-sided polygon, after working problems one through nine in the textbook? And what happens to Archimedes Junior's motivation and self-confidence if, after seventeen immersions in the tub, he had merely succeeded in getting himself soaking wet?

Research Evidence

Despite their frequent espousal of discovery principles, the various curriculum reform projects have failed thus far to yield any research evidence in support of the discovery method. This is not to say that the evidence is negative, but rather that there just isn't any evidence, one way or the other—notwithstanding the fact that these projects are often cited in the "discovery" literature under the heading, "research shows." For one thing, the sponsors of some of these projects have not been particularly concerned about *proving* the superior efficacy of their programs, since they have been thoroughly convinced of this from the outset. Hence in many instances they have not even attempted to obtain comparable achievement test data from matched control groups. And only rarely has any effort been expended to prevent the operation of the crucial "Hawthorne Effect," that is, to make sure that evidence of superior achievement outcomes is attributable to the influence of the new pedagogic techniques or materials in question, rather than to the fact that the experimental group is the recipient of *some* form of conspicuous special attention; that *some*thing new and interesting is being tried; or that the teachers involved are especially competent, dedicated, and enthusiastic, and receive special training, attend expense-free conventions and summer institutes, and are assigned lighter teaching loads.

But even if the sponsors of the curriculum reform movements were all imbued with missionary research zeal, it would still be impossible to test the discovery hypothesis within the context of curriculum research. In the first place, a large number of other significant variables are necessarily operative in such programs. The UICSM program, for example, not only relies heavily on the principle of self-discovery of generalizations, but also on an inductive approach, on nonverbal awareness, on abundant empirical experience, on careful sequential programming, and, above all, on precise, self-consistent, unambiguous, and systematic verbal formulation of basic principles. To which variable, or to which combination of these variables and the "Hawthorne Effect" should the success of this program be attributed? Personally, for reasons enumerated earlier in this paper, I would nominate the factor of precise and systematic verbal formulation rather than the discovery variable. (Students enrolled in the UICSM program learn more mathematics, in my opinion, *not* because they are required to discover generalizations *by themselves*, but because they have at their disposal a systematic body of organizing, explanatory, and integrative principles which are not part of the conventional course in secondary-school mathematics. These principles illuminate the subject for them and make it much more meaningful.)

EVERY CHILD A CREATIVE AND CRITICAL THINKER

One of the currently fashionable educational doctrines giving support to the discovery method movement, is the notion that the school can make every child a creative thinker, and help him discover discontinuously new ideas and ways of looking at things. Creativity, it is alleged, is not the exclusive property of the rare genius among us, but a tender bud that resides in some measure within every child, requiring only the gentle, catalytic influence of sensitive, imaginative teaching to coax it into glorious bloom.

This idea rests on the following questionable assumptions: that one can be creative without necessarily being original; that all discovery activity, irrespective of originality, is qualitatively of one piece—from Einstein's formulation of the theory of relativity to every infant's spontaneous discovery that objects continue to exist even when they are out of sight; that considering the multiplicity of abilities, every person stands a good chance, genically speaking, of being creative in at least one area; and that even if heredity is uncooperative, good teachers can take the place of missing genes.

Hohn's [8] use of the term "creativity" is typical of the prevailing tendency in "discovery" circles to "democratize" the meaning of this concept. A child behaves creatively in mathematics, according to Hohn, when he proposes alternative approaches, grasps concepts intuitively, or displays autonomy, flexibility, and freedom from perseverative rigidity in his discovery efforts. Now one can define words in any way one chooses, and hence can define creativity so that it means nothing more than "autonomous and flexible discovery." But if this is *all* one means, would it not save endless confusion if one used these particular words instead of a term which both connotatively and denotatively implies a rare form of originality?

As a matter of fact, the very same persons who use "creativity" in the more "democratic" sense of the term, also imply in other contexts that the encouragement of *true* creativity (that is, in the sense of original accomplishment) in *every* child, is one of the major functions of the school. This view is implicit in Bruner's [4] position that the school should help every child reach discontinuous realms of experience so that he can create his own interior culture. It is also implicit in the goal of the Inquiry Training Program, namely, that children should be trained to formulate the same kinds of unifying concepts in science which are produced by our most creative scientists (Suchman [9]).

How reasonable now is the goal of "teaching for creativity," that is, in the sense of singularly original achievement? A decent respect for the realities of the human condition would seem to indicate that the training possibilities with respect to creativity are severely limited. The school can obviously help in the realization of existing creative potentialities by providing opportunities for spontaneity, initiative, and individualized expression; by making room in the curriculum for tasks that are sufficiently challenging for pupils with creative gifts; and by rewarding creative achievement. But it cannot actualize potentialities for creativity if these potentialities do not exist in the first place. Hence it is totally unrealistic, in my opinion, to suppose that even the most ingenious kinds of teaching techniques we could devise could stimulate creative accomplishment in children of average endowment.

Even "teaching for *critical* thinking" and "teaching for problem-solving" are somewhat grandiose slogans, although obviously much more realistic than "teaching for creative thinking." To be sure, the critical thinking and problem-solving abilities of most pupils can be improved. But this is a far cry from saying that most pupils can be trained to become good critical thinkers and problem-solvers. Potentialities for developing high levels of these abilities are admittedly much less rare than corresponding potentialities for developing creativity. Nevertheless, there are no good reasons for believing that they are any commoner than potentialities for developing high general intelligence. Also, in my opinion,

> . . . aptitude in problem-solving involves a much different pattern of abilities than those required for understanding and retaining abstract ideas. The ability to solve problems calls for qualities (for example, flexibility, resourcefulness, improvising skill, originality, problem sensitivity, venturesomeness) that are less generously distributed in the population of learners than the ability to comprehend verbally presented materials. Many of these qualities also cannot be taught effectively. Although appropriate pedagogic procedures can improve problem-solving ability, relatively few good problem-solvers can be trained in comparison with the number of persons who can acquire a meaningful grasp of various subject-matter fields [1, p. 23].

From the standpoint of enlightened educational policy in a democracy, therefore, it seems to me that the school should concentrate its major efforts on teaching both what is most important in terms of cultural survival and cultural progress, and what is most teachable to the majority of its clientele. As improved methods of teaching become available, most students will be able to master the basic intellectual skills as well as a reasonable portion of the more important subject-matter content of the major disciplines. Is it not more defensible to shoot for this realistic goal, which lies within our reach, than to focus on educational objectives that presuppose exceptional endowment and are impossible of fulfillment when applied to the generality of mankind? Would it not be more realistic to strive first to have each pupil respond meaningfully, actively, and critically to good expository teaching before we endeavor to make him a good critical thinker and problem-solver?

I am by no means proposing a uniform curriculum and pedagogy for all children irrespective of individual differences. By all means let us provide all feasible special opportunities and facilities for the exceptional child. But in so doing, let us not attempt to structure the learning environment of the *non*-exceptional child in terms of educational objectives and teaching methods that are appropriate for either one child in a hundred or for one child in a million.

References

1 Ausubel, D. P. "In defense of verbal learning," *Educational Theory*, XI (1961), 15–25.

2 Bruner, J. S. *The Process of Education*. Cambridge, Massachusetts: Harvard University Press, 1960.

3 ____, "The act of discovery," *Harvard Education Review*, XXXI (1961), 21–32.

4 ____, "After Dewey what?" *Saturday Review*, June 17, 1961, pp. 58–59; 76–78.

5 Hendrix, Gertrude. "A new clue to transfer of training," *Elementary School Journal*, XLVIII (1947), 197–208.

6 ____, "Prerequisite to meaning," The Mathematics Teacher, XLIII (1960), 334–339.

7 ____, "Learning by discovery," The Mathematics Teacher, LIV (1961), 290–299.

8 Hohn, F. E. "Teaching creativity in mathematics," The Arithmetic Teacher, VIII (1961), 102–106.

9 Suchman, J. R. "Inquiry training: building skills for autonomous discovery," *Merrill-Palmer Quarterly of Behavior and Development*, VII (1961), 148–169.

20 The Effect of Incidental and Experimentally Induced Experience in the Learning of Relevant and Irrelevant Causal Relationships by Children*

David P. Ausubel
Herbert M. Schiff

Introduction

How children learn cause-and-effect relationships, and how the learning process varies with age is not only a crucial problem for learning theory and developmental psychology, but also for education and mental hygiene. It is directly implicated in the learning of school materials related to the physical, biological, and social sciences and is indirectly involved in the individual's rational understanding of his environment and in his adjustment to situations and persons within it.

* *Reprinted from the article of the same title,* Journal of Genetic Psychology, *1954,* **84,** *109–129. By permission of the authors and The Journal Press.*

Most studies in the field of causal thinking have been stimulated by a desire to add or detract support from the conclusions reached by Piaget (9) who postulated the existence of 17 different varieties of causal explanations, each supposedly characteristic of a distinct stage of development in this area. Contrary to Piaget's findings, the consensus of opinion reached by American investigators is that the same qualitative forms of causal thinking can be found among children of all ages beyond the kindergarten level; and that the differences which do prevail between age groups are differences in complexity and breadth of the cause-and-effect problems which can be successfully solved rather than in the underlying type of thinking process involved (2, 4, 5, 7).

The traditional method of investigating causal thinking in children has been naturalistic rather than experimental, that is, data are obtained from the responses given by children to questions seeking explanations of various natural phenomena. Such data are customarily secured in the course of individual interviews with children, the investigator either asking questions such as the reason for the coming of night, or performing demonstrations such as covering a lighted candle with a jar and inquiring why the light went out. Categories of causal thinking are then abstracted by content analysis by several independent judges, and the quality of the product is related as the dependent variable to such independent variables as age (2, 3, 7, 8, 9), intelligence (2, 7, 8), and school experience (2, 7, 8).

In the present study, both the objectives and the procedure are somewhat different from the traditional approach. Instead of investigating changes in the quality of causal thinking with age, we have attempted to identify some of the more important psychological processes involved in causal thinking and to study the relationships between them by means of controlled experimental methods.

We can illustrate what we mean by the component psychological processes involved in causal thinking by relating the following hypothetical story:

An African Bushman goes hunting for tigers one summer evening. As he leaves his hut he notices that there is a quarter moon in the sky. He is successful in his evening's quest. Two weeks later there is a full moon as he starts out on his evening's work, and he returns home unsuccessful. The next time he is careful to wait for a quarter moon before venturing forth; and again he accomplishes his mission. Thereupon he concludes with conviction that tigers can only be successfully hunted when there is a quarter moon in the sky.

To begin with, there is awareness of temporal contiguity, the formation of an association between two events contiguous in time. This association is reinforced by repetition, vividness (the dramatic quality of the event), primacy (the first thing he noticed), and reward (achievement of his goal). Secondly, a generalization is formed, "It seems that a quarter moon is present whenever tigers can be killed." Lastly, there is imputation of a causal relationship between the two events, moon and tiger-killing.

The crucial aspect of this latter process is a judgment regarding the relevance of the antecedent event for the consequence. Mere contiguity is insufficient since innumerable events antecede the consequence and are not taken into account causally, or even noticed. Many factors influence this judgment of relevance. In an animistic culture, for example, the notion that the size of the moon may influence a hunter's marksmanship is not incongruous with the general framework of causal thinking in relation to which a particular judgment of relevance is formed. A second important factor is the general background of experience or sophistication in a given area (6). The Bushman might be more or less naïve about what is relevant for hunting success depending on the extent of his hunting experience. It has been shown, for example, that when adults are required to provide explanations for events completely outside their sphere of competence, they tend to give answers that are remarkably similar to those of children (1, 3, 7). When non-science teachers were shown some simple demonstrations of principles in physics, "there was a marked tendency on the part of these adults to support the views [they had] once stated in the prediction or its explanation, even when these views were in conflict with the observation. There were striking instances of this reluctance to change even when the subject was looking at the phenomenon itself" (7). Deutsche (2) found marked qualitative differences in the responses of the same child to different types of questions, indicating the importance of general familiarity with the area involved for the degree of sophistication characterizing the judgment made of the relevance of a particular antecedent for a particular consequence.

Two other variables also come into play in making this judgment of relevance: (*a*) flexibility in shifting the framework of relevance when new experience is introduced; and (*b*) general logical ability. The latter in turn involves appreciation of the fact that contiguity *per se* does not imply causality, that other relevant variables must be controlled before a causal relationship between two events can be inferred, and that the difference between two successes under one condition and a failure under another condition is hardly significant.

The Problem

In this study we were particularly interested in the problem of age trends in children's judgments of relevance in cause-and-effect sequences. A problem in causal thinking was designed in which children of various ages were shown a teeter-totter which worked on one of two principles: (*a*) a relevant principle according to which that side of the teeter-totter which was longest always fell when the supporting pins were removed; and (*b*) an irrelevant principle, according to which that side on which a red block (as opposed to a green block) was placed was invariably made to fall. In each case the child after an initial demonstration was asked to predict which side would fall until learning as measured by a criterion of three successive correct predictions took place. All of the subjects were presented with both types of learning problems, half of them being presented with the problems in one order and the other half in the reverse order.

By means of this experimental design it was possible to investigate the relative influence of two different variables impinging on the issue of relevance in causal thinking: (*a*) immediate experimentally-induced learning experience; and (*b*) incidental past experience with teeter-totters and with discounting contiguity as a causal principle. It was assumed that both aspects of incidental experience would increase with age, although it was impossible to differentiate between their effects in this study.

Answers were sought to the following questions: (*a*) Do children of different age groups differ in ability to learn relevant and irrelevant causal sequences? (*b*) To what extent does either prior incidental or immediate experimentally-induced *relevant* experience protect a child from learning irrelevant causal relationships? Are there age differences in this function? (*c*) To what extent does immediate experimentally-induced *irrelevant* experience retard the learning of relevant causal sequences? Are age differences observable in the unlearning of irrelevant causal relationships?

METHOD

Population

(*a*) Sixty kindergarten children between the ages of five and six drawn from two classes—a P.T.A. sponsored kindergarten in Champaign, Illinois, and a University of Illinois sponsored kindergarten in Urbana, Illinois. The two groups were roughly comparable in terms of socio-economic status of parents. (*b*) Sixty-six third-grade children drawn from three classrooms in three different elementary schools in Bloomington, Illinois. (*c*) Sixty-six sixth-grade children from two classrooms in different schools in Bloomington, Illinois.

The Bloomington schools that were chosen are publicly supported institutions located in middle-class residential neighborhoods.

Teeter-Totter Apparatus

A small, specially constructed table model is used consisting of fulcrum, board, one weight and underpin for each end of the board, and two wooden screens. The weights are two identical wooden blocks, one painted red, the other green. The board has three notched grooves so that it can be placed on the fulcrum either in dead center, or three-quarters of an inch to the right or left of center.

For the relevant series of trials, the subject is placed two feet from the table directly in front of the teeter-totter. Each end of the board is supported by an underpin, and a block is placed on either side. The fulcrum is visible, and the child can clearly observe whether one side is longer than the other. This fact is further emphasized by the three grooves. The apparatus is put together out of sight of the subject, and he is made to turn around between trials as the settings of the board are changed.

From a preliminary pilot study it was ascertained that eight trials were sufficient for learning if learning were to take place at all; that is, no child who did not learn the task within eight trials was able to learn it no matter how many trials he was given. In the relevant series, the settings are so arranged that the side with the red or green block (the longer side) would fall in random order. In each case the longer side is plainly visible to the child. To avoid positional effects, both falling side (right or left) and color (red or green) are randomly alternated.

In the irrelevant series of trials, the fulcrum is completely obscured by two wooden screens, one placed in front, and the other in back of the fulcrum. These screens are wide enough so that even when the board is placed off center on the fulcrum, they can be adjusted to make both sides of the board projecting from the end of the screens appear equal in length, despite the fact that one side is actually an inch and one-half longer than the other. In the irrelevant series of trials, the apparatus is so manipulated that the side with the red block always falls when the underpins are removed. In order for this to happen the red block is, of course, always placed on the longer side, but from the point of view of the subject, both sides appear equal in length. The falling side (right or left) is also alternated, and a maximum of eight trials is allowed.

For each series (relevant and irrelevant) of trials the child is given an initial demonstration. In the relevant series, the experimenter states the following:

This is a teeter-totter. These blocks are the same size but one is red and one is green. When I pull out these pins one side will fall. Watch and see which side falls (*E* pulls out underpins). Now turn around (*E* makes the setting for Trial 1). All right, turn back. Which side do you think will fall when I pull the pins out this time, the side with the red block or the side with the green block? (*E* records the prediction which *S* makes and then pulls out the underpins.)

For the irrelevant series, *E* states:

Now let's try this another way [child is facing apparatus with the screens in place]. When I pull out these pins one side will fall. Watch and see which side falls (*E* pulls out underpins). Now turn around (*E* makes the setting for Trial 1). All right, turn back. Which side do you think will fall when I pull the pins out this time, the one with the red block or the one with the green block? (*E* records the prediction which *S* makes and then pulls out the underpins.)

Procedure

Each child was tested individually in a private room with only an experimenter and recorder present. In order to minimize communication between children about the experiment, an entire class was tested in either a morning or afternoon school session.

In each age group, two groups of subjects were formed. Group I was tested on the relevant series first and then on the irrelevant series. In Group II the reverse order was used. A child was considered to have learned the series if he made three successively correct predictions within the maximum of eight trials allowed. In computing the total number of trials necessary for learning, the last three correct trials were not counted in the score.

At the conclusion of both series of trials the subject was asked, "How were you able to guess which side would fall?" if he was successful; if he was unsuccessful, he was asked, "What was it that always made one side fall?"

In order to measure the "protective" effect of immediate experience with a relevant series on the learning of an irrelevant series the mean scores of Groups I and II on the irrelevant series could be compared. In order to measure the "contaminating" effect of immediate experience with an irrelevant series on the learning of a relevant series, it would be necessary to compare the mean scores of Groups I and II on the relevant series. For these purposes, however, it was necessary to equate Groups I and II. This was done as follows:

In administering the learning task, each odd-numbered child was placed in Group I and each even-numbered child in Group II. In addition, each child was given a pretest consisting of questions and demonstrations relating to the explanation of natural phenomena. On the basis of both prediction and explanation scores, individuals in Groups I and II were matched. Cases that could not be matched were discarded. Each group therefore had identical means and standard deviations.

Pretest

The pretest consisted of (*a*) four physical demonstrations requiring a prediction from the subject as to what would happen, and also an explanation in each case of what actually did happen; and (*b*) four questions regarding explanations of natural phenomena.

a. *The demonstrations*: (*a*) Here are two pieces of paper the same size. I am going to crush one into a ball and then drop both at the same time. Which one will fall to the table first? (*b*) This is a U tube. I am going to pour a little water down this end. What will happen to the water? (*c*) What will happen if I drop this stone into this full glass of water? (*d*) What will happen if I cover this lighted candle with the jar?

b. *The questions*: (*a*) Where do waves come from? (*b*) Why does night come? (*c*) Where does the wind come from? (*d*) What makes the clouds?

The maximum explanation score possible was eight and the maximum prediction score possible was four. An answer was considered correct if it provided the gist of the physical explanation on a naturalistic basis without necessarily identifying the underlying scientific principle, e.g., "The water would spill over since the stone takes up room too and there isn't room for both"

TABLE 1

Pretest Scores for the Various Age Groups

Age Group	*N*	Prediction Score Mean	Prediction Score *SD*	Explanation Score Mean	Explanation Score *SD*
Kindergarten	46	2.74	0.84	1.22	0.95
Third-grade	54	3.11	0.83	2.67	0.98
Sixth-grade	48	3.33	0.75	4.33	1.62

(demonstration three); "all the air got used up" (demonstration four).

Partial scoring on a qualitative basis was not considered necessary since the pretest was used only for equating Groups I and II and not for determining changes in the quality of causal thinking with age. Table 1 gives the pretest scores for the three grade levels. From this table it can be seen that most of the discrimination between mean scores of grade levels was provided by the explanation score rather than by the prediction score. Only the difference between the means of the kindergarten and sixth grade groups was significant for the prediction score (at 5 per cent level), whereas corresponding differences in relation to the explanation scores were all significant at the one per cent level. Sixth-graders also showed significantly greater variability ($5 > P > 1$) than the other two groups on the explanation score.

TABLE 2

Comparison of Group Variance Within Grade Levels

Grade Level	Variance Ratios
K: Groups I and II	1.63
3rd: Groups I and II	1.74
6th: Groups I and II	1.94

TABLE 3

Means and Standard Deviations by Grade Levels of Number of Trials Required by Group I to Learn Relevant Sequence

GRADE LEVEL	MEAN	*SD*
K	3.70	2.74
3	2.56	2.53
6	0.83	1.74

RESULTS

Homogeneity of Groups I and II at Each Grade-Level

To test our assumption that matching subjects on the basis of pretest scores had actually provided us with comparable groups (i.e., drawn from the same population) within each grade level, the variance ratios were computed for Groups I and II at each grade level and compared with Fisher's tables for the distribution of F. The variance ratios as presented in Table 2 are not significant at the five per cent point indicating homogeneity of population at each grade level.

Grade-Level Differences in the Learning of the Relevant Sequence

By comparing the learning performances of the three Group I's (relevant sequence presented first) on the relevant sequence at the various grade levels, it can be seen that the mean number of trials required for the learning of the relevant relationship consistently decreases with age (see Table 3). The difference between the third and sixth grade groups is significant above the one per cent level, but the difference between the kindergarten and third-grade group is only significant at the 10 per cent level.

The variability of this learning function also decreases with age. Between the kindergarten and third grade groups, however, the difference is negligible; but between the third and sixth grade levels it approaches the 5 per cent level of significance.

Grade-Level Differences in Learning of Irrelevant Sequence

The number of trials required by each grade level to learn the irrelevant sequence is shown in Table 4. There are only negligible differences between age groups with respect to both means and standard deviations. The means of the sixth-grade and third-grade groups are practically identical, while that of the kindergarten group is only slightly and unreliably greater. Hence, there are no significant differences between grade levels in the learning of the irrelevant sequence.

TABLE 4

Means and Standard Deviations by Grade Levels of Number of Trials Required by Group II to Learn Irrelevant Sequence

GRADE LEVEL	MEAN	*SD*
K	3.48	2.25
3	3.07	2.05
6	3.04	2.47

TABLE 5

Differences between Groups I and II at Three Grade Levels on Learning the Irrelevant Sequence

	GROUP I		GROUP II		
GRADE LEVEL	MEAN	*SD*	MEAN	*SD*	$t(M_I - M_{II})$
K	3.61	2.43	3.48	2.25	0.1885
3	3.67	2.67	3.07	2.05	0.9262
6	4.70	2.25	3.04	2.47	2.4337

The Effect of Immediate Relevant Experience on the Learning of the Irrelevant Sequence

By comparing the means of Groups I and II within each grade level (see Table 5), the effect of immediate experimentally induced relevant experience on the learning of an irrelevant sequence can be ascertained. Table 5 shows that in each grade level the means of Group I (which experienced the relevant series first) are greater than the means of Group II; that is, the learning of the irrelevant sequence required a greater number of trials when preceded by relevant experience. However, this difference is only significant for the sixth-grade group (at the 5 per cent level).

The Effect of Immediate Irrelevant Experience on the Learning of the Relevant Sequence

Table 6 demonstrates that at the kindergarten and sixth-grade levels there are only negligible differences between the groups first exposed to irrelevant experience (II) and the groups not so exposed (I) in the learning of the relevant sequence. At the third-grade level, however, there is a difference which is almost significant at the 5 per cent level but not in the expected direction; that is, exposure to the irrelevant sequence apparently facilitates the learning of the relevant sequence at this grade level.

TABLE 6

Differences between Groups I and II at Three Grade Levels on Learning the Relevant Sequence

	Group I		Group II		
Grade Level	Mean	*SD*	Mean	*SD*	$t(M_I - M_{II})$
K	3.70	2.74	3.61	2.84	.1094
3	2.56	2.53	1.41	2.08	1.8539
6	0.83	1.74	0.83	1.74	0

Comparison of Each Group's Performance on the Relevant and Irrelevant Sequence

If we compare separately the learning of the relevant sequence to the learning of the irrelevant sequence in Groups I and II, the same results are obtained for each group (in apparent disregard of which sequence is presented first; see Tables 7 and 8). At the kindergarten level there is only a negligible difference between the learning of the relevant and irrelevant sequences. At the third-grade level, the difference between the learning of the two sequences is significant in Group II at the five per cent level (Table 8), and approaches the five per cent level in Group I. At the sixth-grade level, the corresponding differences exceed the one per cent level of significance for both groups.

TABLE 7

Means and Standard Deviations by Grade Levels for Group I on the Relevant and Irrelevant Sequences

Grade Level	Relevant Sequence Mean	Relevant Sequence SD	Irrelevant Sequence Mean	Irrelevant Sequence SD	$t(M_i—M_r)$
K	3.70	2.74	3.61	2.43	0.1180
3	2.56	2.53	3.67	2.67	1.5678
6	0.83	1.74	4.70	2.25	6.7811

Causal Explanations Offered for Relevant and Irrelevant Sequence

Table 9 shows that in general the frequency of the correct (actual) explanatory principle increases with age for both relevant and irrelevant sequences. Individuals who offered correct explanations also required fewer trials to learn a given sequence. "Redness" was infrequently offered at any grade level as an explanation for the irrelevant sequence. Invariably, more correct explanations were given by a group for the *second* sequence it experienced regardless of whether it was relevant or irrelevant. The explanations "guessed" or "don't know" decreased with

TABLE 8

Means and Standard Deviations by Grade Levels for Group II on the Relevant and Irrelevant Sequences

Grade Level	Relevant Sequence Mean	Relevant Sequence *SD*	Irrelevant Sequence Mean	Irrelevant Sequence *SD*	$t(M_i - M_r)$
K	3.61	2.84	3.48	2.25	0.174
3	1.41	2.08	3.07	2.07	2.954
6	0.83	1.74	3.04	2.47	3.5830

age, and with age tended to occur more frequently in relation to the irrelevant sequence.

Discussion

In accordance with what could reasonably be expected, ability to learn a relevant causal relationship (i.e., that the side of a teeter-totter which is farthest from the fulcrum will fall) is a function of age in children. For kindergarten and third-grade children it represents a challenging task eliciting a wide range of variability in learning performance. For sixth-grade children, however, it constitutes a rather simple learning task since two-thirds of them are able to master it directly without any errors.

Despite considerable overlapping in the distribution of ability between age groups, rate of growth seems to be greater between the ages of eight and 11 than between the ages of five and eight. This is shown by the much greater difference in means and the greater decline in variability in the former age interval. Whether this growth in ability to learn a relevant causal relationship is attributable to greater incidental experience with teeter-totters or to a gain in reasoning ability or both cannot be deduced from these results. To answer this question, it would be necessary to incorporate in the experimental design a learning task which is foreign to children of all ages in our culture.

Parallel results were obtained with respect to the ability to resist the learning of an irrelevant causal relationship. This

TABLE 9

Explanations Offered for Irrelevant and Relevant Sequences

Explanation	Kindergarten						Third-Grade						Sixth-Grade					
	Group I			Group II			Group I			Group II			Group I			Group II		
	N	*T*	*T/N*	*N*	*T*	*T/N*	*N*	*T*	*T/N*	*N*	*T*	*T/N*	*N*	*T*	*T/N*	*N*	*T*	*T/N*
Irrelevant sequence																		
1. Length of Side	1	3	3.0	0	0	—	8	27	3.4	0	0	—	13	57	4.4	6	17	2.8
2. Difference in Weight	3	10	3.3	9	21	2.3	0	0	—	12	30	2.5	1	6	6.0	6	16	2.7
3. Difference in Procedure	9	31	3.4	10	41	4.1	9	30	3.3	9	24	2.7	4	26	6.5	4	17	4.2
4. Redness	2	6	3.0	1	4	4.0	3	8	2.7	1	4	4.0	0	0	—	7	20	2.9
5. "Guessed"; "Don't know"	8	33	4.1	3	14	4.7	7	34	4.9	5	25	5.0	6	24	4.0	1	1	1.0
Relevant sequence																		
1. Length of Side	6	22	2.7	9	17	1.9	16	27	1.7	20	22	1.1	21	10	.47	22	13	0.6
2. Difference in Weight	5	19	3.8	5	29	5.8	2	7	3.5	3	4	1.3	1	0	—	0	0	—
3. Difference in Procedure	5	20	4.0	5	22	4.4	8	28	3.5	0	0	—	0	0	—	2	7	3.5
4. "Guessed"; "Don't know"	7	24	3.4	4	15	3.8	1	7	7.0	4	12	3.0	2	10	5.0	0	0	—

conclusion is supported by two lines of evidence: (*a*) the lack of significant difference between grade levels in the learning of the irrelevant sequence; (*b*) the absence of difference in the kindergarten group between the number of trials required to learn the relevant and irrelevant sequences respectively, and the progressive increase in the corresponding difference in the third- and sixth-grade groups. The kindergarten children can learn an irrelevant sequence as readily as a relevant sequence. The older children, on the other hand, are inhibited in the learning of the irrelevancy by either greater incidental experience with teeter-totters or by growth in the ability to discount mere contiguity as an adequate causal principle. This inhibition is revealed by the facts that the sixth-graders required more trials to learn the irrelevant sequence than the relevant sequence, and that they required as many trials as the younger groups to learn the irrelevant sequence despite evident superiority in learning the relevant sequence.

The influence of immediate, experimentally-induced experience is less apparent and straightforward. Immediate relevant experience has a significant "protective" effect (i.e., inhibits the learning of an irrelevancy) only in the sixth-grade group. In the third-grade group, the protective effect is not statistically significant; while in the kindergarten group no protective effect could be expected since these children are able to learn irrelevancies as readily as relevancies. From these results it can be concluded that immediate relevant experience only has a "protective" effect when the ability to recognize the relevancy is already well established.

Immediate prior experience with an irrelevant sequence does not exert any inhibitory effect on the learning of the relevant sequence at any grade level. At the kindergarten level this is understandable for the reason given above in relation to the "protective" effect. At the sixth-grade level, the relevant causal relationship is apparently so well established that there is no negative transfer effect from experience with the irrelevant sequence.

The suggestive trend at the third-grade level for a positive transfer effect to result from exposure to the irrelevant situation is rather difficult to explain. Perhaps in this case where the ability to perceive the relevant relationship is unstable (only moderately well established), there is less specific perseveration of the irrelevant relationship than a general "sharpening" of perceptivity as a result of the experience. This suggests that any type of immediate experience highlighting causal relationships, even if irrelevant, may increase subsequent ability to perceive relevant causal factors. This interpretation is strengthened by the fact that at the third-grade level more individuals in Group II than in Group I give a correct explanation for the relevant sequence.

These results point in general to the importance of maturation in the ability to learn relevant causal relationships or to avoid learning irrelevant causal relationships. It is not clear, however, whether this maturational effect is produced by the cumulative impact of incidental experience with teeter-totters or to a gain in reasoning ability with respect to making judgments of relevancy. Immediate experience plays a much less important role, and only in relation to inhibiting the learning of irrelevancies (providing that the ability to appreciate the relevant relationship in the training experience is already well established). Immediately preceding experience with an irrelevant causal relationship does not interfere with and (at an intermediate level of stability) may even facilitate the learning of relevant causal sequence.

An interesting finding indicative of the cultural pressures operating against overt acceptance of an irrelevant causal principle is the very small number of individuals at all grade levels who gave "redness" as an explanation for the irrelevant sequence despite the fact that it was the only antecedent cue enabling correct prediction. This could either mean that (*a*) the subjects responded to it subliminally with respect to conscious awareness; or (*b*) that the cue was consciously taken into account in making predictions but was rationalized when an explanation was sought.

CONCLUSIONS

With respect to the learning of a relevant and an irrelevant causal relationship in a teeter-totter problem by kindergarten, third-grade, and sixth-grade children, the following conclusions seem justified:

1. The ability to learn a relevant causal sequence and to inhibit the learning of an irrelevant causal sequence increases with age. Rate of growth of this ability is greater between the ages of eight to 11 than between the ages of five to eight. From this experiment it cannot be ascertained whether the maturational effect is attributable to increased incidental experience with teeter-totters, to growth in reasoning ability, or to both. At the kindergarten level, children are able to learn the irrelevant relationship as readily as the relevant relationship.
2. Immediately preceding experience with the relevant sequence exerts an inhibitory effect on the learning of the irrelevant sequence only when ability to learn the relevant relationship is stable and well established (i.e., only in the sixth-grade group).
3. Immediately preceding experience with the irrelevant sequence inhibits the learning of the relevant sequence at no age level. However, in the third-grade group (where ability to learn the relevant relationship is only moderately well established), it apparently exerts a facilitating effect which is almost significant at the 5 per cent level.
4. Despite the fact that children at all three age levels were able to utilize an irrelevant antecedent cue in learning to predict a consequence, they were reluctant to acknowledge same and in most cases offered relevant explanations for their predictions.

References

1 Abel, T. M. Unsynthetic modes of thinking among adults: A discussion of Piaget's concepts. *Amer. J. Psychol.*, 1932, **44,** 123-132.

2 Deutsche, J. M. The Development of Children's Concepts of Causal Relations. Institute of Child Welfare Monog. No. 13. Minneapolis: Univ. Minn. Press, 1937. P. 104.

3 Hazlitt, V. Children's thinking. *Brit. J. Psychol.*, 1930, **20,** 354-361.

4 Jersild, A. T. Child Psychology. New York: Prentice-Hall, 1947. P. 623.

5 Johnson, E. C., and C. C. Josey. A note on the development of thought forms of children as described by Piaget. *J. Abn. & Soc. Psychol.*, 1931, , 338–339.

6 Munn, N. L. Learning in Children. In *Manual of Child Psychology* (L. Carmichael, *Ed.*). New York: Wiley, 1946. (Pp. 370-449.)

7 Oakes, M. E. Children's Explanations of Natural Phenomena. Teachers College Contributions to Education No. 926. New York: Teach. Coll., Columbia Univ., 1947. P. 151.

8 Peterson, G. M. An empirical study of the ability to generalize. *J. Gen. Psychol.*, 1932, **6,** 90-114.

9 Piaget, J. The Child's Conception of Physical Causality. New York: Harcourt, Brace, 1930. P. 309.

21 Creativity, General Creative Abilities, and the Creative Individual*

David P. Ausubel

Creativity is one of the vaguest, most ambiguous, and most confused terms in psychology and education today. This is particularly unfortunate because "teaching for creativity" has become one of the latest and most flourishing fads and catchphrases on the current educational scene. Partly because of the conceptual confusion surrounding this term, many otherwise hardheaded educators have adopted highly unrealistic educational objectives regarding the nurturance of creativity, and many otherwise well-trained educational and school psychologists have deluded themselves into believing that they are able to identify pupils with unusual potentialities for creativity.

* *Reprinted from the article of the same title,* Psychology in the Schools *1964,* **1,** *344–347. By permission of the author and* Psychology in the Schools.

Creativity versus the Creative Individual

One of the major sources of this conceptual confusion, in my opinion, is the failure to distinguish between creativity as a continuously and normally distributed intellectual-personality trait, on the one hand, and a person manifesting a unique and qualitatively distinctive degree of this trait, on the other. It is true that creativity is not an all-or-none characteristic, but is expressed along a continuum extending from negligible to highly unusual manifestations of the trait. But to be a creative person one must exceed a certain quantitative cut-off point at the upper end of the distribution. This singular degree of creativity also differs qualitatively from lesser degrees of creativity. To be a creative individual, in other words, one must make or be capable of making a uniquely original discovery that is different in kind from ordinary expressions of creativity. Simply any kind of original discovery does not make a person creative, although it obviously constitutes a form of creativity.

This distinction naturally assumes that the criterion for singular originality is cultural or pan-cultural rather than intraindividual. A truly creative person must discover something uniquely original in terms of human experience, not merely something unique in terms of his own experience. Thus when an individual performs in a novel way insofar as his own past experience is concerned, he cannot be regarded as a creative person if his discovery is just a common rediscovery or if his degree of originality is only ordinary. For example, a sixth-grade pupil who writes a commendable poem may be exhibiting a form of creativity, but he does not necessarily establish himself thereby as a creative individual. Similarly, every scientist who formulates and empirically verifies a new proposition does not automatically lay claim to joining the ranks of the creative. All discovery activity is not qualitatively of one piece.

Another way of clarifying the distinction between creativity and the creative individual is to point to the analogous, well-recognized distinction between intelligence and the intelligent individual. Intelligence, like creativity, exists along a continuum.

Everyone, even an idiot, manifests some degree of intelligence. But no one, unless he were an idiot himself, would call an idiot an intelligent person. In other words, one must exceed a certain cut-off point at the upper end of the continuum to be considered an intelligent individual. However, unlike the difference between the creative and noncreative person, the difference between the intelligent and the nonintelligent is probably only a difference in degree rather than a difference in kind. Also, since creativity is less generously distributed in the population than is intelligence, there are many fewer creative than intelligent persons.

Creativity versus the General Creative Abilities

A second major source of conceptual confusion in this area, in my opinion, is the failure to distinguish between creativity as a substantive capacity and the general, content-free creative abilities. True creativity is a unique manifestation of talent in a particular field of human endeavor. It consists of rare sensitivity to particular kinds of intellectual or aesthetic experience, and a rare capacity for making original discoveries or producing original work in a particular area of human achievement. The general creative abilities, on the other hand, are a constellation of problem-solving and personality traits that, like general intelligence, not only facilitate discovery learning, but also help implement the expression of substantive creativity. Genuinely creative persons, for example, tend to surpass noncreative persons in these abilities just as they tend to surpass them in IQ (Taylor, 1961). A certain minimal degree of the general creative abilities, just like a certain minimal degree of intelligence (Torrance, Yamamoto, Schenetzki, Palamutlu and Luther, 1960), is necessary for the actualization of creative potentialities; but beyond this minimum the degree manifested in either case does not crucially affect creative output. The general creative abilities, however, are probably more intrinsically related to creative accomplishment than is IQ. They correlate just as highly with academic achievement as IQ does (Getzels and

Jackson, 1962), but more highly than IQ with research accomplishment and vocational productivity (Taylor, 1961).

The general creative abilities also resemble general intelligence in being continuously and normally distributed. Unlike the situation with respect to substantive creativity, however, differences among individuals are solely differences in degree, not in kind. From a descriptive standpoint, these abilities consist of such intellectual problem-solving traits as sensitivity to the existence of problems; facility in formulating, testing, and reformulating hypotheses; skill in improvising solutions; openness to new experience; and spontaneity and flexibility in approach to problems (Kettner, Guilford and Christensen, 1959). Also involved are such personality traits bearing on problem-solving as perseverance and venturesomeness. But according to many authorities in the field, the distinctive attribute of creativity is divergent thinking ability as measured by such tests as Unusual Uses, Consequences, and Impossibilities (Guilford, Wilson, Christensen and Lewis, 1951). It should be noted, however, that scores on these latter tests are contaminated by verbal fluency, uninhibited self-expression, and deficient self-critical ability. In any case, moreover, neither divergent thinking ability nor any of the other content-free, general creative abilities are constituents of creativity as a substantive capacity. This is not to say, of course, that they are unimportant or not worth measuring. By all means let us identify the divergent thinkers and the spontaneous and flexible problem-solvers in our schools, as long as we do not make the unwarranted inference that we are simultaneously identifying the individuals most likely to be substantively creative in the various fields of human endeavor! Tests of the general creative abilities are not much more suitable than are tests of general intelligence for identifying potentialities for true creative accomplishment.

The general creative abilities by their very nature exhibit considerable generality from one kind of problem-solving task or activity to another (Getzels and Jackson, 1962; Kettner, *et al.*, 1959). Creativity per se, however, manifests little generality of function and becomes increasingly more particularized with increasing age. A person who is creative in one area is not typically more creative in other areas than are non-creative individuals. Multiple creative persons do exist but are exceedingly rare, especially today when the various disciplines are so highly differentiated from each other. Universal geniuses of the Leonardo da Vinci type belong to a long-past era that is unlikely ever to recur. Hence, by definition, no general tests of creativity are possible. Assessments of creativity or of creative potential can only be made in particular fields of achievement by using expert judgments of actual performance or work products that take age and experience into consideration.

Typically, when teachers or school psychologists refer to pupils as being creative, what they really mean is that they exhibit a high degree of the general, creative abilities. For example, a pupil who proposes alternative solutions to arithmetic problems and displays ingenuity and flexibility in problem-solving is often said to be creative. Actually, he is merely outstanding in certain of the general creative abilities.

Teaching for Creativity

A currently popular objective of education is to "teach for creativity"—to make every child an original and creative thinker. This incredible aspiration is based on one or more of five untenable propositions. The first proposition assumes that every child, by definition, has potentialities for unique creativity providing that they are not stifled by the educational system. This, of course, is sheer sentimentality since such potentialities are extremely rare. The second proposition, in accordance with the naïve *tabula rasa* view of human plasticity, asserts that even if a child has no creative potentialities, inspired and sensitive teaching can compensate for missing genes. The third proposition, ignoring the distinction between creativity and the creative individual, advances a watered-down, "democratic" definition of creativity that employs an intraindividual criterion of originality and assumes that all creativity is qualitatively of one piece. By the very same token, however, if this criterion of creativity is used, the educational objective of making every pupil a creative individual becomes so watered down that it becomes virtually meaningless. The fourth proposition simply rests on the previously discussed assertion that the general creative abilities are coextensive with substantive creativity. The final proposition asserts that since the structure of intellect, according to Guilford (1959) and others, consists of about 120 separately identifiable cognitive abilities, every individual stands a good statistical chance of becoming a genius or near-genius with respect to one or more of these abilities. But creativity is no more coextensive with superiority in a particular cognitive ability than it is coextensive with high scores on tests of the general creative abilities.

Although the training possibilities for fostering creativity are severely limited, there are some things that the schools can realistically attempt in this regard. They can help pupils possessing unique creative potentialities actualize them by providing adequate opportunities for spontaneity and individuality, by setting suitably challenging tasks, by rewarding creative accomplishments, and by providing appropriate guidance and encouragement. These same techniques can also be used to further the actualization of more limited and less unique degree of creative potentiality as well as to foster the development of the general creative abilities. No amount of inspired or appropriately designed teaching, however, can generate unique creativity in pupils if the necessary potentialities are lacking. Even the general creative abilities are only slightly susceptible to training; genic factors, I suspect, account for more of their measurable variance than do any manipulable characteristics of the environment.

How important, then, one might legitimately ask, is it to identify pupils with true creative potentialities? Persons belonging to the "genius will out" school of thought would argue that these potentialities will be actualized irrespective of what the school does or fails to do. The realization of creative potentialities, however, like the phenotypic expression of any genic tendencies, is seldom an all-or-none proposition. True, in certain instances the genic factors are so prepotent, or all of the relevant personality, motivational, family, peer, and cultural variables are so overwhelmingly favorable, that a successful outcome is almost inevitable. But in many other instances the influence of these variables is more equivocal, and a successful outcome hinges on the guidance, stimulation, and encouragement that is forthcoming from such agencies as the school.

References

Ausubel, D. P. *The psychology of meaningful verbal learning*. New York: Grune & Stratton, Inc., 1963.

Getzels, J. W. and P. W. Jackson. *Creativity and intelligence*. New York: John Wiley & Sons, 1962.

Guilford, J. P. Three faces of intellect. *Amer. Psychologist*, 1959, **14**, 469–479.

Guilford, J. P., R. C. Wilson, P. R. Christensen, and D. J. Lewis. A factor-analytic study of creative thinking. 1. Hypotheses and description of tests. *Rep. psychol. Lab.*, No. 4. Los Angeles: University of Southern California, 1951.

Kettner, N. W., J. P. Guilford, and P. R. Christensen. A factor-analytic study across the domains of reasoning, creativity, and evaluation. *Psychol. Monogr.*, 1959, **73**, No. 14 (Whole No. 479).

Taylor, C. W. A tentative description of the creative individual. In W. W. Waetjen (Ed.), *Human variability and learning*. Washington, D.C.: Association for Supervision and Curriculum Development, 1961. 62-79.

Torrance, E. P., K. Yamamoto, D. Schenetzki, N. Palamutlu, and B. Luther. *Assessing the creative thinking abilities of children*. Minneapolis: Bureau of Educational Research, University of Minnesota, 1960.

PART V | AFFECTIVE-SOCIAL FACTORS IN LEARNING

Affective-social factors influencing school learning may be grouped under the following headings: motivational variables, personality variables, teacher variables, and group and social variables. In contrast to the cognitive factors considered in Part III, they do not directly affect the availability (retrievability) of the assimilated learning task. They exert instead a nonspecific, catalytic effect on school learning by influencing such mediating variables as the degree of effort and attention. These variables can obviously affect the future availability of the learning task only during the learning period itself; in order for affective-social variables independently to influence the availability of the learned material during the retention interval, another mediating mechanism is necessary. The most probable mechanism in the latter event is an elevation of the availability threshold; but such a mechanism can be invoked only during such relatively rare circumstances in school learning as when elicitation of learned material would produce anxiety or guilt.

The operation of these generalizations regarding the mediation of motivational and attitudinal variables in school retention or forgetting is illustrated by the first two selections in this section. In Selection 22, intention is shown to facilitate retention of school material only when it is operative during the learning period; intention to remember does not influence retention when it is introduced *after* learning is completed. In Selection 23, attitudinal bias for or against controversial material is shown to influence retention largely through the cognitive rather than the affective component of attitude structure: when degree of knowledge is held constant the differential effect of attitudinal bias on retention is eliminated.

Anxiety is one of the more important personality factors in school learning. In Selection 24, neurotic anxiety is differentiated from situational anxiety and its typical genesis in deviant parent-child relationships is traced. Selection 25 describes an experimental study in which neurotic anxiety inhibits the improvising aspects of problem solving and unrealistically raises level of aspiration.

The school's secondary, rather than primary, responsibility for the pupil's mental hygiene and personality development is discussed in Selection 26. Other shibboleths of the mental hygiene movement in education—the cult of extroversion, the inherent and invariable evils of authoritarianism, and various permissivist distortions of democratic discipline—are also considered in this article.

Both the cognitive and motivational problems in educating culturally disadvantaged pupils are discussed in Selection 27, and the outlines of a teaching strategy for coping with them are delineated. With respect to both intrinsic and extrinsic motivation, emphasis is placed on the "retroactive" approach, that is, the approach that initially focuses on the cognitive and interpersonal conditions assuring successful performance and expects suitable motivations stem therefrom, rather than vice versa.

Selection 28 considers the problems of cultural disadvantage in the special context of a racially defined caste as illustrated by the status of Negroes in the United States; the unique ego development of Negro children in America is traced, and its implications for later educational and vocational adjustment are considered. Stress is placed on the principle that the problems of cultural disadvantage cannot be overcome by relying solely on such social and legal changes as desegregation of schools, jobs, and neighborhoods, but the article also presupposes concomitant change in the character structure and achievement level of individual Negroes to be brought about through such factors as individual initiative, improvement of family life, counseling, and their taking maximum advantage of existing educational and vocational opportunities.

In Selection 29, the personality and educational development of Maori children in New Zealand, a group undergoing rapid psychological acculturation to Western civilization, is interpreted as typical of the problem of culturally disadvantaged pupils among ethnic minority peoples and citizens of underdeveloped nations everywhere. Characteristic of Maori, and all culturally disadvantaged, children is extreme poverty and lower social class-status compounded by social demoralization and gross intellectual impoverishment in the home and community environment. What is primarily lacking in such children is not so much appropriate aspirations for academic and vocational success as the absence of the motivations and personality traits necessary for implementing them.

22 The Influence of Intention on the Retention of School Materials*

David P. Ausubel
Seymour H. Schpoont
Lillian C. Robbins

Extrapolating from general principles of educational psychology and from related experimental evidence, many educators and psychologists implicitly believe that intention to remember facilitates the retention of learned verbal materials. Actually, all of the evidence bearing on this issue is ambiguous and inconclusive for one or both of two reasons: the experimental arrangements have been such as (1) to induce intentions to learn rather than to retain, or (2) to make impossible the isolation of the effects of intention on learning from its effects on

Reprinted from the article of the same title,* Journal of Educational Psychology, *1957,* **48, *87-92. By permission of the authors and the American Psychological Association, Inc.*

retention. The present study was designed to overcome these interpretive ambiguities by both introducing explicit intentions to remember for an extended period of time and by experimentally isolating the effects of such intentions from original learning. The latter result could only be insured by introducing intentions to remember *after* completion of the learning task.

Numerous studies have shown that intention to remember influences the quality and longevity of retention. When subjects learn material with the expectation of recalling it for a designated period of time, recall is superior for the expected as against either a shorter or longer interval (2, 3, 8). Lester demonstrated that retention is enhanced by expectation of recall and by foreknowledge of the occurrence and possible effect of interpolated materials (5). Unfortunately, however, since differential intentions to remember were introduced at the time of original learning, these experiments did not isolate the effects of intention on the quality or quantity of what was learned in the first place from its effects on retention per se.

Another group of studies (e.g., 6, 7) has shown that retention is superior and retroactive inhibition less marked when practice is accompanied by "intent to learn" than when learning takes place incidentally. That this difference is largely attributable to superior original learning, however, is demonstrated by the fact that it no longer prevails when *S*s are equated for original mastery of the learning task (1). Heyer and O'Kelly (4), on the other hand, showed that learning under conditions of strong ego-involvement did significantly increase retention even though their ego-involved and control groups could not be differentiated on the basis of original learning outcomes. It is quite possible, however, that the superiority of the ego-involved group on original learning was masked by the inhibitory effect of intense ego-involvement on initial test performance. In any event, the evidence yielded by all of these studies can at best be indirect, because in each instance an explicit experimental set was induced to *learn* material for immediate reproduction rather than to *retain* it for an extended period of time. Furthermore, even if ego-involved intention to learn leads to no demonstrable quantitative superiority in original learning, it may still affect retention by influencing certain qualitative aspects of the learning process.

METHOD

Standardization of Learning Material and Tests of Retention

The learning material used in this study was a passage of approximately 1400 words on the history of opiate addiction. It was selected on the basis of being generally unfamiliar and inaccessible to undergraduate students, but yet learnable and relatively interesting. Two equivalent multiple-choice tests on this material were constructed as follows: 56 five-choice test items were administered to a group of 55 undergraduate students in education three days after they had studied the passage for 25 minutes. Following item analysis, the order of items was rearranged so as to match odd and even items with respect to difficulty and type of question. The revised form of the test was then administered to a different group of 29 undergraduate students in education. The range of scores (number correct) on this test was from 13 to 45 with a mean of 33 and a standard deviation of 7.8. The uncorrected odd-even coefficient of equivalence was .76. For the main experiment the odd and even items respectively constituted the two equivalent forms.

Experimental Procedure

Our experimental population consisted of 97 undergraduate students enrolled in four sections of an educational psychology course at the University of Illinois. Of these, 53 were in the control group and 44 in the experimental group. In order to minimize the possibility and consequences of communication between groups, the control group was handled during the Fall semester and the experimental group during the following Spring semester. The experiment was rationalized as a laboratory exercise and was performed during scheduled class hours. The control *S*s were first instructed to read the passage at their normal reading speed (approximately eight minutes), and then to utilize the remainder of the 25 available minutes to commit the facts and concepts in the passage to memory. It was explained that a multiple-choice examination on the material would be given immediately after the reading was completed. *S*s were assured that the results on the examination would not be made public and would not affect their grades in the course. They were promised, however, that their scores would be returned to them individually, and that the median and frequency distribution of the class scores would be placed on the blackboard so that they could compare their own scores with the class norms. Fourteen days after the original learning and test, an unannounced (surprise) retest was given, utilizing the equivalent form of the test. Hence the control group had no explicit intention to remember the material for the second test.

During the second semester the same procedure, with one exception, was followed for the experimental group. Immediately *after* the *S*s finished the first test, they were informed that a second test on the same material would be given in fourteen days. This announcement presumably induced explicit intentions to retain the previously learned material for an additional two weeks without in any way affecting the quality or quantity of original learning.

Results

Means and standard deviations of learning (test) and retention (retest) scores for control and experimental groups are shown in Table 1. Comparison of test and retest scores indicates that a significant degree of forgetting ($p < .001$) occurred in each group during the two week interval. The mean learning and retention scores made by the two groups were also significantly greater in all instances than the test scores made by different *S*s who answered the test questions without prior study of the learning passage. The product-moment correlation between test and retest scores was .45 ($p < .01$).

Since the means, standard deviations, and variances of the two groups are not significantly different from each other on the learning test, we are justified in comparing control and experimental groups with respect to percentage of retention from test to retest. The respective percentages of 48.5 and 53.9 show only a negligible difference in degree of retention which does not even begin to approach statistical significance.

TABLE 1

Comparison of Control and Experimental Groups on Learning and Retention Tests

	CONTROL GROUP		EXPERIMENTAL GROUP	
	Test	Retest	Test	Retest
Mean	20.1	13.2	19.5	13.6
S.D.	2.53	3.06	2.56	2.58
Corrected Mean*	13.4	6.5	12.8	6.9
Percentage Retained**	48.5		53.9	

*The corrected means were computed by subtracting 6.7 (the mean score of subjects who took the test without studying the material) from the group means of raw scores (number of correctly answered items).

**Corrected means were utilized in computing the percentage of retention from test to retest.

DISCUSSION

The results of the present study do not support the widely held view that intention to remember facilitates the retention of learned verbal material. In reconciling these findings with previously reported studies in this area (2, 3, 5, 8), we can only surmise that intention to remember in these latter studies did not influence the retention process *per se,* but affected various quantitative and qualitative aspects of original learning which indirectly increased the availability of the learned material at a later date.

Obviously, if a student learns material more thoroughly in the first place because he expects to be tested on it several weeks later he will have more available to remember than a student who originally learns less diligently because he does not expect to be tested. However, if the intention to remember is introduced *after* learning takes place it apparently has no influence on the longevity of the learned material. Intention to remember, in other words, affects retention by enhancing learning rather than by increasing the stability of existing memory traces; or, to put it negatively, intention *not* to remember material beyond the date of the examination leads to little subsequent retention not because of any direct influence of this intention on memory traces but because such intentions are invariably associated with superficial and cursory methods of original learning. Hence, teachers who wish to increase the longevity of learning by maximizing intention to remember can only do so by inducing the appropriate intention at the time of original learning. Admonitions to remember once learning is completed, even if they lead to corresponding intentions in the student, do not alter the subsequent fate of memory traces.

One possible qualification of these findings should be considered. Intention to remember in our *S*s might have been relatively weak in the absence of tangible material rewards for superior retention. High retention scores, after all, did not "count" in the sense of improving students' grades. On the other hand, level of ego-involvement was maintained at a reasonably high level by intrinsic desire to cooperate in a research study relevant to the subject matter of the course and by *S*s' incentive of scoring favorably in relation to class norms.

Summary and Conclusions

An attempt was made to ascertain whether explicit intention to remember facilitates retention of learned school materials apart from its influence on original learning. An experimental group of undergraduates studied an historical selection for 25 minutes and was tested on same immediately afterwards by means of a multiple-choice test. *After* this test, an explicit intention to remember was induced by announcing that an equivalent form of the test would be given two weeks later. The same procedure was followed with a control group except that an unannounced retest was given.

The two groups were not significantly different in mean learning scores or in the percentage of material retained from test to retest. It was concluded that intention to remember facilitates retention by enhancing original learning rather than by increasing the stability of existing memory traces.

References

Biel, W. C., and R. C. Force. Retention of nonsense syllables in intentional and incidental learning. *J. exp. Psychol.*, 1943, 32, 52–63.

Boswell, F. D., and W. S. Foster. On memorizing with the intention permanently to retain. *Amer. J. Psychol.*, 1916, 27, 420–426.

Geyer, M. T. Influence of changing the expected time of recall. *J. exp. Psychol.*, 1930, 13, 290-292.

Heyer, A. W. Jr., and L. I. O'Kelly. Studies in motivation and retention. II. Retention of nonsense syllables learned under different degrees of motivation. *J. Psychol.*, 1949, 27, 143–152.

Lester, O. P. Mental set in relation to retroactive inhibition. *J. exp. Psychol.*, 1932, 15, 681–699.

Peterson, J. The effect of attitude on immediate and delayed recall: a class experiment. *J. educ. Psychol.*, 1916, 7, 523–532.

Prentice, W. C. H. Retroactive inhibition and the motivation of learning. *Amer. J. Psychol.*, 1943, 56, 283–292.

Thisted, M. N., and H. H. Remmers. The effect of temporal set on learning. *J. appl. Psychol.*, 1932, 16, 257–268.

23 Cognitive versus Affective Factors in the Learning and Retention of Controversial Material*

Donald Fitzgerald
David P. Ausubel

The phenomena of selective learning and selective forgetting of material involving ego threat has been consistently interpreted in terms of affective mechanisms operating directly on the learning and forgetting processes (Edwards, 1941; Gustafson, 1957; Taft, 1954). Implicit in the interpretive use of affective mechanisms is a denial of the importance of cognitive factors in selective learning and retention. However, despite widespread use of the notion of intrinsic motivational factors in explaining these phenomena, no research to date has unequivocally established the operation of "defense" or "repression"

Reprinted from the article of the same title,* Journal of Educational Psychology, *1963,* **54, *73–84. By permission of the authors and the American Psychological Association, Inc.*

mechanisms in the learning and retention of meaningful material which conflicts with the learner's prevailing attitude structure.

On the other hand, the dependence of learning and retention on cognitive variables has been clearly established (Ausubel and Blake, 1958; Ausubel and Fitzgerald, 1962). The learning and retention of meaningful noncontroversial material have been shown to be directly related to the learner's subject-matter sophistication (Ausubel and Blake, 1958; Ausubel and Fitzgerald, 1962). When existing cognitive structure is generally devoid of subsuming concepts relevant to the learning task, the novel material is poorly learned and rapidly forgotten. This line of research suggests a more parsimonious interpretation of "selective forgetting" than the concepts of defense and repression. In learning "other side" arguments, the conceptual schema constituting the cognitive dimension of attitudes is usually devoid of relevant subsuming ideas to which the new material can be functionally related. The material, therefore, cannot be readily anchored to cognitive structure, competes with existing meanings, and is consequently ambiguous and subject to rapid forgetting. In the case of positive attitudinal bias, it seems reasonable to suppose that the cognitive dimension of attitude structure contains more relevant and appropriate subsuming concepts than in the case of negative bias. Hence the material can be readily anchored to cognitive structure, need not compete with existing meanings, and is therefore less ambiguous and less subject to forgetting. Attitudinal bias might conceivably facilitate or inhibit the *learning* of controversial material by generally raising or lowering levels of effort and concentration. However, once material is learned, it seems more reasonable to attribute differential rates of forgetting to cognitive variables.

In order to differentiate experimentally the respective effects of the cognitive and affective components of attitude on learning and retention in this research, attitude structure is analyzed in terms of the direction and intensity of attitudinal bias (i.e., the affective dimension) and the extensiveness and clarity of the related conceptual schema (i.e., the cognitive dimension). An attitude, therefore, is here considered a structure of ideas which involves organization around a conceptual nucleus and which has affective properties (Peak, 1955). That is to say, an attitude involves both affective and cognitive components. Any meaningful concept or conceptual system which an individual internalizes will be related in some way, along a negative-positive continuum, to his ego structure. What we are here calling an attitude is a conceptual nucleus whose evaluative dimension is either highly positive or highly negative from an affective stand-point. The term "cognitive structure" as used in this paper is synonymous with the cognitive dimension of attitude. In contrast to this cognitive component, the phrase "affective components" refers to the complex of feelings that a particular organization of cognition or perception induces in the subject.

Using this affective-cognitive analysis of attitudes, the main purpose of conducting the experiment reported here was to reexamine the effect of attitudes on the learning and retention of controversial material in an attempt to determine the relative contributions of cognitive and affective variables to the learning-forgetting process. Concurrent with this analysis, the efficacy of a brief introductory passage (an "organizer") in facilitating the learning and retention of controversial materials was tested.

In the present study the following hypotheses were tested: (*a*) The clarity and stability of cognitive structure are positively related to the learning and retention of controversial material. (*b*) Positive attitudinal bias facilities, and negative attitudinal bias inhibits, the learning of controversial material. (*c*) Attitudinal bias has no effect on the *retention* of controversial material. (*d*) The learning and retention of controversial material is proactively facilitated by the introduction of a relevant comparative organizer.

METHOD

Subjects and Learning Passage

Since one purpose of this study was to demonstrate the feasibility of controlled classroom experimentation in this area, 264 junior students of an Illinois high school were used as subjects, and the learning material was related to a traditionally presented unit in United States history.

The experiment was conducted separately in each of 16 American history sections, as one unit in a sequence dealing with the causes of the Civil War. The learning passage consisted of a 2,900-word Southern interpretation of the causes of the Civil War. The material presented a general theme of Northern aggression and acts of violence against the South and, in particular, condemned the Lincoln administration. The regular class unit preceding the experiment considered the same topic as the learning passage but from a Northern point of view. The Southern interpretation was unfamiliar to the subjects and was selected because it conflicted with the culturally biased interpretation of this historical period to which Northern students are continually exposed. By using material which interpreted known facts in an *unfamiliar* controversial way, it was possible both to estimate the clarity and extensiveness of the cognitive dimension of attitude structure (by a pretest covering factual knowledge of the period) and yet to retain the unfamiliarity of the learning passage.

Test on the Learning Passage

Knowledge of the Civil War passage was tested by a 34-item multiple-choice test (five responses) with a split-half reliability of .77. The test was used for measuring both learning and retention. Test questions generally covered points of dispute between Northern and Southern interpretations, the five responses being ordered along a continuum from an appropriate Northern response to a response most appropriate in terms of the learning passage. To insure that subjects responded in terms of the learning passage, the test directions repeated the instruction that the response selected should be "the *one* that seems *most* consistent with the ideas and point of view presented in the passage." Test questions were selected by an item analysis from a larger population of items.

Both learning and retention scores on the test showed a satisfactory range of variability and were distributed normally. It was found on item analysis that eight responses could be given a secondary weighting. Correct primary responses were given a weight of 2, and correct secondary responses were given a weight of 1 point, making a maximum score of 68. Since the test was intended as a power test, no time limit was imposed.

Attitude Inventory

A 20-item attitude inventory was prepared to measure the direction and intensity of attitudinal bias toward Southern actions during the era preceding the Civil War. The inventory consisted of controversial statements directly related to the content of the learning passage. The 20 items were selected from a larger population of items on the basis of a group of expert ratings (senior undergraduate students majoring in social studies) of the statements as indicative of either strong Northern or Southern bias. Only items at the extremes of the judgmental scale which manifested little or no variability in the ratings received were chosen. Approximately half the items selected were indicative of the Northern bias, and half were indicative of Southern bias.

Subjects were asked to rate the items in terms of their own agreement, disagreement, strong disagreement, strong agreement, or uncertainty regarding the sentiments expressed in the various statements. The responses were weighted from one to five (five indicating strong Northern bias), and a total attitude score was determined by summing the item scores and dividing by three (for purposes of computation).

Apart from their self-evident face validity as a measure of Northern-Southern bias, an empirical check, carried out with an independent group of subjects, showed that a correlation of .54 ($p < .001$) existed between attitudinal bias scores and intensity of acceptance or rejection of the passage. The group of students used in validating the inventory was a representative sample of junior year students who could not be used in the main experiment because of a schedule conflict. The mean attitude score of the group responding to the passage in a neutral manner was 22.

The attitude scores showed a satisfactory degree of variability and were normally distributed. Since the mean attitude score of subjects in the middle-third of the subgroup distributions was not significantly different from the established neutral point of 22, the upper-third, middle-third, and lower-third attitude groups were described, respectively, as negatively biased, neutral, and positively biased toward the learning passage.

Test of Verbal Reasoning

The Verbal Reasoning test (Form A) of the Differential Aptitude Test (DAT) battery was used as a measure of the subject's ability to abstract, to generalize, and to understand verbal concepts. Approximately 75% of the experimental population had test scores on file. The DAT Verbal Reasoning test was administered to the remaining 25% immediately after the experimental sequence.

Introductory Passages

Two types of introductory passages were used in this experiment, each about 450 words in length. The experimental group studied a *comparative organizer* which explicitly pointed out, at a high level of abstraction, generality, and inclusiveness, the principal differences between the Northern and Southern positions on the causes of the Civil War. The ideas in the comparative organizer were presented at a much higher level of generality and inclusiveness than the learning passage itself, and were deliberately constructed to increase discriminability between the two sets of concepts. The *control introduction* discussed the *history* of Civil War interpretations and the possibility of the same events being interpreted in many different ways depending upon the perspective of the historian, but it contained no substantive material about these interpretations. This control introduction served two important functions. First, it was methodologically important to provide a control introduction in order that any obtained differences in learning and retention outcomes between the experimental and control groups could be attributed to the particular nature of the organizer (i.e., to its enhancing effects on discriminability) rather than to its presence per se. Second, an organizer could conceivably facilitate learning and retention of controversial materials by reducing the negative bias that induces selective learning. Since one principal purpose of this study was to separate the effects of cognitive and affective factors on the learning and retention of controversial material, it was necessary to provide a control introduction that equated the two groups on "affective set," leaving the cognitive effects of the organizer "free" as an independent variable.

Neither introduction provided any information that could be used in answering the test questions on the learning passage.

Procedure

The sequence began immediately following the completion of the unit of study on the events leading up to the Civil War. On the day preceding Session 1, the subjects were informed that some people from the Bureau of Educational Research would be working with them on the pre-Civil-War period. Every attempt was made to have the teachers feel that the material to be studied was relevant to their purposes. It was suggested to the teachers that the results of the pretest on the pre-Civil-War period could be used for grading purposes if they so wished, and that the scores on the pretest as well as on the retention test would be made available to them.

Session 1. During Session 1, all subjects took the attitude inventory (8 minutes) and the pretest, and then (after assignment to a treatment group) studied either the organizer or the control introduction for 8 minutes. Membership in a treatment group was determined by random assignment. The population of each of the four treatment groups (i.e., experimental learning, experimental retention, control learning, and control retention) was also stratified by sex so that the proportion of males to females would be the same in each group. This was necessary because of the possibility that female subjects might possess higher DAT scores. It was possible to administer both treatments simultaneously because they consisted of identical appearing introductory passages (with identical sets of directions) differing only in content.

To control for the effects of different teacher, test administrator, and classroom climate variables in the 16 sections, the subjects *within each* section were equally divided among the four treatment groups. Since analysis of the data showed that homogeneity of variance prevailed, both on an interclass and intergroup basis for the Civil War pretest, attitude inventory, and learning and retention tests it was considered justifiable to treat the scores of the four treatment groups on each of these instruments as random samples from the same population.

Session 2. The day after Session 1, all subjects read and studied for 28 minutes the learning passage presenting the Southern point of view. Immediately after studying the passage, the experimental and control "learning" groups took the 34-item test on the passage. At the same time the experimental and control "retention" groups took an irrelevant test on Christianity in order to equate the learning and retention groups on procedure. (The topic of Christianity was chosen as maximally dissimilar to the learning passage, and therefore least likely to induce retroactive interference.)

Session 3. Seven days after Session 2 all subjects took the test on the passage as a test of retention. The learning groups' scores on this test were not considered in the retention analysis.

Results and Discussion

Effect of the Organizer on Learning and Retention

As hypothesised, the organizer treatment was significantly effective in facilitating learning and retention of controversial material ($F=5.79$, $p < .05$; see Table 1). Moreover the beneficial effect of the organizer was further demonstrated by the significant treatment effect that emerged (*a*) when an analysis of covariance of attitude levels × treatment × retention was performed with DAT held constant ($F=6.15$, $p < .01$; see Table 2), and (*b*) when an analysis of covariance of pretest levels × treatment × retention, holding DAT constant, was performed ($F=6.98$, $p < .01$; see Table 3). However, when an analysis of covariance of attitude levels × treatment × retention was carried out with *pretest* held constant, the treatment effect was not significant (see Table 4). Hence it can be reasonably inferred that much of the positive treatment effect evident in the preceding two analyses could be attributed to the interaction (in a nonstatistical sense) between the organizer and what we have called the cognitive dimension of attitude structure.

Although there was a tendency for the experimental group to be superior on learning, most of the benefit derived from the organizer was manifested in relation to retention rather than to learning. When subgroup means of *learning* were corrected for their dependence on DAT, there were no significant differences between treatment pairs of upper-third, middle-third, and lower-third or combined pretest levels (means are given in Table 5). However, comparable corrected retention means indicated a significant difference between the treatment means of the combined

TABLE 1

Analysis of Variance of Pretest Levels × Treatment × Retention

Sources	*df*	*SS*	*MS*	*F*
Treatment	1	417	417	5.79**
Pretest levels	2	12890	6445	89.5***
Retention	1	4483	4483	62.3***
Treatment × pretest	2	293	147	2.04
Treatment × retention	1	1	1	
Pretest × retention	2	405	203	2.82*
Treatment × pretest × retention	2	302	151	2.09
Error	252	18082	72	
Total	263	36873		

Note.—Null hypotheses concerning homogeneity of variance accepted.
*$p < .10$.
**$p < .05$.
***$p < .01$.

TABLE 2

Analysis of Covariance of Attitude Levels × Treatment × Retention Holding DAT Constant

Source	df	SS_y	SP	SS_x	Adjusted			
					SS'_y	df'	MS'	F
Treatment	1	417	—157	59	492	1	492	6.15**
Attitude levels	2	671	3732	23192	167	2	84	1.05
Retention	1	4483	590	77	4216	1	1216	15.2**
Treatment × attitude	2	393	241	151	291	2	146	1.83
Treatment × retention	1	1	—6	1970	106	1	106	1.33
Attitude × retention	2	239	110	4074	399	2	200	2.50*
Treatment × bias × retention	2	339	636	1340	118	2	59	
Error	252	30330	45282	197778	19962	251	80	
Total	263	36873	50428	228641	25751	262		

Note.—Null hypotheses concerning homogeneity of variance and regression accepted.
*$p < .10$.
**$p < .01$.

TABLE 3

Analysis of Covariance of Pretest Levels × Treatment × Retention Holding DAT Constant

Source	df	SS_y	SP	SS_x	Adjusted SS'_y	Adjusted df'	Adjusted MS'	Adjusted F
Treatment	1	417	−44	247	433	1	433	6.98**
Pretest levels	2	12890	30278	79882	11568	2	5784	93.3**
Retention	1	4483	680	103	4302	1	4302	69.4**
Treatment × pretest	2	293	347	317	207	2	104	1.68
Treatment × retention	1	1	−5	1587	30	1	30	
Pretest × retention	2	405	−172	256	455	2	228	3.68*
Pretest × treatment × retention	2	302	654	1678	158	2	79	1.26
Error	252	18082	18970	144242	15587	251	62	
Total	263	36873	50708	228312	25611	262		

Note.—Null hypotheses concerning homogeneity of variance and regression accepted.
*$p < .05$.
**$p < .01$.

TABLE 4

Analysis of Covariance of Attitude Inventory Level × Treatment × Retention Holding Pretest Constant

Source	df	SS_y	SP	SS_x	Adjusted			
					SS'_y	df'	MS'	F
Treatment	1	417	268	172	118	1	118	1.74
Attitude inventory level	2	671	1237	2283	72	2	36	
Retention	1	4483	524	61	3745	1	3745	55.1*
Treatment × attitude inventory	2	393	260	273	159	2	80	1.18
Treatment × retention	1	1	−1	34	20	1	20	
Attitude inventory × retention	2	239	73	114	193	2	97	1.43
Treatment × retention × attitude inventory	2	339	299	375	103	2	52	
Error	252	30330	18357	25261	16990	251	68	
Total	263	36873	21017	28573				

Note.—Null hypotheses concerning homogeneity of variance and regression accepted.
$^*p < .01$.

TABLE 5

Means of Pretest Levels on Learning and Retention Corrected for DAT

Pretest Level	Learning M: Experimental	Learning M: Control	Learning M: Total	Retention M: Experimental	Retention M: Control	Retention M: Total
Upper-third	36.7	34.7	35.7	27.9	21.1	24.5
Middle-third	27.0	22.6	24.8	16.9	15.2	16.1
Lower-third	21.1	21.9	21.5	16.9	16.2	16.6
Combined	28.3	26.3	27.3	20.6	17.5	19.1

Note.—N for each subgroup is 22.

levels ($t = 2.31$, $p = .03$; see Table 5 for corrected means), as well as a significant difference between the treatment means in the upper-third pretest level ($t = 2.88$; $p = .007$). This latter result is in contrast to the findings of a previous study in which Ausubel and Fitzgerald (1961) found that organizers differentially benefit subjects with a limited and diffuse cognitive structure. The discrepancy can probably be explained by the nature of the learning tasks involved in the two studies.

In the Ausubel and Fitzgerald (1961) study, the learning task dealt with material which, although unfamiliar in terminology, was directly relatable and in many ways similar to concepts already established in cognitive structure. The learning passage dealt with the principles of Mahayana Buddhism, and the organizer presented Buddhism as a categorical variant of Christianity. The comparative organizer, in other words, presented an organized structure of Buddhist concepts in terms of Christianity, thereby clarifying and reinforcing the main principles of Christianity as well as introducing Buddhism. The organizer could therefore be expected to benefit most those subjects whose knowledge of Christianity was unclear, by first clarifying Christianity concepts before differentiating them from Buddhism. Subjects with an extensive and clear organization of Christianity, on the other hand, could be expected to formulate their own differentiations within the learning task itself, and would thus derive little benefit either from the presented contrasts or from the discussion of Christianity given in the organizer. In the present study, however, the ideas presented in the learning passage were concepts which directly conflicted with existing ideas in cognitive structure rather than constituting variations of existing ideas. Whereas the learning task in the previous study tended to reinforce the existing structure of knowledge, the present study was designed to induce cognitive dissonance and affective stress. In the latter circumstances the data clearly indicate that a prerequisite condition for deriving benefit from the organizer is a clear stable cognitive structure of ideas. In a recent study in which the learning task (endocrinology of pubescence) was not directly relatable to general background knowledge in endocrinology, there was a similar tendency for the organizer to benefit differentially those subjects with the higher general endocrinology scores (Ausubel and Fitzgerald, 1962).

Effect of Cognitive Variables on Learning and Retention

The data clearly established the general dependence of learning and retention on pretest scores. In a pretest levels × treatment × retention covariance analysis holding DAT constant, the significant effect of pretest levels was readily apparent ($F = 93.3$, $p < .01$; see Table 3). However, a significant first-order interaction between pretest levels and retention indicated that the effects of the independent variable differed from learning to retention. From Table 5 it can be seen that this interaction is largely a reflection of the fall off from learning to retention in the upper-third pretest level (difference between means of 11.2) in contrast to the much smaller difference in the lower-third pretest level (difference between means of 4.9). Apparently the tendency for the more knowledgeable subjects to manifest a relatively higher rate of forgetting than the less knowledgeable subjects is a function of the greater ideational incompatibility (cognitive dissonance) of the new material with established knowledge in the former instance. Thus, although a clear and stable cognitive structure enables the subjects to learn antithetical new material more readily, this material, once learned, is more rapidly reduced during the retention interval to the original, established propositions in cognitive structure than when existing ideational structure is less clear and stable. Supporting evidence of the long-term inhibitory effect of cognitive dissonance on retention is seen in the significant inverse relationship of .30 ($p < .01$) between degree of pro-Southern attitude and pretest scores: ideational conflict between existing pro-Southern bias in the individual, on the one hand, and the general pro-Northern cultural bias in the Northern community, on the other, tends to render knowledge about the Civil War period less stable than when the individual shares the cultural bias. The higher rate of forgetting in the more knowledgeable group of subjects also explains in part why the organizer has more of an effect on retention than on learning, and why it differentially benefits the subjects with higher pretest scores.

Further evidence of the dependence of learning and retention on pretest scores is provided by simple and partial correlations. Simple correlations between pretest and learning scores ($r = .67$, $p < .01$) and between pretest and retention scores ($r = .59$, $p < .01$) still remained significant when corrected for their dependence on DAT scores. The partial correlation between pretest and learning with DAT eliminated ($r = .47$, $p = .01$) was not significantly different from a similar partial correlation between pretest and retention ($r = .41$, $p < .01$). A similar analysis of DAT by learning and retention indicated a correlation of .68 ($p < .01$) between DAT and learning which was reduced to .49 ($p < .01$) when pretest was partialed out, and a correlation of .59 ($p = .01$) between DAT and retention which was reduced to .22 (*ns*) when the effect of the pretest was eliminated (see Table 6). Therefore it seems that although the clarity and stability of cognitive structure are significant variables in both the learning

TABLE 6

Partial Correlations of Pretest and DAT Scores with Learning and Retention Scores

Partial Correlation	Test	
	Learning	Retention
Pretest[a]	.47*	.41*
DAT[b]	.49	.22

[a]DAT eliminated.
[b]Pretest eliminated.
*$p < .05$.

and retention of controversial materials, verbal reasoning ability is functionally related only to learning.

Effects of Attitudes and Attitudinal Bias on Learning and Retention

It has been suggested that the facilitating effect of advance organizers is primarily due to their interaction with the cognitive dimension of attitude structure. The main thesis of this paper is that the cognitive dimension of attitude structure is the major variable in the learning and retention of controversial materials. The intent is not to minimize the obvious significance of *extrinsic* motivational factors in a subject's *general* approach to learning and subsequent recall of the learned materials. What is suggested is that the general interpretation often found in the psychological literature that *intrinsic* motivational or affective factors (e.g., attitudinal bias) account for the phenomenon of selective forgetting in relation to learning tasks involving only a moderate amount of ego threat, is untenable. In order to explore this thesis further in relation to the present study, it is first necessary (*a*) to determine the comparability of the present research to previous studies investigating the phenomenon of selective recall, and (*b*) to clearly distinguish between the effects of cognitive and affective factors on the learning and forgetting processes in order to establish their relative importance.

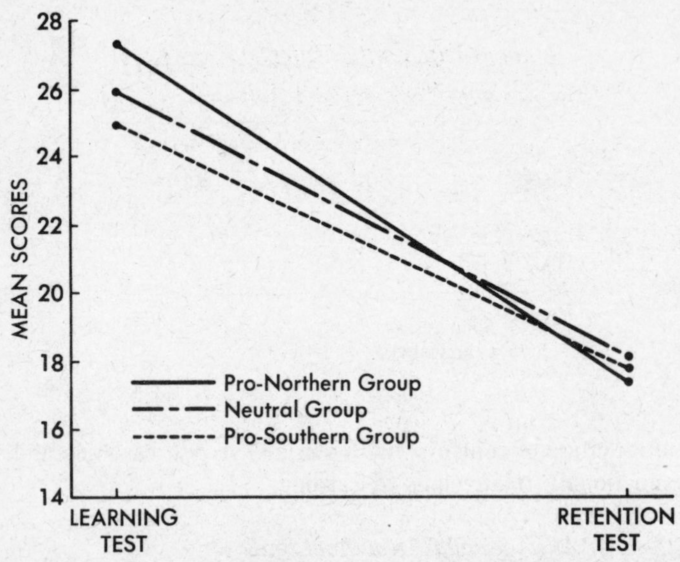

Figure 1 Mean learning and retention scores for different attitude and inventory levels with no statistical control (control group only).

Comparability of This Study to Previous Research No hypotheses were ventured in this study regarding the effect of attitudes (as differentiated from attitudinal bias) on learning and retention, since the nature of this effect has been clearly shown in previous research (Edwards, 1941; Levine and Murphy, 1943; Taft, 1954; Watson and Hartmann, 1939). Nevertheless, an important aspect of the present study is to ascertain the consistency of our general findings with previously demonstrated attitude effects. (Means of the attitude level groups on learning and retention, uncorrected for either pretest or DAT, are shown in Figure 1.)

The principal attitude effect studied in the learning of controversial materials is the phenomenon of differential rates of forgetting for subjects with negative and positive attitudes, respectively. A general indication of the comparability of the findings of the present study to previous research findings can be obtained by comparing the percentages of material forgotten by

TABLE 7

Table of Differential Rates of Forgetting Expressed in Percentages and DF *Index for Four Studies*

Attitude Level	Percentage Forgotten			
	Taft	Present[a]	Levine[b]	Edwards
Negative	42	36	29	13
Positive	37	28	21	8
DF index	1.14	1.29	1.38	1.63
Time-days	3	7	14	21

[a]Results of present study uncorrected for independent variables.
[b]Levine and Murphy's results for anti-Soviet Union materials.

negative and positive attitude groups in the study reported herein to corresponding percentages in those previous studies in which both a test of learning and a test of retention were used. These percentages are given in Table 7, ordered in terms of the retention period (in days) and rendered comparable by a "differential forgetting" (DF) index. This index was computed by dividing the percentage forgotten by the negative attitude group by the percentage forgotten by the positive attitude group. The general consistency of the present research findings with previously reported results is clearly demonstrated.

Attitude and Attitudinal Bias Variables As previously stated, the affective component of attitudes consists of the general complex of feelings that a particular organization of ideas arouses in the subjects. This affective component is synonymous with attitudinal bias. Levels of attitudinal bias are operationally defined, in terms of our statistical model, as attitude inventory scores with the effect of pretest scores (estimate of the *cognitive* dimension of attitudes) held statistically constant. In contrast, attitude levels as such are operationally defined in terms of attitude inventory scores when pretest is uncontrolled. To introduce a control and reduce the error variance in analyzing the effects of attitude levels on learning and retention, DAT was used as a predictor variable.

TABLE 8

Analysis of Covariance[a] *of Attitude Inventory Levels × Retention Holding Pretest Constant*

Source					Adjusted			
	df	SS_y	SP	SS_x	SS'_y	df'	MS'	F
Attitude inventory	2	21	461	10057	313	2	157	2.21*
Retention	1	2250	−1193	633	2817	1	2817	39.7**
Attitude inventory × retention	2	45	−162	738	158	2	79	1.11
Error	126	14193	23084	99892	8859	125	71	
Total	131	16509	22190	111320	12086			

Note.—Null hypotheses concerning homogeneity of variance and regression accepted.
[a] Control group only.
*$p < .13$.
**$p < .01$.

Effect of Attitudes on Learning and Retention An analysis of covariance of attitude levels × retention (control group only) with DAT held constant, shows a suggestive but not significant attitude × retention interaction ($F = 1.11$; see Table 8). This same effect was found by Edwards (1941), Taft (1954), and Gustafson (1957) and was interpreted by these investigators as "repression" due to affective or motivated forgetting. In none of these three studies, however, was the interaction effect as pronounced as in the present study. Direction of interaction is clearly seen in the table of attitude level means corrected for DAT (Table 9). This trend is entirely consistent with the findings of related research. Moreover, the "differential forgetting" effect is more strongly suggested by the above data (with the aid of statistical controls) than in the work of Taft, Levine and Murphy, or Edwards. The DF index for the data in Table 9 with DAT held constant is 1.92. It seems, therefore, that the differential forgetting effect which Edwards (1941) interpreted as due to a "conflict with [the] ego's desires" (p. 34), and Taft (1954) interpreted as due to "defense" and "repression" (p. 27), and which Gustafson (1957) referred to as due to an "affective

TABLE 9

Mean Learning and Retention Scores for Different Inventory Levels Corrected for DAT[a]

Attitude Inventory Level	Control Group *M*		
	Learning	Retention	Learning Retention Difference
Pro-Northern	26.6	14.5	12.1
Neutral	25.8	16.8	9.0
Pro-Southern	27.5	20.9	6.6

Note.—N for each subgroup is 22.
[a] Control group only.

factor in retention" (p. 49), can be attributed to the attitude variable as defined above. It is possible in the present research design, however, to consider the relative importance of the cognitive and affective components of attitude in causing "selective forgetting." Clearly, in the work cited above, and implicitly in most other studies of this phenomenon, the interpretation has been entirely in terms of "affect."

Effect of Attitudinal Bias on Learning and Retention The hypothesis that positive attitudinal bias facilitates and that negative attitudinal bias inhibits the learning of controversial materials was rejected. The differences were in the predicted direction (see Table 10) but were not statistically significant.

The differential forgetting trend reported above and shown graphically in Figure 2, although not within an acceptable range of statistical significance, is comparable to that found in previous studies involving controversial material in which the results were also suggestive but nonsignificant. The central focus of research interest in this area has been on the attitude × retention

TABLE 10

Mean Learning and Retention Scores for Different Attitude Levels, Corrected for Pretest[a]

Attitude Inventory Level	Control Group *M*		
	Learning	Retention	Learning Retention Difference
Pro-Northern	25.1	16.4	8.7
Neutral	25.9	17.6	8.3
Pro-Southern	27.1	19.8	7.3

Note.—*N* for each subgroup is 22.
[a] Control group only.

interaction. This interaction effect has been at least as clearly shown in the present study as it has been in previous research.

However, when pretest is held constant in an analysis of covariance of attitude inventory levels × retention (control group only), the inventory level × retention interaction is reduced from 1.13 (pretest not controlled) to .08 (pretest controlled; see Table 11). Comparison of the differences between learning and retention means, both before and after pretest is controlled, also clearly establishes that whatever attitude × retention interaction occurs is entirely attributable to the cognitive dimension of attitudes. When inventory levels are uncorrected for pretest, the difference between the learning and retention means for the pro-Northern-attitude group is 12.1 compared to 6.6 for the pro-Southern-attitude group (see Table 9). When, however, the effect of pretest scores is eliminated, the corresponding differences for the negative and positive attitude groups are 8.7 and 7.3 (see

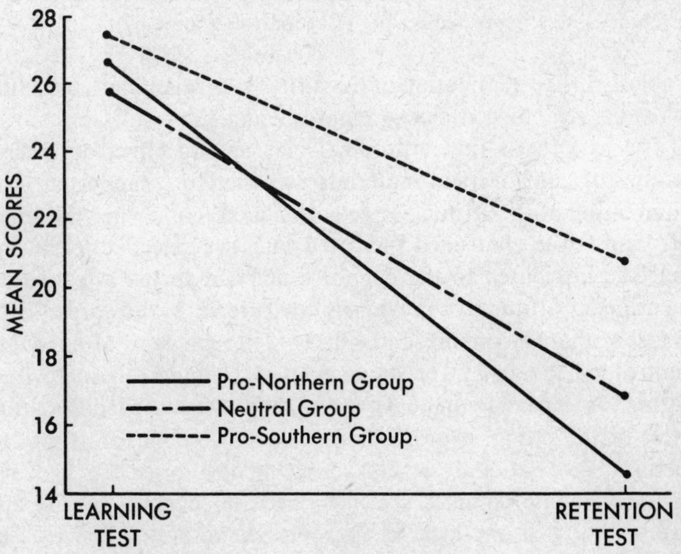

Figure 2 Mean learning and retention scores for different attitude inventory levels, corrected for DAT (control group only).

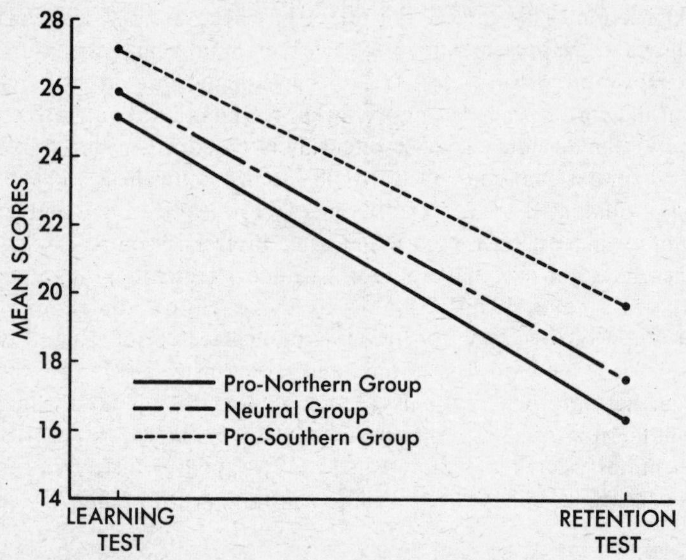

Figure 3 Mean learning and retention scores for different attitude inventory levels, corrected for pre-test (control group only).

Table 10). The elimination of the attitude × retention interaction is readily seen by comparing Figures 2 and 3.

The hypothesis that attitudinal bias has no effect on the retention of controversial materials was therefore supported. The elimination of the attitude × retention interaction when the effect of pretest was controlled indicated that any selective forgetting must be attributed to the cognitive and not to the affective dimension of attitude as previously interpreted by Edwards, Taft, Watson and Hartmann, and others. Through lack of adequate control of the cognitive dimension of attitudes these investigators, in our opinion, have mistakenly attributed differential rates of forgetting in positively and negatively biased groups to intrinsic motivational factors acting on the forgetting process. When adequate controls are introduced it becomes readily apparent that it is the lack of appropriate subsuming concepts in attitude structure that renders "other side" arguments more susceptible to rapid forgetting.

TABLE 11

Analysis of Covariance[a] of Learning and Retention Holding Pretest Constant

Source					Adjusted			
	df	SS_y	*SP*	SS_x	SS'_y	*df'*	*MS'*	*F*
Attitude inventory	2	21	119	674	155	2	78	1.13
Retention	1	2250	66	2	2162	1	2162	31.3*
Attitude inventory × retention	2	45	38	38	11	2	6	.08
Error	126	14193	8360	12492	8598	125	69	
Total	131	16509	8583	13206	10931	130		

Note.—Null hypothesis concerning homogeneity of variance and regression accepted.
[a]Control group only.
*$p < .01$.

Summary and Conclusions

The 264 Illinois high school students studied a passage presenting a Southern interpretation of the Civil War. When general knowledge about the Civil War period was held constant in an analysis of covariance design, the differential effect of attitudinal bias on retention was eliminated. This finding suggests that it is the lack of appropriate subsuming concepts in attitude structure, rather than the direct effect of affective factors on retention processes, that renders "other side" arguments more susceptible to forgetting. Further substantiating the greater relative importance of cognitive factors were the facts that the more knowledgeable *S*s learned more than the less knowledgeable *S*s, and that an organizing passage facilitated retention.

References

Ausubel, D. P., and E. Blake, Jr. Proactive inhibition in the forgetting of meaningful school material. *J. educ. Res.*, 1958, **52,** 145–149.

Ausubel, D. P., and D. Fitzgerald. The role of discriminability in meaningful verbal learning and retention. *J. educ. Psychol.*, 1961, **52,** 266–274.

——, Organizer, general background, and antecedent learning variables in sequential verbal learning. *J. educ. Psychol.*, 1962, **53,** 243–249.

Edwards, A. L. Political frames of reference as a factor influencing recognition. *J. abnorm. soc. Psychol.*, 1941, **36,** 34–50.

Gustafson, Lucille. Relationship between ethnic group membership and the retention of selected facts pertaining to American history and culture. *J. educ. Sociol.*, 1957, **31,** 49–56.

Levine, J., and G. Murphy. The learning and forgetting of controversial material. *J. abnorm. soc. Psychol.*, 1943, **38,** 507–517.

Peak, Helen. Attitude and motivation. In M. R. Jones (Ed.), *Nebraska symposium on motivation: 1955*. Lincoln: Univer. Nebraska Press, 1955. Pp. 149–189.

Taft, R. Selective recall and memory distortion of favorable and unfavorable material. *J. abnorm. soc. Psychol.*, 1954, **49,** 23–28.

Watson, W. S., and G. W. Hartmann. The rigidity of a basic attitudinal frame. *J. abnorm. soc. Psychol.*, 1939, **34,** 314–335.

24 Some Comments on the Nature, Diagnosis, and Prognosis of Neurotic Anxiety*

David P. Ausubel

Anxiety is a ubiquitous phenomenon, and anxiety neurosis is an exceedingly widespread disease. A large proportion of psycho-neurotics who consult general medical practitioners for a variety of somatic complaints are in reality suffering from the physiological manifestations of anxiety. Similarly, a goodly portion of psychiatric practice consists of patients with severe anxiety states whose symptoms are psychological rather than physiological in nature, such as subjective awareness of dread, or compulsive or obsessive defenses against anxiety.

Reprinted from the article of the same title,* Psychiatric Quarterly, *1956,* **30, *77–88. By permission of the author and* The Psychiatric Quarterly and Supplement.

Anxiety and Fear

Anxiety must be differentiated from other kinds of fear-like states. Generically, it refers to an actual phobic response or to a tendency to respond with fear to any *anticipated* situation which is perceived as a potential threat to self-esteem. It differs from ordinary fear in that the source of the threat is referable to the future rather than to the present. A person is fearful when a mad dog lunges for his throat; he is anxious when he contemplates the loss in self-respect that would result from vocational failure. Anxiety differs from feelings of insecurity, which also arise in response to *anticipated* threat, in the fact that the threat is specifically directed against the individual's self-esteem and not against his physical safety. In many situations, however, insecurity and anxiety are aroused concomitantly. The threat of possible vocational failure, for example, is not only damaging to self-regard but also generates genuine apprehension regarding chances for survival.

At one time, anxiety was distinguished from fear on the assumption that a tangible source of threat was always present in the latter reaction, whereas in the case of anxiety the source of threat was presumably vague and nonspecific. Thus, anxiety was regarded as "free-floating" or objectless. Actually this distinction is groundless since the concept of objectless fear is psychologically meaningless. In cases of supposedly "free-floating" anxiety, careful examination invariably reveals that an actual threat is operative, even if it cannot always be identified by the patient. And obviously there is a vast difference between the cryptic concept of "objectless" anxiety and the more parsimonious notion that sometimes the patient is at a loss when it comes to identifying the source of his anxiety. Furthermore, in many undoubted cases of clinical anxiety, patients enjoy relatively complete and precise insight into the objects of their dread.

Other proposed differentiating criteria between fear and anxiety, such as whether the source of the threat is internal or external in origin or whether the fear response is proportionate to the objective degree of danger confronting the individual, are equally unserviceable. As will be seen presently, they merely distinguish between different kinds of anxiety.

Normal versus Neurotic Anxiety

Within the generic meaning of the term, as defined here, one can conceive of several qualitatively different varieties of anxiety arising under basically different conditions of instigation. Situationally, for example, anxiety is generated in medical students when they are confronted with important examinations that jeopardize the achievement of a life goal closely identified with their sense of adequacy. One can induce the same type of situational anxiety experimentally by giving subjects bogus reports which reflect adversely on their competence or personality integration. Anxiety is aroused during transitional periods of personality development, such as adolescence, when individuals have to achieve a new bio-social status and are kept in a prolonged state of uncertainty regarding the outcome. Feelings of hostility can generate anxiety by threatening an individual with loss of status, as a result of antagonizing persons on whom he is dependent.[1] Similarly, feelings of guilt can generate anxiety by exposing an individual to a sullied, reprehensible portrait of himself, at odds with the moral values he has internalized.

These different varieties of anxiety have one property in common which distinguishes them from neurotic anxiety: In each situation described, anxiety is instigated by an objectively dangerous threat to self-esteem. In some instances this threat may be external in origin—as, for example, the crucial examination in the case of medical students, or the need to acquire adult status under conditions of uncertainty in the case of adolescents. In other instances the source of the threat is within the person—it may come from aggressive impulses or from the individual's awareness that he has violated certain of his moral scruples. The important thing in all of these cases—regardless of whether the source of the threat is internal or external—is that the threat is *objectively* capable of impairing self-esteem in normal persons. In all cases, the threat comes from a source distinct from the object that is being threatened; in no case does the threat to self-esteem come from impaired self-esteem itself. In all cases the response to the threat is appropriate and proportionate to the objective degree of jeopardy confronting the individual's self-esteem.

In neurotic anxiety, on the other hand, the essential source of the threat to self-esteem does not lie outside self-esteem but is to be found in a catastrophic impairment of self-esteem itself. Hence, a person suffering from neurotic anxiety apparently over-reacts with fear to a perceived threat. But this over-reaction is an over-reaction only when considered in relation to the ostensible source of the threat to self-esteem—the threat lying outside self-esteem which precipitates the anxiety. It is not an over-reaction when it is considered in relation to the major source of threat to self-esteem which lies within self-esteem itself. An example and an analogy may help to sharpen this distinction.

In a recently-conducted study of the effects of anxiety on learning,[2] individuals who showed either low or high levels of endogenous anxiety were required to solve a stylus maze blindfolded. This situation constituted a mild form of threat to self-esteem. If the subject was not able to solve the problem, he demonstrated to another and to himself that he was not very good at a certain type of learning. Even rats are reputed to learn to solve mazes. For all the subjects of this recent study, the maze represented a novel learning-task in which past experience was not only of no help but was actually a hindrance. Successful solution of the problem could not be accomplished without improvisation.

The low-anxiety subjects with normal self-esteem tended to assume that they could learn to improvise successfully with a little practice. And if they failed, so what? So they weren't good at solving mazes blindfolded. The high-anxiety subjects had a different orientation. Lacking normal self-esteem, they lacked confidence in their ability to cope with new adjustive situations. They were frightened when their habitual visual learning cues were removed, when they had to improvise. And lacking any intrinsic self-esteem they were naturally dependent on the self-esteem they could achieve through successful performance. Thus, they could less afford to say, "So what?" to failure.

What were the results? The high-anxiety subjects apparently over-reacted to the threat to self-esteem emanating from the maze situation. The real threat, however, came from their own impaired self-esteem. And in terms of *that* threat they certainly did *not* over-react. On the first trial of the maze they became panicky and flustered, making a significantly greater number of errors than the low-anxiety subjects. But after the first trial the maze was no longer a new learning task requiring improvisation. It became more and more familiar and "old hat." By the end of 10 trials, there was no longer a significant difference between the two anxiety groups.

The role of novel adjustive situations, that demanded improvisation, in instigating anxiety in neurotically anxious subjects was demonstrated in a corollary experiment. When high-anxiety subjects were allowed to practice on an easier maze, first with and then without vision, they benefited significantly more from this advance preparation than did low-anxiety subjects.

These experiments could defensibly illustrate the following facts about the nature of neurotic anxiety: (a) that an actual threat to the individual apart from his own impaired self-esteem is the precipitating factor; (b) that the most effective threat is a new adjustive situation requiring improvisation, since it hits at the very core of impaired self-esteem (when adjustive situations become routine and familiar they are no longer threatening); (c) that the anxiety response is disproportionate to the objective danger of the threat but *not* to the *actual* degree of threat experienced; and (d) that the major source of threat in neurotic anxiety lies in impaired self-esteem.

The distinction between normal and neurotic anxiety can be further highlighted with an analogy from heart physiology. When a person has a normal, undamaged heart, how can he develop heart failure? It's not very easy. He has to be subjected to tremendous exertion without rest, prolonged exposure to heat, severe pulmonary disease, etc. The threat to cardiac adequacy when one has a normal heart, therefore, lies in an objectively-punishing situation. Less rigorous threats to cardiac adequacy are easily compensated for because of the great reserve power of the heart. If the heart shows signs of beginning to fail when the external pressure increases, the outcome is hardly disproportionate to the degree of strain involved.

But a person with a damaged heart has already exhausted all of his power to compensate for increased external demands. Require him to run up a flight of stairs quickly, and he will be thrown into heart failure. In his case, the source of the threat to cardiac adequacy lies in his own damaged heart muscle, just as the source of the threat to self-esteem in a person with neurotic anxiety lies in his own damaged self-esteem. Certainly he is over-reacting with signs of cardiac insufficiency to a flight of stairs just as the anxiety neurotic is over-reacting to the stylus maze with signs of fear and further impairment of self-esteem. But in neither case is the reaction disproportionate to the actual degree of jeopardy confronting the heart or the self-esteem.

The Origin of Neurotic Anxiety

The crucial question, of course, is: How do anxiety neurotics develop catastrophic impairment of self-esteem so that they over-react with fear to perceived threats to self-esteem? A definitive answer to this question cannot be given at this time because there is as yet no definitive evidence. In the area of personality development, psychology and psychiatry have not yet advanced beyond the stage of hypothesis. This statement is probably difficult to accept, since one has only to open any textbook in the field to find all the answers neatly worked out in great detail with accompanying diagrams. Explanations that are given are not offered as hypotheses, as ways in which personality *could* conceivably develop, but as if they were indisputably-proven, empirical truths. Yet the hard fact remains that existing personality theory is mainly unsystematic and unverified clinical impressionism. No controlled, definitive, longitudinal study has *ever* been conducted relating conditions that bear on personality development in childhood to measurable aspects of adult personality structure. It seems to the writer, therefore, that this situation imposes some obligation of humility and tentativeness on personality theorists who have suggestions to offer.

The writer's own unverified clinical impression of the origin of neurotic anxiety[3] is as follows: An individual can never develop neurotic anxiety as long as he enjoys intrinsic feelings of self-esteem, by which is meant a deep inner conviction that he is important and worth while for himself apart from what he can do or accomplish, and apart from the position he holds in life. As long as he possesses this intrinsic self-esteem, failure in achieving superior competence or status is intense, deeply-felt, discouraging—but always peripheral to basic self-esteem, and, hence, never catastrophic. However, if one has to rely on success in performance, status, or vocation for whatever self-esteem he enjoys, catastrophic impairment following some very traumatic experience is much more possible. Failure is no longer peripheral but central—since there is now no basis for a feeling of worth as a human being. His sense of worth becomes purely a function of his competence or reputation; and little self-regard can remain if these are undermined.

Feelings of intrinsic self-esteem, in the writer's opinion, can only develop in one way—from a child identifying in a dependent sense with his parents. He can do this if he perceives that he is accepted and valued for himself. His all-powerful, omniscient parents can endow all objects, including him, with intrinsic value if they so desire. If they respond to him as a person who is worth while and important in his own right—just because they accept him as such—he tends to react to himself in the same way, since he has no other standards of value but theirs. He thus acquires an intrinsic sense of adequacy, a vicarious status which is derived from his dependent relationship to his parents, and which is independent of his actual competencies. As he becomes older, he will increasingly strive for a more primary status based upon his own accomplishments, and will develop feelings of self-esteem related to them. But there will always remain a residual sense of worth which his parents conferred on him by fiat—when as a child he perceived this to be within their power.

Not all children, however, are fortunate enough to be accepted and intrinsically valued by their parents. Some are rejected outright, and others are accepted but extrinsically valued, that is, accepted only in terms of their potential capacity for enhancing their parents' egos by becoming important and successful individuals. Such children do not undergo dependent identification with their parents since they cannot acquire any vicarious status or intrinsic feelings of self-esteem from such a relationship. From the very beginning, their self-esteem becomes a function of what they are able to do and accomplish, and, hence, becomes very vulnerable to catastrophic impairment.

Of course, vulnerability to catastrophic impairment of self-esteem does not guarantee that such impairment must inevitably occur. However, this catastrophic impairment is frequently for another reason. It seems that when individuals lack intrinsic feelings of self-esteem, they are compensatorily motivated to aspire to higher goals and ambitions than the general run of mankind. This is hardly surprising when one considers that the less adequate an individual really feels, the more need he has to prove his adequacy to himself and others by superior accomplishments. In the maze experiments with anxious subjects, it was found that their levels of aspiration in relation to previous performance and to prior feelings of failure were significantly higher than those of the non-anxious subjects. This means that their aspirations were more unrealistic, that their goals were not only too high, but were also extremely resistive to lowering in the face of realistic indications for so doing.

Thus, it seems reasonable to expect that rejected and extrinsically-valued children who have no intrinsic feelings of self-esteem will tend to set their academic and vocational goals high, and often unrealistically high. If they happen to be extremely able individuals, or less able persons with wealthy fathers, all may go well, and they may achieve in accordance with their aspirations. However, there is no reason to believe that such rejected and extrinsically-valued individuals tend to be more gifted or more frequently related to affluent ancestors. Hence, the chances for large-scale collapse of their grandiose and unrealistic aspirations are rather good; and since they have no intrinsic self-esteem to fall back upon, this defeat is centrally traumatic to self-esteem and possibly catastrophic in its implications. This occurrence precipitates acute anxiety, akin to panic. If recovery occurs without psychosis, it leaves a permanently damaged self-esteem or, in other words, a chronic anxiety neurosis, which may flare up at any time and become acute when the environment becomes too threatening.

Prognosis and Therapy

If this hypothesis about the nature and origin of anxiety is correct, it would seem that the prognosis of neurotic anxiety is not too good. Once an individual's self-esteem has been catastrophically impaired, permanent damage has, in the writer's opinion, been incurred—damage that will forever predispose him to over-react with anxiety to new adjustive situations, or even to old adjustive situations that he has never learned how to handle. The writer has never witnessed a genuine case of anxiety neurosis in which complete cure has been effected. But this does not mean that anxiety neurotics cannot make a good adjustment to life, or that they cannot learn to keep their anxiety within tolerable limits. As long as they can prevent their environment from becoming too threatening, they can keep the triggering-mechanism at bay. This is not so difficult as it sounds. Take practically any new job. Within six weeks, one meets 90 per cent of all the potential situations that can arise. Within a year one meets 99 per cent of such situations. After that, the job is pretty much routine. Also, if one is reaction-sensitive to threat, one becomes fairly adroit at avoiding, circumventing, and by-passing threatening situations. If avoidance is not possible, one can take steps to neutralize the novelty of new adjustive situations by priming one's self in advance. Anxiety neurotics are also hard-working, highly-motivated, ambitious persons. In due time they tend to get ahead, win promotions and acquire job security. All this bolsters self-esteem. Perhaps they don't get as far ahead as they'd like to, but often far enough to keep the level of self-esteem above the threshold of acute anxiety.

In addition, numerous defensive, anxiety-reducing, adjustive mechanisms are available—becoming an "awfully nice guy" who hears no evil and sees no evil; placating everybody in sight, from the boss to the office boy; rationalizing mediocrity through psychosomatic symptoms or paranoid trends; creating an illusion of certainty through compulsion; displacing and concretizing the source of threat through phobias and obsessions, and so on.

Sometimes, of course, things don't work out so well. Some anxiety neurotics have very itchy ambitions that require constant scratching. They expose themselves for years to threatening situations like working for advanced degrees. Others safeguard themselves from threat in a modest, protected environment, but at such a *low* level of accomplishment that self-esteem is depressed below the level of toleration. Hence, acute exacerbations of anxiety arise, with signs of panic and agitation. Most persons recover from these attacks. Others abandon all striving, become reconciled to complete defeat and develop depressive psychoses. Still others abandon adult standards of maturity, and withdraw from the operation of adjusting to social reality. In other words, they develop a reactive schizophrenia.

What can a therapist do for such persons? In the stage of panic, drastic measures are indicated—anything that will reduce anxiety quickly and effectively—the use of reserpine and tolserol, reducing the burden of immediate pressures and demands on the patient, rendering supportive and paternalistic therapy. At this point the patient is incapable of taking any kind of action or making any kind of rational decision by himself. He has to be told what to do if he is to receive the benefit of any help.

In the more chronic stage of anxiety, psychotherapy must first be directed toward preventing acute attacks of anxiety and their dangerous complications. Primarily this means attention to situational conditions. That is, the patient must be helped to an adjustment that is not highly threatening to self-esteem, but at the same time is not pitched at so low a level that no self-esteem is obtainable. Afterward or concomitantly, the following therapeutic goals can be striven for: acquisition of insight into the nature of anxiety; abandonment of exaggerated and distortive defenses; ego-disinvolvement from utterly unrealistic ambitions; avoidance of excessive circumscription of the environment; and increasing tolerance for conscious anxiety. Subjective anxiety is psychologically more uncomfortable but is prognostically more hopeful than the defensive or physiological varieties. And although the two latter kinds of symptoms undoubtedly reduce conscious anxiety, they are, if physiological, more dangerous to health and life. Defensive symptoms, on the other hand, may lead to serious distortions of personality, which are very resistive to change because of their adjustive value.

Some Diagnostic Considerations

What about the diagnosis of neurotic anxiety? The only suggestion that the writer can offer is that valid diagnoses will be made by clinicians who have adequate theoretical and clinical training, and who, above all, possess a special kind of talent—psychological sensitivity or empathy. In the final analysis, correct clinical diagnoses can only be made by accurately perceiving the emotions, attitudes and motivations of other persons. Some clinicians can do this, others cannot.

One might logically suppose that individuals entering the fields of clinical psychology, psychiatry or counseling are especially empathic or psychologically sensitive. But this is not necessarily true, and the same thing might be said for those who are in the field of personality research. Some of these persons would do just as well dealing with the statistical means and sigmas of soybean yield per acre or of life expectancies. Yet because of the type of phenomenology involved in personality, it does not seem possible that we shall ever be able to rule out subjective perceptual skills in identifying various dimensions of personality structure. It is very unlikely that we shall ever be able to diagnose neurotic anxiety by methods similar to those used by physicians in diagnosing anemia or diabetes. We are dealing with phenomena of a higher order of complexity than the concentration of hemoglobin or glucose in the blood stream. As yet, there is no really sensitive *objective* instrument for personality measurement that is reliable or valid enough for purposes of individual prediction. And the writer's guess is that there never will be one.

In the last 20 years, more subtle but also more subjective, instruments than formerly have been devised for measuring personality—the projective tests. But tests that rely on subjective interpretation are no more valid than the skillfulness of the person using them permits them to be. Hence projective tests are mostly useful to the skillful clinician as short-cuts. If the clinician is perceptive, he can make a diagnosis more quickly by using them; if he isn't perceptive, he will mainly use these tests to confirm his erroneous diagnoses.

When one says that a diagnostic instrument is only valid in the hands of a talented user, does this mean that the instrument is capricious and unreliable and ought to be thrown away? Quite the contrary. It means that it ought to be taken out of the hands of non-talented users. Perhaps one physician out of 10 is skillful enough to use the stethoscope in making an accurate diagnosis of difficult pulmonary conditions. Should the medical profession dispose of the stethoscope, or should it refer difficult pulmonary cases to physicians with sensitive auditory perception?

The point the writer is belaboring is that the most important diagnostic tool in the hands of a clinician in psychological medicine is a certain skill or talent which enables him to perceive, and gain insight into, the workings of another's personality. Like all talents, high degrees of it are not generously distributed among the population. If we want to make accurate diagnoses, we shall have to see to it that these psychologically-talented persons become clinical psychologists and psychiatrists, instead of deluding ourselves that personality diagnosis can become an exact and objective science, or that any well-trained person with a Rorschach in his hands can become a good clinician. Is this position unrealistic? It is followed every day in other clinical fields which can lay claim to greater objectivity in diagnostic methods—internal medicine for example.

This does not mean, of course, that a good diagnostician is necessarily a good therapist, since other qualities of personality in addition to psychological sensitivity are necessary for therapy. In other words, empathic ability is a necessary, rather than a sufficient, condition for success in psychotherapy.

Summary and Conclusions

Anxiety is conceptualized as a specific kind of fear-response or tendency to respond with fear to anticipated situations that are perceived as threats to an individual's self-esteem. The characteristic feature of neurotic anxiety is a tendency to apparent over-response to such threats, particularly to those posed by novel adjustive situations. But in terms of the essential or predisposing cause of neurotic anxiety, an existing state of catastrophically impaired self-esteem, the response is not disproportionate to the degree of subjectively experienced threat.

It is postulated that neurotic anxiety only occurs in persons who, as a result of not being accepted and intrinsically valued as children, do not enjoy an intrinsic sense of adequacy which is independent of their performance-ability and success in life. Such individuals are vulnerable to neurotic anxiety because their self-esteem is wholly a function of the realization of their compensatorily exalted and highly tenacious ambitions.

The prognosis for complete cure of neurotic anxiety is regarded with pessimism, but several effective steps can be taken to prevent acute exacerbations of anxiety, that is, states of panic. Accurate diagnoses of neurotic anxiety can only be made by specially empathic clinicians with adequate theoretical and clinical training. Projective tests are useful diagnostic tools in the hands of such clinicians. The fact that these instruments require special skills of a subjective nature in order to be valid does not in any sense destroy their clinical usefulness.

References

1 Horney, Karen: The Neurotic Personality of Our Time. Norton. New York. 1937.

2 Ausubel, D. P.; H. M. Schiff; and M. Goldman: Qualitative characteristics in the learning process associated with anxiety. J. Abnor, and Soc. Psychol., 48: 537-547, 1953.

3 Ausubel, D. P.: Ego Development and the Personality Disorders. Grune & Stratton. New York. 1952.

25 Qualitative Characteristics in the Learning Process Associated with Anxiety*

David P. Ausubel
Herbert M. Schiff
Morton Goldman

Anxiety states are among the most common forms of personality disturbance met with in clinical practice. Unlike psychotic and certain other disabling neurotic conditions (e.g., hysterical paralysis), the sufferer from anxiety remains in good contact with his environment and strives unremittingly for prestige and self-realization (2). It is because of this widespread prevalence of anxiety among persons attempting an adequate reality adjustment that greater insight must be gained into the characteristic adjustive techniques adopted by these individuals.

Reprinted from the article of the same title,* Journal of Abnormal and Social Psychology, *1953,* **48, *537–547. By permission of the authors and The American Psychological Association, Inc.*

Since an integral relationship exists between anxiety and learning, further investigation of this relationship promises to be extremely rewarding in elucidating the nature of both phenomena. On the one hand, there is definitive experimental evidence on the infrahuman level that (*a*) phobic stimuli of low and moderate intensity exert a motivational effect by creating a need for reduction of the discomfort induced by their anticipation, and (*b*) responses which provide this reduction have reinforcing (rewarding) properties (12, 28, 29, 30). On the other hand, anxiety has been shown to influence learning and problem solving adversely in human subjects (4, 6, 7, 13, 20, 22, 26, 34, 36, 37, 40, 41, 44).

What is needed, therefore, is a theoretical conception of anxiety which primarily defines this propensity to respond with fear to threatening stimuli in terms of problem-solving situations. Only within the framework of such a definition can an attempt be made to provide answers to the questions which this study seeks to investigate, i.e., Why does anxiety both disorganize performance and motivate improvement? Does anxiety impair the efficiency of the learning process in all areas or selectively? Do anxiety-ridden individuals approach learning situations differently? If they do employ unique learning techniques or "crutches," how effective are they?

The Methodology of Investigating Human Anxiety

Paradoxically enough, despite his pioneering experimental work on the role of anxiety in learning (both as a motivating agent and selective determinant of the learned response), Mowrer takes a dim view of the possibility of establishing an experimental psychology of anxiety in human subjects (31). His reasons are that human anxiety is both a highly complex experience and one that is potentially too damaging to induce experimentally. If by anxiety he means a propensity to react with fear that is deeply rooted in personality structure, we must obviously concur in his second reservation. However, it is *not* necessary to induce personality anxiety in order to study it experimentally. One can utilize *existing* states of clinical anxiety providing that they can be identified and measured—in relative if not in absolute terms.

Secondly, the manifest complexity of personality anxiety obviates its experimental investigation *only* if one dichotomizes it and fear anticipation in animals in relation to the learning process. The relationship of phobic stimuli to animal learning problems is clear enough. But if one defines human anxiety in Mowrer's terms as the infiltration of imperfectly repressed guilt into conscious awareness, it does become so unnecessarily complex a phenomenon that its intrinsic relation to learning is obscured. This methodological impasse is not presented by our more clinically defensible conception of anxiety as "an acquired reaction-sensitivity in individuals suffering from impaired self-esteem to over-react with fear to any anticipated adjustive situation that contains a further threat to self-esteem" (2). It is largely because of theoretical orientations to anxiety stemming from the psychoanalytic tradition (which place undue emphasis upon repression and ignore its organic connection to everyday learning situation) that there is such a complete dearth of experimental studies dealing with *personality* anxiety.

The trend in recent years has been to study the effects of situationally induced anxiety, i.e., anxiety occurring in uncontrived, life situations; anxiety experimentally generated by social threat, failure experience, conflict, etc.; and anxiety induced by hazards implanted through hypnotic suggestion. An obvious difficulty of this method is the fact that "identical situations usually mean very different things to different people" (14). More important still is the lack of psychological equivalence between situational and personality anxiety. Granted that situational stress alone can enhance or disrupt learning performance, and that personality anxiety is usually evoked in response to external threat. Nevertheless, we submit that the anxiety precipitated by an environmental hazard because of impaired self-esteem (leading to a predisposition to overreact with fear to threat) is both quantitatively and qualitatively different from the anxiety induced by the same external hazard when the personality predisposition is absent. In the first instance, a general predisposition to react with fear is merely released; in the second, the fear response is freshly and specifically instigated in relation to the situation. In the latter case also, since the subject is reacting to the phobic stimulus in terms of its objective hazardness, the response will be more proportionate to the actual danger involved; hence, to an objectively equivalent danger signal there will be less response indicative of disorganization. Finally, it is reasonable to expect that the individual with personality anxiety (in contrast to the normal person exhibiting situational anxiety) develops a number of *habitual* anxiety-reducing "response sets" which qualitatively alter the nature of his learning process.

Thus, the choice of experimental method must be adapted to purpose. If we are not primarily concerned with investigating the reaction of normal persons to catastrophic situations, we must study the effects of existing personality anxiety in appropriate learning situations. Such anxiety may be identified and evaluated for intensity by clinical judgment (7), or by a wide variety of projective techniques (3, 11, 16, 19, 24, 38). Our choice of the Rorschach method (in the absence of an adequate clinical population) was based on the availability of considerable clinical and experimental support for test indices of anxiety (3, 8, 9, 19, 34).

METHOD

Definition of Terms and Operations

For the purposes of this study the term *improvising ability* is defined as the relative capacity of an individual to utilize varied, extemporaneous, and unfamiliar responses (or to free himself from the perseverative influence of a previously acquired and more conventional mode of response which is unadjustive) in the solution of a novel problem.

The operations by which this study proposes to test this ability involve problems the solution of which are especially amenable to motor learning of a trial-and-error variety. It is entirely conceivable, however, that this same ability could be implicated in other types of problem situations which are characteristically solved by "insight," planning, and reasoning.

The specific operations employed in the testing of improvisation are:

The mirror-tracing of a six-pointed star This is ostensibly a test of improvising ability since learning involves the abandonment of established eye-hand coordinations built up over a lifetime in favor of the trial-and-error discovery of an entirely new eye-hand direction relationship. The learning task involves only one tracing of the star.

The blindfold learning of a stylus maze A maze of such difficulty is used as to result in a mean score of 15-20 trials necessary for errorless learning in a group of normal adult *S*s. Each *S* is given ten trials.

Under conditions of absent vision, the maze test is a very novel situation for human *S*s which demands considerable improvisation since spatial orientation is customarily and almost exclusively determined by visual clues.

Preparation is defined as a preliminary and limited period of orientation with the test materials and situation as the result of performing operations of a related but not identical nature, and which are also simpler and less frustrating than the actual test situation.

Desire for preparation is defined as the *S*'s verbal expression of preference for this preliminary period of orientation.

The effect of preparation is determined by dividing a given group of *S*s into two subgroups on the basis of random selection, and then comparing the performance of the subgroup allowed preparation with the performance of the subgroup not allowed preparation. Each subgroup is given preparation on one test (mirror or maze) and not on the other. Preparation is limited on a time or trial basis and is uniform for all *S*s in a given subgroup.

Practice effect is defined as the improvement in score from the first to the tenth maze trial. Regression effect is defined as the occurrence of a poorer performance in a subsequent, as opposed to an immediately preceding, maze trial.

Two indices of *level of aspiration* are determined: (*a*) *goal discrepancy score*, the algebraic difference between level of aspiration for a succeeding trial and score on the immediately preceding trial, and (*b*) *goal tenacity score*, the relationship between goal discrepancy score and the feelings of success or failure relating to the previous performance. These feelings are defined operationally in terms of the *performance discrepancy score*, or the difference between actual performance and the prior level of aspiration for it. The goal tenacity score, therefore, is derived by subtracting performance discrepancy score from the succeeding goal discrepancy score. Hence a positive goal tenacity score indicates that future level of aspiration is being maintained at a high level in relation to prior success or failure experiences.

Over- or underestimation of score is defined as the difference between (*a*) *S*'s estimates of the percentile rank equivalents of his maze error scores on the first and tenth trials of the maze and (*b*) his actual percentile ranks on same. Over- or underestimation of test performance time is defined as the difference between (*a*) *S*'s estimate of elapsed time on each maze trial and (*b*) his actual time score. In each case the actual score is subtracted from the estimate.

The experimental (high) and control (low) anxiety groups are constituted in terms of the upper and lower fifths of a distribution of anxiety scores on the group Rorschach test. In determining the effects of anxiety on the above dependent variables, only the nonpreparation subgroups on a given learning instrument are compared. In ascertaining the relative benefit accruing to the two groups from preparation, the difference between the mean performances of the nonpreparation and preparation subgroups of the high anxiety group is compared to the corresponding difference in the low anxiety group.

Selection of Experimental and Control Groups

The population from which the experimental and control groups were chosen consisted of 285 college students (216 women and 69 men) enrolled in the beginning undergraduate course in education[1] at the University of Illinois. To this entire group the group Rorschach test was administered by the method of Harrower-Erickson (15). The Rorschach pictures reproduced on

[1] The authors are grateful for the cooperation of Professors Harold C. Hand and Gilbert C. Finlay in permitting the use of their classes for this study.

slides were projected onto a screen, *S* writing his own responses to the blots in a printed test booklet. Following this procedure, *S*s were given a preliminary form of the Illinois Personality Inventory, a paper-and-pencil instrument designed to measure subjective, physiological, defensive, and disruptive manifestations of anxiety.

The Rorschach anxiety score was derived by crediting *S* with one point for each anxiety sign manifested in his test booklet. The following test indices, commonly regarded by Rorschach experts (3, 19, 34) as anxiety indications, were used as a guide in determining the anxiety rating for each subject:

1. The total number of card rejections (*rej*).
2. The percentage of responses: to the whole card (*W*); of oligophrenic details (*o*); of unusual details (*Dd*); using human movement (*M*); using form as a sole determinant, and the quality of the form (*F* +, *F*−).
3. Diffuse shading responses (*K*, *KF*, *kF*).
4. The ratio of human detail to complete human figure responses; the ratio of human detail and animal detail to human and animal responses (*Hd: H*; *Hd* + *Ad:H* + *A*).
5. Content analysis: threatening, vague, evasive responses, noncommittal comments, etc.
6. Signs of shading shock (*Sh S*); impoverished content, decline in form quality, irregular succession, avoidance of use of texture, decrease in ability to see popular (*P*) responses, etc.
7. Color balance (*FC: CF* + *C*).

Four of the above Rorschach factors (*Sh S*, *W*, *R*, *Do*,) have been validated as anxiety indicators in an experimental study of stress-induced anxiety, and three others (*P*, *Rej*, and color balance) have received suggestive support (8). We utilized the other signs not validated by Eichler's study on the grounds that clinical evidence (3, 19, 34) is more relevant in an investigation of personality anxiety than validation data secured in relation to situational anxiety. The unlikelihood of situational changes producing all of the Rorschach manifestations associated with a basic personality pattern is borne out by the absence of any change in the Rorschach picture in a group of anxious schizophrenics following the reduction of anxiety by tolserol (26).

The frequency distribution of these Rorschach anxiety scores, ranging from 1 to 10, was markedly skewed to the right, indicating a rather low level of anxiety for the group as a whole. High and low anxiety groups were constituted by counting off the fifty highest and fifty lowest scores from each end of the distribution. The high group included scores from 10 to 5,[2] and the low group scores from 1 to 3.[2] By a process of random selection, each group was divided into two subgroups, I and II. The mean Rorschach anxiety score and the sex distribution for each group and subgroup are given in Table 1.[3]

The Rorschach tests were scored by one of the investigators, and the motor tests of learning were administered by two other experimenters. The latter did not know the anxiety scores of *S*s at the time of testing. The *S*s of the two groups were not informed on what basis they had been chosen. They were assured that the results would be used for research purposes only, and that their anonymity apart from the experimenters would be unconditionally respected. The performance tests—first the mirror tracing test and then the stylus maze test—were administered individually to each *S* with only a single *E* present.

The Learning Tests

Control of preparation Advance preparation was regulated as follows: In the mirror tracing test, *S*s in subgroup I of each group were asked whether prior to the actual performance of the test they would prefer to have an opportunity to practice mirror drawing movements on a blank sheet of paper. At this point, *S* knew that the test required the tracing of a design, but did not know that this was to be a six-pointed star. After this expression of preference was indicated and recorded, all *S*s in subgroup I (regardless of their preference) were required to practice random movements for one minute. The *S*s in subgroup II performed the mirror tracing test directly without any mention of preparation.

[2] To complete the high and low groups, several *S*s with Rorschach anxiety scores of 5 and 3 respectively were randomly selected from a larger number of *S*s with these scores.

[3] The original number of 50 *S*s in each group was reduced to 47 in the high anxiety group and 46 in the low anxiety group as a result of missed appointments.

TABLE 1

Population Characteristics of Groups and Subgroups

	Subgroup I				Subgroup II			
Group	*N*	Male	Female	Mean Rorschach Anxiety Score	*N*	Male	Female	Mean Rorschach Anxiety Score
High anxiety	21	2	19	6.4	26	6	20	6.4
Low anxiety	22	5	17	1.9	24	5	19	2.0
All groups	43	7	36	4.2	50	11	39	4.2

In the stylus maze test (18 turns), *S*s in subgroup II (who had not been allowed preparation on the mirror tracing test) were required to take preparation on another stylus maze with a different and simpler pattern (9 turns). One complete trial run of the practice maze, first without and then with the blindfold, was performed prior to the administration of the test maze. As above, *S*s were also asked to indicate their desire for preparation, and were informed that the two maze patterns were different. Subgroup II took the maze test without any mention of preparation.

The mirror tracing test The *E* placed the mirror drawing apparatus in front of *S*. The picture of the star was covered by a screen which was arranged so as to block *S*'s direct view of the star and of his hand, but allowed him to observe the reflection of same in the mirror. The point of the pencil was placed at the starting point, and *E* assisted *S* in grasping the pencil. *E* stated:

I want to find out how rapidly and accurately you can trace a design while you are looking in the mirror. Trace the outline of the star starting in this direction. Work as rapidly as you can but try to keep on the line; the point of the pencil must always touch the paper. Ready? Go!

The *E* measured elapsed time with a stop watch. The time limit was 10 minutes. At the conclusion of the performance, *S* was asked to estimate the elapsed time and the percentile rank which his performance would earn him in the group.

The stylus maze test An 18-turn stylus maze was used for this study. With the apparatus out of sight, *E* stated:

I want to see how quickly and accurately you can learn the correct path through a maze while you are blindfolded. After I blindfold you I will place a stick in your hand at the beginning of the maze. Your job is to find the correct path that will lead you to the end of the maze, making as few mistakes as possible. If the stick hits an obstruction it means that you have entered a blind alley. Each time you enter a blind alley it will count as an error. You must never lift your stick up out of the grooves.

Always keep it in contact with the hard floor of the maze. Do you understand what is to be done?

The *E* put cotton and a mask over *S*'s closed eyelids, and placed the stick in his hand at the start of the maze indicating the proper direction. The *E* started his stop watch and counted all errors. Exits from blind alleys or backward traversing of the correct path were not counted as errors. After each trial, *S* was asked to estimate elapsed time and percentile rank in his group as above.[4] Level of aspiration for the next trial was obtained as follows: *E* stated, "You made . . . errors in this trial. How many errors do you think you will make on the next trial? Use your very best judgment."

The same procedure was repeated for ten trials. After the tenth trial, level of aspiration for the next trial was ascertained, but the eleventh trial was not performed. The test was terminated during any trial in which *S*'s performance exceeded 10 minutes.

Results

The feasibility of using Rorschach test signs as indices of personality anxiety was confirmed by the finding of significant differences between high and low anxiety groups with respect to total score and one subscale score of the anxiety inventory. On four other subscale scores, differences were not significant but were in the appropriate direction (see Table 6).

Effect of Anxiety on Improvising Ability

Table 2 shows the effects of anxiety on improvising ability. Although the mirror tracing test scores did not differentiate significantly between high and low anxiety groups, the low anxiety group was significantly superior to the high anxiety group with respect to time score ($p = .02$) and error score ($p = .02$) on the *first* trial of the maze. When the scores of all *S*s (including those who failed on the first trial) were utilized in computing the

[4] Estimates of percentile rank were made only after the first and tenth trials.

TABLE 2

Improvising Ability of High and Low Anxiety Groups

Criterion	High Anxiety Group			Low Anxiety Group			Significance Level of Differences Between Means
	N	*M*	σ	*N*	*M*	σ	
Mirror seconds	26	146.5	170.2	24	170.5	130.4	.55
Maze seconds (mean of 10 trials)	21	115.1	57.9	22	109.5	54.1	.74
Maze errors (mean of 10 trials)	21	33.4	24.0	22	30.4	23.1	.69
Maze seconds, 1st trial (all scores)	21	393.6	210.2	22	324.2	211.0	.28
Maze seconds, 1st trial (only passers)	14	290.4	180.8	14	166.6	210.1	.02
Maze errors, 1st trial (all scores)	21	93.1	72.5	22	63.0	51.0	.09
Maze errors, 1st trial (only passers)	14	64.9	53.1	14	28.6	15.1	.015

mean,[5] the significance level of these differences dropped to .28 and .09 respectively, but were in the appropriate direction. The high anxiety group was significantly more variable than the low anxiety group with respect to maze errors on the first trial of the maze.

When the two anxiety groups were compared on the mean of *ten* maze trials, the superiority of the low anxiety group was no longer significant (see Table 2).

Anxiety and Practice Effect

Both low and high anxiety groups benefited significantly from practice as shown by the marked improvement in their performances from the first to the tenth trials of the maze (see Table 3). The practice gain of the high anxiety group, however, was significantly greater ($p = .02$) and more variable ($p < .01$) than that of the low anxiety group for both time and error scores.

When six *S*s in each of the two groups were matched on the basis of error score on the first trial, the difference in practice gain failed to be significant.

The high anxiety group showed significantly less regression effect with respect to maze seconds than the low anxiety group, and a suggestive trend toward fewer regressive errors (see Table 6). On both criteria of regressive effect they were also significantly more variable.

Anxiety and Preparation

There was no significant difference between high and low anxiety groups with respect to expressed desire for preparation on either the maze or mirror tracing tests. Preparation did not produce a significant effect upon mirror tracing performance in either group (see Table 4).

Preparation benefited the high anxiety group more than the low anxiety group on the maze test. When the scores of all [6] *S*s

[5] In calculating the mean and standard deviation when *all* scores were used, *S*s who failed on the first trial were credited with the score achieved by the poorest passing *S*.

[6] See footnote 5.

TABLE 3

Effect of Practice on High and Low Anxiety Groups

Criterion	High Anxiety Group				Low Anxiety Group				Significance Level of Differences					
									Between 1st and 10th Trials High Group		Low Group		Between Practice Gain of High and Low Groups	
	N	1st Trial	10th Trial	Practice Gain	N	1st Trial	10th Trial	Practice Gain	M	σ	M	σ	M	σ
Maze seconds	12	286.3	31.7	254.6	14	166.6	33.3	133.3	.001	.001	.001	.001	.02	<.01
Maze errors	12	60.3	6.1	54.2	14	28.6	5.)	23.5	.001	.001	.001	.001	.02	<.01
Goal discrepancy	12	−14.7	−1.4	−13.3	14	−6.9	−0.9	−6.0	.001	.001	.001	.001	.10	<.01
Goal tenacity	12	24.3	−3.5	27.8	14	−2.7	−0.7	−2.0	.05	.001	.76	.01	.05	>.05

TABLE 4

Effect of Preparation on High and Low Anxiety Groups

Criterion	High Anxiety Group				Low Anxiety Group				Significance Level of Differences		
	Preparation Group		Nonpreparation Group		Preparation Group		Nonpreparation Group		between 2 High Subgroups	between 2 Low Subgroups	between Differences
	N	*M*	*N*	*M*	*N*	*M*	*N*	*M*			
Mirror seconds	21	200.5	26	146.5	22	142.5	24	170.5	.29	.62	.20
Maze seconds (mean of 10 trials)	26	105.3	21	115.1	24	123.9	22	109.5	.55	.34	.29
Maze errors (mean of 10 trials)	26	31.6	21	33.4	24	37.3	22	30.4	.78	.30	.36
Maze seconds, 1st trial (all scores)	26	259.4	21	393.6	24	312.3	22	324.2	.002	.83	.001
Maze seconds, 1st trial (only passers)	24	231.0	14	290.4	19	236.6	14	166.6	.31	.09	.07
Maze errors, 1st trial (all scores)	26	64.2	21	93.1	24	72.0	22	63.0	.11	.52	.10
Maze errors, 1st trial (only passers)	17	61.9	12	60.3	14	59.9	14	28.6	.91	.003	.15

were used in comparing the first trial performances of the preparation and nonpreparation subgroups, the high anxiety group showed greater differences between subgroups than the low anxiety group on both time score ($p < .001$) and error score ($p = .10$). When the scores of passing *Ss* only were used, the comparable differences in favor of the high anxiety group were less significant ($p = .07$ and .15 respectively) but in the same direction. A significantly greater percentage of *Ss* given preparation in the high anxiety group completed the maze on the first trial as against those not given preparation ($p = .01$). The comparable difference in the percentage of successes achieved by the "prepared" subgroup of the low anxiety group was not significant ($p = .15$).

The differential effect of preparation was largely vitiated when computed on the basis of the mean of 10 trials but was in the same direction (see Table 4).

Anxiety and Level of Aspiration

The high anxiety group had a larger goal discrepancy score than the low anxiety group on the first trial of the maze[7] (see Table 5). This difference was almost significant at the .05 level. The high anxiety group was also significantly more variable with respect to goal discrepancy score.

In both high and low anxiety groups, goal discrepancy score declined significantly from the first to the tenth trials (see Table 3) and became less variable. The high anxiety group, however, showed a greater and more variable loss in goal discrepancy score from the first to the tenth trials (see Table 3). As a result, the two groups were almost evenly matched with respect to this score on the tenth trial as well as on the mean of 10 trials.

The high anxiety group significantly exceeded the low anxiety group on the second trial of the maze with respect to goal tenacity score and was also significantly more variable (see Table 5). But whereas the goal tenacity score of the high anxiety group decreased significantly in both magnitude and variability from the first to the tenth trials, the corresponding score of the low

[7] Since we are dealing with scores which decrease with improvement, a negative goal discrepancy score is indicative of a positive goal discrepancy.

TABLE 5

Goal Discrepancy and Goal Tenacity Scores of High and Low Anxiety Groups

Criterion	High Anxiety Group			Low Anxiety Group			Significance Level of Differences	
	N	*M*	σ	*N*	*M*	σ	*M*	σ
Goal discrepancy (mean of 10 trials)	11	—2.6	2.4	14	—3.2	3.1	.53	—
Goal discrepancy, 1st trial (all scores)	19	—24.5	28.7	19	—11.2	13.1	.06	<.01
Goal discrepancy, 1st trial (only passers)	14	—18.7	23.0	14	—6.9	7.3	.07	<.001
Goal tenacity (mean of 10 trials)	11	0.8	5.0	14	—2.4	6.7	.18	—
Goal tenacity, 2nd trial (all scores)	14	20.9	45.4	14	—9.0	23.1	<.05	<.05

TABLE 6

Comparison between High and Low Anxiety Groups on Time Estimate, Percentile Rank Estimate, Regression Effect, and Anxiety Inventory

CRITERION	HIGH ANXIETY GROUP			LOW ANXIETY GROUP			SIGNIFICANCE LEVEL OF DIFFERENCES	
	N	*M*	σ	*N*	*M*	σ	*M*	σ
Mirror seconds estimate*	26	41.2	94.7	24	16.5	110.3	.20	—
Maze seconds estimate* (mean of 10 trials)	12	24.5	36.1	14	14.5	28.9	.41	—
Maze seconds estimate* (1st trial)	21	−76.1	190.3	20	−37.2	110.4	.43	.05
Mirror percentile rank estimate*	26	+1.9	32.1	24	+7.9	29.3	.47	—
Maze percentile rank estimate*	12	−19.5	24.0	14	−23.9	27.1	.68	—
Maze regression seconds	12	52.4	29.3	14	131.1	130.1	.04	<.01
Maze regression errors	12	17.2	12.0	14	34.0	38.8	.13	<.01
I.P.I., Total	21	75.5	25.1	22	59.5	25.5	.04	—
I.P.I., Subjective	21	28.5	9.6	22	20.5	10.7	.01	—
I.P.I., Physiological	21	10.0	7.1	22	7.9	4.0	.22	<.01
I.P.I., Miscellaneous	21	8.2	2.4	22	7.2	2.2	.09	—
I.P.I., Defensive	21	18.6	7.8	22	15.4	6.1	.13	—
I.P.I., Disruptive	21	10.3	5.0	22	8.5	6.4	.31	—

*Actual score has been subtracted from each reported estimate. A positive result, therefore, is an overestimate, and a negative result an underestimate.

anxiety group only showed a significant decrease in variability (see Table 3).

Anxiety and Estimation of Score

No consistent or reliable differences were found between the high and low anxiety groups with respect to the tendency to over- or underestimate elapsed performance time and percentile rank on the maze and mirror tracing tests.

DISCUSSION[8]

Anxiety and Improvisation

We have postulated that "personality" (neurotic) anxiety is the phobic overreaction of an individual with impaired self-esteem to the threat anticipated in adjustive situations. The threatening implications of the latter are derived from their capacity to further impair self-esteem in the face of an inner feeling of inadequacy to cope with them. Normal anxiety, on the other hand, is the fear evoked by anticipation of objectively hazardous threats to self-esteem. Normal *S*s do not display anxiety when confronted with ordinary adjustive situations since they do not lack confidence in their ultimate capacity to acquire the necessary adaptive responses.

As used here, an adjustive problem is one which

> . . . requires the evolution of a new organization of responses. This does not mean that the problem must necessarily be a uniquely new experience for an individual; in fact, many anxiety-producing adjustive situations represent recurrent problems for which the individual has been unable to ever evolve satisfactory enough solutions that would remove the problems in question from the adjustive category. In other words, for a problem to be adjustive, it must involve more than pulling a well-estab-

[8] For general reviews of studies in this area, see Hanfmann (14) and Lazarus, R. S., *et al.* Effects of psychological stress upon performance. *Psychol. Bull.*, 1952, 49, 293–317.

lished, familiar, or routine response pattern out of one's behavior repertory (2, p. 375).

It is precisely with respect to the need for improvising solutions to *new* problems that the individual with personality anxiety experiences feelings of inadequacy. Since they pose an exaggerated threat to his self-esteem and sensitize him to overrespond with fear when he is obliged to face up to them, it follows, therefore, that anxiety can best be mitigated by removing the elements of novelty and improvisation from problem-solving situations. The "response set" of the neurotically anxious individual, therefore, is to avoid putting his improvising ability to the test and to frantically search "his available response repertory for an appropriate solution that would not involve any reorganization of existing patterns" (2, p. 375). And if the problem is one that requires improvisation for solution, this inflexible response set to avoid improvisation will not only inhibit learning, but will also render it impossible until it is eventually abandoned.

Thus, to the panic that results from anticipatory overreaction to any new situation is added the panic resulting from initial failure to make any progress toward solution. The cumulative impact of this disorganization may be disabling enough to induce total blocking of response (16, 41) which, in turn, may stimulate a "face-saving" attempt to produce any kind of response regardless of how inappropriate or unadaptive. Later, with increasing exposure to the problem—providing that the panic is not too catastrophic—the individual may become sufficiently desensitized to its unfamiliarity and fear-instigating properties to recover from his disorganization and adopt a more efficacious (i.e., improvising) response set.

The significantly poorer and more variable maze scores of anxiety *S*s on the *first* trial in our study, followed by gradual recovery and obliteration of the difference between experimental and control groups after *ten* trials, gives support to the theoretical framework outlined above. Diethelm and Jones (7) found significant differences between patients in acute and remissive states of anxiety with respect to maze learning and retention, and performance on the Kohs block test. Similar evidence of the selective impairment of improvisation as opposed to rote learning under anxiety conditions was found by Tomkins (37) and Zander (44). Lantz (20) discovered that items involving thinking were most affected by the administration of test items under stress. The *S*s with high Rorschach anxiety displayed superior ability only in those parts of a comprehensive social science examination testing rote recall, and inferior ability in other portions requiring improvisation in new problem-solving tasks (13).

The failure of the mirror tracing test to differentiate between anxiety and nonanxiety *S*s is interpreted to mean that the task is not sufficiently novel to constitute a threat to the former group. Previous evidence with this test only showed that it was useful in differentiating between delinquent, emotionally unstable, and psychotic patients on the one hand and normals on the other (17, 23, 33, 42). Since it does require a certain amount of persistence, it is reasonable to expect that emotionally unstable individuals would be more prone to discontinue their efforts after failure (10). But lack of persistence is hardly characteristic of anxiety-prone *S*s as shown by experiments requiring prolonged holding of a fixed posture (35).

Mirror drawing, on the other hand, is a much more novel and highly unstructured task. Evidence of impairment of this function in individuals with personality anxiety was reported by Wechsler and Hartogs (41), Hartogs (16), and Ammons (1).

Rigidity in problem orientation naturally has much in common with the response set of avoiding improvisation. The latter behavior may indeed be a major cause of the rigidity shown by anxiety-ridden personalities in learning situations, and persists precisely because it *usually* has anxiety-reducing properties in most of these situations. However, rigidity may also be reflective of other personality variables that are unrelated to anxiety. As might readily be predicted, "rigidity predisposition, as inferred from the Rorschach, correlates positively with performance on materials calling for rote recall . . . but negatively with abstract materials or problems dissimilar to those previously studied, and those problems requiring fresh modes of attack" (13, p. 24). Beier reported rigidity in problem-solving behavior in response to situationally induced anxiety (4). Rigid construction is also characteristic of the performance of anxious individuals on the World Test (27).

Anxiety and Practice Effect

Consistent with our hypotheses regarding the nature of both the disorganizing and motivational effects of anxiety on learning is the differentially greater benefit accruing to the high anxiety group as a result of successive repetitions of the maze. This can be explained as an outcome of (*a*) release from the fear-inspired, nonimprovising response set as increased familiarity with the learning task renders it less novel, and (*b*) the operation of higher motivation in anxiety-ridden personalities. Supporting the motivational hypothesis is the fact that regression effect was smaller and less variable in the high anxiety group, as would be expected wherever a stabilizing influence such as motivation is operating. The high anxiety group also showed evidence of greater motivation in higher initial goal discrepancy and goal tenacity scores.

Detracting from this interpretation is the well-known fact that *S*s with poorer initial scores generally tend to gain more from practice than initially abler *S*s because of the availability of more ceiling for improvement (39). In our study, when small groups of six *S*s each (drawn from the high and low anxiety groups respectively) were matched on the basis of initial score, the differential effect of practice was no longer significant. It should be borne in mind, however, that in such a small sample considerable overlap in anxiety level could easily occur. Also, whereas the difference in initial score in traditional studies of practice effect is mostly attributable to individual difference in native ability, in our study it was highly correlated with level of anxiety. Thus, the higher ceiling available for improvement was less a function of low ability per se than a function of the inhibitory influence of anxiety; and before the high ceiling could be realized through practice, release from this inhibitory influence had to be effected.

Anxiety and Preparation

Added support for the hypothesis that the novelty of a learning problem is the chief precipitant of fear responses in *S*s with personality anxiety is provided by the finding that the latter *S*s benefited more than the control group from exposure to a period of preliminary orientation to the learning situation. Wiltbank (43) had previously found no positive transfer effect in rats from a practice to a test maze until the first maze was fairly well learned. Our control *S*s also failed to benefit from advance preparation. Hence, the significant benefit the high anxiety group derived from the practice maze cannot be attributed to the transfer of *objective* elements in the learning situation.

However, a period of preliminary orientation in the maze situation has great transfer value for the rat because it allays his understandable fear of the unfamiliar laboratory situation (18). Thus, while a maze fails to prove threatening to nonanxious human *S*s it induces both *normal* fear in rats and *neurotic* anxiety in human *S*s suffering from impaired self-esteem.

Anxiety and Level of Aspiration

The significantly higher initial level of aspiration and goal tenacity scores manifested by our high anxiety group confirms previous findings by Eysenck (11) and Hartogs (16). It is consistent with our theoretical conception of anxiety neurotics as individuals lacking in intrinsic self-esteem and therefore compensatorily motivated to aspire to high levels of achievement. This same need for high achievement also makes them initially less flexible in lowering their level of aspiration in the face of failure experiences, thereby giving rise to high goal tenacity scores. But contrary to Hartogs' anxiety *S*s who, subsequent to initial failure, protectively disinvolved their egos from the task by intentionally keeping goal levels far below performance level, our anxiety *S*s merely lowered their aspirational level more than controls did until they approximately equalled the latter's at the end of 10 trials. This difference between ego disinvolvement in Hartogs' experiment and realistic revision of aspirational level in ours can possibly be explained by the higher level of anxiety (and, thus, the greater traumatic effect of initial failure) in Hartogs' cases who were drawn from a clinical population.

Summary and Conclusions

Qualitative changes in the learning process attributable to anxiety were studied in a group of young college students. High and low anxiety groups of 50 *S*s each were constituted from the upper and lower quintiles of a distribution of group Rorschach anxiety scores. A significant difference between these two groups was obtained on the Illinois Personality Inventory, a paper-and-pencil test of anxiety. Each *S* was given a mirror tracing test and a blindfold stylus maze test. Half of the *S*s in each group were allowed advance preparation on each test.

The low anxiety group was significantly superior to the high anxiety group on the first trial of the maze, but this superiority was not maintained over the course of ten trials. No differences were obtained in the mirror tracing test. These results are interpreted as indicative of a deficiency in improvising ability in the high anxiety group brought about by a response set to reduce anxiety by adhering to familiar and stereotyped responses in a novel learning situation.

Anxiety is conceptualized as an "acquired reaction-sensitivity in individuals suffering from impaired self-esteem to overreact with fear to any anticipated adjustive situation that contains a further threat to self-esteem." It is the novel elements of an unfamiliar learning problem which constitute the threat to the anxious individual, and instigate a habitual, anxiety-reducing response set to avoid the improvisation necessary for successful learning.

This interpretation is strengthened by the differentially greater benefit accruing to the high anxiety group from preliminary orientation to the maze task and from successive repetitions of the test maze. Both practice and advance preparation render the learning task less novel and unfamiliar, thereby mitigating the threat it poses, the intensity of the anxiety, and the inhibitory response set it induces. Also operating to differentially enhance the benefit anxiety *S*s derive from practice is a higher level of motivation inferred from significantly greater initial goal discrepancy and goal tenacity scores. These scores gradually decline during the course of the learning task until they reach the level of the low anxiety group.

References

1 Ammons, Carol H. Personality variables in mirror drawing. *Motor Skills res. Exch.*, 1950, **2,** 15.

2 Ausubel, D. P. *Ego development and the personality disorders.* New York: Grune & Stratton, 1952.

3 Beck, S. J. *Rorschach's test.* Vol. II. *A variety of personality pictures.* New York: Grune & Stratton, 1945.

4 Beier, E. G. The effect of induced anxiety on some aspects of intellectual functioning: a study of the relationship between anxiety and rigidity. *Amer. Psychologist,* 1949, **4,** 273–274. (Abstract)

5 Benton, A. L. The experimental validation of the Rorschach test. *Brit. J. med. Psychol.*, 1950, **23,** 45–58.

6 Davis, D. R. Increase in strength of a secondary drive as a cause of disorganization. *Quart. J. exp. Psychol.*, 1948, **1,** 22-28.

7 Diethelm, O., and M. R. Jones. Influence of anxiety on attention, learning, retention and thinking. *Arch. Neurol. Psychiat.*, 1947, **58,** 325-336.

8 Eichler, R. M. Experimental stress and alleged Rorschach indices of anxiety. *J. abnorm. soc. Psychol.*, 1951, **46,** 344-355.

9 Elizur, A. Content analysis of the Rorschach with regard to anxiety and hostility. *Rorschach res. Exch. & J. proj. Tech.*, 1949, **13,** 247-284.

10 Escalona, Sibylle K. *An application of the level of aspiration experiment to the study of personality.* New York: Teachers College, Columbia Univer., 1948.

11 Eysenck, H. J. *Dimensions of personality.* London: Kegan Paul, 1947.

12 Farber, I. E. Response fixation under anxiety and non-anxiety conditions. *J. exp. Psychol.*, 1948, **38,** 111–131.

13 Gaier, E. L. The use of stimulated recall in revealing the relationship between selected personality variables and the learning process. *Psychol. Monogr.*, 1952, **66,** No. 17 (Whole No. 349).

14 Hanfmann, Eugenia. Psychological approaches to the study of anxiety. In P. Hoch and J. Zubin (Eds.), *Anxiety*. New York: Grune & Stratton, 1950. Pp. 51–69.

15 Harrower-Erickson, Molly R. Directions for administration of the Rorschach group test. *Rorschach res. Exch.*, 1941, **5,** 145–153.

16 Hartogs, R. The clinical investigation and differential measurement of anxiety. *Amer. J. Psychiat.*, 1950, **106,** 929–934.

17 Holsopple, J. Q. The social adjustment of delinquents who are unable to inhibit old automatic perceptual responses. *J. soc. Psychol.*, 1932, **3,** 91-96.

18 Jackson, T. A. General factors in transfer of training in the white rat. *Genet. Psychol. Monogr.*, 1932, **11,** 1–59.

19 Klopfer, B., and D. M. Kelley. *The Rorschach technique.* Yonkers, N. Y.: World Book Co., 1942.

20 Lantz, Beatrice. Some dynamic aspects of success and failure. *Psychol. Monogr.*, 1945, **59,** No. 1 (Whole No. 271).

21 Leeper, R. W. A motivational theory of emotion to replace "emotion as a disorganized response." *Psychol. Rev.*, 1948, **55,** 5–21.

22 Lewinski, R. J. The psychometric pattern—anxiety neurosis. *J. clin. Psychol.*, 1945, **3,** 214–221.

23 Louttit, C. M. The mirror tracing test as a diagnostic aid for emotional instability. *Psychol. Rec.*, 1943, **5,** 279–286.

24 Machover, Karen. *Personality projection in the drawing of the human figure*. Springfield, Ill.: Charles C Thomas, 1949.

25 May, R. *The meaning of anxiety*. New York: Ronald, 1950.

26 Mercer, M., and A. O. Hecker. The use of tolserol (myanesin) in psychological testing. *J. clin. Psychol.*, 1951, **7,** 263–266.

27 Michael, J. C., and Charlotte Buhler. Experiences with personality testing in the neuropsychiatric department of a general hospital. *Dis. nerv. System*, 1945, **6,** 205–211.

28 Miller, N. E. Studies of fear as an acquirable drive: I. Fear as motivation and fear-reduction as reinforcement in the learning of new responses. *J. exp. Psychol.*, 1948, **38,** 89–101.

29 Mowrer, O. H. A stimulus-response analysis of anxiety and its roles as a reinforcing agent. *Psychol. Rev.*, 1939, **46,** 553–565.

30 _____,Anxiety reduction and learning. *J. exp. Psychol.*, 1940, **27,** 497–516.

31 _____,*Learning theory and personality dynamics.* New York: Ronald, 1950.

32 Munroe, Ruth L. Prediction of the adjustment and academic performance of college students by a modification of the Rorschach method. *Appl. Psychol. Monogr.*, 1945, No. 7.

33 Peters, H. N. The mirror-tracing test as a measure of social maladaptation. *J. abnorm. soc. Psychol.*, 1946, **41,** 437–448.

34 Rapaport, D. *Diagnostic psychological testing.* Chicago: Yearbook Publishing Co., 1945.

35 Sapirstein, M. R. The effect of anxiety on human after-discharges. *Psychosom. Med.*, 1948, **10,** 145–155.

36 Schafer, R. *The clinical application of psychological tests.* New York: International Universities Press, 1948.

37 Tomkins, S. S. An experimental study of anxiety. *J. Psychol.*, 1943, **15,** 307–313.

38 _____, *The Thematic Apperception Test.* New York: Grune & Stratton, 1947.

39 Tyler, Leona. *Psychology of human differences.* New York: D. Appleton-Century, 1947.

40 Wechsler, D. *The measurement of adult intelligence.* Baltimore: Williams and Wilkins, 1944.

41 Wechsler, D., and R. Hartogs. The clinical measurement of anxiety. *Psychiat. Quart.*, 1945, **19,** 618–635.

42 Weidensall, J. *The mentality of the criminal woman.* Baltimore: Warwick and York, 1916.

43 Wiltbank, R. T. Transfer of training in white rats upon various series of mazes. *Behav. Monogr.*, 1919, **4,** No. 17.

44 Zander, A. A study of experimental frustration. *Psychol. Monogr.*, 1944, **56,** No. 3 (Whole No. 256).

26 Some Misconceptions Regarding Mental Health Functions and Practices in the School*

David P. Ausubel

Most reasonable persons would agree today that the legitimate functions of the school extend beyond the development of intellectual skills and the transmission of subject-matter knowledge. The school also has undeniable responsibilities with respect to mental health and personality development, simply because it is a place where children spend a good part of their waking hours, perform much of their purposeful activity, obtain a large share of their status, and interact significantly with adults, age-mates, and the demands of society. Hence, as long as the organizational, administrative, disciplinary, and in-

Reprinted from the article of the same title, Psychology in the Schools, *1965,* **2,** *99–105. By permission of the author and* Psychology in the Schools.

terpersonal aspects of the school environment inevitably affect the mental health and personality development of its future citizens, it obviously behooves society to arrange these matters as appropriately and constructively as possible. Nevertheless, because the mental hygiene role of the school has been oversold and misrepresented so frequently by educational theorists, I would like to consider in this article what I believe to be some of the more serious misconceptions about mental health functions and practices in the school setting.

The Primary Responsibility of the School

To begin with, I think we need to recognize that the primary and distinctive function of the school in our society is not to promote mental health and personality development but to foster intellectual growth and the assimilation of knowledge. The school admittedly has important responsibilities with regard to the social, emotional, and moral aspects of the pupil's development, but certainly not the primary responsibility; the school's role in intellectual development, however, is incontrovertibly primary. Furthermore, much of the school's legitimate concern with interpersonal relations in the classroom does not stem merely from interest in enhancing healthful personality development as an end in itself. It also reflects appreciation of the negative effects which an unfavorable social and emotional school climate has on academic achievements, on motivation to learn, and on desirable attitudes toward intellectual inquiry. For example, if pupils feel unhappy and resentful about the discipline and social environment of the school, they will neither learn very much while they are in school nor remain much longer than they have to. And if they are goaded by fear to accept uncritically the views of their teachers and to memorize materials they do not really understand, they neither learn how to think for themselves nor build the foundations of a stable and usable body of knowledge.

The Selection and Evaluation of Teachers

Over the past three decades, in selecting and appraising school personnel, educators have tended to overvalue the personality attributes of the teacher and the mental health implications of teacher-pupil relationships, and to undervalue the teacher's intellectual functions and capabilities. But although teacher training institutions and teachers themselves overemphasize the importance of personality and interpersonal factors in the classroom, there is some evidence that pupils are primarily concerned with their teachers' pedagogic competence or ability to teach, and not with their role as kindly, sympathetic, and cheerful adults.[1] Despite the recent trend in such fields as government and business administration to place ability in getting along with people ahead of professional competence, it is self-evidently a dangerous state of affairs when professional personnel in any field of endeavor are judged mainly on the basis of personal qualities. It is obvious that because teachers deal with impressionable children and affect their personality development, they should not have unstable or destructive personalities. Nevertheless, the principal criterion in selecting and evaluating teachers should not be the extent to which their personality characteristics conform to the theoretical ideal promoting healthful personality development, but rather their ability to organize and present subject matter effectively, to explain ideas clearly, and to stimulate and competently direct pupil learning activity.

The Limits of Normality

As was long true in the area of physical hygiene, some educators also tend to exaggerate the seriousness and per-

[1] P. H. Taylor, "Children's Evaluations of the Characteristics of the Good Teacher," *British Journal of Educational Psychology*, 1962, *32*, 258-266.

manence of the effects on mental health of minor deviations from the norm of desirable hygienic practice. There is every reason to believe, however, that a wide margin of safety is the rule both in physical and mental health. Within fairly broad limits, many different kinds of teacher personality structure and ways of relating to children are compatible with normal health and personality development in pupils. This principle applies when either mildly undesirable classroom practices prevail over an extended period of time, or when more serious deviations from optimal standards occur occasionally. In general, children are not nearly as fragile as we profess to believe, and do not develop permanent personality disabilities from temporary exposure to interpersonal practices that fall short of what the experts currently regard as appropriate.

The Cult of Extroversion

In education, as in many other vocational fields, we have succumbed to the cult of the warm, outgoing, amiable, and extroverted personality, and have tended to regard any deviation from this standard as axiomatically undesirable from a mental hygiene standpoint. Formerly a pupil would be referred to the school psychologist if he was boisterous, aggressive, and refractory to discipline. Now it is the child who is reserved, contemplative, and unconcerned about the opinion of his peers who arouses the clinical concern of the child guidance specialist. Similarly, many excellent teachers who happen to be shy and introverted are viewed with alarm by their psychologically oriented superiors. Yet there is absolutely no evidence that they impair their pupils' mental health, even though they may conceivably be less popular as individuals than their extroverted colleagues; and as far as pupils are concerned, it has been definitely established that popularity may be a grossly misleading index of social adjustment. An ostensibly popular individual may be little more than a "stranger in his group" in terms of the depth of his attachments, or may be popular simply because he is docile, conforming, and willing to be directed and "used" by others.[2] Contrariwise, the pupil who is unpopular because of temperamental shyness or strong intellectual interests is not necessarily socially maladjusted or inevitably fated to become so.[3]

The Effects of Authoritarianism

Many educators have uncritically accepted the ethnocentric psychological dictum that only democratic teacher-pupil relationships are compatible with normal mental health and personality development. Yet there are many examples of authoritarian western cultures (e.g., Germany, Italy, Switzerland) in which all of the indices of mental health and mature personality development compare very favorably with those prevailing in the United States. Hence, it is obviously not authoritarianism per se that has damaging mental health consequences, but rather the existence of authoritarian practices in home and school that are incongruous with the general pattern of interpersonal relations in the culture at large. Children *are* able satisfactorily to internalize adult personality traits and mature attitudes toward authority, even in an authoritarian home and school environment, providing that (a) personal, social, and working relationships among adults are similarly authoritarian, and (b) that adults generally make as stringent demands on themselves as they do on young people. In countries like Germany and Switzerland these latter conditions prevail, and therefore authoritarianism in home and school has few adverse effects on mental health and personality development. In New Zealand, on the other hand, authoritarianism in the home and secondary school has more serious effects because it contrasts sharply with the egalitarian and generally relaxed character of vocational and social life in the adult world.

[2] R. M. Wittenberg and J. Berg, "The Stranger in the Group," *American Journal of Orthopsychiatry*, 1952, *22*, 89–97.

[3] D. P. Morris, E. Soroker, and G. Buruss, "Follow-up Studies of Shy, Withdrawn Children. I. Evaluation of Later Adjustments," *American Journal of Orthopsychiatry*, 1954, *24*, 743–754.

Older children and adolescents do not satisfactorily internalize values that are indoctrinated in an authoritarian fashion if the adult culture itself is organized along democratic and egalitarian lines. Under these circumstances they feel unjustly treated and discriminated against; and not only do they tend to resent the authoritarian discipline that is imposed upon them, but also to conform to adult standards only under threat of external compulsion. This is particularly true if they perceive that many adults do not honor these standards but nevertheless presume to punish them whenever they are guilty of lapses. Hence, when adults preach the virtue of hard work, ambition, responsibility, and self-denial, but do not practice these virtues themselves in occupational life, children tend to emulate their example rather than their precepts. They become habituated to striving and working hard under external pressure but fail adequately to internalize these values. Thus when they finally enter the adult vocational world and the customary authoritarian demands for conscientious effort are lifted, the tenuous structure of their disciplined work habits tends to collapse in the absence of genuinely internalized needs for vocational achievement.

Furthermore, when a teen-ager in New Zealand obtains a job he dresses as an adult, is treated as an adult, and, from the age of eighteen, is paid on an adult wage scale. Even in the armed forces where working relationships are traditionally authoritarian, he is treated no differently than anyone else. Neither a shop foreman nor an army sergeant would ever think of using a cane on a seventeen-year-old factory hand or recruit who broke one of the rules or failed to do his work neatly. Yet in the secondary school this same teen-ager is treated very much as a child, wears short pants, and is growled at or caned for similar lapses. Hence, when he perceives the vastly more egalitarian treatment accorded his contemporaries in occupational life and in the military services, it is small wonder that he often feels resentful and sometimes manifests anti-adult and anti-social tendencies.

It also seems reasonable to suppose that as children enter adolescence, disciplinary practices should be progressively liberalized to meet increasing needs for self-determination and growing capacities for self-discipline. Quite paradoxically, however, since the primary school in New Zealand has always been much less authoritarian than the secondary school, and especially so over the past two decades, discipline tends to become stricter, more rigorous, and more explicit as children pass from the former to the latter. It is entirely understandable, therefore, that when the adolescent is unexpectedly subjected to a more restrictive discipline than he was in primary school—despite his greater physical, intellectual, emotional, and social maturity—he tends to become bewildered, dismayed, and resentful.

Attributable in part to the incongruous authoritarianism of the secondary school in New Zealand are many immature attitudes toward authority. First, in public situations, New Zealanders tend to defer excessively to the opinions of authority figures and to overconform to their dictates. Second, coexistent with this exaggerated public deference to authority, particularly among University students, is a puerile species of defiance, and an irresistible impulse to reject traditional values out-of-hand, to take outrageously extreme positions, and to shock the sensibilities of conventional folk with sacrilege, profanity, and the desecration of revered symbols. Third, because of resentment toward a discriminatory type of authoritarianism and overhabituation to external controls, many secondary school pupils fail adequately to internalize recognized social norms and individual restraints. Hence they feel quite justified in violating rules and asserting themselves when authority turns its back. Finally, the distinctive feature of adolescent misbehavior in New Zealand, is simply a more exaggerated and generalized expression of anti-adult feeling and puerile defiance of adult authority. In its most extreme form, bodgieism, it is basically a cult of exhibitionistic nonconformity, out-of-bounds loutishness, and of studiously labored rejection of adult respectability. Among its multiple causes must certainly be counted widespread adolescent resentment of an inappropriately authoritarian type of discipline and subordination relative to other age groups in New Zealand society. It bears some relation to the beatnik movement in the United States, but occurs in a younger age group, is less intellectual in its manifestations, and is more directly aggressive rather than philosophical in its protest.

Distortions of Democratic Discipline

Proponents of democratic classroom discipline believe in imposing the minimal degree of external control necessary for socialization, personality maturation, conscience development, and the emotional security of the child. Discipline and obedience are not regarded as ends in themselves but only as means to these latter ends. They are not striven for deliberately, but are expected to follow naturally in the wake of friendly and realistic teacher-pupil relationships. Explicit limits are not set routinely or as ways of showing "who is boss," but only as the need arises, i.e., when they are not implicitly understood or accepted by pupils.

Democratic discipline is as rational, nonarbitrary and bilateral as possible. It provides explanations, permits discussion, and invites the participation of children in the setting of standards whenever they are qualified to do so. Above all it implies respect for the dignity of the individual, and avoids exaggerated emphasis on status differences and barriers between free communication. Hence it repudiates harsh, abusive, and vindictive forms of punishment, and the use of sarcasm, ridicule, and intimidation.

The aforementioned attributes of democratic classroom discipline are obviously appropriate in cultures where social relationships tend to be egalitarian. This type of discipline also becomes increasingly more feasible as children become older, more responsible, and more capable of understanding and formulating rules of conduct based on concepts of equity and reciprocal obligation. But contrary to what the extreme permissivists would have us believe, democratic school discipline does not imply freedom from all external constraints, standards, and direction, or freedom from discipline as an end in itself. And under no circumstances does it presuppose the eradication of all distinctions between pupil and teacher roles, or require that teachers abdicate responsibility for making the final decisions in the classroom.

Many educational theorists have misinterpreted and distorted the ideal of democratic discipline by equating it with an extreme form of permissiveness. These distortions are most commonly encountered in the United States but have also found acceptance in some New Zealand primary school circles. They have been dogmatically expressed in various psychologically unsound and unrealistic propositions that are considered sacrosanct in many teachers' colleges. Fortunately, however, most classroom teachers have accepted them only for examination purposes—while still in training—and have discarded them in actual practice as thoroughly unworkable.

According to one widely held doctrine, only "positive" forms of discipline are constructive and democratic. It is asserted that children must only be guided by reward and approval; that reproof and punishment are authoritarian, repressive, and reactionary expressions of adult hostility which leave permanent emotional scars on children's personalities. What these theorists conveniently choose to ignore, however, is the fact that it is impossible for children to learn what is *not* approved and tolerated, simply by generalizing in reverse from the approval they receive for behavior that *is* acceptable. Even adults are manifestly incapable of learning and respecting the limits of acceptable conduct unless the distinction between what is proscribed and approved is reinforced by punishment as well as by reward. Furthermore, there is good reason to believe that acknowledgment of wrongdoing and acceptance of punishment are part and parcel of learning moral accountability and developing a sound conscience. Few if any children are quite that fragile that they cannot take deserved reproof and punishment in stride.

A second widespread distortion of democratic discipline is reflected in the popular notion that there are no culpably misbehaving children in the classroom, but only culpably aggressive, unsympathetic, and punitive teachers. If children misbehave, according to this point of view, one can implicitly assume that they must have been provoked beyond endurance by repressive and authoritarian classroom discipline. Similarly, if they are disrespectful, then the teacher, by definition, must not have been deserving of respect. It is true, of course, that much pupil misconduct *is* instigated by harsh and abusive school discipline; but there are also innumerable reasons for out-of-bounds behavior that are completely independent of the teacher's attitudes and disciplinary practices. Pupils are also influenced by factors originating in the home, the neighborhood, the peer group, and the mass-media. Some children are emotionally disturbed, others are brain-damaged, and still others are aggressive by temperament; and there are times when even the best behaved children from the nicest homes develop an irresistible impulse—without any provocation whatsoever—to test the limits of a teacher's forbearance.

Both of the aforementioned distortions of classroom democracy are used to justify the commonly held belief among educators that pupils should not be reproved or punished for disorderly or discourteous conduct. I have, for example, observed classrooms where everybody talks at once; where pupils turn their backs on the teacher and engage in private conversation while the latter is endeavoring to instruct them; and where pupils verbally abuse teachers for exercising their rightful disciplinary prerogatives. Some educators contend that all of this is compatible with wholesome, democratic teacher-pupil relationships. Other educators deplore this type of pupil behavior but insist, nevertheless, that punishment is unwarranted under these circumstances. In the first place, they assert, reproof or punishment constitutes a "negative" and hence axiomatically undesirable approach to classroom management; and, secondly, the misbehavior would assuredly have never occurred to begin with, if the teacher's attitudes had been less autocratic or antagonistic. I have already answered the second group of educators, and to the first group I can only say that I am still sufficiently old-fashioned to believe that rudeness and unruliness are not normally desirable classroom behavior in any culture.

When such misconduct occurs, I believe pupils have to be unambiguously informed that it will not be tolerated and that any repetition of the same behavior will be punished. This action does not preclude in any way either an earnest attempt to discover why the misbehavior occurred, or suitable preventive measures aimed at correcting the underlying causes. But, by the same token, the mere fact that a pupil has a valid psychological reason for misbehaving does not mean that he is thereby absolved from moral accountability or rendered no longer subject to punishment.

Still another related distortion of democratic discipline is reflected in the proposition that it is repressive and authoritarian to request pupils to apologize for discourteous behavior or offensive language. However, if we take seriously the idea that the dignity of the human being is important, we must be willing to protect it from affront; and apology is the most civilized and effective means mankind has yet evolved for accomplishing this goal. In a democratic society nobody is that important that he is above apologizing to those persons whom he wrongfully offends. Everybody's dignity is important—the teacher's as well as the pupil's. It is no less wrong for a pupil to abuse a teacher than for a teacher to abuse a pupil.

If apologies are to have any real significance in moral training, however, it is obvious that, even though they are explicitly requested, they must be made voluntarily, and must be reflective of genuine appreciation of wrong-doing and of sincere regret and remorse. Purely formal and mechanical statements of apology made under coercion are less than worthless. Apologies are also without real ethical import unless their basis is reciprocal, i.e., unless it is fully understood that under comparable circumstances the teacher would be willing to apologize to his pupils.

In seeking to correct these undesirable permissive distortions of classroom democracy, it would be foolhardy to return to the equally undesirable opposite extreme of authoritarianism that flourished in the United States up to a quarter of a century ago, and still prevails in many western nations. Democratic school discipline is still an appropriate and realistic goal for education in a democratic society; hence there is no need to throw away the baby with the bath water. It is only necessary to discard the aforementioned permissivist doctrines masquerading under the banners of democracy and behavioral science, and to restore certain other traditional values that have been neglected in the enthusiasm of extending democracy to home and school.

More specifically, we first have to clear up the semantic confusion. We should stop equating permissiveness with democratic discipline, and realistic adult control and guidance with authoritarianism. Permissiveness, by definition, is the absence of discipline, democratic or otherwise. We should cease instructing teachers that it is repressive and reactionary to reprove or punish pupils for misconduct, or to request them to apologize for offensive and discourteous behavior.

Second, we should stop misinterpreting what little reputable evidence we have about discipline, and refrain from misrepresenting our personal biases on the subject as the indisputably established findings of scientific research. The available evidence merely suggests that in a democratic cultural setting, authoritarian discipline has certain undesirable effects—*not* that the consequences of laissez-faire permissiveness are desirable. As a matter of fact, research studies[4] show that the effects of extreme permissiveness are just as unwholesome as are those of authoritarianism. In the school situation a laissez-faire policy leads to confusion, insecurity, and competition for power among pupils. Assertive pupils tend to become aggressive and ruthless, whereas retiring pupils tend to withdraw further from classroom participation. The child who is handled too permissively at home tends to regard himself as a specially privileged person. He fails to learn the normative standards and expectations of society, to set realistic goals for himself, and to make reasonable demands on others. In his dealings with adults and other children he is domineering, aggressive, petulant, and capricious.

Third, we should stop making teachers feel guilty and personally responsible for all instances of misconduct and disrespect in the classroom. We do this whenever we take for granted, without any actual supporting evidence, that these behavior problems would never have arisen in the first place if the teachers involved were truly deserving of respect and had been administering genuinely wholesome and democratic discipline.

Finally, teachers' colleges should terminate the prevailing conspiracy of silence they maintain about the existence of disciplinary problems in the schools. Although discipline is the one

[4] Ruth Cunningham, *Understanding Group Behavior of Boys and Girls* (New York: Teachers College, Columbia University, 1951).

aspect of teaching that the beginning teacher is most worried about, he receives little or no practical instruction in handling this problem. Many teacher training institutions, as pointed out above, rationalize their inadequacies in this regard by pretending that disciplinary problems are relatively rare occurrences involving the disturbed child, or more typically the disturbed teacher. Due respect for the facts of life, however, suggests that prospective teachers today not only need to be taught more realistic propositions about the nature and purposes of democratic discipline, but also require adequately supervised, down-to-earth experience in coping with classroom discipline.

27 A Teaching Strategy for Culturally Deprived Pupils: Cognitive and Motivational Considerations*

David P. Ausubel

The possibility of arresting and reversing the course of intellectual retardation in the culturally deprived pupil depends largely on providing him with an optimal learning environment as early as possible in the course of his educational career. If the limiting effects of prolonged cultural deprivation on the development of verbal intelligence and on the acquisition of verbal knowledge are to be at least partially overcome, better-than-average strategies of teaching are obviously necessary in terms of both general effectiveness and specific appropriateness for his particular learning situation. Yet precisely the opposite

Reprinted from the article of the same title,* School Review, *1963.* **71, *454–463. By permission of the author and the University of Chicago Press.*

state of affairs typically prevails: the learning environment of the culturally deprived child is both generally inferior and specifically inappropriate. His cumulative intellectual deficit, therefore, almost invariably reflects, in part, the cumulative impact of a continuing and consistently deficient learning environment, as well as his emotional and motivational reaction to this environment. Thus, much of the lower-class child's alienation from the school is not so much a reflection of discriminatory or rejecting attitudes on the part of teachers and other school personnel—although the importance of this factor should not be underestimated; it is in greater measure a reflection of the cumulative effects of a curriculum that is too demanding of him, and of the resulting load of frustration, confusion, demoralization, resentment, and impaired self-confidence that he must bear.

Cognitive Considerations

An effective and appropriate teaching strategy for the culturally deprived child must therefore emphasize these three considerations: (*a*) the selection of initial learning material geared to the learner's existing state of readiness; (*b*) mastery and consolidation of all on-going learning tasks before new tasks are introduced, so as to provide the necessary foundation for successful sequential learning and to prevent unreadiness for future learning tasks; and (*c*) the use of structured learning materials optimally organized to facilitate efficient sequential learning. Attention to these three factors can go a long way toward insuring effective learning for the first time, and toward restoring the child's educational morale and confidence in his ability to learn. Later possible consequences are partial restoration of both intrinsic and extrinsic motivation for academic achievement, diminution of anti-intellectualism, and decreased alienation from the school to the point where his studies make sense and he sees some purpose in learning. In my opinion, of all the available teaching strategies, programmed instruction, minus the teaching-machine format, has the greatest potentialities for meeting the aforementioned three criteria of an effective and appropriate approach to the teaching of culturally deprived pupils.

Readiness

A curriculum that takes the readiness of the culturally deprived child into account always takes as its starting point his existing knowledge and sophistication in the various subject-matter areas and intellectual skills, no matter how far down the scale this happens to be. This policy demands rigid elimination of all subject matter that he cannot economically assimilate on the basis of his current level of cognitive sophistication. It presupposes emphasis on his acquisition of the basic intellectual skills before any attempt is made to teach him algebra, geometry, literature, and foreign languages. However, in many urban high schools and junior high schools today, pupils who cannot read at a third-grade level and who cannot speak or write grammatically or perform simple arithmetical computations are subjected to irregular French verbs, Shakespearean drama, and geometrical theorems. Nothing more educationally futile or better calculated to destroy educational morale could be imagined!

In the terms of readiness for a given level of school work, a child is no less ready because of a history of cultural deprivation, chronic academic failure, and exposure to an unsuitable curriculum than because of deficient intellectual endowment. Hence, realistic recognition of this fact is not undemocratic, reactionary, or evidence of social class bias, of intellectual snobbery, of a "soft," patronizing approach, or a belief in the inherent uneducability of lower-class children. Neither is it indicative of a desire to surrender to the culturally deprived child's current intellectual level, to perpetuate the status quo, or to institute a double, class-oriented standard of education. It is merely a necessary first step in preparing him to cope with more advanced subject matter, and hence in eventually reducing existing social class differentials in academic achievement. To set the same *initial* standards and expectations for the academically retarded, culturally deprived child as for the non-retarded middle- or lower-class child is automatically to insure the former's failure and to widen prevailing discrepancies between social class groups.

Consolidation

By insisting on consolidation or mastery of on-going lessons before new material is introduced, we make sure of continued readiness and success in sequentially organized learning. Abundant experimental research has confirmed the proposition that prior learnings are not transferable to new learning tasks unless they are first overlearned.[1] Overlearning, in turn, requires an adequate number of adequately spaced repetitions and reviews, sufficient intratask repetitiveness prior to intra- and intertask diversification,[2] and opportunity for differential practice of the more difficult components of a task. Frequent testing and provision of feedback, especially with test items demanding fine discrimination among alternatives varying in degrees of correctness, also enhance consolidation by confirming, clarifying, and correcting previous learnings. Lastly, in view of the fact that the culturally deprived child tends to learn more slowly than his non-deprived peers, self-pacing helps to facilitate consolidation.

Structured, Sequential Materials

The principal advantage of programmed instruction, apart from the fact that it furthers consolidation, is its careful sequential arrangement and gradation of difficulty which insures that each attained increment in learning serves as an appropriate foundation and anchoring post for learning and retention of subse-

[1] See R.W. Bruce, "Conditions of transfer of Training," *Journal of Experimental Psychology,* XVI (1933), 343–61; C. P. Duncan, "Transfer in Motor Learning as a Function of Degree of First-task Learning and Inter-task Similarity," *Journal of Experimental Psychology,* XLV (1953), 1–11, and his "Transfer after Training with Single versus Multiple Tasks," *Journal of Experimental Psychology,* LV (1958), 63–72; L. Morrisett and C. I. Hovland, "A Comparison of Three Varieties of Training in Human Problem Solving," *Journal of Experimental Psychology,* LV (1958), 52–55; and J. M. Sassenrath, "Learning without Awareness and Transfer of Learning Sets," *Journal of Educational Psychology,* L (1959), 202–12.

[2] See Duncan, "Transfer after Training with Single versus Multiple Tasks," *op. cit.*; Morrisett and Hovland, *op. cit.*; and Sassenrath, *op. cit.*

quent items in the ordered sequence.[3] Adequate programming of materials also presupposes maximum attention to such matters as lucidity, organization, and the explanatory and integrative power of substantive content. It is helpful, for example, if sequential materials are so organized that they become progressively more differentiated in terms of generality and inclusiveness, and if similarities and differences between the current learning task and previous learnings are explicitly delineated.[4] Both of these aims can be accomplished by using an advance organizer or brief introductory passage before each new unit of material, which both makes available relevant explanatory principles at a high level of abstraction and increases discriminability. Programmed instruction can also be especially adapted to meet the greater needs of culturally deprived pupils for concrete-empirical props in learning relational propositions.

Although programmed instruction in general is particularly well suited to the needs of the culturally deprived child, I cannot recommend the small-frame format characteristic of teaching-machine programs and most programmed textbooks. In terms of both the logical requirements of meaningful learning and the actual size of the task that can be conveniently accommodated by the learner, the frame length typically used by teaching machines is artificially and unnecessarily abbreviated. It tends to fragment the ideas presented in the program so that their interrelationships are obscured and their logical structure is destroyed.[5] Hence it is relatively easy for less able students to master each granulated step of a given program without understanding the

[3] D. P. Ausubel and D. Fitzgerald, "Organizer, General Background, and Antecedent Learning Variables in Sequential Verbal Learning," *Journal of Educational Psychology*, LIII (1962), 243–49

[4] D. P. Ausubel, "The Use of Advance Organizers in the Learning and Retention of Meaningful Verbal Learning," *Journal of Educational Psychology*, LI (1960), 267–72; D. P. Ausubel and D. Fitzgerald, "The Role of Discriminability in Meaningful Verbal Learning and Retention," *Journal of Educational Psychology*, LII (1961), 266–74, and their "Organizer, General Background, and Antecedent Learning Variables in Sequential Verbal Learning," *op. cit.*

[5] S. L. Pressey, "Basic Unresolved Teaching-Machine Problems," *Theory into Practice*, I (1962), 30–37.

logical relationships and development of the concepts presented.[6] In my opinion, therefore, the traditional textbook format or oral didactic exposition that follows the programming principles outlined above, supplemented by frequent self-scoring and feedback-giving tests, is far superior to the teaching-machine approach for the actual presentation of subject-matter content.[7]

Motivational Considerations

Thus far I have considered various environmental factors that induce retardation in the culturally deprived child's intellectual growth, as well as different cognitive techniques of counteracting and reversing such retardation. These factors and techniques, however, do not operate in a motivational vacuum. Although it is possible separately to consider cognitive and motivational aspects of learning for purposes of theoretical analysis, they are nonetheless inseparably intertwined in any real-life learning situation. For example, school failure and loss of confidence resulting from an inappropriate curriculum further depress the culturally deprived pupil's motivation to learn and thereby increase his existing learning and intellectual deficit. Similarly, although a number of practice and task variables are potentially important for effective learning in a programmed instruction context, appropriate manipulation of these variables can, in the final analysis, only insure successful long-term learning of subject matter provided that the individual is adequately motivated.

Doing without being interested in what one is doing results in relatively little permanent learning, since it is reasonable to suppose that only those materials can be meaningfully incorporated on a long-term basis into an individual's structure of knowledge that are relevant to areas of concern in his psychological field. Learners who have little need to know and understand

[6] D. G. Beane, "A Comparison of Linear and Branching Techniques of Programed Instruction in Plane Geometry" ("Technical Report," No. 1 [Urbana: Training Research Laboratory, University of Illinois, July 1962]).

[7] Pressey, *op. cit.*

quite naturally expend little learning effort; manifest an insufficiently meaningful learning set; fail to develop precise meanings, to reconcile new ideas with existing concepts, and to formulate new propositions in their own words; and do not devote enough time and energy to practice and review. Material is therefore never sufficiently consolidated to form an adequate foundation for sequential learning.

The problem of reversibility exists in regard to the motivational as well as in regard to the cognitive status of the culturally deprived pupil, inasmuch as his environment typically stunts not only his intellectual development, but also the development of appropriate motivations for academic achievement. Motivations for learning, like cognitive abilities, are only potential rather than inherent or endogenous capacities in human beings; their actual development is invariably dependent upon adequate environmental stimulation. Cognitive drive or intrinsic motivation to learn, for example, is probably derived in a very general sense from curiosity tendencies and from related predispositions to explore, manipulate, and cope with the environment; but these tendencies and predispositions are only actualized as a result of successful exercise and the anticipation of future satisfying consequences from further exercise and as a result of internalization of the values of those significant persons in the family and subcultural community with whom the child identifies.

Intrinsic Motivation

The development of cognitive drive or of intrinsic motivation for learning, that is, the acquisition of knowledge as an end in itself or for its own sake, is, in my opinion, the most promising motivational strategy which we can adopt in relation to the culturally deprived child. It is true, of course, in view of the anti-intellectualism and pragmatic attitude toward education that is characteristic of lower-class ideology,[8] that a superficially better case can be made for the alternative strategy of appealing to the incentives to job acquisition, retention, and advancement that now

[8] F. Riessman, *The Culturally Deprived Child* (New York: Harper & Row, 1962).

apply so saliently to continuing education because of the rapid rate of technological change. Actually, however, intrinsic motivation for learning is more potent, relevant, durable, and easier to arouse than its extrinsic counterpart. Meaningful school learning, in contrast to most kinds of laboratory learning, requires relatively little effort or extrinsic incentive, and, when successful, furnishes its own reward. In most instances of school learning, cognitive drive is also the only immediately relevant motivation, since the greater part of school learning cannot be rationalized as necessary for meeting the demands of daily living. Furthermore, it does not lose its relevance or potency in later adult life when utilitarian and career advancement considerations are no longer applicable. Lastly, as we know from the high dropout rate among culturally deprived high-school youth, appeals to extrinsic motivation are not very effective. Among other reasons, the latter situation reflects a limited time perspective focused primarily on the present; a character structure that is oriented more to immediate than delayed gratification of needs; the lack of strong internalized needs for and anxiety about high academic and vocational achievement, as part of the prevailing family, peer group, and community ideology,[9] and the seeming unreality and impossibility of attaining the rewards of prolonged striving and self-denial in view of current living conditions and family circumstances, previous lack of school success, and the discriminatory attitudes of middle-class society.[10]

If we wish to develop the cognitive drive so that it remains viable during the school years and in adult life, it is necessary to move still further away from the educational doctrine of gearing the curriculum to the spontaneously expressed interests, current concerns, and life-adjustment problems of pupils. Although it is undoubtedly unrealistic and even undesirable in our culture to eschew entirely the utilitarian, ego-enhancement, and anxiety-reduction motivations for learning, we must place increasingly greater emphasis upon the value of knowing and understanding

[9] A. Davis, "Child Training and Social Class," *Child Behavior and Development,* ed. R. G. Barker, J. S. Kounin, and H. F. Wright (New York: McGraw-Hill Book Co., 1963), pp. 607–20.

[10] *Ibid.*

as goals in their own right, quite apart from any practical benefits they may confer. Instead of denigrating subject-matter knowledge, we must discover more efficient methods of fostering the long-term acquisition or meaningful and usable bodies of knowledge, and of developing appropriate intrinsic motivations for such learning.

It must be conceded at the outset that culturally deprived children typically manifest little intrinsic motivation to learn. They come from family and cultural environments in which the veneration of learning for its own sake is not a conspicuous value, and in which there is little or no tradition of scholarship. Moreover, they have not been notably successful in their previous learning efforts in school. Nevertheless we need not necessarily despair of motivating them to learn for intrinsic reasons. Psychologists have been emphasizing the motivation-learning and the interest-activity sequences of cause and effect for so long that they tend to overlook their reciprocal aspects. Since motivation is not an indispensable condition for short-term and limited-quantity learning, it is not necessary to postpone learning activities until appropriate interests and motivations have been developed. Frequently the best way of motivating an unmotivated pupil is to ignore his motivational state for the time being and concentrate on teaching him as effectively as possible. Much to his surprise and to his teacher's, he will learn despite his lack of motivation; and from the satisfaction of learning he will characteristically develop the motivation to learn more.

Paradoxically, therefore, we may discover that the most effective method of developing intrinsic motivation to learn is to focus on the cognitive rather than on the motivational aspects of learning, and to rely on the motivation that is developed retroactively from successful educational achievement. This is particularly true when a teacher is able to generate contagious excitement and enthusiasm about the subject he teaches, and when he is the kind of person with whom culturally deprived children can identify. Recruiting more men teachers and dramatizing the lives and exploits of cultural, intellectual, and scientific heroes can also enhance the process of identification. At the same time, of course, we can attempt to combat the anti-intellectualism and lack of cultural tradition in the home through programs of adult education and cultural enrichment.

Extrinsic Motivation

The emphasis I have placed on intrinsic motivation for learning should not be interpreted to mean that I deny the importance of developing extrinsic motivations. The need for ego enhancement, status, and prestige through achievement, the internalization of long-term vocational aspirations, and the development of such implementing traits as responsibility, initiative, self-denial, frustration tolerance, impulse control, and the ability to postpone immediate hedonistic gratification are, after all, traditional hallmarks of personality maturation in our culture; and educational aspirations and achievement are both necessary prerequisites for, and way-station prototypes of, their vocational counterparts. Hence, in addition to encouraging intrinsic motivation for learning, it is also necessary to foster ego-enhancement and career-advancement motivations for academic achievement.

As previously pointed out, however, the current situation with respect to developing adequate motivations for higher academic and vocational achievement among culturally deprived children is not very encouraging. But just as in the case of cognitive drive, much extrinsic motivation for academic success can be generated retroactively from the experience of current success in schoolwork. Intensive counseling can also compensate greatly for the absence of appropriate home, community, and peer-group support and expectations for the development of long-term vocational ambitions. In a sense counselors must be prepared to act *in loco parentis* in this situation. By identifying with a mature, stable, striving, and successful male adult figure, culturally deprived boys can be encouraged to internalize long-term and realistic aspirations, as well as to develop the mature personality traits necessary for their implementation. Hence, as a result of achieving current ego enhancement in the school setting, obtaining positive encouragement and practical guidance in the counseling relationship, and experiencing less rejection and discrimination at the hands of school personnel, higher vocational aspirations appear to lie more realistically within their grasp.

Further encouragement to strive for more ambitious academic and vocational goals can be provided by making available abundant scholarship aid to universities, to community colleges, and to technical institutes; by eliminating the color, ethnic, and class bar in housing, education, and employment; by acquainting culturally deprived youth with examples of successful professional persons originating from their own racial, ethnic, and class backgrounds; and by involving parents sympathetically in the newly fostered ambitions of their children. The success of the Higher Horizons project indicates that an energetic program organized along the lines outlined above can do much to reverse the effects of cultural deprivation on the development of extrinsic motivations for academic and vocational achievement.

28 Ego Development among Segregated Negro Children*

David P. Ausubel
Pearl Ausubel

Ego development refers to the orderly series of changes in an individual's self-concept, self-attitudes, motives, aspirations, sources of self-esteem, and key personality traits affecting the realization of his aspirations as he advances in age in a particular cultural setting. It obviously varies from one individual to another within a particular culture or subculture in accordance with significant temperamental traits and idiosyncratic experience. Nevertheless, it manifests a certain amount of intracultural homogeneity or intercultural difference because of culturally institutionalized differences in interpersonal relations; in opportunities for and methods of acquiring status; in prescribed

**Reprinted from the article of the same title in* Education in Depressed Areas *(A. H. Passow, Ed.) New York: Teachers College Press, 1963, pp. 109–141. By permission of the authors, the editor, and the Teachers College Press.*

age, sex, class, and occupational roles; in approved kinds of personality traits; and in the amount and types of achievement motivation that are socially sanctioned for individuals of a given age, sex, class, and occupation.

For all of these reasons the ego development of segregated Negro children in America manifests certain distinctive properties. Negro children live in a predominantly lower-class subculture that is further characterized by a unique type of family structure, by specially circumscribed opportunities for acquiring status, by varying degrees of segregation from the dominant white majority, and, above all, by a fixed and apparently immutable denigration of their social value, standing, and dignity as human beings because of their skin color. Hence, it would be remarkable indeed if these factors did not result in significant developmental differences in self-esteem, in aspirations for achievement, in personality adjustment, and in character structure. In fact the Supreme Court decision of 1954 outlawing school segregation was based primarily on considerations of ego development. It recognized that school and other public facilities cannot be "separate and equal" because enforced and involuntary separateness that is predicated on purely arbitrary criteria necessarily implies an inferior caste status, and thereby results in psychological degradation and injury to self-esteem.

In the context of this conference on the education of culturally disadvantaged groups in depressed urban areas, our interest in the ego development of segregated Negro children obviously transcends mere theoretical considerations. Recent technological and sociological changes are confronting the American Negro with significant new challenges to his traditional role and status in our society. In the past it was possible for him to achieve some measure of stable adjustment to his inferior caste position, unsatisfactory though it was. He more or less accepted his devalued social status and second-class citizenship, aspired to low-level occupational roles requiring little education and training, found work in unskilled and menial occupations, and lived within his segregated subculture shunning contact and competition with whites. But two important changes are currently rendering this type of adjustment less and less tenable. In the first place, automation is rapidly decreasing the need for unskilled and uneducated labor in America. The poorly trained and poorly educated Negro youth who drops out of secondary school as soon as he reaches the minimum legal age, or fails to acquire some post-high-school technical training, finds himself at a much greater disadvantage in today's job market than was true of his father and older brother just a decade ago. He now lives in a wider culture in which a much higher level of educational and vocational training is a prerequisite for occupational adjustment, but he still grows up in a subculture that neither fosters aspirations for such education and training, nor provides the moral and material support necessary for their realization. Second, there are many indications that the Negro is no longer content with his segregated caste status and second-class citizenship. At the same time, however, he possesses a character structure and a repertoire of educational and vocational skills that, on the whole, do not prepare him to compete adequately with whites in the wider culture. In short, he is more desirous of participating in the unsegregated American culture, but lacks the personality traits and intellectual attainments that would enable him to do so effectively.

As educators, our job is to help the Negro child fill the new and more desirable place in American society that technological change and his elders' aspirations for equality are creating for him. Essentially this means altering his ego structure so that he desires and is able to achieve a level of educational and vocational training that would make it possible for him to compete successfully with whites in modern industrial society. It is true, of course, that the Negro's ego structure is largely a reflection of the actual social and legal status he enjoys in our culture; and as citizens it is our obligation to help him achieve equality of opportunity and equality before the law. But status and its reflection in self-esteem depend as much on real achievement as on equality of rights and opportunity. A changed ego structure, as manifested in higher educational and vocational aspirations, in the development of personality traits necessary for realizing these aspirations, and in the actual achievement of higher educational and vocational qualifications, can do as much to improve the Negro's status in society, and hence enhance his self-esteem, as can amelioration of his social and legal status. If, on the other hand, the Negro community cannot obtain our support in helping to mold the Negro youth's ego structure in ways that will eventually improve his competitive position in the employment market, he can only look forward to becoming permanently unemployable and subsisting on public assistance. This latter state of affairs would not only tend to perpetuate the Negro's lower-class and inferior caste position with its attendant adverse effects on ego development, but would also increase racial tensions and encourage anti-social behavior.

In this paper we propose to do three things. First, we would like to consider the personality development of the segregated Negro child as a special variant of the more typical course of ego development in our culture. Here the approach is normative, from the standpoint of a personality theorist interested in subcultural differences. In what ways does the ego development of segregated Negro children differ from that of the textbook child growing up in the shadow of our dominant middle-class value system? Second, we would like to consider some kinds of and reasons for individual differences within this underprivileged group. Do all Negro children in the Harlem ghetto respond in the same way to the impact of their segregated lower-class environment? If not, why not? Are there social class, sex, and individual differences among Negro children? Questions of this type would be asked by a personality theorist concerned with idiosyncratic and group variability within a subcultural setting, or by a psychiatrist treating the behavior disorders of such children in a Harlem community clinic. Finally, we propose to consider the implications of this material for such practical issues as educational practice and desegregation.

Overview of Ego Development in White Middle-Class Children

Before turning to a description of ego development in segregated Negro communities, it may be helpful to examine briefly the typical middle-class model with which it will be compared. In doing this we do not mean to imply that the developmental pattern in suburbia is necessarily typical of the

American scene. Obviously only a minority of America's children live in the ecological equivalent of suburban culture. Nevertheless it is still a useful model for comparative purposes because it reflects the value system that dominates such official socializing institutions in our society as the school, the church, the youth organizations, the mass media, and the child-rearing manuals. Hence, it is the most widely diffused and influential model of socialization in our culture. It is the official model that most parents profess to believe in regardless of whether or not they practice it. It is the model that would most impress foreign anthropologists as typical of American culture.

The infant in suburbia, as in many other cultures, may be pardoned for entertaining mild feelings of omnipotence (7). Out of deference for his manifest helplessness, his altruistic parents are indulgent, satisfy most of his needs, and make few demands on him. In view of his cognitive immaturity, it is hardly surprising then that he interprets his enviable situation as proof of his volitional power than as reflective of parental altruism. As he becomes less helpless and more responsive to parental direction, however, this idyllic picture begins to change. His parents become more demanding, impose their will on him, and take steps to socialize him in the ways of the culture; and by this time the toddler has sufficient cognitive maturity to perceive his relative impotence and volitional dependence on them. All of these factors favor the occurrence of satellization. The child surrenders his volitional independence and by the fiat of parental acceptance and intrinsic valuation acquires a derived or attributed status. As a result, despite his marginal status in the culture and manifest inability to fend for himself, he acquires feelings of self-esteem that are independent of his performance ability. He also internalizes parental values and expectations regarding mature and acceptable behavior.

In suburbia, derived status constitutes the cornerstone of the child's self-esteem until adolescence. Beginning with middle childhood, however, forces are set in motion which bring about preliminary desatellization from parents. Both in school and in the peer group he is urged to compete for a primary status based on his academic proficiency, athletic prowess and social skills. School and peer groups legislate their own values, impose their own standards, and also offer him a subsidiary source of derived status insofar as they accept him for himself in return for his loyalty and self-subordination. All of these factors tend to devalue the parents and to undermine their omniscience in the child's eyes. The home becomes only one of several socializing agents that foster the development of aspirations for academic and vocational success and of the pattern of deferred gratification necessary to achieve them. Nevertheless, until adolescence, parents remain the major socializing agents and source of values in the child's life. Compared to the derived status obtained from parents, the primary status available in school and peer group plays only a subsidiary role in the total economy of ego organization.

Ego Development in Young Negro Children

Social-class factors

Many of the ecological features of the segregated Negro subculture that impinge on personality development in early childhood are not specific to Negroes as such, but are characteristic of most lower-class populations. This fact is not widely appreciated by white Americans and hence contributes to much anti-Negro sentiment: many characteristic facets of the Negro's value system and behavior pattern are falsely attributed to his racial membership, whereas they really reflect his predominant membership in the lower social class. Nevertheless, these characteristics are commonly offered as proof of the alleged moral and intellectual inferiority that is supposedly inherent in persons of Negro ancestry and are used to justify existing discriminatory practices.

Lower-class parents, for example, are generally more casual, inconsistent, and authoritarian than middle-class parents in controlling their children, and resort more to harsh, corporal forms of punishment (30, 31, 70, 71, 74). Unlike middle-class fathers, whose wives expect them to be as supportive as themselves in relation to children, the lower-class father's chief role in child rearing is to impose constraints and administer punishment (74). Even more important, lower-class parents extend less succorant care and relax closely monitored supervison much earlier than their middle-class counterparts (29, 30, 35, 54). Lower-class children are thus free to roam the neighborhood and join unsupervised play groups at an age when suburban children are still confined to nursery school or to their own backyards. Hence, during the pre-school and early elementary-school years, the lower-class family yields to the peer group much of its role as socializing agent and source of values and derived status. During this early period lower-class children undergo much of the desatellization from parents that ordinarily occurs during middle childhood and preadolescence in most middle-class families. They acquire earlier volitional and executive independence outside the home and in many cases assume adult responsibilities such as earning money and caring for younger siblings. Abbreviated parental succorance, which frustrates the dependency needs of middle-class children and commonly fosters overdependence (100), has a different significance for and effect on these lower-class children. Since it reflects the prevailing subcultural norm, and since the opportunity for early anchorage to a free-ranging peer group is available, it tends to encourage the development of precious independence.

This pattern of precocious independence from the family combined with the exaggerated socializing influence of the peer group, although characteristic of both white and Negro lower-class children, does not necessarily prevail among all lower-class minority groups in the United States. Both Puerto Rican (3) and Mexican (75) children enjoy a more closely-knit family life marked by more intimate contact between parents and children. In Mexican families, maternal and paternal roles are also more distinctive, masculine and feminine roles are more clearly delineated in childhood, and the socializing influence of the peer group is less pronounced (75).

The working-class mother's desire for unquestioned domination of her offspring, her preference for harsh, punitive, and suppressive forms of control, and her tendency to maintain considerable social and emotional distance between herself and her children are probably responsible in part for the greater prevalence of the authoritarian personality syndrome in lower-class children than in middle-class children (36, 53, 69). Lower-class children tend to develop ambivalent attitudes toward authority figures and to cope with this ambivalence by making an exaggerated show of overt, implicit compliance, by maintaining formally appropriate social distance, and by interacting with these figures on the basis of formalized role attributes rather than as persons. Their underlying hostility and resentment toward this arbitrary and often unfair authority is later expressed in such displaced forms as scape-goating, prejudice, extremist political and religious behavior, ethnocentrism, and delinquency (36, 53, 69).

Much of the significant relationship between social-class status and school achievement undoubtedly reflects pervasive social-class differences in cognitive orientation and functioning that are operative from early childhood (15). Middle-class children are trained to respond to the abstract, categorical, and relational properties of objects, whereas lower-class children are trained to respond more to their concrete, tangible, immediate, and particularized properties. This difference in perceptual disposition is carried over into verbal expression, memory, concept formation, learning and problem-solving. Hence, since schools place great emphasis on the learning of abstract relationships and on the abstract use of language, lower-class children, on the average, experience much greater difficulty than middle-class children in mastering the curriculum.

Racial Factors

All of the foregoing properties of the lower-class environment also apply to the segregated Negro community. Most authorities on Negro family life agree that well over 50 per cent of Negro families live at the very lowest level of the lower-class standard (56). In addition, however, Negro families are characterized by a disproportionate number of illegal and loosely connected unions (56). Illegitimacy is a very common phenomenon and is associated with relatively little social stigma in the Negro community (20); nevertheless, illegitimate Negro children, especially at the older age levels, are significantly inferior to their legitimate counterparts in IQ, school achievement, and personal adjustment (59).

Negro families are much more unstable than comparable lower-class white families. Homes are more apt to be broken, fathers are more frequently absent, and a matriarchal and negative family atmosphere more commonly prevails (25, 28, 34, 56). Thus the lower-class Negro child is frequently denied the benefits of bi-parental affection and upbringing; he is often raised by his grandmother or older sister while his mother works to support the family deserted by the father (34). One consequence of the matriarchal family climate is an open preference for girls. Boys frequently attempt to adjust to this situation by adopting feminine traits and mannerisms (28).

Negro family life is even more authoritarian in nature than is that of the lower social class generally. "Children are expected to be obedient and submissive" (56), and insubordination is suppressed by harsh and often brutal physical punishment (28, 31, 56). "Southern Negro culture teaches obedience and respect for authority as a mainspring of survival" (51). Surveys of high-school and college students show that authoritarian attitudes are more prevalent among Negroes at all grade levels (50, 51, 108).

Being a Negro also has many other implications for the ego development of young children that are not inherent in lower-class membership. The Negro child inherits an inferior caste status and almost inevitably acquires the negative self-esteem that is a realistic ego reflection of such status. Through personal slights, blocked opportunities, and unpleasant contacts with white persons and with institutionalized symbols of caste inferiority (segregated schools, neighborhoods, amusement areas, etc.)—and more indirectly through mass media and the reactions of his own family—he gradually becomes aware of the social significance of racial membership (45).

As a consequence of prejudice, segregation, discrimination, inferior status, and not finding himself respected as a human being with dignity and worth,

> . . . the Negro child becomes confused in regard to his feelings about himself and his group. He would like to think well of himself but often tends to evaluate himself according to standards used by the other group. These mixed feelings lead to self-hatred and rejection of his

group, hostility toward other groups, and a generalized pattern of personality difficulties (58, p. 146).

Segregation

> . . . means that the personal worth, of either a white or Negro person, is measured solely by group membership regardless of individual merit. Such a measure is realistically false and of necessity distorts the developing self-image of Negro and white children as well as their view of each other. Under these psychological circumstances the Negro child, for example, is burdened with inescapable inferiority feelings, a fixed ceiling to his aspiration level which can constrict the development of his potentialities, and a sense of humiliation and resentment which can entail patterns of hatred against himself and his own group, as well as against the dominant white group (14, p. 151).

The Negro child perceives himself as an object of derision and disparagement (45), as socially rejected by the prestigeful elements of society, and as unworthy of succorance and affection (34); and having no compelling reasons for not accepting this officially sanctioned negative evaluation or himself, he develops a deeply ingrained negative self-image (14, 123).

It does not take long for Negro children to become aware of the unfavorable implications of their racial membership. In interracial nursery schools, most children show some type of racial awareness at the age of three (115), and this awareness increases rapidly between the ages of 3 and 7 (116). Once aware of racial differences, they soon learn that "skin color is important, that white is to be desired, dark to be regretted" (68). Very significantly, racial self-recognition develops later in Negro than in white children (77, 116); in the light of doll play evidence indicating that they resist identifying with their own stigmatized racial group (23), this delay in racial self-recognition can only be interpreted as reluctance in acknowledging their racial membership.

All of the sociometric rejection and maltreatment experienced by Negro children in a mixed group cannot, of course, be attributed to their inferior caste status alone. Some of the victimization undoubtedly reflects the dynamics of a majority-minority group situation. Thus, when white children are in the minority, the values, judgments, and verbal expression of the Negro majority tend to prevail (96). Under these conditions, Negroes curse whites but the latter do not openly retaliate despite revealing anti-Negro prejudice to white investigators (96).

In addition to suffering ego deflation through awareness of his inferior status in society, the Negro child finds it more difficult to satellize and is denied much of the self-esteem advantages of satellization. The derived status that is the principal source of children's self-esteem in all cultures is largely discounted in his case since he can only satellize in relation to superordinate individuals or groups who themselves possess an inferior and degraded status. Satellization under such conditions not only confers a very limited amount of derived status but also has deflationary implications for self-esteem. We can understand, therefore, why young Negro children resist identifying with their own racial group, why they seek to shed their identities (34), why they more frequently choose white than Negro playmates (116), why they prefer the skin color of the culturally dominant caste (23, 47, 68), and why they tend to assign negative roles to children of their own race (116). These tendencies persist at least into late adolescence and early adult life, insofar as one can judge from the attitudes of Negro college students. These students tend to reject ethnocentric and anti-white ideologies and to accept authoritarian and anti-Negro propositions (114).

Ego Development in Older Negro Children and Adolescents

Social-class Factors

During middle childhood and preadolescence the ego development of the segregated Negro child also reflects the influence of both general social class factors and of more specific racial factors. As already pointed out, early experience in fending for himself both in the wider culture and in the unsupervised peer group, as well as in exercising adult-like responsibilities, accomplishes precociously much of the desatellization from and devaluation of parents characterizing the ego development of middle-class children during this period.

In these developments, the school plays a much less significant role among lower-class than among middle-class children. The lower-class child of school age has fewer illusions about parental omniscience for the teacher to shatter, and is coerced by the norms of his peer group against accepting her authority, seeking her approval, or entering into a satellizing relationship with her (30). School can also offer him very little in the way of either current or ultimate primary status. His parents and associates place no great value on education and do not generally encourage high aspirations for academic and vocational success, financial independence, or social recognition (30, 54, 97). It is hardly surprising, therefore, that lower-class children are less interested in reading than are middle-class children, have lower educational aspirations, take their schoolwork less seriously, and are less willing to spend the years of their youth in school in order to gain higher prestige and more social rewards as adults (30, 54, 97).

Even if they equalled middle-class children in these latter respects, academic achievement would still be quite a valueless reward for a child who soon comes to realize that professional status is beyond his grasp (30). Hence, anxiety regarding the attainment of internalized needs for vocational prestige does not drive the lower-class child to excel in school (30). Also, because of low achievement and discriminatory treatment, he fails to obtain the current rewards of academic success available to middle-class school children (30). On what grounds could a child immersed in an intellectually impoverished environment be expected to actualize his genic potentials for verbal and abstract thinking, when he is unmotivated by parental pressures, by ambitions for vocational success, or by the anxiety associated with realizing these ambitions?

Lower- and middle-class adolescents differ markedly both in their social value systems and in their vocational interests. Middle-class youths and their parents are more concerned with community service, self-realization, altruistic values, and internalized standards of conduct (60, 112), and prefer demanding, responsible, and prestigeful occupational pursuits (88, 89, 103). They also make higher vocational interest scores in the literary, esthetic, persuasive, scientific and business areas than do lower-class adolescents. The latter adolescents and their parents, on the other hand, place greater stress on such values as money, security, respectability, obedience, and conformity to authority, and tend to prefer agricultural, mechanical, domestic service, and clerical pursuits (88, 89, 103).

The lower-class child's *expressed* levels of academic and vocational aspirations often appear unrealistically high (34), but unlike the analogous situation in middle-class children, these do not necessarily represent his *real* or functional levels of striving. They more probably reflect impairment of realistic judgment under the cumulative impact of chronic failure (99) and low social status (48), as well as a compensatory attempt to bolster self-esteem through the appearance rather than the substance of aiming high. Lacking the strong ego involvement which the middle-class child brings to schoolwork, and which preserves the attractiveness of academic tasks despite failure experience (98), he quickly loses interest in school if he is unsuccessful. Finally, since he does not perceive the eventual rewards of striving and self-denial as attainable for persons of his status, he fails to develop to the same degree as the middle-class child the supportive traits of ego maturity necessary for the achievement of academic and vocational success (30). These supportive traits include habits of initiative and responsibility and the "deferred gratification pattern" of hard work, renunciation of immediate pleasures, long-range planning, high frustration tolerance, impulse control, thrift, orderliness, punctuality, and willingness to undergo prolonged vocational preparation (30, 54, 86, 97).

Despite having less deep-seated anxiety with respect to internalized needs for academic achievement and vocational prestige, children of lower-class families exhibit more signs of personality maladjustment than do children of middle-class families (4, 6, 57, 101, 102, 111). This greater degree of maladjustment is largely a response to the greater vicissitudes and insecurities of daily living; to the greater possibility and actual occurrence of failure in an educational and vocational world dominated by middle-class standards in which they are greatly disadvantaged;

to inner tensions engendered by conflict between the values of the family and those of the dominant middle-class culture; to feelings of shame about family background that are associated with impulses to reject family ties; to feelings of guilt and anxiety about these latter impulses (102); and to the personal demoralization and self-derogation that accompany social disorganization and the possession of inferior social status (5, 7, 111). In most instances, of course, the symptoms of maladjustment are uncomfortable rather than disabling; but the generally higher level of anxiety, and the more frequent occurrence of motivational immaturity in lower-class children and adolescents, also increase the incidence of such serious disorders as schizophrenia, drug addiction, and anxiety neurosis and its various complications (7, 57, 111). Proneness to delinquency is, of course, higher among lower-class adolescents because of greater family and social disorganization, the deep-seated resentments and aggressive impulses attributable to socio-economic deprivation, the influence of organized, predatory gangs, and the tacit encouragement offered by the lower-class value system and the slum-urban teen-age cult of thrills, kicks, self-indulgence, violence, and non-conformity.

Racial Factors

All of the aforementioned factors inhibiting the development of high level ego aspirations and their supportive personality traits in lower-class children are intensified in the segregated Negro child. His overall prospects for vertical social mobility, although more restricted, are not completely hopeless. But the stigma of his caste membership is inescapable and unsurmountable. It is inherent in his skin color, permanently ingrained in his body image, and enforced by the extra-legal power of a society whose moral, legal, and religious codes proclaim his equality (123).

It is proper to speak of a stigma as being "enforced" when the stigma in question is culturally derived rather than inherent in the physical existence of the mark per se (that is, a mark of inferiority in *any* culture such as lameness or blindness). Dark skin color is a stigma in our culture only because it identifies a culturally stigmatized caste. When we speak of the stigma being "inherent in his skin color," we mean that it is a stigma which the Negro inherits by virtue of being born with that skin color in a culture that places a negative valuation on it. Hence the stigma "inheres" in the skin color. But this does not imply that dark skin color is inherently (that is, apart from a particular set of cultural values) a mark of inferiority; the stigma is only inherent for the individual insofar as he acquires it by cultural definition rather than by anything he does.

Hence, since a culturally derived stigma refers to an identifying characteristic of a group which has been relegated to an inferiority status position in society, the stigma can only be perpetuated as long as the culture provides some mechanism for *enforcing* the low status position of the group in question. In the absence of cultural enforcement the stigma would vanish in as much as it is not inherent in the characteristic itself but is merely a symbol of membership in an inferior caste. In our society (unlike the Union of South Africa), there are no laws which explicity create an inferior caste status for the Negro; even segregation statutes accord him a separate rather than an inferior status. Hence the "mark" is enforced extra-legally by preserving through informal social practices the social inferiority of which the mark is but a symbol.

If this situation exists despite the authority of God and the Constitution, what basis for hope does the Negro child have? It is not surprising, therefore, that, in comparison with lower-class white children, he aspires to jobs with more of the formal trappings than with the actual attributes of social prestige; that he feels impotent to strike back at his tormentors; that he feels more lonely and scared when he is by himself; and that he gives more self-deprecatory reactions when figuratively looking at himself in the mirror (34). He may have less anxiety about realizing high-flown ambitions than the middle-class child, but generalized feelings of inadequacy and unworthiness make him very prone to overrespond with anxiety to any threatening situation. In view of the general hopelessness of his position, lethargy, apathy, submission, and passive sabotage are more typical than aggressive striving of his predominant reaction to frustration (95, 105).

Rosen (95) compared the educational and vocational aspirations of Negro boys (age 8 through 14) and their mothers to those of white, Protestant Americans, French Canadians, American Jews, Greek-Americans, and Italian-Americans. The mean vocational aspiration score of his Negro group was significantly lower than the mean scores of all other groups except the French Canadian. Paradoxically, however, 83 per cent of the Negro mothers aspired to a college education for their sons.[1] Rosen concluded that although Negroes have been

> . . . exposed to the liberal economic ethic longer than most of the other groups . . . their culture, it seems, is least likely to accent achievement values. The Negro's history as a slave and depressed farm worker, and the sharp discrepancy between his experience and the American Creed, would appear to work against the achievement values of the dominant white group. Typically, the Negro life-situation does not encourage the belief that one can manipulate his environment, or the conviction that one can improve his condition very much by planning and hard work (95, p. 55).
>
> . . . Negroes who might be expected to share the prevalent American emphasis upon education, face the painfully apparent fact that positions open to educated Negroes are scarce. This fact means that most Negroes, in all likelihood, do not consider high educational aspirations realistic, and the heavy drop-out in high school suggests that the curtailment of educational aspirations begins very early (95, p. 58).

Ethnicity was found to be more highly related to vocational aspirations than was social class; sizable ethnic and racial differences prevailed even when the influence of social class was controlled. These results are consistent with the finding that white students tend to prefer "very interesting jobs," whereas Negro students are more concerned with job security (106).

The relatively low vocational aspirations of Negro children are apparently justified by the current facts of economic life. Negroes predominate in the unskilled occupations, receive less pay than whites for equivalent work, and exceed the percentage figured for whites in degree of unemployment (43, 105). In skilled occupations, Negroes are excluded at all educational

[1] Another datum at variance with the general trend of the evidence is Grossack's finding that female Negro students in the South score significantly higher on need achievement measures than do comparable white females, and that the males of both groups are not significantly different (52).

levels (120): higher educational qualifications in Negroes are less frequently associated with higher-level vocational pursuits than they are in the case of whites (119). Thus,

> . . . from long experience Negroes have learned that it is best to be prepared for the absence, rather than the presence of opportunity—or, at most, to prepare and strive only for those limited opportunities which have been open in the past. . . . Like most other people, Negroes tend to accept the views that prevail in the larger society about their appropriate role in that society, [and aspire and prepare] for only those positions where they are confident of acceptance (110, p. 461).

Negro children and lower-class white children who attend schools with a heterogeneous social class and racial population are in a more favorable developmental situation. Under these conditions, the unfavored group is stimulated to compete more aggressively, even to the point of unrealism (16, 109), with the more privileged group in every-day contracts and in aspirational behavior (16). In their self-judgments they compare themselves with *actual* models, who in fact are only slightly better off than they are, and hence do not feel particularly inferior (34). Negro children in segregated schools, on the other hand, are not only deprived of this stimulation, but in comparing themselves to other children paradoxically feel more depressed and less able to compete adequately (34), despite the fact that their actual contacts are confined to children in the incapsulated community who share their socio-economic status. Apparently then, they must use idealized mass media models as the basis for comparison.

Negro children are placed in the same ambivalent, conflictful position with respect to the achievement values of western civilization as are the children of many native peoples experiencing acculturation and the socio-cultural impact of rapid industrialization. On the one hand, exposure to the new value system and its patent and alluring advantages makes them less able to accept the traditional values of their elders; on the other hand, both loyalty to their families and the excluding color bar established by the dominant group make it difficult for them to assimilate the new set of values (9, 11, 12, 35, 81). Resentment and hostility toward the rejecting whites, as well as disillusionment regarding white middle-class values and institutions, predispose them arbitrarily and indiscriminately to repudiate the aspirations and personality traits valued by the dominant culture. These negativistic tendencies are even manifested in speech patterns: minority group children tend to reject the accepted model of speech that is symbolic of superordinate status in a social order that accords them only second-class membership (2).

Further abetting these tendencies toward resistive acculturation are many organized and institutionalized forms of nationalism and counter-chauvinism. Among the Maori, "resistance took the form of unadaptive but adjustive messianic and magical cults, emphasis on moribund and ceremonial features of the ancient culture, and indiscriminate rejection of progressive aspects of European culture" (9, p. 221). Numerous parallels can be found among the American Negro—for example, the Father Divine and Black Muslim movements.

One of the most damaging effects of racial prejudice and discrimination on the victimized group is that it provides an all-embracing rationalization for personal shortcomings, lack of striving, and antisocial conduct.

> Some Negroes use the objective injustice of [creating scapegoats] as an opportunity to relieve or ward off feelings of personal inadequacy, self-contempt, or self-reproach by projecting all the blame onto white prejudice and discrimination. For other Negroes, however, reaction-formation becomes a main defense against the negative racial image. . . . Thus they may develop extremes of moralistic, prudish, and compulsively meticulous attitudes [to disprove the stereotype] (14, p. 152).
>
> The Negro child is offered an excuse for anti-social behavior and evasion of social responsibility through feeling deprived of the social rewards for self-denial which are part of a healthy socialization process. But since these reactions are at variance with the democratic ideal of many other teachings to which children of both races are exposed at home, at church, and at school, they arouse of necessity feelings of inner conflict, confusion, anxiety, and guilt. These constitute liabilities for optimal adjustment (14, p. 152).
>
> A continuing set of small incidents, closed doors, and blocked opportunities contribute to feelings of insecurity and mistrust and lead to the

building of faith only in immediate gratifications and personal possessions (14, p. 148).

Withdrawal from Competition An important factor helping to perpetuate the Negro's inferior social status and devalued ego structure is his tendency to withdraw from the competition of the wider American culture and to seek psychological shelter within the segregated walls of his own subculture. Such tendencies are particularly evident among middle-class Negroes who, instead of providing the necessary leadership in preparing their people to take advantage of new vocational opportunitites in the emerging desegregated culture, often seek to protect their own vested interests in segregation. Negro businessmen, professionals, and teachers, for example, largely owe their clientele, jobs, and incomes to the existence of segregated institutions; furthermore, in the segregated community they do not have to meet the more stringent competitive standards prevailing in the wider culture (42, 93, 120). An additional complication is the fact that even though they "cannot escape altogether the discrimination and contempt to which Negroes are generally subjected" (42, p. 299), they tend to identify with the values and ideology of the white middle-class and to dissociate themselves from other Negroes (42, 93, 107, 110, 114). Together with pride of race and grudging affirmation of their racial identity, members of intellectual Negro families "are led to assert their superiority over other Negroes, and look down on those who are 'no account,' shiftless, and 'mean' " (93, p. 240).

The degree to which Negro potential can be developed in America depends, according to Smuts (110),

> . . . not only on the willingness of the white community to grant greater opportunity to Negroes in the struggle for integrated schools and equal access to jobs; but it also depends at least as much on what the Negro community does to help its own members prepare themselves for new opportunities. . . .In a democracy, how well the individual develops and utilizes his potential depends not only on the opportunities that come his way as a youth and a man, but equally on his own determination to seek and make the most of opportunity (p. 456).

In the past the real world that Negroes had to adjust to included segregation, discrimination, absence of opportunity. But the facts are changing and a new kind of adjustment is called for (p. 461). . . . The development of high ambition and firm self-confidence among Negro youth is one prerequisite for the fuller development of Negro potential (p. 462). . . .In a competitive society integration means competition, and successful competition requires at least equal preparation (p. 458). . . .Negroes will not be able to take full advantage of [new] opportunities unless they improve their preparation for work (p. 458). . . . Negro children cannot develop an image of themselves as free and equal members of American society unless they see their elders actually living that role (p. 463).

Educational Aspirations and Achievement of Negro Children Partly as a result of unequal educational opportunities, Negro children show serious academic retardation. They attend school for fewer years and, on the average, learn much less than white children do (5, 17, 21, 82, 110, 113). One of the chief reasons for this discrepancy is the inferior education and training of Negro teachers who themselves are usually products of segregated education. The inequality of educational facilities exists not only in the South (5, 17, 127), but also in the urban North as well, where, for the most part, de facto segregation prevails (110, 113). Eighty-four per cent of the top 10 per cent of Negro graduates in one southern high school scored below the national mean on the Scholastic Aptitude Test (17). Thus the incentive of reaching the average level of proficiency in the group is not very stimulating for Negro children, since the mean and even the somewhat superior child in this group are still below grade level. Teachers in segregated schools also tend to be overly permissive and to emphasize play skills over academic achievement; they are perceived by their pupils as evaluating them negatively, and as more concerned with behavior than with schoolwork (34).

Even more important perhaps as a cause of Negro educational retardation is the situation prevailing in the Negro home. Many Negro parents have had little schooling themselves and hence are unable to appreciate its value. Thus they do not provide active, wholehearted support for high-level academic performance by demanding conscientious study and regular attendance from their children. Furthermore, because of their large families and their own meager schooling they are less able to provide help with lessons. Keeping a large family of children in a secondary school constitutes a heavy economic burden on Negro parents in view of their low per capita income and the substantial hidden costs of "free" education. The greater frequency of broken homes, unemployment, and negative family atmosphere, as well as the high rate of pupil turnover (25, 104), are also not conducive to academic achievement.

Negro pupils are undoubtedly handicapped in academic attainment by a lower average level of intellectual functioning than is characteristic of comparable white pupils. In both northern and southern areas, particularly the latter, Negro pupils have significantly lower IQ's (19, 39, 80, 82), and are retarded in arithmetic, reading, language usage, and ability to handle abstract concepts (17, 82). The extreme intellectual impoverishment of the Negro home *over and above* its lower social-class status reflects the poor standard of English spoken in the home and the general lack of books, magazines, and stimulating conversation. In view of the educational and psychological inequality of segregated schools, the inferior intellectual status of Negro homes, and the negative motivational effects of membership in a socially stigmatized group, any inferences from the lower IQ's and educational retardation of Negro pupils regarding *innate* differences in intelligence are obviously unwarranted. Organic brain damage, however, is a more frequent occurrence in Negro children because of inadequate prenatal care and nutrition and because of the higher incidence of prematurity (85).

Similar kinds of family and community factors depress the vocational strivings and accomplishments of Negro youth. Practically all of the following description of the occupational aspirations of Maori adolescents in New Zealand applies to the Negro in America:

> Maori parents are less sophisticated than their [European] counterparts about vocational matters and are accordingly less capable of assisting their children with appropriate information, advice, and guidance. . . . In view of their smaller incomes and larger families, Maori parents are also more reluctant to commit themselves to supporting plans requiring

long-term vocational preparation (9, p. 623).

. . . Maori parents tend to adopt more permissive and laissez-faire attitudes than [European] parents toward their children's vocational careers. Despite occasional and inconsistent displays of authoritarianism in this regard, they are usually content to let them drift. They apply fewer coercive pressures and extend less support and encouragement in relation to the long-term occupational ambitions of their children. Their own values concerning vocational achievement and the example they set their children also tend to encourage the adoption of a short-term view. In practice they make few demands for the deferment of immediate hedonistic satisfactions and for the internalization of supportive traits consistent with high academic and occupational attainment (p. 623).

. . . [Still] another factor limiting the vocational achievement of Maori youth is the relatively low occupational status and morale of Maori adults. Young people lack the encouragement [of visible emulatory models], of a tradition and a high current standard of vocational accomplishment in the ethnic group. They are also denied the practical benefits of guidance and financial backing that would follow from the existence of such a standard and tradition. On the other hand, they are discouraged by the marginal economic position of their elders [and] by social demoralization (p. 624).

Maori pupils also receive less encouragement from their peers than [European] pupils do to strive for vocational achievement. Not only is occupational success less highly valued in the Maori than in the European peer culture, but the greater availability of *derived status*—based solely on membership in and intrinsic acceptance by the group—also removes much of the incentive for seeking *primary status* based on individual competence and performance. In districts where community morale is low and juvenile delinquency flourishes, vocational achievement tends to be negatively sanctioned (p. 624).

Low vocational aspirations, of course, are in large a reflection of the distressingly high rate of unemployment among Negro youth in the urban slums. Conant reports that in one large city 48 per cent of male Negro high school graduates and 63 per cent of non-graduates were unemployed (25).

The tone is not one to encourage education or stimulate ambition. One often finds a vicious circle of lack of jobs and lack of ambition; one leads to the other. It is my contention that the circle must be broken both by upgrading the educational and vocational aspirations of slum youth and, even more important, by finding employment opportunity for them, particularly for high school graduates. It does no good whatever to prepare boys and girls for non-existent jobs (25, p. 36).

Finally, because of their precocious desatellization and emancipation from parents, Negro youths have greater needs for *immediate* financial independence. They therefore find psychologically more intolerable a prolonged period of psychological dependence on parents, such as would be required in preparing for a profession.

Personality Adjustment The destructive impact of prejudice, discrimination, segregation, an inferior caste status on self-esteem, in addition to the usual mental hygiene consequences of lower social class membership, result in a much higher incidence of behavior disorders in Negroes than in whites (51, 111, 128). Personality disturbance is also more highly correlated with intelligence test scores in Negroes than in whites (94). Quite understandably, both high anxiety level (83, 94) and suppressed feelings of aggression (61) are prominent symptoms of Negro maladjustment. Overt expression of these same aggressive impulses leads to a juvenile delinquency rate that is two to three times as high as among white teen-agers (37, 38). The occurrence of delinquent behavior is abetted by the high rate of unemployment (25) and by many characteristic features of lower-class Negro family life, such as illegitimate births, broken homes, desertion, neglect, employment of the mother, intra-familial violence, harsh punishment, and tolerance for minor dishonesties (20). Under these circumstances, aggressive antisocial behavior may be considered both a form of individual and social protest (38), as well as an effective means of obtaining and maintaining status in the peer group of the lower-class Negro subculture (22). Drug addiction, on the other hand, represents a particularly efficient type of "dead-end" adjustment for the hedonistic, motivationally immature adolescent who refuses to face up to the responsibilities of adult life (10, 41).

Sex Differences

One of the most striking features of ego development in the segregated Negro community is the relatively more favored position enjoyed by girls in comparison to the middle-class model. It is true that middle-class girls have certain advantages over boys in early ego development. Since girls perceive themselves as more highly accepted and intrinsically valued by parents (13) and have a more available emulatory model in the home (84), they tend to satellize more and longer. In addition to enjoying more derived status in the home, they can also acquire more primary status from household activities (84) and from school achievement. The opportunity for acquiring primary status in school is greater for girls than for boys because of their superior verbal fluency and greater conformity to adult authority, and because school success is less ambivalently prized by their peers. In general, girls are less negativistic (46), more amenable to social controls (66), and less alienated from adults.

Middle-class boys, however, are not excessively disadvantaged. Their mothers tend to prefer them to girls (100), and their fathers are responsible and respected status figures in the home and the principal source of economic security. Furthermore, although girls enjoy more current primary status during childhood, boys have higher ultimate aspirations for primary status; their aspirational level both for laboratory tasks (121) and for possessions and achievement (24) are higher. Unlike boys, girls do not *really* expect to prove their adequacy and maintain their self-esteem as adults by means of their vocational accomplishments. Their fathers are satisfied if they are "pretty, sweet, affectionate, and well-liked" (1). Finally, the superordinate position of men in our society, and the accompanying male chauvinism, is reflected in childhood sex roles. From an early age boys learn to be contemptuous of girls and their activities; and although girls retaliate in kind by finding reasons for deprecating the male sex, they tend to accept in part the prevailing view of their inferiority (65). Whereas boys seldom if ever desire to change sex, girls not infrequently wish they were boys (124). The male counterpart of a "tomboy" who relishes sewing and reads girls' books is indeed a rarity.

In contrast to this picture, we find girls in the *segregated* Negro community showing much greater relative superiority in academic, personal, and social adjustment (34). They not only outperform boys academically by a greater margin, but do so in all subjects rather than only in language skills (34). These girls have higher achievement needs (44, 52) and a greater span of attention; they are more popular with classmates; they show more mature and realistic aspirations; they assume more responsible roles; and they feel less depressed in comparing themselves with other children (3). Substantially more Negro girls than Negro boys complete every level of education in the United States (110). Adequate reasons for these differences are not difficult to find. Negro children in this subculture live in a matriarchal family atmosphere where girls are openly preferred by mothers and grandmothers, and where the male sex role is generally deprecated. The father frequently deserts the family and in any case tends to be an unreliable source of economic and emotional security (28, 34). Hence the mother, assisted perhaps by her mother or by a daughter, shoulders most of the burdens and responsibilities of child rearing and is the only dependable adult with whom the child can identify. In this environment male chauvinism can obtain little foothold. The preferential treatment accorded girls is even extended to opportunities for acquiring ultimate primary status. If the family pins all of its hopes on one child and makes desperate sacrifices for that child, it will often be a daughter in preference to a son.[2] Over and above his handicaps at home, the Negro boy also faces more obstacles in the wider culture in realizing his vocational ambitions, whatever they may be, than the Negro girl in fulfilling her adult role expectations of housewife, mother, nurse, teacher, or clerical worker (34).

It seems, therefore, that Negro girls in racially incapsulated areas are less traumatized than boys by the impact of racial discrimination. This is precisely the opposite of what is found in studies of Negro children from less economically depressed and less segregated environments (45, 117). The discrepancy can be attributed perhaps to two factors: (1) the preferential treatment

[2] In lower-class Puerto Rican and Mexican families, just the opposite situation is to be found; that is, male dominance and superiority prevail (40, 49, 75).

accorded girls in the incapsulated community is more pervasive, unqualified, and continuous, and (2) the fact that, unlike Negro girls in mixed neighborhoods, these girls are less exposed to slights and humiliation from white persons. However, because of less tendency to internalize their feelings and greater openness in their social organization, Negro boys are able to adjust more easily than girls to the initial impact of desegregation (18).

Individual Differences in Reactions to the Segregated Negro Environment

Only extreme cultural determinists would argue that all children in the incapsulated Negro community necessarily respond in substantially identical ways to the impact of their social environment. Although common factors in cultural conditioning obviously make for many uniformities in personality development, genically determined differences in tempermental and cognitive traits, as well as differential experience in the home and wider culture, account for much idiosyncratic variation. Would it be unreasonable, for example, to anticipate that an intellectually gifted Negro child in this environment might have a different fate than an intellectually dull or average youngster; that an active, assertive, outgoing, and tough-skinned child might react differently to discriminatory treatment than one who is phlegmatic, submissive, sensitive, and introverted?

Differences in early socializing experience with parents are probably even more important, especially since they tend to generalize to interpersonal behavior outside the home. At this point it is worth noting that, generally speaking, racial discrimination affects children indirectly through their parents before it affects them directly through their own contacts with the wider culture. This indirect influence is mediated in two ways. (1) General parental attitudes toward the child are undoubtedly determined in part by the parent's own experience as a victim of discrimination. Some racially victimized parents, seeking retribution through their children, may fail to value them intrinsically and may place exaggerated emphasis on ego aggrandizement. Others may be so preoccupied with their own frustrations as to reject their children. Still others may accept and intrinsically value their children, and through their own example and strength of character encourage the development of realistic aspirations and mature, self-disciplined behavior. (2) Parents transmit to their children some of their own ways of responding to discrimination, such as counter-aggression, passive sabotage, obsequious submission, or strident counter-chauvinism. Individual differences such as these undoubtedly explain in part why some Negroes move into unsegregated neighborhoods and transfer to unsegregated schools when these opportunities arise, whereas other members of the race choose to remain in the segregated environment. The decision to transfer or not to transfer to an unsegregated school, for example, was found to be unrelated to both social class status and academic ability (27).

Much inter-individual variability therefore prevails in the reactions of children to minority group membership. Fortunately, sufficient time is available for establishing some stable feelings of intrinsic adequacy within the home before the impact of segregation on ego development becomes catastrophically destructive. It was found, for example, that Negro children who are most self-accepting also tend to exhibit more positive attitudes toward other Negro and white children (117), and that Negro college students who identify most with their own race tend to be least prejudiced against other minority groups (64). Hence, while appreciating the generally unfavorable effects of a segregated environment on all Negro children, we may conclude on the more hopeful note that the consequences of membership in a stigmatized racial group can be cushioned in part by a foundation of intrinsic self-esteem established in the home (7, 76).

Implications for Education

Before Negroes can assume their rightful place in a desegregated American culture, important changes in the ego structure of Negro children must first take place. They must shed feelings of inferiority and self-derogation, acquire feelings of self-confidence and racial pride, develop realistic aspirations for occupations requiring greater education and training, and develop the personality traits necessary for implementing these aspirations. Such changes in ego structure can be accomplished in two different but complementary ways. First, all manifestations of the Negro's inferior and segregated caste status must be swept away—in education, housing, employment, religion, travel, and exercise of civil rights. This in itself will enhance the Negro's self-esteem and open new opportunities for self-fulfillment. Second, through various measures instituted in the family, school and community, character structure, levels of aspiration, and actual standards of achievement can be altered in ways that will further enhance his self-esteem and make it possible for him to take advantage of new opportunities.

Desegregation

Desegregation, of course, is no panacea for the Negro child's personality difficulties. In the first place, it tends to create new problems of adjustment, particularly when it follows in the wake of serious community conflict. Second, it cannot quickly overcome various longstanding handicaps which Negro children bring with them to school "such as their cultural impoverishment, their helplessness or apathy toward learning, and their distrust of the majority group and their middle-class teachers" (14, p. 158); nor can it compensate for "oversized classes, inappropriate curriculums, inadequate counseling services, or poorly trained or demoralized teachers" (14, p. 158). Yet it is an important and indispensable first step in the reconstitution of Negro personality, since the school is the most strategically placed social institution for effecting rapid change both in ego structure and in social status. A desegregated school offers the Negro child his first taste of social equality and his first experience of first-class citizenship. He can enjoy the stimulating effect of competition with white children and can use them as realistic yardsticks in measuring his own worth and chances for academic and vocational success. Under these circumstances, educational achievement no longer seems so pointless, and aspirations for higher occupational status in the wider culture acquire more substance.

It is also reasonable to anticipate that white children will be prejudiced and continue to discriminate against their Negro classmates long after desegregation accords them equal legal status in the educational system. Attitudes toward Negroes in the South, for example, are remarkably stable, even in periods of rapid social change involving desegregation (130), and are not highly correlated with anti-Semitic or other ethnocentric trends (50, 62, 90, 91). Prejudice against Negroes is deeply rooted in the American culture (92) and is continually reinforced both by the socio-economic gain and by the vicarious ego enhancement it brings to those who manifest it (14, 55, 95). It is hardly surprising, therefore, that racial prejudice is most pronounced in lower social-class groups (125) and that these groups constitute the hard core of resistance to desegregation (63, 118); anti-white prejudice is similarly most pronounced among lower-class Negroes (26, 126). Increased physical contact per se between white and Negro children does little to reduce prejudice (78, 122), but more intimate personal interaction under favorable circumstances significantly reduces social distance between the two groups (62, 73, 129).

Artificial attempts to end de facto school segregation, caused by neighborhood segregation of Negroes in particular urban slums, are socially and psychologically unsound (25). It is not only impractical to transport white children to schools in distant, predominantly Negro neighborhoods just for the purpose of maintaining the principle of racially mixed classes, but it also victimizes individual white children and thereby increases racial tensions. Unless de facto segregation is accomplished by the gerry-mandering of school districts, and unless schools in Negro districts are *actually* inferior, it seems more reasonable to work for the elimination of this type of school segregation by directly attacking its underlying cause, that is, neighborhood segregation (25).

Community Action

The support of parents and of the Negro community at large must be enlisted if we hope to make permanent progress in the education of Negro children.

One needs only to visit . . . a [slum] school to be convinced that the nature of the community largely determines what goes on in the school. Therefore to attempt to divorce the school from the community is to engage in unrealistic thinking, which might lead to policies that could wreak havoc with the school and the lives of children (25, p. 20).

Whatever can be done to strengthen family life and to give the fathers a more important role in it will make a significant contribution to the development of Negro potential (110, p. 462).

Working with mothers and getting them to adopt a more positive attitude toward school is an important first step in improving the educational achievement of urban Negro children (25). Typically only 10 per cent of Negro parents are high-school graduates and only 33 per cent complete elementary school (25). Thus enrollment of parents in adult-education programs would significantly raise the cultural level of the Negro home and "stimulate an interest in newspapers, magazines and possibly even books. One of the troubles. . . is that when the children leave the school they never see anyone read anything—not even newspapers" (25, p. 25). The "Higher Horizons" project in New York City is a good example of a recent attempt to discover academically talented children in slum areas and encourage them to aspire to college education. This program embodies cultural enrichment, improved counseling and instruction, and the sympathetic involvement of parents.

Counseling

Because of current grave inadequacies in the structure of the lower-class urban Negro family, the school must be prepared to compensate, at least in part, for the deficiencies of the home, that is, to act, so to speak, *in loco parentis*. Teachers in predominantly Negro schools actually perform much of this role at the present time. As one Negro teacher said to Conant:

We do quite well with these children in the lower grades. Each of us is, for the few hours of the school day, an acceptable substitute for the mother. But when they reach about 10, 11, or 12 years of age, we lose them. At that time the "street" takes over. In terms of schoolwork, progress ceases; indeed many pupils begin to go backward in their studies (25, p. 21).

It is apparent, therefore, that trained counselors must assume the role of parent substitute during pre-adolescence and adolescence. They are needed to offer appropriate educational and vocational guidance, to encourage worthwhile and realistic aspirations, and to stimulate the development of mature personality traits. In view of the serious unemployment situation among Negro youth, they should also assist in job placement and in cushioning the transition between school and work. This will naturally require much expansion of existing guidance services in the school.

Research has shown that Negro children's distrust of white counselors and authority figures in general makes it

> . . . difficult for a white counselor to create an atmosphere wherein a Negro could gain insight. . . . The fundamental principle of counseling—to view the social or personal field as the counselor does—is difficult to attain in such a situation. The white person can only imagine, but never know, how a Negro thinks and feels, or how he views a social or personal situation. The cultural lenses which are formulated from unique milieus are not as freely transferable as it is assumed, or as we are led to believe (87, p. 188).

Educational Measures

Specially trained teachers and smaller classes are obviously required to cope with the difficulties of educating culturally disadvantaged minority group children. Emphasis must be placed on acquiring such basic intellectual skills as reading, writing, and arithmetic before any attempt is made to teach algebra, literature, science, or foreign languages. In many urban high schools today, pupils who cannot read at a fifth grade level, and who cannot speak or write grammatically or do simple arithmetical calculations, are subject to irregular French verbs, Shakespearean drama, and geometrical theorems. Nothing more educationally futile or better calculated to destroy educational morale could be imagined! Slow readers and pupils with other educational disabilities should be identified early and given intensive remedial work (25). Going even one step further, Professor Strodtbeck of the University of Chicago is attempting to teach underprivileged children to read at the age of 4, combining instruction with personal attention and affection, in order to forestall later reading difficulties (79).

If Negro youth is to be adequately prepared for the changing job market, more realistic pre-vocational courses, integrated in some instances with work experience programs, should be established in the "general" urban high schools (25). In connection with vocational education, Conant makes these important four points:

> First and foremost, vocational courses should not replace courses which are essential parts of the required academic program for graduation. Second, vocational courses should be provided in grades 11 and 12 and not require more than half the student's time in those years; however, for slow learners and prospective dropouts these courses ought to begin earlier. Third, the significance of the vocational courses is that those enrolled are keenly interested in the work; they realize the relevance of what they are learning to their future careers, and this sense of purpose is carried over to the academic courses which they are studying at the same time. Fourth, the type of vocational training programs should be related to the employment opportunities in the general locality (25, p. 44).

Opportunities should also be made available for part-time high school study in conjunction with trade apprenticeships, as well as for more advanced vocational training in community colleges and technical institutes. For underprivileged urban students capable and desirous of pursuing a regular course of university studies, programs such as the previously described "Higher Horizons" project, supplemented by liberal scholarship aid, are necessary. Finally, a special public works and job training program is currently needed to alleviate the calamitous problem of unemployment among urban youth (25).

Summary and Conclusions

The ego development of segregated Negro children in the United States manifests various distinctive properties, both because Negroes generally occupy the lowest stratum of the lower-class subculture, and because they possess an inferior caste status in American society. Their inferior caste position is marked by an unstable and matriarchal type of family structure, by restricted opportunities for acquiring educational, vocational, and social status, by varying degrees of segregation from the dominant white majority, and by a culturally fixed devaluation of their dignity as human beings. The consequences of this regrettable state of affairs for Negro children's self-esteem and self-confidence, for their educational and vocational aspirations, and for their character structure, interpersonal relations, and personality adjustment, constitute the characteristic features of their ego development.

Beginning in the pre-school period, the Negro child gradually learns to appreciate the negative implications of dark skin color for social status and personal worth. Hence he resists identifying with his own racial group and shows definite preference for white dolls and playmates. This reluctance to acknowledge his racial membership not only results in ego deflation, but also makes it difficult for him to identify with his parents and to obtain from such identification the derived status that universally constitutes the principal basis of self-esteem during childhood. Much of the derived status that white children obtain from their parents is made available to the Negro child by virtue of his membership in an unsupervised peer group, which accordingly performs many of the socializing functions of the white-middle-class home. This is especially true for the Negro boy who often has no adult male with whom to identify in the frequently fatherless Negro family, and who finds maleness deprecated in his matriarchal and authoritarian home. Early experience in fending for himself results in precocious social maturity, independence, and emancipation from the home.

During pre-adolescence and adolescence, segregated Negro children characteristically develop low aspirations for academic and vocational achievement. These low aspirations reflect existing social class and ethnic values, the absence of suitable emulatory models, marked educational retardation, restricted vocational opportunities, lack of parental and peer group support, and the cultural impoverishment of the Negro home. Because of loyalty to parents and rejection by the dominant white group, Negro adolescents develop ambivalent feelings toward middle-class achievement values and the personality traits necessary for their implementation. In many instances they use the objective facts of racial prejudice and discrimination as a rationalization for personal inadequacies, apathy, lack of striving, and antisocial behavior. The seeming hopelessness of attaining adequate vocational and social status in the wider American culture induces many Negro youths to withdraw from contact and competition with whites, and to seek the psychological shelter of their own segregated subculture. Girls tend to develop a more mature ego structure than boys because of their favored position in the home, but face greater adjustment problems during desegregation. The detrimental effects of segregation and inferior caste status on Negro ego development naturally vary from one child to another depending on ability, temperament, and the degree of intrinsic self-esteem and ego maturity that can be acquired within the home environment.

The problem of raising aspirational and achievement levels among Negro youth is presently acute because Negroes can no longer adjust comfortably to their segregated caste status, and because automation has eliminated many of the unskilled jobs which formerly made some type of stable economic adjustment possible. Two different but complementary approaches are available in dealing with this problem. The more general approach, which primarily applies to educators in their role as citizens, involves the elimination of existing racial barriers in housing, education, employment, religion, and civil rights. The more specific educational approach is to attempt, through various family, school and community measures, an upgrading of the Negro child's aspirational level, standards of achievement, and character structure that will both enhance his self-esteem and enable him to take advantage of new opportunities.

In the educational sphere, school desegregation is an indispensable prerequisite for raising aspiration and achievement levels, but obviously cannot compensate, in and of itself, for the long-standing educational handicaps of the Negro child or for existing inadequacies in schools, teachers, curriculums, and counseling services. Before we can expect any permanent improvement in the educational performance of Negro children, we must strengthen Negro family life, combat the cultural impoverishment of the Negro home, and enlist the support and cooperation of Negro parents in accomplishing this objective. More intensive guidance services, utilizing Negro personnel, are required to provide the socializing and supportive functions that are currently lacking in many Negro homes. Other important needs are smaller classes, specially trained teachers, abundant remedial facilities, the provision of expanded and more realistic vocational education, and a public works program to alleviate the explosively dangerous problem of unemployment among urban Negro youth.

References

1 Aberle, D. F., and K. D. Naegele. "Middle-Class Fathers' Occupational Roles and Attitudes Toward Children," *Amer. J. Orthopsychiat.*, 1952, 22:366–378.

2 Anastasi, Anne, and F. A. Cordova. "Some Effects of Bilingualism upon the Intelligence Test Performance of Puerto Rican Children in New York City," *J. educ. Psychol.*, 1953, 44:1–19.

3 Anastasi, Anne, and C. DeJesus. "Language Development and Non-verbal IQ of Puerto Rican Preschool Children in New York City," *J. abnorm. soc. Psychol.*, 1953, 48:357–366.

4 Angelino, H., J. Dollins, and E. V. Mech. "Trends in the 'Fears and Worries' of School Children as Related to Socioeconomic Status and Age," *J. genet. Psychol.*, 1956, 89:263–276.

5 Ashmore, H. S., *The Negro and the Schools*, Chapel Hill, N.C.: University of North Carolina Press, 1954.

6 Auld, B. F., "Influence of Social Class on Personality Test Response," *Psychol. Bull.*, 1952, 49:318–332.

7 Ausubel, D. P., *Ego Development and the Personality Disorders*, New York: Grune & Stratton, 1952.

8 ____, "Ego Development Among Segregated Negro Children," *Ment. Hyg.*, 1958, 42:362–369.

9 ____, "Acculturative Stress in Modern Maori Adolescence," *Child Develpm.*, 1960, 31:617–631.

10 ____, "Causes and Types of Drug Addiction: a Psychosocial View," *Psychiat. Quart.*, 1961, 35:523–531.

11 ____, "The Maori: A Study in Resistive Acculturation," *Soc. Forces*, 1961, 39:218–227.

12 ____, *Maori Youth*, Wellington, New Zealand: Price, Milburn, 1961.

13 ____, et al., "Perceived Parent Attitudes as Determinants of Children's Ego Structure," *Child Develpm.*, 1954, 25:173–183.

14 Bernard, Viola W., "School Desegregation: Some Psychiatric Implications," *Psychiatry*, 1958, 21:149–158.

15 Bernstein, B., "Some Sociological Determinants of Perception: an Enquiry into Sub-cultural Differences," *Brit. J. Sociol.*, 1958, 9, 159–174.

16 Boyd, G. F., "The Levels of Aspiration of White and Negro Children in a Non-segregated Elementary School," *J. soc. Psychol.*, 1952, 36:191–196.

17 Bullock, H A., "A Comparison of the Academic Achievements of White and Negro High School Graduates," *J. educ. Res.*, 1950, 44:179–192.

18 Campbell, J. D., and Marian R. Yarrow, "Personal and Situational Variables in Adaptation to Change," *J. soc. Issues*, 1958, 14:29–46.

19 Carson, A. S., and A. I. Rabin, "Verbal Comprehension and Communication in Negro and White Children," *J. educ. Psychol.*, 1961, 51:47–51.

20 Cavan, Ruth S., "Negro Family Disorganization and Juvenile Delinquency," *J. Negro Educ.*, 1959, 28:230–239.

21 Clark, K. B., "The Most Valuable Hidden Resource," *Coll. Bd. Rev.*, 1956, No. 29, 23–26.

22 ____, "Color, Class Personality, and Juvenile Delinquency," *J. Negro Educ.*, 1959, 28:240–251.

23 ____, and M. P. Clark, "Racial Identification and Preference in Negro Children," *in* T. M. Newcomb and E. L. Hartley (Eds.), *Readings in Social Psychology*, New York: Holt, 1947, pp. 169–178.

24 Cobb, H. V., "Role-Wishes and General Wishes of Children and Adolescents," *Child Develpm.*, 1954, 25:161–171.

25 Conant, James B., *Slums and Suburbs: A Commentary on Schools in Metropolitan Areas*, New York: McGraw-Hill, 1961.

26 Cothran, T. C., "Negro Conceptions of White People," *Amer. J. Social.*, 1951, 56:458–467.

27 Crockett, Harry J., "A Study of Some Factors Affecting the Decision of Negro High School Students to Enroll in Previously All-White High Schools, St. Louis, 1955," *Soc. Forces*, 1957, 35:351–356.

28 Dai, B., "Some Problems of Personality Development in Negro Children," *in* C. Kluckhohn and H. A. Murray (Eds.), *Personality in Nature, Society and Culture*, New York: Knopf, 1949, pp. 437–458.

29 Davis, A., *Deep South: a Social Anthropological Study of Caste and Class*, Chicago: University of Chicago Press, 1941.

30 ——, "Child Training and Social Class," *in* R. G. Barker, J. S. Kounin, and H. F. Wright (Eds.), *Child Behavior and Development*. New York: McGraw-Hill, 1943, pp. 607–620.

31 ——, and J. Dollard, *Children of Bondage*, Washington, D.C.: American Council on Education, 1940.

32 Davis, A., and R. J. Havighurst, Social class and color differences in child rearing. *Amer. sociol. Rev.*, 1946, 11:698–710.

33 Deutsch, Martin P., Minority group and class status as related to social and personality factors in scholastic achievement. *Soc. appl. Anthropol. Monogr.*, 1960, No. 2.

34 ——, et al. "Some Considerations as to the Contributions of Social, Personality, and Racial Factors to School Retardation in Minority Group Children," paper read at American Psychology Association, Chicago, September 1956.

35 De Vos, G., and H. Miner, "Algerian Culture and Personality in Changes," *Sociometry*, 1958, 21:255–268.

36 Dickens, Sara L., and C. Hobart, "Parental Dominance and Offspring Ethnocentrism," *J. soc. Psychol.*, 1959, 49:297–303.

37 Dinitz, S., Barbara A. Kay, and W. C. Reckless, "Group Gradients in Delinquency Potential and Achievement Score of Sixth Graders." *Amer. J. Orthopsychiat.*, 1958, 28:598–605.

38 Douglass, J. H., "The Extent and Characteristics of Juvenile Delinquency Among Negroes in the United States," *J. Negro Educ.*, 1959, 28:214–229.

39 Dreger, R. M., and K. S. Miller, "Comparative Psychological

Studies of Negroes and Whites in the United States," *Psychol. Bull.,* 1960, 57:361–402.

40 Fernandez-Marina, R., E. D. Maldonado-Sierra, and R. D. Trent, "Three Basic Themes in Mexican and Puerto Rican Family Values," *J. soc. Psychol.,* 48:167–81, 1958.

41 Finestone, H., "Cats, Kicks, and Color," *Soc. Probl.,* 1957, 5:3–13.

42 Frazier, E. F., "The Negro Middle Class and Desegration," *Soc. Probl.,* 1957, 4:291–301.

43 Frumkin, R. M., "Race, Occupation, and Social Class in New York," *J. Negro Educ.,* 1958, 27:62–65.

44 Gaier, E. L., and Helen S. Wambach, "Self-evaluation of Personality Assets and Liabilities of Southern White and Negro Students," *J. soc. Psychol.,* 1960, 51:135–143.

45 Goff, R. M., *Problems and Emotional Difficulties of Negro Children,* New York: Bureau of Publications, Teachers College, Columbia University, 1949.

46 Goodenough, F. L., "Anger in Young Children," *Inst. Child Welf. Monogr.,* 1931, No. 9.

47 Goodman, M. E., *Race Awareness in Young Children.* Cambridge, Mass.: Addison-Wesley, 1952.

48 Gould, R., "Some Sociological Determinants of Goal Strivings," *J. soc. Psychol.* 1941, 13:461–473.

49 Green, Helen B., "Comparison of Nurturance and Independence Training in Jamaica and Puerto Rico with Consideration of the Resulting Personality Structure and Transplanted Social Patterns," *J. soc. Psychol.* 1960, 50:27–63.

50 Greenberg, H., A. L. Chase, and T. M. Cannon, "Attitudes of White and Negro High School Students in a West Texas Town Toward School Integration," *J. appl. Psychol.,* 1957, 41:27–31.

51 Greenberg, H., and D. Fane, "An Investigation of Several Variables as Determinants of Authoritarianism," *J. soc. Psychol.,* 1959, 49:105–111.

52 Grossack, M. M., "Some Personality Characteristics of Southern Negro Students," *J. soc. Psychol.,* 1957, 46:125–131.

53 Hart, I., "Maternal Child-Rearing Practices and Authoritarian Ideology," *J. abnorm. soc. Psychol.,* 1957, 55:232–237.

54 Havighurst, R. J., and H. Taba, *Adolescent Character and Personality,* New York: Wiley, 1949.

55 Herr, D. M., "The Sentiment of White Supremacy: an Ecological Study," *Amer. J. Sociol.,* 1959, 64:592–598.

56 Hill, M. C., "Research on the Negro Family," *Marriage fam., Living,* 1957, 19:25–31.

57 Hollingshead, A. B., and F. C. Redlich, *Social Class and Mental Illness,* New York: Wiley, 1958.

58 Jefferson, Ruth B., "Some Obstacles to Racial Integration," *J. Negro Educ.* 1957, 26:145–154.

59 Jenkins, W. A., "An Experimental Study of the Relationship of Legitimate and Illegitimate Birth Status to School and Personal Adjustment of Negro Children," *Amer. J. Sociol.,* 1958, 64:169–173.

60 Kahn, M. L., "Social Class and Parental Values," *Amer. J. Sociol.,* 1959, 64:337–351.

61 Karon, B. P., *The Negro Personality,* New York: Springer, 1958.

62 Kelly, J. G., J. E. Ferson, and W. H. Holtzman, "The Measurement of Attitudes Toward the Negro in the South," *J. soc. Psychol.,* 1958, 48:305–317.

63 Killian, L. M., and J. L. Haer, "Variables Related to Attitudes Regarding School Desegregation Among White Southerners," *Sociometry,* 1958, 21:159–164.

64 Kirkhart, R. O., "Psychological and Socio-psychological Correlates of Marginality in Negroes," *Dissert. Abstr.,* 1960, 20:4173.

65 Kitay, P. M., "A Comparison of the Sexes in Their Attitudes and Beliefs About Women: a Study of Prestige Groups," *Sociometry,* 1940, 3:399–407.

66 Koch, H. L., Some Personality Correlates of Sex, Sibling Position, and Sex of Siblings Among Five- and Six-Year-Old Children," *Genet. Psychol. Monogr.,* 1955, 52:3–51.

67 Kvaraceus, W. C., "Culture and the Delinquent," *NEA J.,* 1959, 48:14–16.

68 Landreth, C., and B. C. Johnson, "Young Children's Responses to a Picture and Inset Test Designed to Reveal Reactions to Persons of Different Skin Color," *Child Develpm.,* 1953, 24:63–79.

69 Lipset, S. M., "Democracy and Working-Class Authoritarianism," *Amer sociol. Rev.,* 1959, 24:482–501.

70 Maas, H., "Some Social Class Differences in the Family Systems and Group Relations of Pre- and Early Adolescents," *Child Develpm.,* 1951, 22:145–152.

71 Maccoby, Eleanor, P. K. Gibbs, et al., "Methods of Child Rearing in Two Social Classes," *in* W. E. Martin and C. B. Stendler (Eds.), *Readings in Child Development.* New York: Harcourt, Brace, 1954, pp. 380–396.

72 McLure, W. P., "Challenge of Vocational and Technical Education," *Phi Delta Kappan*, 1962, 44:212–217.

73 Mann, J. H., "The Effect of Interracial Contact on Sociometric Choices and Perceptions," *J. soc. Psychol.*, 1959, 50:143–152.

74 Markley, Elaine R., "Social Class Differences in Mothers' Attitudes Toward Child Rearing," *Dissert Abst.*, 1958, 19:355–356.

75 Maslow, A. H., and R. Diaz-Guerrero, "Delinquency as Value Disturbance," *in* J. G. Peatman and E. L. Hartley, (Eds.), *Festschrift for Gardner Murphy*, New York: Harper, 1960, pp. 228–240.

76 Milner, Esther, "Some Hypotheses Concerning the Influence of Segregation on Negro Personality Development," *Psychiatry*, 1953, 16:291–297.

77 Morland, J. K., "Racial Recognition by Nursery School Children in Lynchburg, Virginia," *Soc. Forces*, 1958, 37:132–137.

78 Neprash, J. A., "Minority Group Contacts and Social Distance," *Phylon*, 1953, 14:207–212.

79 *The New York Times*, Sunday, March 11, 1962.

80 North, R. D., *The Intelligence of American Negroes*, New York: Anti-Defamation League of B'nai B'rith, 1954.

81 Omari, T. P., "Changing Attitudes of Students in West African Society Toward Marriage and Family Relationships," *Brit. J. Sociol.*, 1960, 11:197–210.

82 Osborne, R. T., "Racial Differences in Mental Growth and School Achievement: a Longitudinal Study," *Psychol. Reps.*, 1960, 7:233–239.

83 Palermo, D. S., "Racial Comparisons and Additional Normative Data on the Children's Manifest Anxiety Scale," *Child Develpm.*, 1959, 30:53–57.

84 Parsons, T., "Age and Sex in the Social Structure of the United States," *Amer. sociol. Rev.*, 1942, 7:604–616.

85 Pasamanick, B., and Hilda Knobloch, "The Contribution of Some Organic Factors to School Retardation in Negro Children," *J. Negro Educ.*, 1958, 27:4–9.

86 Pawl, J. L. H., "Some Ego Skills and Their Relation to the Differences in Intelligence Between the Middle and Lower Classes," *Dissert. Abstr.*, 1960, 21:368.

87 Phillips, W. B., "Counseling Negro Students: an Educational Dilemma," *Calif. J. educ. Res.*, 1959, 10:185–188.

88 Pierce-Jones, J., "Socio-economic Status and Adolescents' Interests," *Psychol. Reps.*, 1959, 5:683.

89 ——, "Vocational Interest Correlates of Socio-economic Status in

Adolescence," *Educ. psychol. Measmt.*, 1959, 19:65–71.

90 Pompilo, P. T., "The Relationship Between Projection and Prejudice with a Factor Analysis of Anti-Semitic and Anti-Negro Attitudes," unpublished doctoral dissertation, Catholic University, Washington, D. C., 1957.

91 Prothro, E. T., "Ethnocentrism and Anti-Negro Attitudes in the Deep South," *J. abnorm. soc. Psychol.*, 1952, 47:105–108.

92 Raab, E., and S. M. Lipset, M., *Prejudice and Society*, New York: Anti-Defamation League of B'nai B'rith, 1959.

93 Record, W., "Social Stratification and Intellectual Roles in the Negro Community," *Brit. J. Sociol.*, 1957, 8:235–255.

94 Roen, S. R., "Personality and Negro-White Intelligence," *J. abnorm. soc. Psychol.*, 1960, 61:148–150.

95 Rosen, B. C., "Race, Ethnicity, and the Achievement Syndrome," *Amer. sociol. Rev.*, 1959, 24:47–60.

96 Rosner, J., "When White Children Are in the Minority," *J. educ. Sociol.*, 1954, 28:69–72.

97 Schneider, L., and S. Lysgaard, "The Deferred Gratification Pattern: a Preliminary Study," *Amer. sociol. Rev.*, 1953, 18:142–149.

98 Schpoont, S., "Some Relationships Between Task Attractiveness, Self-evaluated Motivation, and Success or Failure," unpublished doctoral dissertation, University of Illinois, Urbana, Ill., 1955.

99 Sears, P. S., "Levels of Aspiration in Academically Successful and Unsuccessful Children," *J. abnorm. soc. Psychol.*, 1940, 35:498–536.

100 Sears, R. R., et al., "Some Child-Rearing Antecedents of Aggression and Dependency in Young Children," *Genet. Psychol. Monogr.*, 1953, 47:135–234.

101 Sewell, W., and A. O. Haller, "Social Status and the Personality Status of the Child," *Sociometry*, 1956, 19:113–125.

102 ——, "Factors in the Relationships Between Social Status and the Personality Adjustment of the Child," *Amer. sociol. Rev.*, 1959, 24:511–520.

103 ——, and M. A. Strauss, "Social Status and Educational and Occupational Aspiration," *Amer. sociol. Rev.*, 1957, 22:67–73.

104 Sexton, Patricia C., "Social Class and Pupil Turn-over Rates," *J. educ. Sociol.*, 1959, 33:131–134.

105 Siegel, A. I., and P. Federman, *Employment Experiences of Negro Philadelphians: A Descriptive Study of the Employment Experiences, Perceptions, and Aspirations of Selected Philadelphia*

Whites and Non-Whites. Wayne, Pa.: Applied Psychological Services, 1959.

106 Singer, S. L., and B. Stafflre, "A Note on Racial Differences in Job Values and Desires," *J. soc. Psychol.,* 1956, 43:333–337.

107 Smith, B. F., "Wishes of High School Seniors and Social Status," *J. educ. Sociol.,* 1952, 25:466–475.

108 Smith, C. U., and J. W. Prothro, "Ethnic Differences in Authoritarian Personality," *Soc. Forces,* 1957, 35:334–338.

109 Smith, M. G., "Education and Occupational Choice in Rural Jamaica," *Soc. econ. Stud.,* 1960, 9:332–354.

110 Smuts, R. W., "The Negro Community and the Development of Negro Potential," *J. Negro Educ.,* 1957, 26:456–465.

111 Srole, L., T. S. Langner, S. T. Michael, M. K. Opler, and T. A. C. Rennie, *Mental Health in the Metropolis: the Midtown Manhattan Study,* New York: McGraw-Hill, 1962.

112 Stafflre, B., "Concurrent Validity of the Vocational Values Inventory," *J. educ. Res.,* 1959, 52:339–341.

113 *The Status of the Public School Education of Negro and Puerto Rican Children in New York City,* New York: Public Education Association, 1955.

114 Steckler, G. A., "Authoritarian Ideology in Negro College Students," *J. abnorm. soc. Psychol.,* 1957, 54:396–399.

115 Stevenson, H. W., and N. G. Stevenson, "Social Interaction in an Interracial Nursery-School," *Genet. Psychol., Monogr.,* 1960, 61:37–75.

116 Stevenson, H. W., and E. C. Stewart, A developmental study of racial awareness in young children. *Child Develpm.,* 1958, 29:399–409.

117 Trent, R. D., "An Analysis of Expressed Self-Acceptance Among Negro Children," unpublished doctoral dissertation, Teachers College, Columbia University, New York, 1954.

118 Tumin, M. M., "Readiness and Resistance to Desegregation: a Social Portrait of the Hard Core," *Soc. Forces,* 1958, 36:256–263.

119 Turner, R. H., "Negro Job Status and Education," *Soc. Forces,* 1953, 32:45–52.

120 ____, "Occupational Patterns of Inequality," *Amer. J. Sociol.,* 1954, 59:437–447.

121 Walter, L. M., and S. S. Marzolf, "The Relation of Sex, Age, and School Achievement to Levels of Aspiration," *J. educ. Psychol.,* 1951, 42:285–292.

122 Webster, S. W., "The Influence of Interracial Contact on Social

Acceptance in a Newly Integrated School," *J. educ. Psychol.*, 1961, 52:292–296.

123 Wertham, F., "Psychological Effects of School Segregation," *Amer. J. Psychother.*, 1952, 6:94–103.

124 West, J., *Plainville, U. S. A.*, New York: Columbia University Press, 1945.

125 Westie, F. R., "Negro-White Status Differentials and Social Distance," *Amer. Sociol. Rev.*, 1952, 17:550–558.

126 ——, and D. Howard, "Social Status Differentials and the Race Attitudes of Negroes," *Amer. sociol. Rev.*, 1954, 19:584–591.

127 Wilkerson, D. A., "Conscious and Impersonal Forces in Recent Trends Toward Negro-White School Equality in Virginia," *J. educ. Sociol.*, 1959, 32:402–408.

128 Wilson, D. C., and E. M. Lantz, "The Effect of Culture Change on the Negro Race in Virginia as Indicated by a Study of State Hospital Admissions," *Amer. J. Psychiat.*, 1957, 114:25–32.

129 Yarrows, Marian R., J. O. Campbell, and L. J. Yarrow, "Acquisition of New Norms: a Study of Racial Desegregation," *J. soc. Issues*, 1958, 14:8–28.

130 Young, R. K., W. M. Benson, and W. H. Holtzman, "Change in Attitudes Toward the Negro in a Southern University," *J. abnorm. soc. Psychol.*, 1960, 60:131–133.

29 Psychological Acculturation in Modern Maori Youth*

David P. Ausubel

To anyone concerned with cross-cultural and dynamic aspects of adolescent personality development, modern Maori culture offers almost unlimited research opportunities. In western culture, children at adolescence are expected to strive more for *primary status* based on their own efforts, competence, and performance ability and to strive less for *derived status* predicated on their personal qualities and their dependent relationship to and intrinsic acceptance by parents, relatives, and peers. Concomitantly, in support of this shift in the relative importance and availability of primary and derived status, adolescents are expected to be less dependent than children on the ap-

**Reprinted from the article of the same title in* Problems of Youth: Transition to Adulthood in a Changing World. *(H. Sherif and C. W. Sherif, Eds.) Chicago: Aldine, 1965, pp. 110–128. By permission of the author, the editors, and the Aldine Publishing Company.*

proval of their elders, to play a more active role in formulating their own goals, and to relate more intimately to peers than to parents. They are also under greater pressure to persevere in goal striving despite serious setbacks, to postpone immediate hedonistic gratification in favor of achieving long-range objectives, and to exercise more initiative, foresight, executive independence, responsibility, and self-discipline (Ausubel, 1954).

But what happens to adolescent development in cultures such as the Maori where the importance of derived status is not so deemphasized during and after adolescence as in western civilization, and where youth and adults alike continue to obtain a substantial portion of their self-esteem from a broad-based system of mutual psychological support, emotional interdependence, and reciprocal obligations? (Beaglehole and Beaglehole, 1946; Ritchie, 1956) What course does adolescent personality development take when the culture is less concerned than ours with personal ambition, self-enhancing achievement, and other self-aggrandizing features of primary status, and when it places greater stress on task-oriented motivation, kinship obligations, the enhancement of group welfare and prestige, and the social values of working cooperatively toward common objectives? (Beaglehole and Beaglehole, 1946) Do traits important for implementing achievement goals (*e.g.*, persistence, self-denial) develop when the attainment of vocational success is considered less important as either a reason for living or a criterion of status in the community? (Beaglehole and Beaglehole, 1946)

Are personality outcomes markedly different when peers rather than parents are the principal socializing agents and sources of derived status prior to adolescence? (Ritchie, 1956) Or when rapprochement with parents and the adult world occurs during adolescence, instead of abrupt emancipation from the home and general alienation from the adult community? (Mulligan, 1956; Ritchie, 1956) Or when adolescents assume the role of junior adults instead of living in a separate world of peripheral status (school and peer group) as in our society? (Ritchie, 1956)

To add further interest to the problem of modern Maori adolescence, the above description by the Beagleholes is more typical of an earlier period in the post-withdrawal[1] phase of Maori acculturation, while Ritchie's and Mulligan's accounts describe the current scene in an isolated and relatively backward rural Maori community. The present-day Maori in more progressive rural areas and in urban centers are generally much more acculturated. Although the perpetuative device of extreme physical, social and psychological withdrawal, which preserved an attenuated version of traditional Maori culture in the face of external pressures to change, is still a factor to be reckoned with, it is a less vigorous social reality today than a decade ago. In the struggle to dominate orientations and emotional identification of the coming generation of Maori adults, adolescence constitutes the major psychological battleground for the conflicting claims of two contrasting cultures. The Maori adolescent is still caught midway between two worlds, but in most districts of New Zealand he is considerably closer to the *pakeha*[2] side than previous investigators have pictured him.

Problem and Research Design

The present study presented in this chapter was concerned with the psychological mechanisms of this cultural tug-of-war and its influences on the outcome of Maori adolescence. The study sought to identify culturally determined uniformities and differences in the personality structure and development of Maori and *pakeha* adolescents and how they are transmitted to the developing individual. More specifically, it

[1] The Maori, a Polynesian people, migrated to New Zealand about A.D. 1350, probably from the Society Islands. Initial contact with the Europeans, beginning in 1769, was largely characterized by the incorporation of selected aspects of European goods and technical processes into traditional Maori social and economic organization without any fundamental changes in the value system. Threatened, however, by massive European colonization and coercive alienation of their land, contrary to treaty guarantees, the Maori were forced into war with the British colonists. Catastrophically defeated but not annihilated after a dozen years of bitter conflict (1860-1872), they withdrew, resentful and disillusioned, into reservation-like areas and villages. Emergence from this withdrawal and entrance into the mainstream of New Zealand life first began in earnest with the onset of World War II and is still continuing, despite growing indications of color prejudice and discrimination.

[2] *pakeha*—a person of predominantly European descent in the context of New Zealand race relations, *i.e.*, a non-Maori.

sought (1) to identify Maori-*pakeha* uniformities and differences in expressed and internalized levels of academic and vocational aspiration and in the motivations underlying these aspirations; (2) to identify Maori-*pakeha* uniformities and differences in supportive personality traits important for the realization of achievement goals; and (3) to relate these motivational and other personality differences to cultural and interpersonal factors and mechanisms that account for their transmission from one generation to the next.

Another focus of research concern was on urban-rural differences in aspirational patterns among Maori adolescents and on the relative magnitude of Maori-*pakeha* differences in urban and rural areas. An attempt was also made to assess the relative magnitude and significance of Maori-*pakeha* differences by comparing them to urban-rural differences.

In addition to their theoretical significance for general problems of adolescent personality development (*e.g.*, cross-cultural uniformities and differences; the impact of acculturation), findings such as these obviously have important practical implications in the direction and organization of education and vocational guidance for Maori youth. The data have particular relevance to the serious problems of keeping Maori youth in school beyond the age of fifteen and of increasing Maori representation in the professions and skilled trades.

The general plan was to utilize one rural and one urban group of Maori male adolescents and comparable groups of *pakeha* adolescents from the same localities. Partly because subjects would be more easily accessible, and partly because one focus of inquiry was on academic aspirations, only young adolescents attending school were studied. Fifty Maori and fifty *pakeha* subjects in each sample (urban and rural) were drawn from the same secondary schools and were matched individually on the basis of form, course, ability group and father's occupation. The purpose of using matched groups of Maori and *pakeha* pupils and both urban and rural samples was to distinguish distinctively Maori personality traits from those assimilated from *pakeha* culture; and to isolate the effects of Maori culture on personality from the effects induced by the inequalities in such factors as occupation, social class status, urban-rural residence and academic aptitude on Maori and *pakeha* populations. Because of generally higher *pakeha* than Maori I.Q.'s in the same ability groupings, and the unavailability of sufficient subjects, it was not possible to match subjects on the basis of I.Q. Separate matchings were conducted for the Maori-*pakeha* and the urban-rural comparisons.

The procedures and instruments used in this study included: structured academic and vocational interviews with pupils; Test of Occupational Prestige Needs; Achievement Imagery Test (McLelland, *et al.*, 1953); Vocational Tenacity Test (Ausubel, *et al.*, 1953); Responsiveness to Prestige Incentives Test (Ausubel, 1951); Teachers' Ratings of motivational and aspirational traits; and participant observation at community functions (tribal committee and tribal executive meetings, *huis, tangis,*[3] weddings, sports meetings, birthday parties, etc.), and informal interviews with parents, teachers, Vocational Guidance Officers, Maori Welfare Officers, community leaders and clergymen.

There is no such thing as a "typical" Maori community, and no attempt was made in this study to use a stratified sample representative of the Maori population in New Zealand. These findings may be properly generalized only to Maori communities similar to those described here, *i.e.*, to urban provincial centers, and to relatively prosperous Maori rural districts with roughly equal numbers of Maori and *pakeha* inhabitants and with better than average race relations. Implications from these findings for the educational and vocational achievement of Maori youth *as a whole* are only tentative and suggestive, and would have to be confirmed by research on a more representative sample of Maori adolescents (*i.e.*, drawn from the various main types of Maori districts) before they could be generalized more widely.

THE FINDINGS

Matched groups of Maori and *pakeha* secondary school pupils exhibited a striking measure of over-all similarity in educational and vocational aspirations, underlying

[3] *hui*—a large Maori gathering; *tangi*—ceremonial Maori mourning rites.

motivations for achievement, supportive traits, and perceptions of both prevailing opportunities and family and peer group pressures for achievement. This finding supports the view that many (but by no means all) of the traits commonly regarded as typically Maori largely reflect low occupational and social class status, predominantly rural residence, and environmentally stunted verbal intelligence. Some Maori-*pakeha* differences may have been obscured in part either because of insufficient sensitivity of the measuring instruments or because of their transparency to the subjects. This possibility, however, is discounted both by the adequate range of variability obtained for the various instruments, and by the substantial degree of intercultural uniformity found with those measures where transparency was impossible. In fact, obtained Maori-*pakeha* differences are probably overestimates of true differences since the *pakeha* sample was favored by several factors that could not be controlled by matching.

The major finding of this study was that there was much greater similarity between Maori and *pakeha* pupils in their *expressed* educational and vocational aspirations than there was in those factors necessary to internalize and implement these aspirations; namely, underlying needs and motivations for achievement, supportive traits, and perceived pressures and opportunities for academic and occupational success. In terms of overall magnitude and prestige of academic and vocational aspirations, Maori and *pakeha* samples were not significantly different. Even though the stated aspirations of Maori pupils are not later internalized and implemented to the same extent as those of *pakeha* pupils—because of the absence of suitable cultural, family, and peer group pressures and supports—there was no reason to believe that they were insincere or did not correspond to genuine intentions at the time they were reported. Maori aspirations were especially expansive in relation to more remote goals (*i.e.,* School Certificate, university, hypothetical vocational ambitions) unconstrained by current reality considerations, and were more restrained in relation to less distant goals (*i.e.,* end-of-the-year marks, improvement of scholastic standing in the class).

Maori pupils' assimilation of *pakeha* academic and vocation aspirations—despite inadequate later internalization and implementation—is a datum of tremendous cultural and psychological significance. It constitutes an all-important first step in the taking-over of *pakeha* achievement patterns, and is indicative of a degree of acculturation that undoubtedly was not present twenty or even ten years ago. Maori acculturation has evidently proceeded to the point where it can sustain the *generation,* if not the *implementation,* of European educational and occupational ambitions. The development of these aspirations during late childhood and early adolescence is facilitated by considerable contact with the school and with the wider *pakeha* culture, and by relatively poor communication with parents and the Maori adult community. As this communication improves and as Maori adolescents begin to perceive more accurately the lack of strong cultural and family pressures for educational and vocational achievement, their ambitions not only fall far short of realization but are also drastically lowered.

Pakeha pupils had higher occupational prestige needs than Maori pupils and considered vocational achievement a more important life goal.[4] They also gave higher ratings to such factors as prestige, wealth, and advancement as reasons for seeking occupational and academic success. Maori pupils, on the other hand, were more highly motivated by task-oriented ("interest in studies," "liking job") and group welfare ("to help others") considerations. Urban *pakeha* pupils were more highly rated by teachers than were their Maori counterparts on such supportive traits as persistence, attentiveness, conscientiousness, planning, and initiation of activity; and in the rural school, *pakeha* pupils did more studying for examinations.

Because of poor parent-child communication in our Maori sample, obtained Maori-*pakeha* differences in *perceived* family pressures and opportunities for educational and vocational achievement were less striking than those that actually prevail, which were noted in the course of participant observation and informal interviews. Nevertheless, *pakeha* parents were still perceived as demanding higher school marks and as prodding more

[4] All differences reported in this paper were significant at the .05 level of confidence or better.

about homework than Maori parents. *Pakeha* pupils were more optimistic than their Maori age-mates about the chances of achieving occupational success; they saw fewer obstacles in their path. Another indication of defective Maori parent-child communication was the fact that only about one-quarter of the Maori pupils had any insight into the existence of blatant anti-Maori discriminatory practices in employment.

As predicted, Maori-*pakeha* differences were greater in the urban than in the rural environment. Despite being more highly acculturated than rural Maoris, urban Maoris have not yet assimilated the urban *pakeha* pattern as completely as rural Maoris have assimilated the rural *pakeha* pattern. This, of course, is largely because of the recency of Maori migration to the cities. Not only is rural life much closer than urban to his indigenous pre-*pakeha* culture, but the Maori has had at least a hundred years more time to accustom himself to it.

With progressive urbanization of the Maori population, urban-rural differences among Maori adolescent pupils are becoming increasingly more important, even though these differences in aspirational and motivational traits are currently less conspicuous than corresponding uniformities. Many factors undoubtedly contributed to the finding that Maori pupils in our urban sample were closer to *pakeha* norms in these traits than were rural Maori pupils. These factors include the selective migration to the city of vocationally more ambitious youth, the greater acculturation of longstanding urban residents, the difficulty of practicing Maori cultural values in the city, and the lack of exposure to the traditional practices and influence of Maori elders and of the Maori peer group.

Differences between urban and rural Maori pupils were most marked in their expressed educational and vocational aspirations, prestige motivation, desire for occupational success, and supportive traits. Urban pupils strove more for top marks and for higher class standing, had higher occupational prestige needs, made higher scores on the Achievement Imagery Test, and valued occupational achievement more highly. They also spent more time on homework and in studying for examinations. Although they saw more obstacles in their path they were more hopeful of eventually achieving vocational success. On the other hand, consistent urban-rural differences were not found in relation to task-oriented and group welfare motivation and perceived family pressures for achievement. It seems, therefore, that urban surroundings may encourage *pakeha* aspirations, motivations and supportive traits without immediately weakening Maori motivations. Since Maori parents were only recent arrivals to the city, they apparently did not play an important role in transmitting *pakeha* achievement patterns to their children; urban children did not perceive that their parents demanded any higher educational and vocational achievement than did the parents of rural pupils. Urban parents, however, seemed to be less authoritarian than their rural counterparts, and to have less contact with and control over their children; they generally played a less important role in determining their children's choice of career.

Contrary to our hypothesis, urban-rural differences were slightly greater in the Maori than in the *pakeha* sample. The original prediction was based on the assumption that because they were relatively recent urban residents, the Maori population would have assimilated the urban pattern of achievement less completely than their *pakeha* countrymen. Although this factor was undoubtedly operative, it was apparently more than offset by the tremendous change—and hence the great impact—involved when a Maori moved to the city.

With the progressive advance of Maori acculturation and migration to urban centers, the increase in urban-rural differences among the Maori people has been paralleled by a corresponding decrease in the magnitude of Maori-*pakeha* differences. A credible hypothesis supported by our data would be that Maori acculturation with respect to aspirational patterns has proceeded to the point where, in rural areas, Maori and *pakeha* pupils are more similar to each other than are urban and rural Maori adolescents. In the city, however, Maori youth are, *relatively speaking*, not quite so far along on the acculturation continuum. Maori and *pakeha* pupils are still more different from each other than are matched urban and rural pupils within the Maori population.

Factors Affecting Maori Vocational Achievement

Parental Influences

Maori parents are less sophisticated than their *pakeha* counterparts about vocational matters, and are accordingly less capable of assisting their children with appropriate information, advice and guidance. Even if they were more capable in these respects, however, they would still be handicapped in transmitting helpful insights from their own life experiences because of the conspicuous estrangement and lack of adequate communication existing between them and their children, expecially in urban centers. Because of their smaller incomes and larger families, Maori parents are also more reluctant to commit themselves to supporting plans requiring long-term vocational preparation. Many are greatly confused about the standards of behavior they should properly expect and demand from their adolescent children, and others are ambivalent about letting the latter leave home in search of better vocational opportunities.

Maori parents tend to be more permissive and laissez-faire than *pakeha* parents about their children's vocational careers. Despite occasional and inconsistent displays of authoritarianism in this regard, they are usually content to let them drift. They apply fewer coercive pressures, but also give less support and encouragement to the long-term occupational ambitions of their children. Their own values concerning vocational achievement—and the example they set their children—also tend to encourage the adoption of a short-term view. In practice they seldom demand the deferment of immediate hedonistic satisfactions or the internalization of supportive traits consistent with high academic and occupational attainment. It is small wonder, therefore, that Maori adolescents are unable to resist the lure of immediate "big money" in unskilled laboring jobs. Although in early adolescence they tend to lack adequate insight into their parents' lack of genuine commitment to educational and vocational achievement, Maori pupils in our sample perceived fewer family pressures regarding these matters than did *pakeha* pupils.

Peer Group Influences

Maori pupils also receive less encouragement from their peers than *pakeha* pupils do to strive for vocational achievement. Not only is occupational success less highly valued in the Maori peer culture, but the greater availability of *derived status*—based solely on membership in and intrinsic acceptance by the group—also removes much of the incentive for seeking *primary status* based on individual competence and performance. In districts where community morale is low and *bodgieism*[5] flourishes, vocational achievement tends to be deprecated.

Cultural Influences

Maori culture characteristically places greater emphasis on derived than on primary status, and on the task-oriented and group welfare features of primary status, rather than its self-aggrandizing aspects. Less concerned with achieving occupational prestige, the Maori is also less willing than the *pakeha* to internalize traits important for implementing achievement goals, *i.e.*, to develop initiative, foresight, self-denial and self-discipline, to persevere in the face of adversity, and to defer immediate pleasure in favor of remote vocational goals. He values personal relationships, derived status, and kinship ties above material possessions and occupational prestige; in his eyes, helpfulness, generosity, hospitality, and sociability count for more than punctuality, thrift, and methodicalness.

Many Maori attitudes towards work, which stem both from his indigenous and current value system and from his pre-*pakeha* organization of economic life, impede his vocational adjustment. In the first place, he is less accustomed than the *pakeha* to regular and steady employment, and he finds dull, monotonous labor less congenial than the *pakeha* does. The concept of thrift for vocational or economic purposes is foreign to him. He has greater ties of kinship and sentiment to the locality of his birth and is less eager to migrate to other districts. He does not value

[5] A form of adolescent cultism in New Zealand and Australia comparable to the former American *zoot-suit* movement.

work as an end in itself, as a badge of respectability, or as a means of getting on in the world. Lastly, he is more dependent than the *pakeha* on the psychological support of an intimate group in his work environment.

Another factor limiting the vocational achievement of Maori youth is the relatively low occupational status and morale of Maori adults. Young people lack the encouragement of a tradition and a high current standard of vocational accomplishment. They are also denied the practical benefits of guidance and financial backing that would follow from the existence of such a standard and tradition. Morever, they are discouraged by the marginal economic position of their elders, by social demoralization (*i.e.*, wretched housing and sanitation, alcoholism, apathy, neglect of children) in many communities, and by the institutionalization of a period of occupational drifting during late adolescent and early adult life. Compounding this situation are the overly casual, "She'll be right" attitude that is generally rampant in New Zealand, and the absence of sufficient incentive for a young person to acquire a trade or profession. This is largely a function of an undifferentiated national wage scale which places a tremendous premium on unskilled manual labor.

Racial Prejudice

Finally, discriminatory employment practices deriving from color prejudice and from the popular stereotype of the Maori as lazy, undependable, and capable of only rough, manual labor, tend to bar Maoris from many higher status occupations in banks, commerical establishments, private offices, shops, and skilled trades. Maori boys desiring apprenticeships usually must migrate to urban centers where they face further discrimination in obtaining suitable board and lodging. The denial of equal occupational opportunity to Maori youth constitutes the most serious and prognostically least hopeful factor impeding Maori vocational achievement—color prejudice is not only deeply ingrained and increasing in the *pakeha* population, but its existence is also categorically denied by both the people and government of New Zealand.

Factors Affecting Maori Educational Achievement

Home Influences

Despite their high educational aspirations, incomparably fewer Maori than *pakeha* pupils take or pass the School Certificate Examination, enter the upper forms of post-primary school, attend the university, or obtain a university degree. Home factors are largely responsible for this situation. Many Maori parents have had little schooling themselves, and hence are unable to appreciate its value or see much point in it. Although they accept the necessity for post-primary education, they do not give active, wholehearted support for high level academic performance by demanding conscientious study and regular attendance from their children.

Maori pupils tend to lead two discrete lives—one at school, and one at home in the *pa*.[6] There is little carryover from school to home, but probably much more in the other direction. Conflict between home and school standards exists until middle adolescence and is resolved into a dichotomy of behavior: each standard prevails in its own setting. Thereafter, parental values, reinforced by increased contact with the Maori adult community, tend to predominate over the influence exerted by the school and the wider *pakeha* culture.

Maori parents are less vitally concerned with their children's educational achievement than are *pakeha* parents, and they are also less capable of helping them with their lessons. Because of their larger families they seldom even have time to do so. Living more frequently in outlying rural areas, they are less able to consult with headmaster and teachers. Divided responsibility for children, because of the common Maori practice of adoption and the greater informality and irregularity of marital arrangements, further compounds this situation.

Keeping a large family of children in secondary school constitutes a heavy economic burden on Maori parents in view of their

[6] *pa*—Maori village.

low per capita income and the substantial hidden costs of "free" education. Maori pupils have more onerous household, dairying, and gardening chores to perform than their *pakeha* classmates, and seldom have a quiet place in which to do their homework. Their parents may take them to another district during the sheep-shearing season. They are further handicapped by inadequate lighting and late hour social activities in the home, and frequently by serious malnutrition.

Cultural Influences

Maori cultural values regarding achievement have had a less adverse effect on the educational than on the vocational accomplishments of Maori youth. In the first place, acculturative progress has been greater in the educational sphere. Secondly, since motivations for educational achievement are referable to the less remote future, they are influenced less by the values of the peer group and of the adult Maori community. But although Maori intellectual traditions and traditional respect for learning have been seriously eroded, the loss has not been adequately compensated for by a corresponding acquisition of European intellectual values and pursuits. The modern Maori tends to be distrustful of book learning, intellectuals, and higher education. This attitude is, in part, a reflection of residual disenchantment with *pakeha* education, stemming from the Maori Wars and subsequent withdrawal.

Other limiting factors in the current cultural situation of the Maori include the relatively low educational attainment of most Maori adults, the absence of a strong, academic tradition, residence in remote areas where there are only district high schools or no post-primary facilities whatsoever, and serious staffing problems in most Maori district high schools. But since the percentage of Maoris attending secondary schools is progressively increasing, many of these problems will gradually disappear.

Adjustive Difficulties

Coming as they frequently do from small rural schools where they are in the majority, know all their fellow pupils, and enjoy intimate personal relationships with their teachers, Maori pupils experience considerable difficulities in adjusting to the new secondary school environment. Less well prepared academically for post-primary studies, and less accustomed to impersonal and authoritarian teacher attitudes, they often develop serious feelings of personal inadequacy. In many secondary schools also, teachers adopt covertly antagonistic and overtly patronizing attitudes towards Maori pupils. They accept them on sufferance only, feeling that it is a waste of time, effort, and money to educate Maoris since they "only go back to the mat" (revert to Maori ways of behavior). Hence, they offer the latter little encouragement to remain in school beyond the minimal leaving age. Some university lecturers also manifest similar intolerant and unsympathetic attitudes. Maori students at the universities encounter color prejudice in seeking board and lodging and must often contend with patronizing treatment and social aloofness from their fellow students.

Stunting of Verbal Intelligence

Maori pupils are undoubtedly handicapped in academic achievement by a lower average level of intellectual functioning than is characteristic of comparable *pakeha* pupils. In both our urban and rural samples, particularly the latter, Maori pupils had significantly lower Otis I.Q.'s than their *pakeha* classmates. They were also retarded in arithmetic, English usage, and ability to handle abstract concepts. This retardation is attributable to two main factors: (1) the status of the Maori people as a generally underprivileged lower-class minority group with unusually large families; and (2) special disabilities associated with problems of acculturation. Pointing to an environmental, not a genic, origin for these differences are the facts that urban I.Q.'s were higher than rural I.Q.'s in both Maori and *pakeha* samples, and that the Maori-*pakeha* difference was significantly lower in the urban than in the rural sample. The extreme intellectual impoverishment of the Maori home *over and above* its rural or lower social class status comes from the poor standard of both Maori and English spoken in the home and the general lack of books, magazines, and stimulating conversation.

The low average level of intellectual functioning among Maori pupils cannot be dismissed simply as a function of test bias or of "language difficulty." The inability to handle verbal concepts that leads to low intelligence test scores is undoubtedly of environmental origin; nevertheless, the individuals are still no more competent to handle analogous verbal materials in educational and vocational situations than if it were hereditary.

Bilingualism

The widely held view that the bilingualism of the Maori child causes his educational retardation is not adequately supported by research data. Competent observers have failed to note any negative relationship between bilingualism, on the one hand, and school marks or passes on School Certificate English, on the other. Cook Islanders, Fijians, and Samoans tend to be more bilingual than Maoris, and yet are academically more successful in New Zealand secondary schools and universities. Although rigorous research is urgently needed in this area, it may be tentatively concluded that the language retardation of Maori secondary school pupils is attributable to the poor standard of English spoken in the home and to the generally impoverished intellectual environment in Maori rural districts, rather than to bilingualism itself. When Maori children grow up in the intellectually more stimulating urban environment, mental and language retardation are markedly reduced.

Acculturative History and Personality Development

Acculturative History

The source of current Maori values regarding educational and vocational achievement lies in the pre-*pakeha* Maori culture and in the distinctive features of Maori acculturative history since contact with Europeans was established by Captain Cook in 1769. In the early phases of Maori acculturation, *pakeha* goods and technical processes were simply incorporated into the traditional Maori system of social and economic organization. The Maori sought to retain as far as possible his land, his social institutions, and his distinctive way of life, while at the same time acquiring all the benefits of European technology. But in accepting colonization and British sovereignty he naïvely placed his trust in treaty guarantees and failed to reckon realistically with the predatory designs of the colonists, who were determined to obtain the most desirable land in New Zealand and to establish the supremacy of their own economic and political system. When no more land could be obtained by sharp practices, or questionable, coercive or frankly illegal means, the colonists finally resorted to war and confiscation, and after a dozen years of bitter conflict eventually gained their ends.

The war and the confiscations left bitterness, disillusionment, and resentment in the Maori camp. The Maori lost confidence in himself and in the *pakeha.* European motives, values, customs, education, and religion became suspect. The Maori withdrew from contact with the *pakeha* and surrendered to apathy, despondency, demoralization, and stagnation. He lived in isolated villages and reverted to a subsistence type of agricultural economy supplemented by land clearing and seasonal labor for *pakeha* farmers and for the railways and public works departments. Various messianic, superstitious and nationalistic "adjustment cults" flourished during this period of withdrawal. Although the old communal system of common ownership, cooperative labor organized under the direction of chief and *tohunga,*[7] and sharing of the harvest among the kinship group was largely abondoned, much of Maori social organization and cultural values tended to remain intact.

The perpetuation of Maori culture during this period (1872–1939) was possible because of the vigor and adaptive qualities of indigenous cultural institutions; strong needs, nourished by smoldering bitterness and resentment, to reject *pakeha* ways of life arbitrarily; organized efforts to preserve as far as possible the central values and institutions of pre-*pakeha* culture; and semi-complete physical, social and psychological withdrawal, in

[7] *tohunga*—in former times a priest or expert craftsman, in more recent times a practitioner of Maori folk medicine and magic.

reservation-like areas, from erosive contact with European culture. This is the classical pattern of *resistive acculturation* in post-defeat withdrawal situations, contrasting sharply with *assimilative acculturation*, such as has taken place in Hawaii. Between these two extremes is *adaptive acculturation*, that is, incorporation of material and ideational elements of the new culture into the existing social and ideological structure (*e.g.*, Fiji, Western Samoa).

Emergence from withdrawal was facilitated by the convergence of several factors—the gradual weakening of bitterness, resentment, and suspicion of the *pakeha*, the paternalistic policies of the New Zealand government, the desire of the better educated younger generation to obtain *pakeha*-type jobs, overseas experience during World War II, and the effect of new highways, schools, automobiles, telephones, and the wireless in reducing the isolation of the Maori village. The phenomenally rapid growth of the Maori population and the shrinking of Maori land resources had also created a serious problem of unemployment in rural areas. Thus, when attractive new jobs opened up in the cities during World War II, young Maoris were ready to enter the mainstream of New Zealand life.

Yet, neither the emergence-from-withdrawal process nor the reversal of seventy years of experience in actively resisting *pakeha* culture were phenomena that could be accomplished overnight. A strong residuum of traditional values, ingrained mechanisms of resistance to acculturation, and deep-seated tendencies to reject *pakeha* values indiscriminately still remained among the older generation. Thus, even though young Maori adolescents are currently able to assimilate the *pakeha* pattern of educational and vocational aspiration, they still fail to internalize and implement it adequately, largely because of insufficient support and pressures from their parents, older siblings and peers, and the adult Maori community.

The post-withdrawal phase of Maori acculturation has been characterized by the following major developments stemming from the re-establishment of contact with the *pakeha*: (1) gradual disintegration of Maori village life and social organization as isolation decreased and the young people migrated to the cities; (2) the growth of a youthful urban proletariat and of serious youth and social problems (crime, juvenile delinquency, bodgieism) associated with excessively abrupt urban acculturation; (3) the revival of latent anti-Maori racial prejudice in the *pakeha* population as a result of suddenly increased interracial contact under unfavorable conditions; (4) the growth of supra-tribal racial nationalism as a manifestation of national self-consciousness, as a reaction against color prejudice, and as a compensation for the weakening of tribal loyalties and of traditional cultural practices; (5) notable advancement along many social and economic fronts, *i.e.*, income, health, education, entrance into industrial and skilled occupations and into some professions; and (6) the establishment of self-government at a community level.

Regarding the future, only two alternatives seem credible: gradual cultural assimilation of the Maori to the *pakeha* way of life without appreciable racial mixture; or the establishment of the Maori people as a highly and progressively more acculturated ethnic community within the larger framework of New Zealand social, political, and economic life, enjoying a certain measure of cultural autonomy and separateness even in the status of underprivileged, second-class citizens. To the writer the latter alternative seems the more likely possibility in view of the residual vigor of various Maori psychological traits, the growing problem of color prejudice, and the development of Maori supra-tribal nationalism. Perpetuation of the indigenous value system hardly seems likely now, since village life is decaying and withdrawal is no longer possible, rapid urbanization is taking place, and youth is becoming disinvolved from traditional practices. Overt expressions of *Maoritanga*[8] will become less important as ends in themselves and more important as tangible expressions of racial nationalism.

Sources of Maori Motivational Traits

The ultimate source of Maori-*pakeha* differences in adolescent personality development may be attributed to two core aspects of traditional Maori value structure dealing with the basis of

[8] "Maorihood" or Maori way of life.

self-esteem: greater emphasis on *derived status* throughout the entire life cycle of the individual; and less emphasis on the self-aggrandizing aspects and greater emphasis on task- and group-oriented aspects of *primary status*. The Maori of old valued primary status highly as a proper source of self-esteem, and fostered achievement motivation in youth by encouraging appropriate supportive traits. But the self-aggrandizing features of primary status (*i.e.*, personal ambition, individualism, competitiveness, compulsive need to work, relentless anxiety-driven drives to succeed), although not unknown, were not so highly emphasized as in *pakeha* society. Greater stress was laid on mastery of skills for their socioeconomic importance, pride of craftsmanship, and the personal satisfactions of meritorious accomplishment; on kinship obligations, the enhancement of group welfare and prestige, the personal-social values of cooperative effort towards a common goal, and *inter*-tribal competition; and on the satisfactions associated with working together in an intimate, personal context of reciprocal psychological support. These characteristics of primary status and the continued importance of derived status engendered and made valuable the traits of mutual helpfulness and cooperative effort in bearing economic burdens, and of generosity, hospitality, and concern for the welfare of kinsmen.

This cultural orientation towards status and self-esteem was modified by the Maori's subsequent acculturative history. Several factors militated against acceptance of the *pakeha* achievement pattern. In the first place, lingering resentment towards the *pakeha* and disillusionment with their values, motives and practices fostered an attitude of rejecting *pakeha* ways simply because they were *pakeha*. Secondly, it was difficult for the task- and group-oriented Maori to accept the self-aggrandizing aspects of *pakeha* primary status and the supportive traits that went with it, and to grow accustomed to *pakeha* working conditions. Thirdly, he was handicapped in utilizing *pakeha* channels to primary status by his lack of education and training for *pakeha* jobs, by lack of familial indoctrination in *pakeha* values, by general unfamiliarity with *pakeha* vocational opportunities, and by discriminatory attitudes on the part of many *pakehas*. Lastly, the residual vitality of the traditional Maori value system created basic needs and provided basic satisfactions for those needs which the *pakeha*-pattern could not easily gratify.

On the other hand, traditional channels for implementing the Maori pattern of primary status, and its associated social organization and leadership devices, were no longer functional. Any type of constructive achievement was greatly hampered by the widespread demoralization, lassitude, and feelings of hopelessness and impending cultural obliteration that gripped the Maori people in the first three decades following the civil wars. Hence, the easiest solution for most Maoris seemed to lie in de-emphasizing the importance of *all kinds* of primary status and achievement motivation and in making exaggerated use of the psychological support offered by derived status.

Distinctive cultural expectations with respect to primary and derived status also influenced indirectly the nature of adolescent aspirational patterns. The kinds of childhood and adolescent role and status experiences available to children were determined parallel with these expectations. These factors were relevant: Maoris were used to getting the major portion of derived status from group rather than from parental sources, and so tended to greater dependence on and comformity to the group. Peers and siblings were the major socializing agents during childhood, with a resulting tradition of more equalitarian relationships and reciprocal obligations. Since early satellizing relationships to parents were weak or nonexistent, there was no need for resatellization to peers during adolescence. There was less pressure to repudiate derived status and to strive for a great amount and self-aggrandizing form of primary status, and in general less discontinuity between childhood and adolescence. The direct influence of the cultural ideology on the types of aspirations adolescents internalized was thus reinforced by actual experience with particular kinds of status satisfactions and equalitarian relationships in the peer group—experience that was consonant with the cultural value system and therefore sanctioned by it.

The aspirational and motivational traits of Maori adolescents are undoubtedly influenced by the fact that Maoris are predominantly members of lower social class groups. By using matching procedures that controlled for social class, however, it was possible to eliminate the effects of relative social class status on our

Maori-*pakeha* differences. Intelligence is another variable that is significantly related to educational and occupational aspirations, but the small Maori enrollment in our two schools precluded the possibility of matching pupils on this basis. It is extremely unlikely, however, that our Maori-*pakeha* differences in aspirational traits would have been materially reduced if it had been possible to adopt this procedure.

Conclusion: Transmission of Maori Aspirational and Motivational Traits

In accounting for the transmission of the distinctive Maori pattern of aspirational, motivational, and supportive traits from one generation to the next, our logical point of departure must lie with the heritage of pervasive and interlocking cultural values regarding primary and derived status that functioned in the pre-*pakeha* Maori culture and was subsequently modified by acculturation. The cumulative effects of (1) recurrent exposure to these values and observation of culturally stereotyped role models, and (2) actual participation during childhood and adolescence in analogous types of role and status experience, are that this ideology is gradually internalized by the developing individual. This occurs through the operation of these mechanisms: primacy and exclusiveness of exposure; prerational identification on the basis of personal and group loyalties; implicit and explicit indoctrination; the development of particular needs and the experience of particular satisfactions (canalization); incidental learning; prestige suggestion; the pressure of group expectations and demands; and the application of internal and external sanctions (reward and punishment, shame and guilt, disapproval, threat of exclusion, induced anxiety).

From our data it was clear that young Maori adolescents in our urban and rural samples had for the most part successfully assimilated the *pakeha* pattern of educational and vocational aspiration. These aspirations reflected the prevailing *pakeha* achievement ideology which they encountered in school and in the wider culture, as well as the expressed but superficial desires of their parents. Parents, however, basically identified with the Maori orientation towards primary and derived status and generally had no deep emotional commitment to *pakeha* achievement values. They did not *really* encourage the implementation of these aspirations by voicing appropriate expectations, making unequivocal demands, dispensing suitable rewards and punishments, and insisting on the development of the necessary supportive traits. However, because of poor communication between parents and children, this situation was not clearly perceived by Maori secondary school pupils. Thus, during early adolescence, although they frequently revert to parental standards in the home environment, the influence of the school and of *pakeha* culture generally tends to predominate in developing educational and vocational aspirations and conforming to *pakeha* work standards.

Later on, however, as relationships and communication with parents and the adult community improve, the influence of Maori cultural values, as mediated through parents and peers, begins to prevail. Educational and vocational aspirations, achievement motivation, and essential supportive traits fail to become adequately internalized. Eventually, as the possibility of implementation progressively recedes, the aspirations are either lowered or abandoned. Concomitantly, Maori adolescents also become progressively more aware of the actual obstacles standing in the way of their vocational success because of *pakeha* prejudice and discrimination. This perception of the relative unavailability of the promised rewards of self-denial and striving also tends to make them abandon or modify their earlier aspirations. Other important factors that contribute to the lack of internalization and implementation of educational and occupational aspirations include traditional Maori attitudes towards work, acute social demoralization in some Maori communities, and the absence of adequate guidance and traditions of high scholastic and vocational accomplishment in most Maori families.

On the basis of our data it appears likely that significant Maori-*pakeha* differences in achievement orientation may be reasonably anticipated for at least another generation. They will be gradually obliterated, however, by the increasing urbanization of the Maori people, and by progressive improvement in both the cultural level of the Maori home and the parents' concern for their children's educational and vocational advancement. The next generation of Maori parents will probably be able to sustain the internalization and implementation along with the instigation of *pakeha* aspirations for achievement. Racial discrimination will undoubtedly make it more difficult for Maoris to implement their aspirations; but depending on the magnitude of the handicap imposed, this situation may either stimulate greater striving, as in the case of the Jews and Greeks in the United States (Rosen, 1959), or may promote an attitude of apathy and hopelessness, as is partly true in the case of the American Negro, who often perceives the cards as so overwhelmingly stacked against him that striving seems futile. In any event, the achievement ideology of the Maori will certainly reflect his predominantly lower social class status, becoming in time more and more similar to that of the lower-class *pakeha*.

References

Ausubel, D. P., 1951. Prestige motivation of gifted children. *Genet. Psychol. Monogr.*, 43, 53–117.

——, 1954. *Theory and Problems of Adolescent Development.* (New York: Grune & Stratton.)

Ausubel, D. P., H. M. Schiff, and Marjorie P. Zeleny, 1953. Real-life measures of academic and vocational aspirations in adolescents: relation to laboratory measures and adjustments. *Child Devel.*, 24, 155–168.

Beaglehole, E., and Pearl Beaglehole, 1946, *Some Modern Maoris.* (Wellington, New Zealand: Council for Educational Research.)

McLelland, D. C., J. W. Atkinson, R. A. Clark, and E. L. Lowell, 1953. *The Achievement Motive.* (New York: Appleton-Century-Crofts.)

Mulligan, D. G., 1957. *Maori Adolescence in Rakau.* (Wellington, New Zealand: Dept. of Psychology, Victoria University of Wellington.)

Ritchie, J. E., 1956. *Basic Personality in Rakau.* (Wellington, New Zealand: Dept. of Psychology, Victoria University of Wellington.)

Rosen, B. C., 1959. Race, ethnicity and the achievement syndrome. *Amer. sociol. Rev.*, 24, 47–60.

PART VI MEASUREMENT AND EVALUATION

Measurement and evaluation are integral aspects of the educational enterprise. They are perhaps most crucial in monitoring the outcomes of school learning to provide necessary feedback—both to pupils, with respect to the success or failure of their learning efforts, and to teachers and curriculum specialists, with respect to the effectiveness of instructional techniques and materials. Measurement also plays an important role, however, in quantifying those significant cognitive, affective, personality, and motivational characteristics of pupils that influence learning outcomes. Among these significant characteristics, intelligence has long enjoyed a preeminent position; but adjustment, personality, anxiety level, degree of open- or closed-mindedness, interests, aspirations, values, and cognitive style have also claimed the attention of measurement specialists.

Selection 30 is concerned with the validity of teachers' ratings of the adjustment and aspirations of their pupils. Such ratings, as a measuring instrument, have the obvious advantages of being easily obtainable and of being based on frequent and prolonged observation of behavior under a wide variety of conditions. In addition, when computed as averages of several raters they exhibit considerable *reliability* as to traits that can be unambiguously defined and that are objectively observable. More doubtful is the extent to which they are *valid* or to which they actually measure what they purport to measure.

The validity of teachers' ratings of adjustment can be determined in part by their degree of correspondence with such other measures of adjustment as scores on paper-and-pencil personality and anxiety inventories and scores on "projective" tests (such as the Rorschach test) which also purport to measure levels of adjustment and anxiety. (Projective tests are based on the principle that significant dimensions of personality are revealed by the ways in which subjects interpret or structure stimulus materials that are inherently unstructured or ambiguous in meaning.) This degree of correspondence was found to be disappointingly low—largely because teachers' judgments of adjustment are contaminated by their knowledge of pupils' scholastic performance and sociometric status (the extent to which they are accepted by their classmates).

Another contaminating factor is whether the rating teachers view anxiety as a disabling personality trait indicative of maladjustment or as a factor promoting adjustment in the school environment. In any case it is obvious from the low intercorrelations among the teachers' ratings, projective scores, and personality inventory scores that all three instruments appear to be measuring quite different facets of adjustment which show little overlap.

Teachers' ratings of pupils' scholastic aspirations appear to be even less valid than their ratings of adjustment. These aspiration ratings, too, are highly contaminated by the teachers' knowledge of pupils' academic standing. Teachers apparently assume that there is a one to one correspondence between scholastic aspiration and scholastic performance and seem to ignore the fact that such variables as scholastic aptitude, persistence, self-discipline, adjustment, and anxiety level affect the extent to which academic aspiration is implemented in achievement. Moreover, the significantly negative correlations obtained between "real-life" measures of scholastic aspiration and teachers' ratings of aspirational traits cast doubt on their validity.

30 Validity of Teachers' Ratings of Adolescents' Adjustment and Aspirations*

David P. Ausubel
Herbert M. Schiff
Majorie P. Zeleny

This study was concerned with the relationship between teachers' ratings of adjustment and aspirational traits in adolescents and various other self-report, objective, and projective measures of the same characteristics.

Teachers' ratings are frequently used for diagnostic, prognostic, guidance, and research purposes because of their ready accessibility and quantifiability. Moreover, when employed as averages of several raters and in relation to traits (a) which are overtly manifest and objectively observable in everyday behavior and (b) which can be specifically and unambiguously defined (*8, 20, 21*), such ratings enjoy considerable reliability. A further advantage of teachers' ratings is the fact that they can be based

Reprinted from the article of the same title,* Journal of Educational Psychology, *1954*, **45, *394–406. By permission of the authors and The American Psychological Association, Inc.*

on frequent and prolonged observation of behavior under a variety of conditions.

With respect to teachers' ratings of adjustment, the main problem was to ascertain the kinds of relationships that prevail between these observational appraisals of personality traits involved in adaptation to the school environment and such other criteria of adjustment as absence of overt behavioral symptomatology or relatively low degree of deviancy with respect to the more general personality trends measured by projective instruments. To what extent do these different instruments measure similar, overlapping, or even entirely discrete aspects of the global concept of adjustment? A secondary problem had to do with the bases on which teachers' ratings of adjustment are made. To what extent are they related to ratings of aspirational traits and to pupils' scholastic competence and sociometric status?

The second major problem dealt with in this study was the relationship between teachers' ratings of aspirational traits and "real life" measures of level of aspiration. In a sense this question raises the problem of the validity of such ratings.

METHOD

Population

The subjects in this study consisted of fifty students comprising, with the exception of a few absentees, the entire junior class of University High School[1] in Urbana, Illinois. The mean age of these students was 15.8 years, and the distribution by sex was twenty-four boys and twenty-six girls. A majority of students in this school come from professional homes, the parents generally holding academic appointments at the University of Illinois. Admission to the school, however, is unrestricted except for the payment of a small nominal tuition fee.

[1]The authors acknowledge the cooperation and administrative assistance of Professor Charles M. Allen, Principal, and of the staff of University High School in collecting these data.

Teachers' Ratings

Five current teachers of each student were asked to make ratings at the end of the school year. In all, the ratings of fifteen teachers (eight male and seven female) were involved. Students were rated on a five-point scale on general adjustment (defined in terms of personality integration and emotional stability) and on three aspirational traits (persistence, scholastic competitiveness and academic aspiration). To minimize "halo effect," the teachers were requested to rate all students on a single trait before proceeding to consideration of the next trait. The ratings of five teachers were averaged to provide a mean rating for each student on four traits.

"Real Life" Measures of Aspiration

"Real life" indices of aspirational level included both academic and vocational measures. The former consisted of (a) academic goal discrepancy—the algebraic difference between the student's expressed academic aspiration for the current school year and his composite grade point average for the preceding four semesters; and (b) academic performance estimate—the algebraic difference between the student's estimate of his cumulative high-school standing and his actual four-semester grade point average. Prediction of academic standing was made on a six-point scale (well below average to upper few), and academic aspiration was expressed in terms of a five-point scale (get by to upper few). Grade point average was computed from actual grades which in this school are officially recorded on a five-point scale but are not divulged to students.

Three measures of level of vocational aspiration were utilized: (a) vocational prestige needs—the student's total weighted score on the level of interests, part of the Lee-Thorpe Occupational Interest Inventory[2] (*15*); (b) vocational tenacity—a composite

[2]This is a measure of general level of job prestige desired by an individual. The subject is presented with thirty triads of occupational activities in each of which area of work involved is held relatively constant while level of job prestige is varied. Total score is computed from the subject's preferences in each triad appropriately weighted in terms of job prestige.

standard score on a hypothetical level of aspiration test consisting of three hypothetical situations in which the subject is successively requested to suppose that he is preparing for a career in medicine, engineering, and a skilled trade, respectively, and that in the course of his vocational preparation he meets serious obstacles of a specified nature. In each of these situations, four alternatives are presented ranging from maintenance of the original goal at all costs (high vocational tenacity) to complete abandonment of the original vocational goal (low vocational tenacity). The subject's choice in each situation, appropriately weighted, is converted into a standard score, and all three standard scores are added to yield a composite score; (c) vocational unreality—the total discrepancy between each of the subject's nine percentile scores on the Kuder Preference Record (*14*) and the corresponding mean percentile scores of persons in his occupation of choice as given in the manual for this test.

Measures of Adjustment

In addition to teachers' rating of adjustment, the following indices of adjustment were employed: (a) M.M.P.I. adjustment score—total adjustment score on the Minnesota Multiphasic Personality Inventory (*11*). In deriving total adjustment scores, raw scores on each of the subscales were first converted into standard scores. Since a positive standard score on a given subscale indicated a degree of deviancy with respect to the trait measured that was greater than the mean score characterizing our population, a measure of total personality deviancy could be computed for each subject by merely summing all of his positive standard scores on the various subscales.[3] Finally, by reversing the sign of the total standard score, a measure of adjustment was obtained in which a high score was indicative of relatively good adjustment. (b) Rorschach adjustment score—an adjustment score derived from the Rorschach group test administered in accordance with the procedure developed by Harrower and

[3]Since a negative standard score is indicative of deviancy on the masculinity-femininity subscale, negative standard scores on this scale were added to the other standard scores to obtain total M.M.P.I. adjustment score (prior to final reversal of sign).

Steiner (*10*), and scored in accordance with the system developed by Klopfer and Kelley (*13*). The adjustment score represents the total number of entries made in Munroe's check list[4] (*18*) expressed as a standard score with the sign reversed so that a high score is indicative of good adjustment. (c) Rorschach anxiety score—the total number of occasions specified signs of anxiety appeared in the subject's protocol. Criteria of anxiety included fifteen commonly accepted signs such as diffuse shading responses, signs of shading shock, high number of card rejections, threatening or evasive responses, high percentage of oligophrenic responses, etc. (*9, 13, 19*). Each time one of these fifteen anxiety signs occurred, the subject was credited with one point. Thus, high Rorschach anxiety scores are indicative of relatively high levels of anxiety and vice versa. (d) Composite adjustment score—the algebraic sum of the subject's standard M.M.P.I., Rorschach adjustment and teachers' adjustment rating scores. (e) I.P.I. anxiety score—total score on a paper-and-pencil inventory designed to measure anxiety level (Illinois Personality Inventory). (f) Sociometric status—the mean sociometric rating earned by each student when rated sociometrically by all of his classmates on a five-point scale ("definitely not wanted as a friend" to "wanted as a best friend"). (g) Grade point average—the student's cumulative grade point average over four semesters computed on a five-point scale. As in the case of sociometric status, a numerically high score is at the desirable end of the scale.

RESULTS AND INTERPRETATION

Reliability and Generality of Measures

The reliability (generality over-raters) of teachers' ratings is shown in Table 1. For each trait the mean intercorrelation (computed by the squared r method) between the ratings of five teachers on the same pupils was obtained. This was corrected by the Spearman-Brown formula to indicate the predicted reliability

[4]This check list proposes criteria for a 'normal' range of responses for each type of scoring determinant. Entries in the check list, therefore, represent deviancy from the proposed limits of normalcy.

TABLE 1

Intercorrelations among Personality Traits as Rated by Teachers

	ADJUSTMENT	PERSISTENCE	SCHOLASTIC COMPETITIVENESS	ACADEMIC ASPIRATION
Adjustment	.90*	.71	.60	.42
Persistence	—	.87*	.81	.73
Scholastic Competitiveness	—	—	.83*	.79
Academic Aspiration	—	—	—	.90*

NOTE: All coefficients of correlation in this table are significant beyond the one percent level of confidence.

*Mean intercorrelation between five teachers' ratings of subjects on same trait computed by 'squared r' method, and corrected by Spearman-Brown formula to indicate the predicted reliability of the combined judgments of five raters.

of the average rating of five teachers. Application of the correction formula was considered justifiable since an average of five ratings is more reliable than a single rating in the same sense and to the same predictable degree that a ten-item test is more reliable than a two-item test. The resulting reliability coefficients approximate the range of magnitude generally obtained with combined teachers' ratings.

Table 1 also shows that teachers' ratings exhibit considerable generality over traits. This is not necessarily indicative of "halo effect" since the three aspirational traits both closely resemble each other and are not logically unrelated to adjustment. Furthermore, the intercorrelations among aspirational traits are higher than the correlations between these latter traits and adjustment.

The reliability[5] of academic goal discrepancy and of academic performance estimate scores could not be ascertained, but there was a high degree of relationship between these two different indices of level of academic aspiration. Vocational tenacity scores on the three different kinds of situations (i.e., medicine, engineering, and skilled trade) exhibited a degree of generality which was proportionate to the degree of similarity between the vocations. The test-retest reliability of the level of interests scores on the Occupational Interest Inventory (identical with our measure of vocational prestige needs) is given as .88 in the test manual (*15*). The reliability of vocational unreality scores could not be determined. Vocational prestige needs were significantly related to both vocational unreality and vocational tenacity in boys, but correlations between academic and vocational measures of level of aspiration were not significant.

It was not feasible for either technical or administrative reasons to obtain reliability coefficients for the Rorschach measures, the M.M.P.I. adjustment score, or the composite adjustment score. Intercorrelations among Rorschach adjustment score, M.M.P.I. adjustment score and teachers' rating of ad-

[5]A more definitive presentation and discussion of the reliability, generality, and psychological significance of "real life" measures of level of aspiration are given in a previous paper (*5*). The more relevant findings are summarized here to provide some objective basis for appraisal of these measures.

justment (see Table 2) were generally non-significant except for the correlation between the latter two measures in our female subjects. The correlations between each of these three measures and composite adjustment score were spuriously high because each measure was a component part of the composite score. M.M.P.I. adjustment score was the most representative component of the composite measure in boys, and teachers' rating of adjustment enjoyed comparable status among girls.

Thus, it appears that the aspects of adjustment measured, respectively, by teachers' observational ratings of classroom behavior, a self-report index of behavioral deviancy with respect to various syndromes in psychopathology, and a projective measure of general personality integration are relatively unrelated to each other in our sample of adolescents. If all three measures are equally valid, they must all be measuring quite different aspects of adjustment which (except for M.M.P.I. and teachers' ratings in girls) show no significant overlap whatsoever. The same type of relationship holds true for self-report (I.P.I.) and Rorschach measures of anxiety which were not significantly correlated. This latter datum is not in accord with the previously reported finding of a significantly positive relationship between these two measures of anxiety in a population of college students (*4*).

More in accordance with expectations, I.P.I. anxiety scores correlated negatively with composite and M.M.P.I. adjustment scores, and with teachers' ratings of adjustment in girls, and with Rorschach adjustment scores in boys. The relationships between Rorschach anxiety scores and other measures of adjustment were not significant. At least among our adolescent girls, therefore, high levels of anxiety as measured by the I.P.I. tended to be associated with poor adjustment and vice versa. A possible explanation for this sex difference might lie in the prevailing cultural attitude that high levels of striving (and of the anxiety that accompanies such striving) are more acceptable and compatible with good adjustment in boys than in girls. In support of this interpretation was the fact that teachers' adjustment ratings were more consistently negatively related to boys' than to girls' academic goal discrepancy scores and academic performance estimates (see Table 4).

TABLE 2

Intercorrelations among Adjustment Scores

	Rorschach Anxiety		M.M.P.I. Adjustment		Teachers Adjustment		Anxiety Level (I.P.I.)		Sociometric Status		Composite Adjustment	
	Boys	Girls	Boys	Girls	Boys	Girls	Boys	Girls	Boys	Girls	Boys	Girls
Rorschach Adjustment	−.24	−.19	.31	−.21	−.26	−.09	*−.40	−.32	−.17	.30	**.59	.40
Rorschach Anxiety	—	—	−.11	.01	−.21	−.16	.36	.06	−.17	−.22	−.21	−.20
M.M.P.I. Adjustment	—	—	—	—	.05	**.57	−.06	**−.56	.04	.13	**.79	**.61
Teacher Adjustment	—	—	—	—	—	—	.03	**−.52	**.75	**.64	*.40	**.79
Anxiety Level (I.P.I.)	—	—	—	—	—	—	—	—	.03	.01	.17	*−.45
Sociometric Status	—	—	—	—	—	—	—	—	—	—	*.44	**.59

*Significant at the five percent level.
**Significant at the one percent level.

Relationship between Teacher's Ratings and Other Measures of Adjustment

As already noted, teachers' rating of adjustment was not significantly related to Rorschach adjustment score in either sex, but was positively related to M.M.P.I. adjustment score in girls ($p. < .01$). Teachers' rating of adjustment was also significantly more highly related to composite adjustment score in girls than in boys, although in each case the coefficient of correlation was spuriously high. Rorschach anxiety score was not significantly correlated with teachers' rating of adjustment, but I.P.I. anxiety score was negatively related to the latter score in girls ($p. < .01$).

It would appear, therefore, that for our population of adolescents, teachers' ratings of adjustment are a more valid and psychologically meaningful measure in relation to girls than in relation to boys. Appraisal of boys' adjustment status is very possibly complicated in the minds of teachers by the fact that certain traits related to extremely high levels of striving (and the associated anxiety) are regarded as unfavorable for adjustment by mental hygienists, but are nevertheless accepted as desirable in connection with our cultural ideal of masculine success. In the case of girls, on the other hand, teachers are apparently less confused by contradictory criteria of adjustment. Supporting this interpretation are (a) the significantly negative correlation between girls' I.P.I. anxiety scores and teachers' adjustment ratings, in contrast to the approximately zero coefficient of correlation between the corresponding scores of boys, and (b) the more consistent tendency for teachers' ratings of adjustment to be correlated negatively with objective indices of academic level of aspiration in the case of girls (see Table 4).

A clue regarding the bases on which teachers' ratings of adjustment are made appears in the moderately high degree of positive relationship found between these ratings and (a) ratings on aspirational traits, (see Table 1), and (b) pupils' sociometric status and grade point average (see Table 3). The composite portrait of a pupil who receives a high teachers' rating on adjustment is an individual who is perceived by teachers as persistent and scholastically competitive, who is highly accepted by his classmates and who has a superior scholastic record. Table 4 also shows that his academic aspirations tend to be more com-

TABLE 3

Correlations between Teachers' Ratings and Various Measures of Adjustment

Measures of Adjustment	Teachers Ratings							
	Adjustment		Persistence		Scholastic Competitiveness		Academic Aspiration	
	Boys	Girls	Boys	Girls	Boys	Girls	Boys	Girls
M.M.P.I. Adjustment	.05	**.57	−.06	−.02	−.01	−.05	−.16	−.24
Rorschach Adjustment	−.26	−.09	−.03	−.14	−.28	.22	−.12	.30
Rorschach Anxiety	−.21	−.16	−.19	.02	−.14	−.10	−.12	−.17
Anxiety Level (I.P.I.)	.03	**−.52	−.30	**−.52	−.38	−.20	−.30	−.34
Composite Adjustment	*.40	**.79	*.44	**.57	.23	**.53	−.04	**.70
Sociometric Status	**.75	**.64	**.54	*.48	*.46	*.42	*.40	*.39
Grade Point Average	**.59	**.61	**.78	**.72	**.92	**.84	**.61	**.71

*Significant at the five percent level.
**Significant at the one percent level.

mensurate with his past academic performance as evidenced by the negative correlation between academic goal discrepancy and teachers' adjustment rating. In addition, if the pupil is a girl, she will tend to have high M.M.P.I. and composite adjustment scores and a low I.P.I. anxiety score.

Table 3 also shows the relationships between teachers' ratings of aspirational traits and other non-rating scale indices of adjustment. Aspirational ratings were not significantly related to M.M.P.I. and Rorschach adjustment scores or to Rorschach anxiety ratings. A puzzling negative relationship (p. < .01) prevailed between girls' I.P.I. anxiety scores and teachers' ratings on persistence. Teachers' ratings of aspirational traits were significantly correlated with composite adjustment in girls; in the case of boys this was only true with respect to persistence.

In general, as one might expect, grade point average was more highly correlated with aspirational ratings than with ratings of adjustment, but the reverse held true for sociometric status (see Table 3).

Relationship between Teachers' Ratings and "Real Life" Measures of Aspiration

Table 4 shows that there is a pronounced tendency for academic goal discrepancy scores to be negatively correlated with such highly related teachers' ratings as scholastic competitiveness, persistence, and academic aspiration. Thus, students who expressed relatively high academic aspirations for the future in the light of previous scholastic performance tended to receive ratings from teachers which were indicative of relatively low aspirational level. This same tendency prevailed with respect to academic performance estimate, but was significant only for girls, and in only two out of three instances. Generally speaking, relationships between teachers' ratings of aspirational traits and measures of vocational aspiration were not statistically significant and exhibited no consistent trend with respect to direction.

This negative relationship between "real life" measures of academic aspiration and teachers' ratings of aspirational traits (ostensibly based on motivational behavior in an academic setting) casts doubt upon the validity of the latter measures. It confirms findings in a previous study with intellectually gifted

TABLE 4

Correlations between Teachers' Ratings and 'Real Life' Measures of Level of Aspiration

'Real Life' Measures of Level of Aspiration	Adjustment		Persistence		Scholastic Competitiveness		Academic Aspiration	
	Boys	Girls	Boys	Girls	Boys	Girls	Boys	Girls
Academic Goal Discrepancy	*−.43	*−.49	**−.57	**−.59	**−.52	**−.57	−.30	*−.44
Academic Performance Estimate	−.20	*−.46	−.20	*−.43	−.38	*−.48	−.15	−.31
Vocational Prestige Needs	−.25	−.10	.16	.11	.31	.23	.35	.25
Vocational Tenacity	−.11	−.19	−.04	−.15	.22	*.45	.34	.37
Vocational Unreality	−.31	−.22	−.13	.37	−.08	.27	−.03	.33

*Significant at the five percent level.
**Significant at the one percent level.

sixth-graders (*1*) in which the writer failed to obtain significant relationships between teachers' ratings of aspirational traits and a measure of prestige motivation (i.e., relative tendency to respond to an incentive of personal prestige by increasing work output over the level achieved under conditions of anonymity). Another supportive finding in this latter study was a zero correlation between these same ratings and pupils' self-ratings on aspirational traits (*1*). Lewis (*16*), on the other hand, obtained very significant differences between "educationally retarded" and "educationally accelerated" gifted children aged nine to fourteen with respect to teachers' ratings on perseverance and ambitiousness.

Although educational performance (holding other factors constant) is perhaps a more definitive criterion of the validity of ratings of aspirational traits than either self-ratings or objective test measures, it should be realized that such evidence of validity is largely circular when the ratings are made by teachers. Since teachers' ratings of motivation are substantially based on academic performance, the latter criterion can hardly be considered independent. In the present study, correlations of .61 to .92 were obtained between teachers' ratings of aspirational traits and grade point average (see Table 3).

Taking all of the evidence into consideration, there is certainly good reason for questioning the validity of teachers' ratings of pupils' aspirational characteristics. This lack of validity is apt to be even more serious in the case of adolescent pupils, judging from the findings of the present study and from the relatively poor insight of teachers into high-school pupils' interests (*6*) and sociometric status (*7*). Also, at least with respect to the latter function, teachers' perceptual ability has been shown to decrease markedly with increasing age of pupils (*3, 17*).

Summary and Conclusions

Teachers' ratings of adjustment and aspirational traits were obtained for a class of fifty juniors in a University high school and related to various other self-report, objective, and projective measures of the same characteristics. The following conclusions can be reached with respect to our particular sample of adolescent boys and girls, and deserve to be tested on a more representative population:

1) Averages of five teachers' ratings of adjustment and aspirational traits enjoyed high split-half reliability.
2) Rorschach adjustment score, teachers' adjustment rating, and M.M.P.I. adjustment score were not significantly intercorrelated except for the latter two measures in the case of girls. Thus, all three instruments appear to be measuring quite different aspects of adjustment showing little or no overlap.
3) High level of anxiety, as measured by the Illinois Personality Inventory (I.P.I.) was consistently associated with poor adjustment in girls. This was not true of boys. The suggestion was offered that anxiety, especially the variety associated with high striving, is more compatible with and culturally acceptable as evidence of good adjustment in boys than in girls.
4) Teachers' ratings of adjustment appear to be more meaningful and psychologically valid for girls than for boys in as much as they were correlated in the appropriate direction with M.M.P.I. and composite adjustment scores and with I.P.I. anxiety score. This sex difference is attributed to the prevailing cultural ambivalence regarding the adjustive value of anxiety for boys in the light of their social sex rôle. In the case of girls, teachers' ratings of adjustment also tended to be more consistently correlated in the negative direction with "real life" measures of level of academic aspiration.
5) Teachers tended to give high adjustment ratings to pupils whom they perceived as persistent and scholastically competitive, who were highly accepted by their classmates, who had superior scholastic records, and whose academic aspirations were commensurate with past academic achievement.
6) Teachers' ratings of pupils' aspirational traits were very highly related to the latter's scholastic standing. Hence, academic performance can not be used as an independent criterion of the validity of these ratings.
7) In view of the reliably negative correlations obtained between "real life" measures of level of academic aspiration and teachers' ratings of aspirational traits, the validity of the latter measure seems highly questionable.

References

1 Ausubel, D. P., "Prestige motivation of gifted children." *Genet. Psychol. Monogr.*, 1951, 43, 53–117.

2 Ausubel, D. P., and H. M. Schiff. "A level of aspiration approach to the measurement of goal tenacity." *J. gen. Psychol.*, (in press).

3 Ausubel, D. P., H. M. Schiff, and E. B. Gasser. "A preliminary study of developmental trends in sociempathy: Accuracy of perception of own and others' sociometric status. *Child Developm.*, 1952, 23, 111–118.

4 Ausubel, D. P., H. M. Schiff, and M. Goldman. "Qualitative characteristics in the learning process associated with anxiety." *J. abnorm. soc. Psychol.*, 1953, 48, 537–547.

5 Ausubel, D. P., H. M. Schiff, and M. P. Zeleny. " 'Real life' measures of level of academic and vocational aspiration in adolescents: Relation to laboratory measures and to adjustment." *Child Developm.* (in press).

6 Baker, H. L., "High-school teachers' knowledge of their pupils." *Sch. Rev.*, 1938, 46, 175–190.

7 Bonney, M. E., "Sociometric study of agreement between teacher judgments and student choices." *Sociometry*, 1947, 10, 133–146.

8 Cronbach, L. J., *Essentials of Psychological Testing.* New York: Harper, 1949.

9 Eichler, R. M., "Experimental stress and alleged Rorschach indices of anxiety." *J. abnorm. soc. Psychol.*, 1951, 46, 344–355.

10 Harrower, Molly R., and M. E. Steiner, *Large Scale Rorschach Techniques: A Manual for the Group Rorschach and Multiple-choice Test.* Springfield, Ill.: Charles C Thomas, 1945.

11 Hathaway, S. R., and J. C. McKinley, *The Minnesota Multiphasic Personality Inventory.* Minneapolis: Univer. of Minnesota Press, 1943.

12 Kelly, E. L., and D. W. Fiske, *The Prediction of Performance in Clinical Psychology.* Ann Arbor, Michigan: Univer. of Michigan Press, 1951.

13 Klopfer, B., and D. M. Kelley, *The Rorschach Technique.* New York: World Book Co., 1946.

14 Kuder, G. F., *Revised Manual for the Kuder Preference Record.* Chicago: Science Research Associates, 1946.

15 Lee, E. A., and L. P. Thorpe, *Occupational Interest Inventory, Advanced Form A.* Los Angeles: California Test Bureau, 1946.

16 Lewis, W. D. "A comparative study of the personalities, interests and home backgrounds of gifted children of superior and inferior educational achievement." *J. genet. Psychol.*, 1941, 59, 207–218.

17 Moreno, J. L., *Who Shall Survive?* Washington, D. C.: Nervous and Mental Disease Publishing Co., 1934.

18 Munroe, Ruth L., "Prediction of the adjustment and academic performance of college students by a modification of the Rorschach method." *Appl. Psychol. Monogr.*, 1945, No. 7.

19 Rapaport, D., *Diagnostic Psychological Testing.* Chicago: Yearbook Publishing Co., 1945.

20 Symonds, P. M., *Diagnosing Personality and Conduct.* New York: Appleton-Century, 1931.

21 Terman, L. M., and M. Oden, *The Gifted Child Grows Up: 25 Years' Follow-up of a Superior Group.* Stanford, Calif.: Stanford Univer. Press, 1949.

Index

U

V